"This book makes a major contribution to the study of legal discourse and to our understanding of variation in professional communication practices across cultures. An outcome of a major international research project, the volume contains a series of studies focusing on the language used in international commercial arbitration documents, presenting a range of analyses, insights and perspectives on legal language in such diverse contexts as Malaysia, Brazil, India, Japan, Finland, the UK and Iran. The editors and contributors have done an excellent job in weaving together the diverse threads of this complex topic and in presenting a multidisciplinary perspective on legal language and its socio-political and communicative consequences in both national and global contexts. I am sure that this valuable book will be widely read and be of great benefit to teachers, scholars and all those interested in legal discourse."
– *Ken Hyland, Professor, Institute of Education, University of London*

"This book makes an important contribution to fields of international law, discourse analysis and intercultural communication. It will be an invaluable resource for legal scholars, applied linguists, legal translators and anyone interested in the influence of language and culture on law and legal process."
– *Rodney Jones, Associate Professor, Department of English and Communication, City University of Hong Kong*

What exactly is legal about legal language? What happens to legal language when it is used across linguistic, national, socio-political, cultural, and legal systems? In what way is generic integrity of legal documents maintained in multilingual and multicultural legal contexts? What happens when the same rule of law is applied across legal systems?'

By bringing together scholars and practitioners from more than ten countries, representing various jurisdictions, languages, and socio-political backgrounds, this book addresses these key issues arising from the differences in legal or sociocultural systems. The discussions are based not only on the analysis of the legal texts alone, but also on the factors shaping such constructions and interpretations.

Given the increasing international need for accurate and authoritative translation and use of legal documents, this important volume has considerable contemporary relevance in a globalized economy. It will appeal to discourse analysts, commercial consultants, legal trainers, translators, and applied researchers in professional communication, especially in the field of legal writing and languages for specific purposes.

Vijay K. Bhatia is Professor in the Department of English and Communication, City University of Hong Kong. **Christopher N. Candlin** is Senior Research Professor in the Department of Linguistics, Macquarie University, Australia. **Jan Engberg** is Associate Professor in the Department of Language and Business Communication, Aarhus School of Business, Denmark.

Legal Discourse across Cultures and Systems

Hong Kong University Press thanks Xu Bing for writing the Press's name in his Square Word Calligraphy for the covers of its books. For further information, see p. iv.

Legal Discourse across Cultures and Systems

Edited by

Vijay K. Bhatia
Christopher N. Candlin
Jan Engberg

with the assistance of

Jane Lung

香港大學出版社
Hong Kong University Press

Hong Kong University Press
14/F Hing Wai Centre
7 Tin Wan Praya Road
Aberdeen
Hong Kong

Hardback ISBN 978-962-209-851-0
Paperback ISBN 978-962-209-852-7

British Library Cataloguing-in-Publication Data
A catalogue record for this book is available from the British Library.

Secure On-line Ordering
http://www.hkupress.org

Printed and bound by Pre-Press Limited, Hong Kong, China.

Hong Kong University Press is honoured that Xu Bing, whose art explores the complex themes of language across cultures, has written the Press's name in his Square Word Calligraphy. This signals our commitment to cross-cultural thinking and the distinctive nature of our English-language books published in China.

"At first glance, Square Word Calligraphy appears to be nothing more unusual than Chinese characters, but in fact it is a new way of rendering English words in the format of a square so they resemble Chinese characters. Chinese viewers expect to be able to read Square Word Calligraphy but cannot. Western viewers, however are surprised to find they can read it. Delight erupts when meaning is unexpectedly revealed."

— Britta Erickson, *The Art of Xu Bing*

Contents

Acknowledgements

This volume investigates the linguistic and discoursal properties of legal documents used in international commercial arbitration contexts, focusing on their construction, interpretation, and use in international arbitration practice. The aim is to provide a better understanding of legal language seen from an international perspective, in particular with a focus on cross-cultural factors in the context of international arbitration practice. The work presented in this collection has been accomplished with the support of a Competitive Earmarked Research Grant awarded by the UGC Research Grant Council in Hong Kong (project No. 9040474 entitled *Generic Integrity in Legislative Discourse in Multilingual and Multicultural Contexts*). Contributions in this volume are drawn from, but not restricted to, the presentations made at the international conference in Hong Kong (2–4 October 2003) on *Law and Language in International Arbitration*, where members of this international research project presented their findings to a wider community of legal and arbitration scholars and practitioners. The conference was organized by the RGC funded CERG project and co-sponsored by Hong Kong International Arbitration Centre, The WTO Law and Dispute Resolution Centre and the Department of English and Communication, City University of Hong Kong. The editors gratefully acknowledge the support given by these organisations. The volume represents a unique collection of contributions, bringing together not only linguists and legal academics, but also arbitration practitioners. The editors gratefully acknowledge the participation of these established scholars from these related fields to contribute to this multidisciplinary understanding of the use of language in international commercial arbitration. We fully appreciate the time and effort they have spared to make this project a successful example of international and multidisciplinary collaboration. Special thanks are also due to Dr Jane Lung for willingly offering all the editorial assistance to make this volume possible.

Vijay Bhatia
Christopher Candlin
Jan Engberg

Contributors

Vijay K. Bhatia is Professor of English at the City University of Hong Kong. His main research interests are genre analysis of professional discourse, including legal, business, newspaper, advertising and other promotional genres; ESP (theory and practice); simplification of legal and other public documents; cross-cultural and disciplinary variation in professional discourse. He has published in many international journals in these areas. He has worked on a number of projects, the most recent of which is 'Generic Integrity in Legal Discourse in Multilingual and Multicultural Contexts', an international project in which 15 countries participated. He is also on the editorial advisory boards of several international journals. His book on *Analysing Genre: Language Use in Professional Settings* (1993) is widely used by researchers interested in genre theory and practice. His more recent book *Worlds of Discourse* (2004) has appeared in the *Advances in Applied Linguistics* series.

Christopher N. Candlin is Senior Research Professor in the Department of Linguistics of Macquarie University, Sydney. He was the Foundation Executive Director of the Australian Government's National Centre for English Language Teaching and Research from 1987 to 1998, and also established the Research Centre in Language in Social Life, also at Macquarie. He has held Professorships at Lancaster, UK, the City University of Hong Kong, and the UK Open University, and holds Honorary Professorships at the Universities of Lancaster, Nottingham and Cardiff in the UK. He currently holds a Leverhulme Trust Visiting Research Professor in the Centre for Health Communication Research at Cardiff University. His current research is in the fields of professional communication, particularly in healthcare and law, and its application to professional development and practice, and in disciplinary discourses in the academy and their interface with the world of work. He is a member of the editorial boards of several international journals, including *Text & Talk, Journal of Sociolinguistics, Language Awareness, Journal of English for Specific Purposes, Language Teaching Research and Communication in Medicine*, and co-edits (with Srikant Sarangi) the new *Journal of Applied Linguistics*. From 1996 to 2002, he was President of the International Association of Applied Linguistics.

Marta Chroma, Head of the Foreign Language Department of the Charles University Law School in Prague, teaches legal linguistics and legal translation to both students of law and students of linguistics. Her research is based upon comparative study of the Czech laws and language on the one hand and the Anglo-American system of law and legal English on the other. She focuses on the issues of linguistics and legal interpretation of legal texts for the purposes of translation, as well as issues of equivalence and conceptual analysis for the purposes of lexicography. Her latest work is *Legal Translation and the Dictionary* (2004).

Jan Engberg is Associate Professor in the Faculty of Language and Business Communication of the Aarhus School of Business, Denmark. His PhD thesis was a contrastive study of German and Danish civil court judgments with relevance for special genres, cognitive aspects of domain specific discourse and communication in LSP settings. The focus of his research is on communication and translation in the field of law. He is co-chair of the section on LSP communication of the German Association for Applied Linguistics (GAL) and co-editor of the international journals *Hermes* and *LSP & Professional Communication.*

Paola Evangelisti Allori is Professor of English and Director of the Language Centre at the University for Sport Science (IUSM) in Rome. Her main research interests focus on the comparative description of English, particularly the uses of English in different academic and professional settings. She has published extensively in the fields of cross-disciplinary and cross-cultural discourse analysis and of contrastive rhetoric. Among her recent publications are *Academic Discourse in Europe* (1998), *English in Academic and Professional Settings* (2002, co-edited with E. Ventola), *Language and Legal Concepts across Systems and Cultures* (forthcoming, co-edited with V. Bhatia and C. N. Candlin).

Celina Frade is a Lecturer of English for Specific Purposes in the Multidisciplinary Institute, Rural University of Rio de Janeiro, and has a PhD in Linguistics. She has done extensive research mainly on legal English, and published several articles on the topic. She has also taught legal English reading skills to Brazilian legal professionals. She is currently working on the design of ESP courses for other academic and professional areas for the undergraduate and postgraduate levels at the institute.

Maurizio Gotti is Professor of English Linguistics and Director of the Language Centre at the University of Bergamo. He is currently President of the Italian Association of University Language Centres and Director of CERLIS, the research centre on specialized languages based at the University of Bergamo. From 1999 to 2001 he was President of the Italian Association of English Studies. From 2000 to 2004 he was President of the European Confederation of University Language Centres. His main research areas are the features and origins of specialized discourse, and his publications include *Robert Boyle and the Language of Science* (1996), *Specialized Discourse: Linguistic Features and Changing Conventions* (2003), and *Investigating Specialized Discourse* (2005). He is a member of the editorial board of national and international journals, and edits the *Linguistic Insights* series.

Azirah Hashim is the Dean of the Faculty of Languages and Linguistics and a Professor in the English Language Department of the University of Malaya, Kuala Lumpur. Her research interests include genre analysis, academic and professional discourse and varieties of English. She is currently involved in two international projects, 'World Englishes and Miscommunication', and 'Advertising in Asia', and is the Malaysian representative for the English in Southeast Asia Conference series.

Dorothee Heller is Associate Professor of German Linguistics at the University of Bergamo. Her research is mainly concerned with genre analysis, pragmatics and historiography with special attention to LSP, and her publications include *Wörter und Sachen: Grundlagen einer Historiographie der Fachsprachenforschung* (1998). Her current research focuses on academic discourse from a comparative perspective (German vs. Italian).

Kusum Dhanania, the National Academy of Legal Studies and Research (NALSAR) University of Law, Hyderabad, India. She has co-authored a paper with Sandhya Gopakumaran, "Marwari business discourse: An analysis" (2005), published in *Asian Business Discourse(s) Part I* (1995).

Peter Malanczuk, is Dean and Chair Professor in the School of Law of the City University of Hong Kong, and Founding Director of the WTO Law and Dispute Resolution (MAArbDR) Centre. He is also Honorary Professor in several universities: Peking University, China University of Political Science and Law, Nankai University, Shenzhen University and Nanjing University. Previously he has been Distinguished Visiting Professor at Hong Kong University (2001); Chair of International Law and Founding Director of the GLODIS-Institute (Institute of Globalization, International Economic Law and Dispute Settlement), Erasmus University Rotterdam (1997–01); Chair of International Law and International Relations, University of Amsterdam (1990–1997); and Legal Assistant of the President of the Iran-United States Claims Tribunal in The Hague (1986–89). He has also been Visiting Professor at several universities, including Michigan Law School, University of California, Berkeley and Moscow State University. He has published extensively on general international law, international economic and trade law, state responsibility, international arbitration and dispute settlement, environmental law, human rights, international criminal law, telecommunications and space law, European Community law, and comparative constitutional and administrative law.

Yasunobu Sato is a Professor of the Graduate Program of Human Security and the Graduate School of Arts and Sciences at the University of Tokyo. He was admitted to the Bar of Japan in 1984. He has been the Attorney-at-law, Sato Law Office, Takahashi Law Office (1984–1988); Foreign Associate, United Nations Centre for Human Rights (Geneva); Cleary, Gottlieb, Steen & Hamilton (New York, Washington D.C.); Loef Claeys Verbeke (Amsterdam, Brussels) (1988–1991); Legal Officer, United Nations High Commissioner for Refugees (UNHCR) Canberra, Australia); Human Rights Officer, United Nations Transitional Authority in Cambodia (UNTAC) (1991–1993); and Senior Associate, Mitsui, Yasuda, Wani & Maeda, 1993–1999 (1995–1997, seconded to Counsel, European Bank of Reconstruction and Development [EBRD]).

Susan Šarčević is Professor in the Faculty of Law of the University of Rijeka (Croatia) where she teaches legal English, legal German and EU terminology. She has published extensively on legal translation, legal lexicography and multilingual communication in the law (in English,

German and Croatian) and has been invited to lecture on legal translation worldwide. She is a translator of legal texts and reviser of legal texts in English.

Girolamo Tessuto is a Lecturer in English Language in the Law Faculty of the University of Naples II. He has extensive experience in language teaching for specific purposes at both undergraduate and postgraduate levels, and professional experience at the European Parliament. His main research interests are in the fields of ESP (legal language in a variety of application) and applied terminology and translation studies. Besides research articles in the same fields, his recent publications include *Discorso giuridico e repertorio lessicale del diritto penale di Common Law,* (2001); *The Language of Common Law Made Simple* (2002); *English for Law Made Simple* (2003).

Christopher Wing To is Adjunct Professor of Law and Engineering at the City University of Hong Kong and is currently the Secretary General of the Hong Kong International Arbitration Centre. He is a Panel Member (Arbitrator) at several institutions: the International Arbitrators of the Australian Centre for International Commercial Arbitration, the Korean Commercial Arbitration Board, the China International Economic Trade Arbitration Commission, the Kuala Lumpur Regional Arbitration Centre and the Singapore Institute of Arbitrators. He is a Fellow of the Chartered Institute of Arbitrators and a Fellow of the Hong Kong Institute of Arbitrators. He was appointed Chairman of the Inter-Pacific Bar Association Dispute Resolution and Arbitration Committee in 2006.

Anna Trosborg is Professor of English and Reader in Business Communication at Aarhus School of Business, Denmark. She has been conducting extensive research on professional discourse since 1989. Her recent academic publications are in the fields of L2 teaching and learning, business pragmatics, genre analysis, legal speech acts, and business communication. She is currently teaching intercultural business communication and negotiation.

Introductory

1

Concepts, Contexts and Procedures in Arbitration Discourse

Vijay K. Bhatia, Christopher N. Candlin and Jan Engberg

HISTORY AND BACKGROUND

Although legal language has long been the focus of attention for legal philosophers and sociologists (Austin, 1962; Mellinkoff, 1963; Searle, 1965, Allen, 1957; Atkinson and Drew, 1979; to mention only a few), its attraction for linguists and discourse analysts has been of relatively recent origin. Legal language started attracting somewhat adverse publicity in the mid-seventies, when campaigns for reforms in legislative expression gained momentum, especially in the USA and the UK (see Renton Committee Report, 1975). Popularly known as the Plain English Campaign, it brought into focus the question of incomprehensibility of legal expression from the point of view of not only the ordinary people but also of legislators. In the last two decades legal writing has assumed unprecedented significance not only for linguists, language and legal educators, but also for sociologists, critical theorists, writing specialists, translators and social reformers. In particular, there have been a number of studies focusing on the construction, interpretation, use and simplification of legal documents from the perspective of a variety of legal systems and languages. The works of Bhatia (1982, 1983, 1987, 1993) on the analysis of legal documents; Candlin and Maley (1994), and Candlin and others (1987, 1995) on client consultation, arbitration and dispute resolution; Charrow and Charrow (1978) on the comprehensibility of legal documents; Fredrickson (1995) on the analysis of Swedish and American legal language; Gunnarsson (1984) on the comprehensibility of legal Swedish; Maley (1985, 1987, 1994) on judicial and legislative discourse; and Trosborg (1991, 1997) on pragmatic aspects of legal discourse and legal translation, are only a few of the pioneering examples of recent work of interest in legal discourse.

Accompanying this is a valuable and interesting body of research related to the simplification of legal documents. There are two important approaches to reforms in legal writing. The first approach introduces simplification in legal writing as Plain English, where it is widely believed that legal documents can be expressed more or less in ordinary everyday English. Eagleson's work (1991) on the use of Plain English is insightful and encouraging. He has been able to convince a number of stakeholders in legal affairs, including government departments and legal firms, especially in Australia, about the possibility of achieving a reasonably high degree of legal specification without the excessive use of complex grammatical devices. Unfortunately, however, this view is not shared by a wide majority of legal professionals from the drafting community (Renton Committee Report, 1975, Thomas, 1985), who claim that it is impossible to achieve the required specification of scope in legal expression without the use of a complex array of qualifications and other grammatical resources. Bhatia (1982, 1993), in this context, proposed a different approach to rewriting legislation known as 'easification' of legal documents, where it is claimed that although it is possible to some extent to avoid unnecessary use of complex contingencies without sacrificing the essential integrity of the legal documents, it is not always possible to write legal documents in ordinary English without sacrificing a desirable and detailed specification of legal scope, especially if these documents are required to serve legislative purposes in the context of legal systems in western democracies. He suggests the use of a variety of 'easification devices' without compromising the essential integrity of the legislative genre to make them more readily accessible to its users, which may include lay readers as well as legislators.

There is also a vast body of literature on interpretation of statutes and other forms of legislation (Bennion, 1997, Cross, Bell and Engle, 1995, Dickerson, 1975, Eskridge, 1994, Evans, 1990, Gifford, 1990, and others). Some of them codify criteria for the interpretation of statutes, often incorporating linguistic aspects of statute construction and interpretation (Bennion, 1997), sometimes based on rules of logic, syntax, and punctuation. However, the principles of statutory interpretation discussed there do not materially differ from those applicable to the interpretation of documents generally. The most common treatment is based on the use of deductive reasoning, interpretation of individual words and phrases, or on the elaboration of meaning of words and phrases. There is very little available on the lexico-grammar of legislative writing. The most interesting work on legal interpretation from the point of view of different legal systems comes from MacCormick and Summers (1991). They compare statutory interpretation based on a set of common questions applied to nine different countries. The questions addressed interpretative issues such as the general origins of interpretation within legal systems, statutory gaps and gap-filling, the role of constitutional law, the effect of statutory provisions prescribing interpretative method, and the nature of collisions between statutes and other norms, often discussing how they are resolved. However, it is interesting to note that in the context of such a diversity of systems, MacCormick and Summers put forward a universal thesis that amounts to claiming that all systems share a common core of major types of arguments which provide good reasons for interpretative decisions. They also point to major variations in types of arguments and patterns of justification in the different systems, including differences in structure, logic, and style of the opinions in the higher courts. The authors also explain these variations are rationally grounded in political, institutional, cultural, and other factors present in the systems.

All these studies are insightful and stimulating for those interested in the construction, interpretation, use, and rewriting of legal discourse. However, most of these studies focus on the use of English in various legal genres and, as a result, on contexts which are essentially those of common law countries. There are only a few studies which have focused on languages and legal systems other than English. Even then, most of these have so far invested their efforts in the analysis and use of legal language embedded in specific legal cultures and essentially monolingual settings.

In recent years, however, we have seen an unprecedented increase in the dismantling of socio-cultural, disciplinary and national barriers, especially in the context of co-operation and collaboration in international trade and business. Creation of massive international free trade zones, and the opening up of major political economies in the last few years have accelerated moves towards intense competition to capture international markets and the merger of corporations to form huge multinational conglomerates. With the increase in these and similar other trends towards a globalisation of socio-cultural, business and communication issues, law is fast assuming an international perspective rather than retaining a purely national concern. An excellent example of this trend became visible in the early nineteen eighties when most of the countries of Western Europe combined to create a common European market. The need for a common European legal framework in order to introduce legislative instruments and the necessity to translate such legal instruments in all the languages has become a serious issue (Lang, 1989). The task was much more complex than simply creating a new legislative framework because this newly created instrument was meant to be interpreted within the contexts of a diversity of individual legal systems and languages of the member countries of western Europe, especially when one needed to interpret issues such as those of human rights, international agreements and contracts, freedom of speech, freedom of trade, protection of intellectual property, all of which have very strong socio-political and cultural constraints.

More recently, especially in context of the return of Hong Kong to the People's Republic of China and the creation of the SAR, the need to interpret one set of laws in the context of the other has become important. Whenever two languages and/or legal systems come in contact with each other, problems in the interpretation of statutes and regulations and in the translation of legal intentions from one language and/or one system to the other assume serious importance. As one example, in the periods immediately preceding and following the handover of the territory of Hong Kong, there were several cases where sections of the Basic Law were construed and interpreted rather differently by the parties concerned. The underlying issues in relation to statutory interpretation in many of these cases could either be traced back to differences between two drafting systems, which may include differences in languages, legal systems, or other socio-cultural factors. In the existing research on legal language, however, there has been very little attention paid to issues that arise as a result of differences in legal or socio-cultural systems. For example, we have some indication of how legal Danish is constructed, used and interpreted within the Danish legal system; we have some idea of how Swedes write their laws and use legal Swedish to negotiate justice in the courts of law in Sweden; we have considerable understanding of how legal English functions in the countries of the Commonwealth; but we know very little about how a particular legal language, be it English, Danish or Chinese, would handle a legal issue when it arises as a result of an interaction with another legal system, language or socio-cultural expectations. How, for example, should the issue of intellectual property protection law be construed, interpreted and used in Hong Kong SAR and the UK? To what extent and by what linguistic means should the two countries specify the scope of legislation? To what extent will the scope be constrained by the legal system in which it will be established?

To what extent will it be constrained by the linguistic resources available in the language in which it is written? Issues like these are crucial for the construction, interpretation and use of legal language across languages and legal systems. These issues are also extremely relevant when one translates legal expressions from one language or legal system into another. A number of these issues have been identified by several senior solicitors in Hong Kong (see Candlin and Bhatia, 1998).

A number of questions arise from the above review of legal discourse. One of the main questions is: what exactly is legal about legal language? More specifically, what happens to legal discourse when it is constructed, interpreted and used across linguistic, national, socio-political, cultural, and legal systems? In what way is generic integrity of legislative statements and other legal documents maintained in multi-lingual and multicultural legal contexts? What happens when the same rule of law is applied across legal systems?

This volume is an attempt to address some of these questions by contributing to the basic knowledge of legal language typically used in international commercial arbitration, and to suggest implications of this for legal practice, legal translation, and legal practitioner training. The discussions in this volume constitute one of the major outcomes of an international project, 'Generic Integrity in Legal Discourse in Multilingual and Multicultural Contexts'. The project investigated this challenge by focusing on international arbitration laws seen from the standpoint of a number of international contexts. As part of the project, academics and practitioners from, or focusing on, Brazil, the Czech Republic, the People's Republic of China, Denmark, Finland, France, Germany, Hong Kong, India, Italy, Japan, Malaysia, South Africa, and the United Kingdom have been involved in parallel investigations into such processes within their respective jurisdictions for several years. These international teams of researchers have also focused on analyses across their own jurisdictions in order to identify common elements in arbitration legislation as they are constructed and interpreted across multilingual and multicultural contexts. The research is based not only on the analysis of the texts of the legislation alone, but also on the factors shaping such constructions and interpretations. In the process, differences characteristic of, or resulting from the peculiarities of historical, socio-political, cultural, economic and legal developments in the sites concerned have also been taken into account.

The motivation for this research derived from the increasing international need for accurate and authoritative translation and use of legal documents across languages, translations which would both preserve the integrity of the source documents and would provide a robust representation of the legislation in question. Such translations would also need to convey appropriately in both languages the pragmatic and functional intentions and implications of the original document in question, addressing such issues as of degree of qualification, specification of scope, issues of closed versus open-endedness and other matters concerned with complex contingency. Although all legal documents in all languages address these issues, they do so in distinctive and also in overlapping ways, partly as a consequence of the different languages in which they are constructed, partly because of the socio-political and cultural differences of the societies in question and of their legal systems, and partly as a consequence of the ways in which these systems construct and interpret issues such as legal authority, agency and responsibility. The discourse of law, in particular, relating to contract and arbitration, has considerable contemporary relevance in the context of international, inter-linguistic and inter-cultural social actions in an increasingly globalized economy. This comparative legal and commercial interest is matched by a parallel linguistic and discourse analytical interest in the relationship between language and globalisation. A number of diverse communities of practice, such as discourse analysts, commercial consultants, legal trainers, translators, and applied researchers in professional and institutional communication, especially in the field of legal writing and languages for specific purposes, undoubtedly exercise a keen interest in legal discourse across disciplines, languages, cultures, and legal systems.

This introductory chapter has three major objectives: firstly, to identify and bring into focus some of the main *concepts* and *constructs* in the field of comparative legal discourse; secondly, to identify and characterise the main *contexts*, socio-political, institutional, professional, in terms of which comparative legal discourse can be studied, and where such study is practically relevant; and finally, to identify and outline an integrated set of appropriate discourse analytical and other methodological *procedures* that enable the grounded study of legal writing so as to provide substantive, relevant, and usable accounts of value to practitioners in various fields.

LEGAL DISCOURSE

Legal language plays an important role in the construction, interpretation, negotiation and implementation of legal justice. Through a limited set of legal genres an attempt is made to create and maintain a model world of rights and obligations, permissions and prohibitions. Although, in principle, this model world is required to be consistent with the vision that individual states or nations have of the society, in practice, it is often constrained by the changing socio-political realities of the specific nations, legal systems, and cultures. Therefore, to regulate the real world of human behaviour as and when it is found to be inconsistent with the model world, these rules and regulations are judiciously interpreted and applied through a system of courts to negotiate and invariably enforce desired behaviour (Bhatia, 1982). The so-called model world is thus created by imposing rights and obligations, permissions and prohibitions through legislation, and this, in most western democratic systems, is seen as the will of the elected representatives of the people in the parliament.

This view of law and legal justice requires most genres, especially legislation, to be written "with mathematical precision ... to provide a complete answer to virtually every question that can arise" (Sir Charles Davis in Renton Committee Report 1975). This requirement gives legal genres their unique integrity, often characterized in terms of their use of lexico-grammatical and discoursal resources that are rarely found in other disciplinary or professional genres. As pointed out in Bhatia (1982, 1993), legal genres are characterized by their use of a complex range of qualifications often strategically positioned at syntactic points where they are unlikely to attract any ambiguous or unintended interpretation, thus making them clear, precise, unambiguous and all-inclusive at the same time (see Bhatia, 1982, 1993, for a detailed discussion). However, there are several other factors that make this claim somewhat problematic: the legal system, the language, the socio-political and the cultural context within which a specific instance of legal discourse is embedded. One of the main issues arising from this variation is the extent to which the integrity of a specific legal genre is likely to be maintained when it crosses linguistic, socio-political, cultural or legal boundaries in the present-day global business, trade or other professional environment. These issues of diversity in construction and interpretation of legal discourse acquire a more serious importance when we see law losing its jurisdictional character in this rapidly changing corporate world of international trade and commerce.

LEGAL DISCOURSE IN INTERNATIONAL ARBITRATION: THE PROJECT

In order to investigate what happens to the same legislative genre when it is written, interpreted, and used across linguistic, socio-political, cultural and legal jurisdictional boundaries, a group of researchers from more than ten countries representing various jurisdictions, languages, cultures and socio-political backgrounds collaborated on an international project[1] to study international arbitration laws written, interpreted and used in various jurisdictions, including Brazil, China, Hong Kong, India, Japan, Malaysia, and a number of European countries, such as Denmark, England, Finland, France, Germany, and the Czech Republic (for details see the website http://gild.mmc.cityu.edu.hk/) The investigation involved thirteen distinct languages, such as English, Chinese, Czech, Danish, Finnish, German, Hindi, Italian, Japanese, Hong Kong, Bahasa Malaysia, Portuguese and Czech, which drew upon several distinct legal systems, such as the common law, the civil code, Islamic law, and a number of others in use in countries such as Brazil, Japan, Denmark, Finland, and the Czech Republic.

There appeared to be considerable overlap in all the international arbitration laws in different countries as they were invariably adopted from the UNCITRAL Model Law (1985) provided by the United Nations Organization or from the Geneva Convention of 1962. The main objective of the international project was to develop a basic understanding of legal discourse across languages, socio-political and cultural boundaries, and legal systems. However, its primary focus was on the investigation of generic integrity of legislative documents used in multinational and multilingual contexts so as to enhance our understanding of the construction, interpretation and use of legislative discourse in international contexts, and to assist legal writers, translators, and practitioners of law in functioning more effectively internationally. In order to investigate the generic integrity of legislative documents, the investigation drew on a multidimensional and multi-perspective approach to research, one which required the following tasks.

1. Documentation of background reports on individual countries, in particular about their legal systems, focusing especially on the way

1 RGC (HKSAR) funded Cerg Project (No. 9040474) on 'Generic Integrity of Legal Discourse in Multilingual and Multicultural Contexts'.

laws are written, interpreted, and used, choice of language(s), historical traditions in arbitration and conciliation, etc, in each of these countries. These documentations were meant to be used as a broad and rich context within which one could explain some of the findings of the analyses of not only the construction and interpretation of arbitration laws, but also the processes and procedures used in specific arbitration cases (See Bhatia, Candlin, Engberg, and Trosborg, 2003).

2. Analyses of the linguistic and discoursal properties of various subsets of international arbitration laws from different languages, language varieties, cultures and legal systems, focusing, in particular, on the nature and use of qualifications, specification of scope, all-inclusiveness, expressions of contingency, intertextuality and interdiscursivity, and degrees of control and transparency. The analyses offer a grounded account of the drafting and interpretative practices within specific contexts by focusing on a set of critical and relevant sites of engagement, incorporating specific moments of application of the laws under investigation, especially where certain aspects of these laws are invoked during the negotiation of justice (see Bhatia, Candlin and Gotti, 2003 for the analyses of arbitration laws from European countries, and Bhatia and Engberg, 2004 for the analyses of other international laws from outside Europe).
3. Comparing country specific laws with one another taking as a basis the UNCITRAL Arbitration Model Law provided by the United Nations, focusing in particular on areas which have been constructed differently in an attempt to offer explanations and implications of such divergences, often taking evidence from some of critical agreements, contracts, cases, and judgments in international arbitration. The present volume includes much of the comparative analysis of international arbitration laws.

The comparative analyses in the present volume based on a range of arbitration laws also attempt to provide some discussion of the issue of generic integrity of legal discourse in multilingual and multicultural legal contexts, and perhaps offers some answers to the question: "What happens to legislative discourse when it is constructed, translated, interpreted, used, or exploited across national, legal, socio-political, economical, and cultural boundaries"? Explanation of some of the issues is offered by reference to socio-cultural, economic and political, linguistic and legal factors based on the background studies of the legal systems of these two countries, and also on the expert reactions and commentaries by legal specialists, both from the academy and from legal practice.

In addition to the comparative and contrastive analyses of alternative textualizations, the chapters in this volume also provide useful insights for applications in translation of legal genres, especially with regard to the degree to which generic integrity is maintained in the practice of translation and legal drafting of legislative documents. In doing so it provides guidelines for the training of legal draftspersons and translators, with particular reference to inter-cultural sensitivity, with the aim of ensuring greater international acceptability of such translated and drafted texts. In brief, the volume is an attempt to test the validity of the generic integrity hypothesis, focusing in particular on the necessary interplay between genre, linguistic realisation and the underpinning legal systems and philosophies and practices of law in different societies. However, before taking up some of the main issues identified and discussed in this volume, we introduce some of the main findings in this area. These have been raised in earlier volumes published by the project and form the basis of some of the major issues emerging from the analyses of arbitration laws from a number of national and legal contexts (Bhatia, Candlin, Engberg and Trosborg, 2003; Bhatia, Candlin, and Gotti, 2003; Bhatia and Engberg, 2004; and Bhatia, Engberg, Gotti, and Heller, 2005)

As we indicated earlier, one of the main objectives of the project has been to investigate generic integrity, by which we mean stability in the characteristics of a genre across languages, socio-political contexts, and cultures. In short, to explore the differences and similarities to be found when arbitration laws from different countries are compared. How high, for example, is the proportion of overlap, thus indicating a high degree of generic integrity across cultures?

In the project, the cross-cultural investigation of genres connected to arbitration has been carried out in two different ways. One way has been to examine texts written in English, but which originate from cultures where English is not the national legal language, and to compare the results of this scrutiny with a text written originally in English, that is, the UNCITRAL Model Law, 1985. A second direction has been to look at arbitration texts written in official legal languages other than English and once again to compare these with the above-mentioned texts written originally in English. In both cases, the focus has been on cross-cultural differences and similarities. In the second group, differences and similarities between legal cultures may be observed in an unmediated way as texts are written directly in the language of the relevant legal cultures but where results may be influenced by systematic differences between the languages. In the first group, on the other hand, differences and similarities must be observed through the filter of translation (as the texts are written in a language different from the national language of the culture). Here it is possible to compare the results more directly as the language used in all the investigated texts is the same. So, both approaches have their advantages and disadvantages. Put together, they give us a rather detailed picture of differences and similarities.

OVERVIEW OF INVESTIGATIONS

The work being presented here draws on the research of a number of independent researchers working around a common core. Most of the analyses on which this overview is based have a wider scope than merely that of contributing to addressing the central question. We begin, therefore, by summarising earlier work we have already published so as to identify the main issues which arise.

In the edited volume by Bhatia, Candlin, Engberg and Trosborg (2003), a number of national legal systems are presented in general and with a special focus on relationships between national language(s) of law in various countries and national systems of arbitration.[2] The contributions in the volume have served as contextual background for the individual contrastive analyses, but will not be treated further here.

The studies in the project focused on two major genres: *statutes and executive orders* that function as the national or international statutory authority for international commercial arbitration, and *arbitration rules* of individual chambers of commerce, which govern the arbitration procedures. The second genre may be seen as concrete instantiations of procedural rules within the framework set up by the first genre. Most of the investigation has been directed at statutes. Accordingly, we begin with some of the important insights which result from the analyses of arbitration rules as they give us a useful overview of possible aspects on which to focus when examining the larger collection of research works.

---

2 The following countries have been covered in the volume: Brazil, People's Republic of China, The Czech Republic, Denmark, Finland, Germany, Hong Kong, India, Italy, Japan, Malaysia, Spain, and the Republic of South Africa.

Arbitration rules

Here the relevant articles are those of Belotti (2003), Facchinetti (2003) and Garzone (2003), investigating Italian, English, French and Swedish arbitration rules written in or translated into English. Arbitration rules connected to the specific national cultures have been investigated together with the UNCITRAL Rules, which are a set of model rules issued internationally by the United Nations. In these texts, the most important element of generic integrity relates to the macrostructure of the texts. There are major overlaps in terms of topics covered, in their macrostructures as well as in their order of appearance. So on these grounds, it may be stated safely that what we have here are examples of a cross-cultural genre.

One important general difference among the texts under study lies in their different contextual situations, i.e. their different national contexts rather than some international setting. On the one hand, Belotti (2003, 32) finds a general tendency for both national arbitration rules and for the UNCITRAL rules to be more reader-friendly from the point of view of, for example, manageable sentence length and syntactic complexity. In his view, this general characteristic probably derives from the fact that arbitration rules are always meant for business people rather than for legal experts. However, Belotti (2003, 38) and Facchinetti (2003, 169–170) also find that Italian rules are more detailed, concrete and easy to process than those of the UNCITRAL model. In particular the national texts demonstrate a higher degree of textual simplicity on a number of different levels than does the international text. In principle, this characteristic could be due to the differences between the model law and the concrete rules of specific chambers of commerce in one national jurisdiction, which may be a consequence of two different types of context (national vs. international, abstract vs. concrete).

Table 1.1 Number of words in arbitration rules under scrutiny (Garzone 2003, 186)

Arbitration rules by countries	Number of words
English rules	8,266 words
French rules	6,277 words
Swedish rules	4,055 words

However, the study by Garzone (2003, 214) shows that the UNCITRAL rules are much less complex than the national English rules, whereas the Swedish rules are even less complex than the French ones, especially in terms of their average sentence length. This shows that despite the shared generic integrity of the genre in question across these contexts, especially in the field of macro- and move structure, there are major differences in the stylistic features of the realisations of rules in English. The legal writing is heavily influenced by the underlying national legal culture. This influence may be seen, as indicated earlier, in terms of the syntactic complexity as well as in the number of words contained in the texts.

Another indicator is the use of modal auxiliaries: French and Swedish rules show more variation in the choice of modals as well as a less consistent use of *shall* than English and UNCITRAL law. This characteristic may be attributed to the fact that civil law legal cultures (like Sweden and France) traditionally use fewer modal auxiliaries and a greater variety of different expressions of the modality than common law legal cultures (England) and the English of international contracts (Garzone 2003, 206–208).

The investigation of arbitration rules from different cultures thus shows that although a number of successful efforts have been made to harmonize the content of such rules there is still visible a substantial influence of national legislation and drafting practices, even when texts are written in English (Garzone 2003, 211–215; 216). Generic integrity seems to be strongest at macro level (although national legislations may also have a differentiating influence here), whereas differences are more visible at micro level due to variations in drafting practices.

Statutes on arbitration

The general picture arising from the investigation of arbitration rules encourages the finding that generic integrity is primarily the function of overlapping macro-structures, whereas cultural differences operate primarily at the micro level. This is also true of the arbitration statutes, which have been the focus of attention in several papers, some of which are the following:

Scotland (Dossena 2003)
England (Tessuto 2003)
Finland (Salmi-Tolonen 2003)
Denmark (Engberg / Rasmussen 2003)
Germany (Engberg 2004, Engberg/Heller 2002, Heller 2003)

Italy (Giannonni 2003)
Spain (Chierichetti 2003)
Czech Republic (Chroma 2003)
Malaysia (Hashim 2004)
India (Bhatia/Candlin 2004)
China (Bhatia/Candlin 2004, Trosborg 2004)
Brazil (Frade 2004)

The texts under study have been compared to either the UNCITRAL Model Law 1986 or to the Geneva Convention of 1962, on which international model law is based.

Concerning similarities among the investigated texts, we note a high degree of cross-cultural overlap in the area of macro- and move structure of these texts. The general principle of text structuring in statutes is that of conditional argumentation (Heller 2003, 295). This implies that a number of topics are treated in the texts and that the structuring principle is a combination of conditions and consequences (qualifications, Bhatia 1993, 115) which serve as a basis for argumentation by courts or arbitrators. The topic is divided into a number of articles, each containing some kind of legislative provision or definition, although the number of articles, and especially their internal subdivision, may differ considerably. Finally, the analyses in the project show that all-inclusiveness and precision are guiding principles in the structuring of statutory texts, with the proviso that the characteristic of generality, fuzziness and vagueness acquires major importance in most cases (Frade 2004, 67–71).[3] The relative importance of these three kinds of characteristics may differ across cultures.

Many of the analyses explicitly state that the underlying national legal system and the drafting traditions of the specific legal culture studied play a substantial role in shaping concrete texts, even in the case of internationally oriented texts such as the statutes on international commercial arbitration. We illustrate some of these different traditions in what follows.

Generally, there is a basic difference between the contexts of the concrete national statutes on the one hand, and those of general international conventions (UNCITRAL Model Law, Geneva Convention),

3 For more discussions of the balance between these two aspects, see Bhatia/Engberg/Gotti/Heller (2005) and Engberg/Heller in this volume.

on the other. This difference derives from the fact that the international texts establish a framework with the specification of a number of alternatives to choose among, whereas a national statute relies more on the generality of the text. As a consequence, national statutes display fewer instances of bi- and multinomials than the international texts. The following example from the UNCITRAL Model Law illustrates the point.

Fig. 1.1 Bi- and multinomials in UNCITRAL Model Law article 26 (Frade 2004, 61)

Article 26. Expert appointed by arbitral tribunal

(1) Unless otherwise agreed by the parties, the arbitral tribunal

{ (a) may appoint one or more experts to report to it on specific issues to be determined by the arbitral tribunal;
(b) may require }

{ to give the expert any relevant information
or to produce
or to provide access to }

{ any relevant documents
goods
or property }

for his inspection.

However, it is interesting to see that the texts investigated from other countries also display this characteristic:

Table 1.2 Number of bi- and multinomials in Danish, Chinese and Italian texts

	International text	National statutory text	Difference
Denmark (Engberg/Rasmussen, 2003, 120)	63	24	-62 %
China (Bhatia/Candlin 2004, 20)	10	3	-70 %
Italy (Giannonni 2003, 231)	231	125	-46 %

Furthermore, Frade (2004, 62) states that bi- and multinomials are used very sparsely in the Brazilian statute on Arbitration. Consequently, the national statutes are shorter than the international texts (Italy: 5,291 vs. 4,067; Denmark: 1,483 vs. 848; China: 669 vs. 341).[4]

In the Indian text, however, we see exactly the opposite situation:

Table 1.3 Number of bi- and multinomials in Indian text

	International text	National statutory text	Difference
India (Bhatia/Candlin 2004, 20)	10	16	+ 60 %

In the same way, in the analysis of the Malaysian text (Hashim 2004) and of the English text (Tessuto 2003) a number of examples of complex bi- and multinomials are reported, although without exact quantitative data. However, it is clear from the studies that complex bi- and multinomials are not rare in the Malaysian and English texts. This indicates that we can hardly identify the use of bi- and multinomials as an aspect of generic integrity across legal cultures. Rather, the use of bi- and multinomials is dependent on the type of legal system of the underlying legal culture. Denmark, China, Italy are civil-law countries and have a significantly lower incidence of bi- and multinomials, whereas India, England, and Malaysia are common-law countries, and they show a much higher incidence of these lexico-grammatical features.

Interestingly, although a precise quantitative analysis of bi- and multinomials in the German statute is lacking, Heller (2003, 292; 294; 309) notes that the recent German statute she analysed is much more complex than the former version of the German statute. Moreover, this higher complexity is also due to the use of bi- and multinomials. The number of conditionals is more or less constant from one version of the German statute to the other, but bi- and multinomials have been used more frequently when formulating conditionals in the recent version in order to achieve a higher degree of precision than the traditional civil-law drafting style of German statutes is capable of. The result is interesting because it is one of the rare examples where a national statute has taken over a convention from a foreign tradition, probably due to translation, adoption or closer approximation.

4 Not all analyses look at the whole texts, but concentrate upon comparable parts. Both the Chinese and the Italian text has been compared to the UNML, but the analysis of the Chinese text only covers three articles in UNML and their corresponding sections in the Chinese statute.

The observed differences may be attributed to differences in the importance of all-inclusiveness and precision, respectively. According to the general function of statutes in legal systems, modern national statutes have to achieve all-inclusiveness and precision. However, depending upon the basic legal approach, different traditional strategies are adopted in the studied texts: Civil-law jurisdictions seem to opt for all-inclusiveness, using more abstract wording and therefore generally both fewer words and fewer bi- and multinomials than the international texts on which the national statutes are based; common-law countries, on the other hand, opt for precision, generally achieved via more words and more bi- and multinomials than the international texts. The German statute is a special case in that it follows many of the traditional conventions of German statutes, but in its structuring rather opts for a non-traditionally high degree of precision, as it contains a higher number of conditions, a trait which normally leads to a higher degree of explicitness (Heller 2003, 295).

Following the same line of argument, we see differences in the use of modal auxiliaries. Common-law texts have a relatively high proportion of explicitly expressed modality in the format of modal auxiliaries. Civil-law texts, on the other hand, often use simple present or future tense and thus express the modality in a more indirect way (see for example Chierichetti 2003, 54–55). This is further supported by Garzone (2003) in the investigation of the arbitration rules.

Summarizing the results

If we look at the issue of generic integrity in the case of the two genres under scrutiny (statutes and arbitration rules), macro- and move structure are very stable across cultures concerning both genres. All-inclusiveness and precision also seem to belong to the cross-cultural characterising traits of texts of the genre, but the focus may shift between them and, as a consequence, textual realisations like the use of bi- and multinomials are not part of the overall characteristics of the genre across cultures. Their relative importance is dependent on the degree of importance accorded to the characteristic of precision by the respective legal cultures. Here, a first-level division between common-law and civil-law cultures becomes important. We may thus postulate two general sub-types of the genre on this basis.

Finally, most analyses show that national drafting traditions at various textual levels, which include lexico-grammar as well as arrangements of qualifications within the structure of statutory clauses, are generally the dominating factor: Statutes on international commercial arbitration are written so that they meet the traditional standards of the underlying legal culture, irrespective of the language used (English or the national language). As a matter of fact, the analyses undertaken as part of the project only found one example of a text where this description does not fit, viz. the recent German statute. Here, although many of the traditional characteristics of the genre in the German legal culture are to be found, Heller argues that the textual structuring differs considerably from the former version of the same statute — and thus from the traditional standards — in being more deeply structured and thus more explicit and precise. It would be interesting to investigate more thoroughly whether a new development is on its way here, breaking up the divisions between the two major blocks represented in the analyses of the project, viz. that of civil-law and common-law countries.

A preliminary answer thus to one of the central questions of the project, viz. the degree of generic integrity in the statutory genres under scrutiny, is that a number of similarities have been found, mainly at higher textual levels; that general contextual factors like the quest for all-inclusiveness and precision are stable across cultures, but that national traditions also play a considerable role. As already discussed, despite the fact that international commercial arbitration is a field more likely to move towards greater harmonization, legal genres are still deeply rooted in their national cultures.

MAIN ISSUES OF FOCUS IN THE PRESENT VOLUME

In contrast to already published work, which has also been briefly referred to above, the chapters in this volume address some of the major issues emerging from these studies and do so in a more comparative way, taking these concerns further, raising more theoretical issues and discussing their implications for legal drafting, translation and legal practice. In the following we identify some of these general issues and discuss the contributions made by authors of this volume.

Vagueness and indeterminacy

Vagueness and indeterminacy in statutory texts create a dilemma in law. The basic assumption is that society must be governed by the rule of law and not on the basis of individual beliefs or actions. However, it is also obvious that indeterminacy and vagueness are typically inherent characteristics of law, thus making interpretation a necessary and important aspect of legal application.

In international commercial arbitration this aspect of interpretation assumes greater importance because of several factors. Firstly, arbitration is inherently characterised by a relatively lower degree of formalisation and a higher degree of negotiability than is the case in normal litigation, and secondly, it often involves procedural rules of one country, but where the parties may to a large extent (depending on the chosen forum and the relevant arbitration rules) decide the procedural rules for their dispute themselves. This means that at least hypothetically, rules for international commercial arbitration will encourage a high degree of vague expressions which may facilitate negotiation between the parties and the arbitrators.

Engberg and Heller investigate vague expressions in arbitration laws and claim that they are typically essential as discretion markers because the flexible nature of arbitration discourse makes relatively more room for interpretation. They further argue that qualifying expressions, although integral features of legislative provisions, do not necessarily eliminate vagueness. This is chiefly because of the presence of 'internal' qualifiers which contribute significantly to the negotiation of scope and application.

Globalization of legal practice

Economic globalization exercises a significant effect on relations among institutions, organizations and actors across societies, cultures and legal systems, through both law and language. It tends to influence all forms of legal relations through the creation and recreation of new forms of expression for the construction of professional practices and identities (Fairclough 2001).

Economic globalization not only creates conditions for universalization of trade and investment practices — often influenced by dominant American modes of thinking — but also creates conditions for the development of a parallel implementation of legal approaches based on the common law tradition. The globalization of law presupposes its operational autonomy *vis-à-vis* other national laws, serving to undermine the autonomy of nations in regard to their law practices.

Frade analyzes the implications of legal globalization in the context of Brazil, a Portuguese-speaking and civil law country, but one which is fully integrated into global economy. She emphasises the adjustments that need to be made to comply with the latest requirements for becoming "legally global" through the enactment of the Brazilian Arbitration Law and the implications this has on national legal practice, culture, discourse and education. She points out how national legal discourse tends to display a new texturing of meanings to reflect the "generalized tensions between international practices and local traditions" (Fairclough 2001: 25–26), while at the same time legal education and professional training calls for a new perspective for training 'international lawyers' to achieve "core international legal competence" (Orban III 2001: 53).

Litigation v. arbitration

Commercial activities in the present-day world of intense corporate competition have become increasingly complex. Conflicts of various kinds arise and are resolved in various ways through litigation, arbitration, mediation, conciliation or negotiation. Litigation in the common law countries is adversarial and power-laden, and discourse processes are constrained by legal authority and absence of any choice, making discourse in the litigation process typically monologic (Bakhtin, 1984). Other mechanisms, in comparison, are essentially devoid of the imperatives of adversarial process, and hence can be viewed as dialogic in nature.

Arbitration, although like litigation in its adjudicatory process, allows dialogue with no legal mandates as long as this is acceptable to the parties to the conflict. In contrast, a judge in a litigation process is allowed to perform only within the boundaries of specific legal mandates, whether they be legislative authorities or legal precedents. In arbitration, the emphasis is on settling the dispute and winning the case.

Commercial Arbitration proceedings can be, and often are influenced by conventional legal practice in a typically adversarial framework. From the point of view of disputants arbitration should be viewed as negotiation and conciliation and must take place in a dialogic mode instead of the adversarial mode, (which is) clearly seen as monologic. The intensely dialogic and dynamic nature of commercial arbitration mechanism is more visible in the context of the multi-cultural and globalized nature of economic and business activities.

Based on arbitration proceedings in India, Dhanania argues that commercial arbitration proceedings are increasingly being influenced by judicial processes, and hence are less consistent with the principles of negotiation and settlement, and their dialogic modes of interaction. These proceedings, she argues, are becoming mere replicas of the judicial process in private settings. Such adversarial resolution of disputes is contrary to the spirit of arbitration of commercial conflicts.

Based on arbitration practices in Japan, Sato proposes the concept of hybrid dispute processing, which combines some of the basic dispute processing elements such as conciliation, arbitration, and litigation. He identifies the need to recognize the evolution of Alternative Dispute Resolution (ADR) and to cope with the problems arising from an increasing 'colonization' of arbitration by litigation in international commercial contexts. He discusses several examples of hybrid dispute processing from various international contexts, especially Japan, and points out that such hybrid dispute resolution will contribute to harmonization of dispute processing from various dispute cultures scores the world.

Socio-cultural constraints on arbitration: Harmonization of legal discourse

Normative discourse (statutes and regulations) varies in countries with different constitutional, sociocultural and economic conditions in order to adapt to different cultural, linguistic and legal environments, depending on local customs and traditions, legal systems, nature of disputes, procedural aspects, linguistic issues, cultural contexts, and other socio-economic constraints. In the contexts of global trade and commerce, law is increasingly being interpreted in a more international than a purely jurisdictional perspective, which is more centrally relevant to international commercial arbitration than to any other legal domain. It would be interesting to investigate the extent to which cultural elements influence such differentiation in the construction, interpretation, and use of arbitration laws and procedures in various countries. Considering culture as a set of traditions and social practices typical of a specific professional community — in this case, legal practitioners involved in arbitration procedures — one may find interesting variations in arbitration laws and practices in different countries and legal systems, especially when one considers the conditions and constraints within which legal texts are framed and the actual situations in which such texts are used and interpreted.

Features such as the choice of technical lexis, the use of specific syntactic formations, for example binomial/multinomial expressions, complex prepositions, and nominalizations, the transparency and spread of information, concerns for conceptual or terminological unambiguity and explicit textual schematization, are indicative of the emphasis normally placed by common law legislation on precision and detailed specification of legal action in specific circumstances. The civil law, on the other hand, shows a divergent behaviour, paying more attention to simpler syntactic formulations, lower level of information density, extensive use of simple and compound sentences, and the use of common lexical forms.

Gotti, based on his analysis of arbitration laws from different countries, points out textual, conceptual and stylistic discrepancies that arise in the process of establishing closer harmonization in legal normative discourse at a global level. He argues that harmonization becomes particularly difficult when 'model' texts have to be adopted in various contexts. Such contexts give rise to interesting differentiations in the resulting texts that can be attributed not only to the languages in which the final texts are expressed but also to the different cultural traits and legal traditions of the communities for which they are meant. In particular, he finds significant variations in the specification of information in the various texts, which he claims are due to the differences in socio-cultural expectations and practices that constrain social behaviour in local contexts.

His analysis confirms the influence of cultural constraints in texts that are the result of a translation or a re-writing process used in international arbitration. While the main objective of using UNCITRAL Model Law was to create greater harmonization in various country specifications, Gotti, on the contrary, finds that this kind of total harmonization is clearly lacking. A more realistic objective might be to strive for a common understanding of terms and practices rather than total adoption and blind acceptance of proposed models. This might be achieved through the exercise of flexibility and non-involvement in decreeing rules for domestic arbitration, and emphasizing the freedom of action of individual states and the discretion of the institutions involved.

Confidentiality in arbitration

Arbitration is generally seen to be a private matter unless the agreements provide otherwise. It is assumed that any sensitive evidence, documentation or matters raised in the proceedings will not be made public. In other words, contrary to the situation in court proceedings, personal confidences, trade secrets, business processes and reputations are effectively safeguarded.

Confidentiality, cost-effectiveness and flexibility in settling commercial disputes are some of the key aspects in arbitration as against litigation. Parties often weigh some of these advantages when they decide whether to refer the dispute to arbitration rather than litigation. However, there are substantial international differences in the existence and scope of the duty of confidentiality. Privacy ranks relatively low as the most important attribute of arbitration, in spite of an expectation that the proceedings will be conducted in the absence of strangers to the arbitration and that their business and personal confidences will be kept in strict confidence. The International Court of Arbitration (ICA) Rules of Arbitration provide for the protection of trade secrets and confidentiality of the award and the privacy of the hearings.

The confidential and informal nature of arbitration not only protects parties from potentially inconsistent jury awards, settlements and punitive damages that carry large liability, but also from public scrutiny and embarrassing criticism. In the case of labour disputes, arbitration is much preferred, since this allows the preserving of a positive employer-employee relationship with a greater possibility of employee reinstatement during the pendency of the dispute.

To, in his study of confidentiality in arbitration, mediation and litigation considers these issues from an international perspective taking into account case laws on arbitration and mediation from a number of prominent legal systems, including those in Australia, Hong Kong, the People's Republic of China, Sweden, Singapore, the United Kingdom, and the United States of America.

Arbitral awards

Unlike arbitration laws and rules which rely heavily on the use of typical lexico-grammatical features for clarity, precision, unambiguity and all-inclusiveness (Bhatia, 1993), modern English arbitral awards rely more on content. Awards are presented and expressed in modern, plain and effective English, and as such are readily comprehensible to the lay as well as to specialist audiences.

Tessuto argues that although the main purpose of arbitral awards is to provide simple, cost effective ways of resolving disputes, the arbitrator's attitude is equally important, especially his or her socio-culturally-institutionalised judgment in contexts where social behaviour needs to be controlled, and justified.

Multicultural tribunals

Malanczuk, on the basis of his first hand experience of the Iran-United States Claims Tribunal, argues for the multi-cultural composition of the arbitrators in tribunals. This tribunal was created under unique circumstances, considering the diverse ideological premises of the parties, their political and military confrontation, and the volume of the economic interests at issue, and this was often reflected in the difficulties of its operation in practice. In that particular instance, Iran and the United States each appointed three arbitrators from their own countries. Since their national legal systems were as different as their languages, cultures and religion, these differences were further complicated by the diversity of the backgrounds and legal traditions of the third-country arbitrators from Sweden, Germany, Switzerland, Argentina, Poland, Finland, Netherlands and Italy. This made tribunal proceedings and decision in terms both of the procedure and the substantive law truly multicultural, offering a broad field of study for the meaning of the clash of legal cultures in international arbitration.

Translation

In the context of the globalization of international trade, the number of international disputes submitted to arbitration has increased tremendously in recent decades with actors from all continents speaking and writing in a multitude of languages. As a result of the acceptance of international instruments such as the UNCITRAL Model Law on International Commercial Arbitration, a high degree of harmonization has been achieved in national arbitration laws. The Model Law has been accepted in whole or in part by a large number of states and jurisdictions, many of which have incorporated it into their national law largely by an indirect process of translation. Although mostly behind the scenes, translation plays a vital role in numerous aspects of international arbitration, including the translation of legal documents for the proceedings, the translation of national arbitration laws into world languages, the translation of institutional procedural rules and standard arbitral clauses, the production of multilingual instruments of international arbitration law and others. However, multilingualism in the law can be effective only if those affected by the instrument are guaranteed equality before the law, regardless of the language of the text. Although the authentic texts of a legal instrument are presumed to be equal in meaning, effect and intent, there is always a risk of linguistic diversity and error when translation is involved. If the divergences and errors are harmless, it is a less serious problem; however, in cases where more serious ambiguities are noticed, they can be potentially misleading, posing a threat to uniform interpretation and application. This assigns a serious responsibility to translators of legal documents. Šarčević, in her chapter, rightly argues that despite the growing use of English, translation plays a significant role not only in the globalization but also in the harmonization of international arbitration. However, she concedes that the process of legal translation can be risky even for native speakers if they have not participated in the drafting process and have no contact with the drafters of the authentic text or texts. Since the ultimate purpose of arbitration legislation is to resolve disputes, not to create new ones, translators have the difficult task of anticipating how the target text will be interpreted and applied by users of different legal, linguistic and cultural backgrounds (cf. Šarčević 2000: 72). The cause for concern is greater, she adds, when a similar divergence exists in the authentic texts of multilateral instruments of international law, which are interpreted and applied by national courts and arbitrators from diverse legal systems and cultures.

One of the most difficult aspects of legal translation is the issue of terminology, and Chroma, in her chapter, outlines some of the key terminological issues relevant for the translation of arbitration laws and procedures. She argues for a conceptual approach to terminology in legal translation which relies on the choice of seemingly equivalent terms in two or more different legal systems using two or more different languages as the vehicles of legal information, always based on the comparison of the scope (intension), applicability (in various contexts and genres), the purpose and effect of legal concepts. She recommends extensive conceptual analyses of key terms to avoid the potential risk of choosing translational equivalents which would not be adequate in the target legal system and, hence misleading or incomprehensible for the ultimate recipients.

To sum up, research reported in this volume has reinforced the necessity to pay attention to issues of both the language and the law as a means of harmonizing procedures in the construction, interpretation and use of legal language in international legislative contexts. This volume is intended to take the realisation of this necessity forward in close international cooperation with established researchers and practitioners in language and law. The descriptive, interpretive and explanatory approach to the analysis of legislative data has enabled the contributors to this volume to highlight the significance of language analysis to an understanding of international arbitration laws in multilingual and multicultural legal jurisdictions.

REFERENCES

Allen, L. E. (1957) Symbolic Logic: A Razor-Edged Tool for Drafting and Interpreting Legal Documents. *Yale Law Journal* 66.

Atkinson, J. M. and Drew, P. (1979) *Order in Court: The Organization of Verbal Behaviour in Judicial Settings*. London: Macmillan.

Austin, J. L. (1962) *How to Do Things with Words*. New York: Oxford University Press.

Bahktin, M. M. (1984) *Problems of Dostoevsky's Poetics*. Ed. and trans. Caryl Emerson. *Theory and History of Literature*, Volume 8. Manchester: Manchester University Press.

Belotti, U. (2003) Generic Integrity in Italian Arbitration Rules. In Bhatia, Candlin and Gotti (eds.), 19–40.

Bennion, F. (1997) *Statutory Interpretation* (3rd Ed.). London: Butterworths.

Bhatia, V. K. (1982) *An Investigation into Formal and Functional Characteristics of Qualifications in Legislative Writing and Its Application to English for Academic Legal Purposes*. Ph.D. thesis, University of Aston in Birmingham.

Bhatia, V. K. (1983) Simplification v. Easification: The Case of Legal Texts. *Applied Linguistics* 4, 1: 42–54.

Bhatia, V. K. (1987) Textual-Mapping in British Legislative Writing. *World Englishes* 6, 1.

Bhatia, V. K. (1993) *Analysing Genre — Language Use in Professional Settings*. London: Longman.

Bhatia, V. K. and Candlin, C. N. (2004) Analysing Arbitration Laws across Legal Systems. *Hermes* 32: 13–43.

Bhatia, V. K., Candlin, C. N., Engberg, J. and Trosborg, A. (eds.) (2003) *Multilingual and Multicultural Contexts of Legislation: An International Perspective*. Bern: Peter Lang.

Bhatia, V. K., Candlin, C. N. and Gotti, M. (eds.) (2003) *Legal Discourse in Multilingual and Multicultural Contexts: Arbitration Texts in Europe*. Bern: Peter Lang.

Bhatia, V. K. and Engberg, J. (2004) Special Issue of *Hermes, Journal of Linguistics*, Volume 32.

Bhatia, V. K., Engberg, J., Gotti, M. and Heller, D. (eds.) (2005): *Vagueness in Normative Texts*. Bern: Peter Lang.

Candlin, C. N. and Bhatia, V. K. (1998) *Legal Communication: A Study to Investigate the Communicative Needs of Legal Professionals*. Hong Kong: Law Society of Hong Kong.

Candlin, C. N., Bhatia, V. K. and Jensen, C. (2002) Must the Worlds Collide? Professional and Academic Discourse in the Study and Practice of Law. In Cortese, P. and Riley, P. (eds.), *Domain Specific English: Textual Issues: From Communities to Classrooms*. Tübingen: Peter Lang.

Candlin, C. N. and Maley, Y. (1994) Framing the Dispute. *International Journal for the Semiotics of Law* 7, 19: 75–99.

Candlin, C. N. and Maley, Y. (1997) Intertextuality and Interdiscursivity in the Discourse of Alternative Dispute Resolution. In Gunnarsson, B.-L., Linell, P., and Nordberg, B. (eds.), *The Construction of Professional Discourse*. London: Longman.

Candlin, C. N., Maley, Y., Koster, P. and Crichton, J. (1995) *Lawyer-Client Conferencing: A Report to the Law Foundation of the NSW*. Sydney: Law Foundation of NSW.

Candlin, C. N. and Uehara, R. (1987) The Structural and Discoursal Characteristics of 'Voir Dire'. In Coleman, H. (ed.), *Language and Work*, The Hague: Mouton de Gruyter.

Charrow, V. and Charrow, R. (1978) *The Comprehension of Standard Jury Instructions: A Psycholinguistic Approach*. Arlington, VA: Center for Applied Linguistics.

Chierichetti, L. (2003) El arbitraje en España. Con unos apuntes para un análisis lingüistico con la Ley Modelo de UNCITRAL. In Bhatia, Candlin, and Gotti (eds.), 41–61.

Chroma, M. (2003) The Language of Arbitration: From Intent to the Act. In Bhatia, Candlin, and Gotti (eds.), 63–86.

Cross, R., Bell, J. and Engle, G. (1995) *Statutory Interpretation*. London: Butterworths (3rd ed.).

Dickerson, R. (1975) *The Interpretation and Application of Statutes*. Boston: Little, Brown and Company.

Dossena, M. (2003) Arbitration in Scotland: Local Specificity and International Homogeneity. In Bhatia, Candlin, and Gotti (eds.), 87–109.

Eagleson, R. D. (1991) *The Plain English Movement in Australia and the United Kingdom*. In Steinberg, E. T. (ed.), *Plain Language — Principles and Practice*. Detroit: Wayne State University Press.

Engberg, J. (2004) Redehintergründe von Gesetzestexten — ein Sonderfall? In Letness, Ole and Lindemann, Beate (Hrsg.): Diathese, Modalität, Deutsch als Fremdsprache. Festschrift für Oddleif Leirbukt zum 65. Geburtstag. Tübingen: Stauffenburg, 197–210.

Engberg, J. and Wølch Rasmussen, K. (2003) Danish Legal Language in

International Commercial Arbitration. In Bhatia, Candlin and Gotti (eds.), 111–154.

Eskridge, W. (1994) *Dynamic Statutory Interpretation*. Cambridge, MA: Harvard University Press.

Evans, J. (1990) *Statutory Interpretation: Problems of Communication*, Auckland: Oxford University Press.

Facchinetti, R. (2003) The 1998 Rules of the International Court of Arbitration as Implemented in Italy. In Bhatia, Candlin and Gotti (eds.), 155–76.

Fairclough, N. (2001) *Discurso e mudança social* [Discourse and social change]. Brasilia: Editora UnB.

Frade, C. (2004) Generic Variation across Legislative Writing: A Contrastive Analysis of the UNCITRAL Model Law and Brazil's Arbitration Law. *Hermes* 32: 45–75.

Fredrickson, K. (1995) *American and Swedish Written Legal Discourse: The Case of Court Documents*. Ph.D. dissertation, University of Michigan.

Garzone, G. (2003) Arbitration Rules across Legal Cultures: An Intercultural Approach. In Bhatia, Candlin and Gotti (eds.), 177–220.

Giannoni, D. S. (2003) The UNCITRAL Model and Italian Statute Law: A Linguistic and Topical Description. In Bhatia, Candlin and Gotti (eds.), 221–246.

Gifford, D. (1990) *Statutory Interpretation*. North Ryde, NSW.: Law Book.

Gunnarsson, B. (1984) Functional Comprehensibility of Legislative Texts: Experiments with a Swedish Act of Parliament. *Text* 4: 71–105.

Hashim, A. (2004) Aspects of Content and Language in the Malaysian Arbitration Act. *Hermes* 32: 77–98.

Heller, D. (2003) Prinzipien der Textgestaltung und der Gebrauch von Konditionalsätzen im deutschen Schiedsverfahrensrecht. In Bhatia, Candlin and Gotti (eds.), 287–312.

Heller, D. and Engberg, J. (2002) Verwendungskonventionen deontischer Modalmarker im deutschen Schiedsverfahrensrecht. In Gotti, M., Heller, D. and Dossena, M. (eds.), *Conflict and Negotiation in Specialized Texts*. Bern: Peter Lang, 165–188.

Lang, J. T. (1989) The Place of Legislation in European Community Law. *Statute Law Review* 10, 1.

MacCormick, D. N. and Summers, R. S. (1991) *Interpreting Statutes: A Comparative Study*, Aldershot: Dartmouth.

Maley, Y. (1985) Judicial Discourse: The Case of the Legal Judgment. In J. E. Clark (ed.) *The Cultivated Australian: Festschrift for Arthur Delbridge*. Hamburg: Helmut Buske Verlag, 159–173.

Maley, Y. (1987) The Language of Legislation. *Language and Society* 16: 25–48.

Maley, Y. (1994) The Language of the Law. In Gibbons (ed.) *Language and the Law*. London: Longman.

Maley, Y., Candlin, C. N., Koster, P., and Crichton, J. (1995) Orientations in Lawyer-Client Interviews. *Forensic Linguistics* 2(1).

Mellinkoff, D. (1963) *The Language of the Law*. Boston: Little Brown Co.

Orban, III, F. A. (2001) Legal Globalisation: The Challenges for In-House Counsel. *ACCA Docket* 19(2): 48–62.

Renton, D. (1975) *The Preparation of Legislation*. A Report of a Committee Appointed by The Lord President of the Council. London: HMSO.

Salmi-Tolonen, T. (2003) Arbitration Law as Action: An Analysis of the Finnish Arbitration Act. In Bhatia, Candlin and Gotti (eds.), 313–336.

Šarčević, S. (2000) *New Approach to Legal Translation*. 2nd ed. The Hague-London-Boston: Kluwer Law International.

Searle, J. R. (1965) *Speech Acts: An Essay in the Philosophy of Language*. Cambridge: Cambridge University Press.

Tessuto, G. (2003) Legislative Discourse in Arbitration Language: The English 1996 Arbitration Act and the UNCITRAL Model Law. In Bhatia, Candlin and Gotti (eds.), 337–379.

Thomas, R. (1985) *Plain English and the Law*, *Statute Law Review* 9, 3: 144.

Trosborg, A. (1991) An Analysis of Legal Speech Acts in English Contract Law. *Hermes* 6: 65–90.

Trosborg, A. (1997) *Rhetorical Strategies in Legal Language: Discourse Analysis of Statutes and Contracts*. Tübingen: Gunter Narr.

Trosborg, A. (2004) Regulative Strategies in Arbitration Law. Uncitral Model Law on International Commercial Arbitration (UNCITRAL) compared with Arbitration Law of the People's Republic of China. *Hermes* 32: 99–115.

UNCITRAL Model Law 1985.

Perspectives and Issues

2

Mixing Legal Cultures in International Arbitration: The Iran-United States Claims Tribunal

Peter Malanczuk

INTRODUCTION

At an early stage of the work of the Tribunal, the late Richard B. Lillich characterized the Iran-United States Claims Tribunal as the most significant body in arbitral history.[1] Now that the Tribunal, after more than 20 years of its existence, seems to be coming towards the end of its work, with only a few cases left to decide or to settle, it may be the right moment to reconsider this assessment with some more hindsight and discuss the lessons that may be learnt from the Tribunal in mixing legal cultures.[2]

Much has been written on the Tribunal in general as well as on more specific aspects of its work.[3] Among the more recent literature, the

1. R. B. Lillich (ed.), *The Iran-United States Claims Tribunal 1981–1983*, 1984.
2. The present author was Legal Assistant to the President of the Tribunal, Professor Karl-Heinz Böckstiegel, and to Professor Bengt Broms, Chairman of Chamber One, from 1986 to 1989, and continued to work with Professor Böckstiegel on the finalization of cases concerning the expropriation of American oil companies for some years thereafter, while holding a Chair of International Law at the University of Amsterdam. The current chapter is based upon an earlier version published as Peter Malanczuk, "The Iran-United States Claims Tribunal in The Hague — Some Reflections on a Unique Institution of International Dispute Settlement Moving towards the End of Its Work", in: Volkmar Götz, Peter Selmer, and Rüdiger Wolfrum (eds.), *Liber amicorum Günther Jaenicke — Zum 85. Geburtstag*. (Vol. 135. Beiträge zum ausländischen öffentlichen Recht und Völkerrecht, Max Planck Institute for Comparative Public Law and International Law, Jochen Abr. Frowein/Rüdiger Wolfrum eds.). Berlin/Heidelberg/New York: Springer-Verlag, 1998, pp. 221–238.
3. See, for example, N. G. Ziadé, Selective Bibliography on the Iran-United States Claims Tribunal, *ICSID Review — Foreign Investment Law Journal* 2 (1987), 534 et seq.; B. Maiwald, *Das Iran-United States Claims Tribunal*, 1987; K.-H. Böckstiegel, Zur Bedeutung des Iran-United States Claims Tribunal für die Entwicklung des internationalen Rechts, in: *Festschrift*

extremely valuable survey of the jurisprudence of the Tribunal by Judge George H. Aldrich, one of the American members of the Tribunal from the very beginning, should be specially mentioned.[4] As to many details concerning the establishment, operation and case law of the Tribunal reference can be made to the existing publications. The following is therefore restricted to a rather basic outline of the most important features of the Tribunal to provide the reader with the necessary background. It then addresses the output of the Tribunal. Finally, an attempt is made to briefly evaluate the work of the Tribunal.

BACKGROUND

The Tribunal was created by the Algiers Declarations[5] in 1981 as part of

---

der Rechtswissenschaftlichen Fakultät zur 600-Jahr-Feier der Universität Köln, 1998, 610 et seq.; Charles N. Brower, The Iran-United States Claims Tribunal After Seven Years: A Retrospective View from the Inside, *Arbitration Journal*, No. 34 (December 1988), 16 et seq.; N. Wühler, Zur Bedeutung des Iran-United States Claims Tribunal für die Rechtsfortbildung, in: K.-H. Böckstiegel (ed.), *Rechtsfortbildung durch internationale Schiedsgerichtsbarkeit*, 1989, 94–124; K.-H. Böckstiegel, Zur Praxis der internationalen Streiterledigung. Überlegungen am Ende der Tätigkeit als Präsident des Iran-United States Claims Tribunal, in: G. Ress (ed.), *Wissenschaftliches Kolloquium zum Völkerrecht, Europarecht und Verfassungsrecht anlässlich des 75. Geburtstages von Professor Dr. Günther Jaenicke (Universität des Saarlandes. Vorträge, Reden und Berichte aus dem Europa-Institut / Nr. 166)*, 1989, 5–25; R. Khan, *The Iran-United States Claims Tribunal*, 1990; Charles N. Brower, The Iran-United States Claims Tribunal, *RdC* 224 (1990-V), 123–396; J. A. Westberg, *International Transactions and Claims Involving Government Parties — Case Law of the Iran-United States Claims Tribunal*, 1991; A. Avanessian, *The Iran-United States Claims Tribunal in Action*, 1993; W. Mapp, *The Iran-United States Claims Tribunal: The First Ten Years 1981–1991*, 1993; A. Mouri, Striking a Balance between the Finality of Awards and the Right to a Fair Judgment: What is the Contribution of the Iran-U.S. Claims Tribunal, *The Finnish Yearbook of International Law* 4 (1993), 1–97; A. Mouri, Aspects of the Iran-United States Claims Tribunal, *Asian Yearbook of International Law* 2 (1994), 61–85; P. Malanczuk, *Akehurst's Modern International Law*, 7th ed 1997, reprint 1998, 259–60, 262, 267, 276, 296–8. Further literature is cited below.

4. G. H. Aldrich, *The Jurisprudence of the Iran-United States Claims Tribunal — An Analysis of the Decisions of the Tribunal*, 1996.
5. Declaration of the Government of the Democratic and Popular Republic of Algeria (General Declaration); Declaration of the Government of the Democratic and Popular Republic of Algeria concerning the Settlement of Claims by the Government of the United States of America and the Government of the Islamic Republic of Iran (Claims Settlement Declaration); Undertakings of the Government of the United States of America and the Government of the Islamic Republic of Iran with respect to the Declaration of the Government of the Democratic and Popular Republic of Algeria (Undertakings), *ILM* 20 (1981), 224 *et seq*. See S.A. Riesenfeld, United States-Iran Agreement of 19 January 1981 (Hostages and Financial Arrangements), *EPIL* 8 (1985), 522.

the solution to the Tehran hostages crisis[6] mediated by the Algerian Government: on 19 January 1981, the last day of office of President Carter, Iran released the fifty-two hostages held at the American embassy in Tehran, and the United States transferred about US$8 billion from the Iranian assets it had frozen[7] to trust accounts held by Algeria at the Bank of England. The Iran-United States Claims Tribunal was established to settle the numerous claims which each of the two state parties and its nationals had against the other state, ranging from a few thousand dollars in some cases to almost US$12 billion in the largest case (the *Foreign Military Sales* case brought by Iran against the United States).[8] More than 3,800 cases were filed, with the total of the financial amounts involved estimated to be in the vicinity of some US$50 billion.

As an unprecedented mechanism in inter-state claims settlement procedures, a special "Security Account" holding US$1 billion was created at a subsidiary of the Dutch Central Bank to pay for awards rendered by the Tribunal against Iran, with the additional obligation for Iran to replenish the account, once it fell below US$500 million.[9] Iran repeatedly abided by this obligation, making use, *inter alia*, of the interest that accrued to the Security Account on a separate account, in conformity with a decision of the Tribunal.[10] In view of the political difficulty of transferring money from Iran directly into the Security Account, another method used to fill it up was to divert parts of Iranian assets frozen elsewhere, for example in London, which had to be released according to the Tribunal. In politically sensitive cases there were sometimes also complicated diplomatic moves to influence the Algerian Central Bank, in the name of which the Security Account was established in Holland, concerning its required signature for payments out of the Security Account. In the 1990s Iran started to refuse replenishment of the Security Account and the United States filed Case No. A28 requesting the Tribunal to order Iran to do so.[11]

---

6. See *Tehran Hostages* case, Order, *ICJ Rep*. 1979, 7–21; Judgment, *ICJ Rep*. 1980, 3–65; Malanczuk, *Akehurst's*, op. cit., 259–60; 126–127.
7. See Executive Order No. 12170 (14 November 1979), Federal Register 65729 (1979). Assets of Iran in all subsidiaries of American banks abroad were also frozen.
8. Case No. B1.
9. Para. 7 of the General Declaration.
10. See the Decision of the Full Tribunal in *Islamic Republic of Iran* v. *United States of America*, DEC 12-A1-FT (Issue I).
11. See Aldrich, *Jurisprudence*, op. cit., 5 note 5.

The Security Account is not available for Awards rendered in favour of Iran. Thus, if an American party who has lost the case refuses to pay an Award of the Tribunal, Iran must seek to enforce it. In one such case the US Government supported Iran before American courts with the argument that there is an international treaty obligation arising from the Algiers Accords to enforce Tribunal Awards also in the United States.[12] Probably, this support was also motivated by the consideration that it was useful for American claimants to have a clear precedent if the Security Account should be empty at some stage in the future.

The jurisdiction of the Tribunal to give final and binding decisions covers four areas:

1. claims of nationals of the United States against Iran and claims of nationals of Iran against the United States, and any counterclaim which arises out of the same contract, transaction or occurrence that constitutes the subject matter of that national's claim, if such claims and counterclaims are outstanding on the date of this Agreement, whether or not filed with any court, and arise out of debts, contracts (including transactions which are the subject of letters of credit or bank guarantees), expropriations or other measures affecting property rights;[13]
2. official claims of the United States and Iran against each other arising out of contractual arrangements between them for the purchase and sale of goods and services;[14]
3. disputes on whether the United States has met its obligations undertaken in connection with the return of the property of the family of the former Shah of Iran, Reza Pahlevi;[15] and
4. other disputes concerning the interpretation or application of the Algiers Accords.[16]

---

12. In *Gould Marketing* the U.S. Ninth Circuit Court of Appeal found that awards of the Tribunal are enforceable in the United States under the Federal Arbitration Act and the 1958 New York Convention on the Recognition and Enforcement of Foreign Arbitral Awards, *IALR* 3 November 1989, 18011. In *Gould Marketing, Inc.* v. *Ministry of Defense of the Islamic Republic of Iran*, Award No. 136–49/50–2 (29 June 1984), reprinted in 6 *Iran-U.S. C.T.R.*, 272, the Tribunal had ordered Gould to pay almost US$3 million, plus interest, to the Ministry which Gould refused. See D. J. Bederman, *AJIL* 84 (1990), 556 et seq.
13. Claims Settlement Declaration, Article II (1).
14. Article II (2).
15. General Declaration, para. 16.
16. Para. 17. See John R. Crook, Applicable Law in International Arbitration: The Iran-U.S. Claims Tribunal Experience, *AJIL* 83 (1989), 278 et seq.

Matters that were expressly excluded from the Tribunal's jurisdiction were claims related to the seizure of the American embassy in Tehran and injury to US nationals or their property as a result of popular movements in the course of the Islamic Revolution which were not acts of the Government of Iran; and claims arising out of contracts that specifically provided for the sole jurisdiction of the Iranian courts.[17]

With regard to the substantive law to be applied, the Tribunal was given a rather broad scope of discretion:

> The Tribunal shall decide all cases on the basis of respect for law, applying such choice of law rules and principles of commercial and international law as the Tribunal determines to be applicable, taking into account relevant usages of the trade, contract provisions and changed circumstances.[18]

The constitution of the Tribunal and its procedural rules were laid down in the "Tribunal Rules",[19] a specially adapted version of the UNCITRAL Arbitration Rules which the United Nations had negotiated in 1976 as a model for conducting international commercial arbitration[20] and now found the first larger (and successful) test in practice.[21] The adaptation of the UNCITRAL Rules was necessary because they are designed for the ad hoc arbitration of single cases, while the Tribunal, although not a permanent body, is a semi-institutionalized form of arbitration that was endowed with a large case load requiring procedural coordination.

With respect to language, Article 17 of the UNCITRAL Rules provides as follows:

17. Paras. 8 and 11.

18. Claims Settlement Declaration, Article V.

19. For the provisional and final text adopted in March 1982 and May 1983 see *Iran-US CTR* 2 (1983–I), 405, amended once in 1984, *Iran-US CTR* 7 (1984–III), 317.

20. *ILM* 15 (1976), 701 *et seq.*

21. See K.-H. Böckstiegel, Applying the UNCITRAL Rules: The Experience of the Iran-United States Claims Tribunal, *International Tax and Business Lawyer* 4 (1986), 266 et seq.; J. J. van Hof, *Commentary on the UNCITRAL Arbitration Rules. The Application by the Iran-US Claims Tribunal*, 1991; S. A. Bakers/M. D. Davis, *The UNCITRAL Arbitration Rules in Practice — The Experience of the Iran-United States Claims Tribunal*, 1992; I. Dore, *The UNCITRAL Framework for Arbitration in Contemporary Perspective*, 1993; D. D. Caron/M. Pellonpää, *The UNCITRAL Arbitration Rules as Interpreted and Applied*, 1995.

Text of UNCITRAL Rule

Article 17

1. Subject to an agreement by the parties, the arbitral tribunal shall, promptly after its appointment, determine the language or languages to be used in the proceedings. This determination shall apply to the statement of claim, the statement of defence, and any further written statements and, if oral hearings take place, to the language or languages to be used in such hearings.
2. The arbitral tribunal may order that any documents annexed to the statement of claim or statement of defence, and any supplementary documents or exhibits submitted in the course of the proceedings, delivered in their original language, shall be accompanied by a translation into the language or languages agreed upon by the parties or determined by the arbitral tribunal.

The Tribunal Rules stated that Article 17 of the UNCITRAL Rules "is maintained unchanged" and added the following Notes:

Notes to Article 17

1. As used in Article 17 of the UNCITRAL Rules, the term "parties" means the two Governments.
2. In accordance with an agreement of the Agents, English and Farsi shall be the official languages to be used in the arbitration proceedings, and these languages shall be used for all oral hearings, decisions and awards.
3. In accordance with the provisions of Article 17 of the UNCITRAL Rules, the following documents filed with the Tribunal shall be submitted in both English and Farsi, unless otherwise agreed by the arbitrating parties:
   (a) The Statement of Claim and its annexes.
   (b) The Statement of Defence, and any counter-claim, including any annexes.
   (c) The reply (including any annexes) to any counter-claim.
   (d) Any further written statement (e.g. reply, rejoinder, brief), including any annexes, which the arbitral tribunal may require or permit an arbitrating party to present.
   (e) Any written request to the arbitral tribunal to take action or any objection thereto.
   (f) Any Challenge to a member.
4. The arbitral tribunal shall determine in each particular case what other documents, documentary exhibits and written evidence, or what parts thereof, shall be submitted in both English and Farsi.
5. Any disputes or difficulties regarding translations shall be resolved by the arbitral tribunal.

All major documents before the Tribunal must therefore be submitted in both languages. Hearings are conducted on the basis of simultaneous translation. The Tribunal has a special translation division of its own. Deliberations, however, which are confidential, are normally conducted in English only.

The Tribunal consists of nine members, three Iranians, three Americans and three from third states. The President of the Tribunal is selected from the third-party arbitrators. Most cases are decided by Chambers of three arbitrators. The "Full Tribunal" of all nine members only decides on the international law disputes between the parties and in some particularly important cases, such as the complex *Foreign Military Sales* case (Case No. B1) between the two Governments. It does not operate as an appeal body with regard to the decisions of the individual Chambers. The awards of the Tribunal are final and binding. Under the UNCITRAL Rules an important provision is made for the appointment by the Secretary General of the Permanent Court of Arbitration of an Appointing Authority for the Tribunal.[22] The Chief Judge of The Netherlands Supreme Court, Charles Moons, was appointed in his personal capacity as the Appointing Authority to rule on challenges to arbitrators (of which there were quite a number in the history of the Tribunal) and to appoint third-country arbitrators and the President when the party-appointed arbitrators fail to agree. The expenses of the Tribunal are shared equally between the two Governments.

The Tribunal was created under unique circumstances, considering the diverse ideological premises of the parties, their political and military confrontation, and the volume of the economic interests at issue, and this was often reflected in the difficulties of its operation in practice. The Tribunal even had to interrupt its work for a longer period, following an unprecedented event in the history of international arbitration when, in 1984, two Iranian arbitrators physically attacked a Swedish arbitrator.[23] A vivid personal account of the "traumatic events of 1984" has been recently published by an eyewitness, Judge George H. Aldrich. In view of the scarcity of documented information on what actually happened in the so-called "Mangard incident", his account deserves to be quoted at some length. The incident is also characteristic for the degree and kind of difficulties the Tribunal had to face in its earlier phase. At that time,

---

22. Article 6.
23. The so-called "Mangard incident"; see the Documents Arising from the Episode of 3 September 1984, *Iran-US CTR* 7 (1984-III), 281.

the Iranian members of the Tribunal and the Agent of the Government of Iran, according to Judge Aldrich,

> were very unhappy that presiding members could be appointed without their consent or, indeed, could remain in office once they became dissatisfied with them. They disliked Judges Mangard and Riphagen intensely, and they demonstrated their feelings on many occasions, yet they had not been successful in inducing them to resign. Moreover, their efforts to persuade the Central Bank of Algeria to refuse to authorize payment from the Security Account of certain Awards (e.g., to dual nationals or when the Iranian judge refused to sign the Award) had proved unavailing, and their efforts to attack some Awards in Dutch courts had been abandoned after the Second Chamber of the Dutch Parliament had passed legislation in early 1984 that would have limited considerably the bases for any such challenges. The Iranian rhetoric in deliberations had become increasingly insulting — particularly in the heated Full Tribunal deliberations on the dual national issue in *Case No. A18*. On 9 April 1984, The Secretary General of the Tribunal received a telephone threat that 'Lagergren and his people had only a few days'. Nevertheless, the Tribunal, the American Government, and, I believe, the Iranian Government were astonished at the length to which Judges Kashani and Shafeiei were prepared to go in an effort to bring down the Tribunal structure.
>
> The Full Tribunal was scheduled to hold an administrative meeting on the morning of 3 September 1984. As Judge Mangard walked toward the meeting room, he was accosted by Judges Kashani and Shafeiei, who tried to push him toward the front door and out of the building. When I arrived at the bottom of the stairs, I heard and saw the melée and hurried to investigate. The American agent (John Crook) and one of the Iranian legal assistants (Moshen Aghahosseini) were trying to move Kashani away. I asked Shafeiei, who had apparently just stopped hitting Mangard, what was going on, and he just looked embarrassed, so I pushed through the crowd of onlookers and yanked Kashani's hand off Mangard's tie, as Mangard's face was turning blue. The Tribunal guard called the police, and they escorted Judge Mangard to his apartment.[24]

After citing from a diary which Judge Aldrich kept on Tribunal events concerning a revealing conversation he had with Judge Kashani, the author continues:

24. Aldrich, *Jurisprudence*, op. cit., 24–25.

> On 5 September 1984, President Lagergren issued Presidential Order No. 27 in which he determined that 'a situation exists in which the conduct of arbitration in an appropriate manner is, for the time being, not feasible' and postponed all proceedings. The President also sent a letter to all members of the Tribunal and the two agents in which he said the use of violence was 'utterly alien to the spirit of arbitration' and that 'such an incident should not have occurred, and must not be allowed to recur'.
>
> Nevertheless, Judge Kashani remained obdurate. On 7 September, the *New York Times* quoted him as saying: 'If Mangard ever dares to enter the tribunal chamber again, either his corpse or my corpse will leave it rolling down the stairs.' My efforts to persuade Judge Shafeiei to distance himself from Kashani were also unavailing, although his language was much more civil.[25]

Later, following a challenge to Judges Kashani and Shafeiei submitted by the United States to the Appointing Authority, Iran finally recalled Kashani and Shafeiei and replaced them by two new Iranian members, Judges Hamid Bahrami Ahmadi and Seyed Mohsen Mostafavi Tafreshi in November 1984. This incident did not stop the settlement process for which a Special Chamber was established to issue Awards on Agreed Terms, but it did disrupt the proceedings of the Tribunal for about half a year.

On the whole, however, in spite of the continuing disruption of diplomatic relations and the confrontation between Iran and the United States outside of the Tribunal, it was later able, under some cumbersome security arrangements and supported at the height of its activities by a large staff of up to 100 persons, to develop a professional working atmosphere leading to a large body of decisions. Even in the autumn of 1987, by when Iran and the United States were in direct military engagement with each other in the Gulf during the war between Iraq and Iran,[26] there was a large oral hearing in the Peace Palace in The Hague concerning a claim by Iran for the delivery of military equipment held back by the United States, with generals and other high-ranking military officers in uniform represented on both sides, which the Tribunal managed to conduct quietly.

25. Ibid., 26.

26. I. F. Dekker/H. H. G. Post, *The Gulf War of 1980–1988*, 1992.

The Tribunal also continued its business while the two Governments were engaged in legal battles before the International Court of Justice in the *Airbus* case[27] and in *the Oil Platforms* case.[28]

OUTPUT OF THE TRIBUNAL

The success of the Iran-United States Claims Tribunal is demonstrated by the number of cases, most of which had been filed by US nationals and companies that have so far been brought to a decision or a settlement. As of 24 January 2003,[29] the Tribunal had issued 600 Awards (including Partial Awards and Awards on Agreed Terms) and more than 80 Interlocutory and Interim Awards, terminated almost 900 cases by Order or Decision, and filed more than 130 Decisions. The total number of cases finalized was more than 3,936. As regards Oral Proceedings, the Tribunal had held more than 470 Hearings or Pre-hearing Conferences.

However, it must be taken into account that 2,388 so-called "small claims" of less than US$250,000 had been terminated by an Award on Agreed Terms in 1990[30] on the basis of a settlement agreement reached between the two governments, under which Iran accepted to pay the lump sum[31] of US$105 million.[32] These claims were settled internally in the United States by the US Foreign Claims Settlement Commission (FCSC), which also dealt with US Government claims against Iran for the repayment of fifteen loans made as part of a long-term economic development programme.[33] In the end, of the about 3,100 claims before it, the FCSC (which completed its work in February 1995) issued 1,066 awards to 1,075 claimants in the total amount of US$41,570,936.31, plus US$44,984,859.31 in interest.

The Commission dismissed 578 claims, either because the claimants so requested or because they could not be located. The rest of 1,422 claims

27. *Case Concerning the Aerial Incident of 3 July 1988 (Islamic Republic of Iran v. United states of America)*, ICJ Order of 13 December 1989 (discontinuance order).
28. Oil Platforms (Islamic Republic of Iran v. United States of America), ICJ Judgment of 6 November 2003.
29. See *Iran-United States Claims Tribunal Communiqué* No. 05/1 of 24 January 2005.
30. Award on Agreed Terms No. 483-CLTDs/86/B38/B76/B77-FT, filed 22 June 1990.
31. See R. B. Lillich, Lump Sum Agreements, *EPIL* 8 (1985), 367–72.
32. See *AJIL* 84 (1990), 891–5 for details.
33. See Richard B. Lillich/David J. Bederman, Jurisprudence of the Foreign Claims Settlement Commission: Iran Claims, *AJIL* 91 (1997), 436–465.

were denied. It is quite likely that the proportion of the relevant claims dismissed, or only recognized partially, would have been much higher if the Tribunal would have had to adjudicate upon them. But it is also clear that an efficient handling of these "small claims" in reasonable time would not have been feasible under the existing structure and procedure of the Tribunal. Be that as it may, it is noticeable that it even took the FCSC, a national body and not an international arbitral institution with all its inherent complications, almost five years to deal with some 3,100 claims before it.

Moreover, about 240 other Awards mentioned in the Tribunal's statistics were also Awards on Agreed Terms or Partial Awards on Agreed Terms, recording settlements by the parties. It must be borne in mind, that it is one of the important functions of the Tribunal, like any other arbitral body, to encourage the settlement of disputes among the parties themselves, rather than having to decide on them. Obviously, however, such settlements and the Awards recording them are practically of very little, if any, significance for the development of the law. The matter is different with regard to the awards issued by the US Foreign Claims Commission on the basis of the settlement reached with Iran, which has been mentioned above, because of the legal criteria that have been applied by the Commission.[34]

The total amount awarded to US parties and paid out of the Security Account was more than US$2.1 billion (excluding interest). The total amount (excluding interest) awarded to Iran and Iranian parties (not payable out of the Security Account) was more than US$1 billion. More than US$500 million of this total amount was paid to Iran on the basis of a Tribunal award ordering the return of frozen Iranian assets held at the New York Federal Reserve Bank.[35] Moreover, in the *Foreign Military Sales* case, the Tribunal by Order filed on 21 September 1990 terminated arbitral proceedings with regard to an Iranian request for interim measures and attached settlement agreement pursuant to which the United States was obliged to pay US$200,000,000 into the Security Account. With this compromise the United States secured that the money it had to transfer would at least be available for the future payment of Awards in favour of successful American claimants.

As to substance, the decisions of the Tribunal cover the entire range of international commercial transactions and foreign investment and

34. See Lillich/Bederman, op. cit.
35. Award No. 306-A15 (I: G)-FT.

important aspects of public international law and arbitral procedure, although not always in a coherent way. To give an illustration, the legal issues that the Tribunal has addressed include, for example, the nationality of claims of individuals and corporations,[36] claims of dual nationals,[37] the meaning of "controlled entities", indirect claims, the admissibility of counterclaims, interim measures of relief,[38] choice of law, formation and validity of international contracts, interpretation of contracts, breach of contract, termination of contracts, *force majeure, clausula rebus sic stantibus*, damages for breach of contract, lost profits, bank guarantees and standby letters of credit, currency conversion rates, exchange controls,[39] unjust enrichment, export licences, taxes and social security levies, interest, costs, prescription, treaty interpretation,[40] state responsibility, expulsion of aliens,[41] expropriation of foreign property, standard of compensation and valuation,[42] and, as has been noted above, almost any conceivable aspect of the procedure of international arbitration

---

36. *Flexi-Van Leasing Inc. v. Islamic Republic of Iran*, Order of 15 December 1982; *General Motors Corporation v. Government of the Islamic Republic of Iran*, Order of 18 January 1983; confirmed by the Full Tribunal in *Islamic Republic of Iran v. United States of America*, DEC 45-A20-FT, *Iran-US CTR* 11 (1986-II), 271. See also C. Staker, Diplomatic Protection of Private Business Companies: Determining Corporate Personality for International Law Purposes, *BYIL* 61 (1990), 155 et seq.
37. See *Case No. A/18*; P.E. Mahoney, The Standing of Dual Nations Before the Iran-United States Claims Tribunal, *Virginia JIL* 24 (1984), 695; P. McGarvey-Rosendahl, A New Approach to Dual Nationality, *Houston JIL* 11 (1986), 305; D. J. Bederman, *Saghi v. Islamic Republic of Iran*, AWD 544-298-2, Iran-United States Claims Tribunal, January 22, 1993, *AJIL* 87 (1993), 447–52; Bederman, Nationality of Individual Claimants before the Iran-United States Claims Tribunal, *ICLQ* 42 (1993), 119 *et seq.*; Bederman, Historic Analogues of the UN Compensation Commission, in R. B. Lillich (ed.), *The United Nations Compensation Commission: Thirteenth Sokol Colloquium*, 1995, 257–310; D. S. Mathias, The Weighing of Evidence in a Dual National Case at the Iran-United States Claims Tribunal, *NYIL* 26 (1995), 171–89.
38. See David D. Caron, Interim Measures of Protection: Theory and Practice in Light of the Iran-United states Claims Tribunal, *ZaöRV* 46 (1986), 465 et seq.
39. See Allahyar Mouri, Treatment of the Rules of the International Law of Money by the Iran-US Claims Tribunal, *Asian Yearbook of International Law* 3 (1993), 71–110.
40. See K.-H. Böckstiegel, zur Auslegung völkerrechtlicher Verträge durch das Iran-United States Claims Tribunal, in: *Festschrift für Karl Doehring*, 1989, 119 et seq.
41. See Malanczuk, *Akehurst's*, op. cit., 262 with references.
42. See M. Fitzmaurice/M. Pellonpää, Taking of Property in the Practice of the Iran-United States Claims Tribunal, *NYIL* 19 (1988), 53–178; J. A. Westberg, Applicable Law, Expropriatory Takings and Compensation in Cases of Expropriation: ICSID and Iran-United States Claims Tribunal Case Law Compared, *ICSID Rev.* 8 (1993), 1–28; A. Mouri, *The International Law of Expropriation as Reflected in the Work of the Iran-United States Claims Tribunal*, 1994; G. H. Aldrich, What Constitutes a Compensable Taking: The Decisions of the Iran-United States Claims Tribunal, *AJIL* 88 (1994), 585–610; G. H. Aldrich, *Jurisprudence*, op. cit., 171–276.

under the amended version of the UNCITRAL Rules. This broad range of legal issues reflects the "mixed nature" of the Tribunal and it has given rise to some controversy on whether it is public or private.[43] Dr. Allahyar Mouri, in an instructive article on the matter, arrives at the following conclusion:

> ... the main problem is that the nature of the Tribunal can be properly identified, neither through its awards and decisions nor, consequently, through the interpretation of commentators and other fora. Its interpretation of its own nature and that of its awards, the latitude of its jurisdiction and extent of its power would suggest that the Tribunal is a combination of a number of different creatures, and yet none of them. At times it acts not only like a lion that rules the land but like an eagle that controls the sky. Yet in other instances it acts like neither of these beings. It can neither roar nor fly. Those who venture to face this twentieth century griffin never know whether they have to tackle an eagle or a lion, neither or both.[44]

In fact, the Tribunal has been operating both as an international tribunal deciding on state responsibility, for example, in expropriation and expulsion cases, and as a body to determine the private law obligations relevant to the disputes before it.[45] The Tribunal itself has been content to merely note the following in this respect:

> While this Tribunal is clearly an international Tribunal established by treaty and while some of its cases involve disputes between the two Governments and involve the interpretation and application of public international law, most disputes (including all of those brought by dual nationals) involve a private party on one side and a Government or Government-controlled entity on the other, and many involve primarily issues of municipal law and general principles of law. In such cases it is the rights of the claimant, not of his nation, that are to be determined by the Tribunal. This should be contrasted with the situation of espousal of claims in international law ... .[46]

43. See D. D. Caron, The Nature of the Iran-United States Claims Tribunal and the Evolving Structure of International Law, *AJIL* 84 (1990), 104–56.
44. A. Mouri, Iran-United States Claims Tribunal: The Birth of a Twentieth Century Griffin, *The Finnish Yearbook of International Law*, 7 (1996), 180–243, at 243.
45. See Grant Hanessian, "General Principles of Law" in the Iran-U.S. Claims Tribunal, *Columbia Journal of Transnational Law* 27 (1989), 307–352, at 350–351.
46. Case No. A/18 (6 April 1984), 5 *Iran-U.S. C.T.R.*, 251, 261–262.

At any rate, whatever its "true nature", the Tribunal is a prime example for the blurring in practice of the distinction between public and private law on the international level with regard to economic transactions. There is an old dispute since the writings of Georg Erler[47] and Georg Schwarzenberger[48] on whether the subject of international economic law should include relevant national law and private international law aspects or be limited to the field of public international law. This matter is beyond the scope of the present article,[49] but it must be admitted that the experience of the Iran-United States Claims Tribunal supports the view of those who advocate an integrated approach in the study of the law governing international economic relations.[50]

Another special feature is the multi-cultural composition of the arbitrators of the Tribunal and its staff. The three arbitrators appointed by Iran and the three arbitrators appointed by the United States, of course, were own nationals. Their national legal systems are as different as their languages, cultures and religion. In addition, this mixture was further blended by the diversity of the background and legal traditions of the third-country arbitrators and Presidents that were appointed during the life of the Tribunal: nationals of Sweden, Germany, Switzerland, Argentina, Poland, Finland, Netherlands and Italy. The decision-making of the Tribunal, in terms both of the procedure and the substantive law, applied offers a broad field of study for the meaning of the clash of legal cultures in international arbitration.[51]

47. G. Erler, Wirtschaftsrecht, Internationales, in: Strupp/Schlochauer, *Wörterbuch des Völkerrechts*, Bd. III, 1960/62, 862; see also G. Erler, *Grundprobleme des internationalen Wirtschaftsrechts*, 1956, 9 et seq., 17 et seq.
48. G. Schwarzenberger, *Economic World Order?*, 1970, 4. See also his earlier Hague Academy Lecture in *RdC* 117 (1966-I), 7.
49. For a discussion see P. Malanczuk, *"Globalization": Challenges to International Economic Law and the Settlement of International Disputes*, Inaugural Lecture, Erasmus University Rotterdam, 1998.
50. For such an integrated approach see, for example, E.-U. Petersmann, International Economic Theory and International Economic Law: on the Tasks of a Legal Theory of International Economic Order, in: R. St.J. Macdonald/D. M. Johnston, *The Structure and Process of International Law*, 1983, 251; M. Herdegen, *Internationales Wirtschaftsrecht*, 2nd edn 1995, 3 et seq.
51. See generally on the topic Stefan N. Frommel and Barry A. K. Rider (eds.), *Conflicting Legal Cultures in Commercial Arbitration — Old and New Issues* (Kluwer Law International: The Hague-London-Boston 1999).

EVALUATION

The fact that the Tribunal still exists and has been able to function under such delicate circumstances is in itself quite surprising. Now the work of the Tribunal is nearing its end. It has only a few cases left, such as some Iranian Government claims against the United States Government and a number of disputes between the two Governments concerning the interpretation of and compliance with the Algiers Accords.

Years ago, many of the senior staff of the Tribunal had already moved on to new tasks at the United Nations Compensation Commission for Claims Against Iraq in Geneva (a body which is not arbitral or judicial in nature, and which was imposed by the UN Security Council upon Iraq after the invasion of Kuwait).[52] But it is difficult to predict how long the Tribunal will continue to exist. Since its inception in 1981, every year the expectation has been repeated that the Tribunal would not last longer than two to three more years and it has proved to be wrong. Now another three to five years, perhaps with a reduced structure of the Tribunal, might be an educated guess, but surely it is no more than a guess. However, the heydays of one of the most remarkable institutions in the history of international dispute settlement are certainly over. Although there will always be criticism as regards specific issues and cases,[53] for example, concerning the alleged slowness of the Tribunal, it can be said that the Tribunal has largely done justice to the parties before it. It may also ultimately contribute to the normalization of relations between the two countries. At any rate, it has assisted in defusing an explosive political situation and provided the two alienated Governments with a point of direct diplomatic contact. Perhaps it is so, in the words of George Aldrich, "that the work of the Iran-United States Claims Tribunal will be seen as

52. See R. B. Lillich (ed.), *The United Nations Compensation Commission*, 1995; P. Malanczuk, International Business and New Rules of State Responsibility? — The Law Applied by the United Nations (Security Council) Compensation Commission for Claims against Iraq, in: K.-H. Böckstiegel (ed.), *Perspectives of Air Law, Space Law and International Business Law for the Next Century*, 1996, 117–164; Malanczuk, *Akehurst's*, op. cit., 398–399 with further references.

53. There are, of course, some much more critical voices as to the general contribution of the Tribunal to the development of the law, as correctly observed by Menno Kamminga, Staatsaansprakelijkheid jegens individuen: beginselen en procedures, Preadvies, *Mededelingen van de Nederlandse Vereiniging voor Internationaal Recht* 115, 1997, 15. See, for example, David Lloyd Jones, The Iran-United States Claims Tribunal: Private Rights and State Responsibility, *Virginia Journal of International Law* 24 (1983–84), 259–285; Christine D. Gray, *Judicial Remedies in International Law*, 1987, 181–185.

an encouragement of more frequent use of international tribunals for compulsory settlement of legal disputes between States and between States and private parties."[54] The question is, of course, whether the work of the Tribunal could have effectively proceeded without the peculiar mechanism of the Security Account that was born out of a rather unique historical situation and built upon a large amount of frozen financial assets. Generally speaking, states still remain reluctant to accept compulsory dispute settlement mechanisms on the international level.[55]

Returning to Richard B. Lillich's assessment of the Tribunal, to which reference was made at the beginning of this contribution, it is a good conclusion to cite from his introductory remarks at the Second Joint Conference of the American Society of International Law and the Nederlandse Vereiniging voor Internationaal Recht in The Hague in 1993. As Chairman of the Panel on "The Iran-US Claims Tribunal: Its Contribution to International Law and Practice" he stated the following:

> Some of you may recall that in certain remarks I made to the American Society of International Law — remarks that have been quoted both out of context and [in]correctly in writings in recent years — I said the Iran-US Claims Tribunal is the largest and most important international arbitration to date, and it surely will influence the development of international law well into the coming century. This is a statement that has been criticized in some writings about the Tribunal, but it is a statement that I certainly would subscribe to today. Indeed, I would underscore it because all of us working in the field appreciate the fact that the decisions of the Tribunal are having a significant impact on every aspect not only of claims adjudication, but of international arbitration in general ...[56]

The present writer shares this view.[57] The most long-lasting impact of the Tribunal's work is likely to flow from the many hundred contentious cases it has decided and the persuasive value of its jurisprudence beyond

---

54. See Aldrich, *Jurisprudence*, op. cit., 43.
55. See Malanczuk, *Akehurst's*, op. cit., Chapter 18: Peaceful settlement of disputes between states, 273–305; Malanczuk, Streitbeilegung, einvernehmliche, in: Ignaz Seidl-Hohenveldern (ed.), *Lexikon des Rechts — Völkerrecht*, 2nd ed. 1998.
56. The American Society of International Law/Nederlandse Vereniging voor Internationaal Recht, *Contemporary International Law Issues: Opportunities at a Time of Momentous Change, Proceedings of the Second Joint Conference Held in The Hague, The Netherlands,* 22–24 July 1993, 1.
57. See Malanczuk, *Akehurst's*, op. cit., 298.

the specific cases that were at issue. The published decisions of the Tribunal,[58] now approaching thirty volumes, constitute an invaluable collection of materials and jurisprudence on issues of public international law, international commercial law and the procedure of international arbitration, which as a source for the development of the law will not be so easily surpassed in the future. They are a gold mine that is still to be fully discovered by international courts and tribunals in the future.

---

58. *Iran-United States Claims Tribunal Reports* (since 1983, first published by Grotius, now by Cambridge University Press). The latest volume 34 (1998), edited by Karen Lee has appeared in 2004.

3

Hybrid Dispute Processing in Japan: Linking Arbitration with Conciliation

Yasunobu Sato

INTRODUCTION: PROBLEMS IN THE DISPUTE PROCESSING IN JAPAN

There are mixed responses with respect to the existing practice of international arbitration in Japan, in which the arbitrator virtually dictates the conciliation method. American lawyers largely criticised it (Ragan, 1991). Nevertheless, there is also favourable interpretation contending that the practice enables more flexible solutions for individual cases (Tashiro, 1995 and Neuman, 1998). Aside from this, for more than a decade, Japan's bar associations have engaged in civil and commercial dispute processing services, as alternative to domestic litigation, through an office called the "Bar Association's Arbitration Centre." Reportedly, this can trace its beginning to a construction arbitration service mostly by practising lawyers attached to Japan's Ministry of Construction. Concerning the name "arbitration centre," most cases brought there come without an arbitration agreement and, in actual practice, nearly all of them are processed by *Assen* (informal conciliation, hereinafter called "mediation" although it is not accurate translation)[1] or *Chôtei*

1 "*Assen*" in Japanese is apt to be used in the manner less official and with simpler or handier implication than "*Chôtei*." Thus, the former is interpreted as "informal conciliation." There does not seem to be any consistent official distinction between them. In this context, it is like distinguishing between mediation and conciliation in English terminology. In the common law jurisdiction, the word of mediation is preferred, while that of conciliation is favoured in the continental law jurisdiction. Incidentally in the UNCITRAL context, the latter seems to be used in general, including mediation in common law jurisdiction,

(conciliation). This may be due to the fact that historically in Japan there have been few cases which include an arbitration clause in the contract. The objective of these centres obviously has been to provide a way to solve disputes among citizens involving small sums of money, which does not justify the cost of a formal lawsuit (Ohkawa, 1990). In almost all cases of arbitration awards, the purpose of obtaining them are solely to give an appearance of arbitration awards to the settlement agreements in order to gain enforceability. Accordingly such a practice has been criticised with respect to its competence as legitimate arbitration procedure (Hayakawa, 1999). Further, there is criticism that it is a mixture of arbitration and conciliation created by the mingling of the two processes. This is because there is no clear distinction between conciliation and arbitration procedures. The practice of identifying a conciliator with an arbitrator is not unusual. The critics also contend that it materially deteriorates the natural justice, in particular, concerning the removal of prejudice in arbitration, and that it will result in shrinkage of conciliation caused by concern about the abuse of unfavourable statements made by the parties in the conciliation process.

In the background of these practices lies a paternalistic dispute processing practice known as an "attempt of settlement," a form of conciliation led by the judge in charge of the litigation case under the Japanese Code of Civil Procedure ("the CCP"). This practice seeks "settlement-in-litigation" having the same effect as a judgment (the CCP, Article 98). This particular domestic legal practice, however, has been decried as forced conciliation taking advantage of the public authority of court decision.

On 1 August 2003, the "Law on Arbitration" ("the new Law") was finally promulgated and it entered into force on 1 March 2004.[2] It replaced the "Law on Procedure of Public Notice and Procedure of Arbitration," ("the old Law").

---

although it is distinguished from conciliation in its manner and principle. Just for convenience, hereinafter, in this paper, *Assen* will be called mediation implying informal conciliation since mediation seems less formal than conciliation.

2 Its English translation is available at: http://www.jseinc.org/index_e.htm/. Also see Sato, 2005.

THE CONCEPT OF HYBRID DISPUTE PROCESSING

Basic types of dispute processing

To better understand the concept of hybrid dispute processing requires first identifying the basic patterns of procedures. As procedures seeking an agreement for resolution of the dispute among the disputing parties, there are (1) negotiation among the parties; and (2) mediation or conciliation, both of which aim at achieving settlement between the parties by a neutral third party intervention. Mediation and conciliation can be distinguished based on whether the neutral third party tries to persuade the parties with proposed mediation/conciliation terms.

In contrast, as procedures seeking resolution by means of enforcement of umpiring by a neutral third party, there are (1) a court decision grounded on state authority[3] and (2) arbitration, in other words, decision by a private tribunal. In arbitration, both procedure and criteria for decision are subject to an agreement between the parties. Arbitration, in generic terms, may grow and in the coming century emerge as a major way to process and resolve trans-national disputes dealing with highly specialised subjects. At the same time respect of diversity is mandatory. On the other hand, the existence of equitable measures is essential to guard against infringement on the right of access to the courts and the assurance of natural justice (due process). In this context, within the limit that does not contradict public policy, maximal respect for party autonomy in dispute processing is indispensable.[4]

Dispute processing and conceptual differences regarding the value of justice

'**Agreement** between the disputing parties' and '**enforcement** by a third party' exist as distinct components in dispute processing in theory. However, they are hard to distinguish with respect to application in practice, despite technically being two extremes. Actual dispute processing

3 In addition to court judgment available through litigation, there are settlement-in-court (settlement-in-litigation and settlement prior to filing, which are explained below), civil and family conciliation, umpiring and procedures for decisions in non-litigation case.

4 The opinion that development or advancement of the arbitration practice may contribute to promotion of the right to access to justice and to the realisation of natural justice.

in fact is a combination of both with countless variations. In arbitration cases where agreement between the parties and enforcement by a third party are a typical *hybrid dispute processing* combined as essential elements, the concept of arbitration itself is difficult to define universally.

Specifically, between agreement and enforcement lies a peripheral area of *persuasion* or *compromise*, the former obtaining agreement based on enforcement while the latter accepting enforcement by agreement. This applies, as well, to negotiation among parties on equal terms. Based on enforcement, the other party is convinced and, in short, bows to a concession, that is, compromise. The point here is whether the method of enforcement is justifiable persuasion. If so, enforcement can be called justice. Generic justice includes both justice in the result, i.e., substantive justice and justice in the procedures, i.e., procedural justice (Taniguchi, 1985: 35). Depending on form of justice to be weighed, in the actual dispute processing, interpretation of the concept of arbitration can vary in the extreme.

Japanese convention of conciliation gives the highest priority to persuasion based on "*jôri*" (the principle of sound reason) underlying the law.[5] Its aim is to realise substantive justice by conciliation in accordance with ideal norms. From this particular viewpoint of conciliation, arbitration can be interpreted as dispute processing similar to conciliation.[6] This same conclusion can be reached from the standpoint of litigation in Japan. Seeking truth inquisitively, the court respects harmony (conciliation oriented). The court tries to apply law to a case not for substantive justice through enforcement of judgment but through persuasive or educational technique, such as settlement-in-litigation.

By contrast, procedural justice is important under adversarial trial routine by the parties' initiatives, in which the jury finds facts (a jury trial) and the judge decides on the rights and duties by applying law to the facts. Disputing parties confront each other in this process, which gives rise to various rules for procedural justice ("natural justice" or "due process") for fairness. In this common law jurisdiction, arbitration is

5 Article 1 of the Law on Civil Conciliation states, "Aims at resolution that matches the actual environment in a manner that prevails in *jôri* (reason) and through mutual concession by the parties concerned."

6 Akira Mikazuki states his understanding that, technically as a type of norms, laws established as ground for judicial judgment, should be included as part of *ex aequo et bono* that will form the very pillar of arbitration and *jôri* (reason), which in turn constitute the base of conciliation: Mikazuki, 1984).

similar to litigation and forms a totally different concept from mediation, which demands smooth negotiation without evaluation by the mediator. In this context, mixing arbitration with conciliation is viewed as denying individual concepts. It may be possible to place European continental law between them, as it permits *arbitrato irrituale od. arbitrato libero* or *amicable composition* from the legal viewpoint of an inquisitive litigation.

Traditional dispute processing in Japan and its reform

Historically, in Japan, conventional arbitration has not been independent of conciliation in concept (Kawashima, 1967). Late in the 19th century (during the *Meiji* era) such traditional dispute processing was abandoned as obsolete, replaced by modern conciliation based on German law and duly stipulated in the CCP. This led to hiding traditional and paternalistic dispute processing in Japan's authoritative legal practice, reflecting continental legal convention. Then, in the early 1900s, to rectify the shortcomings of the CCP, the very system formerly dropped as outdated was revived as conciliation. Until the end of World War II, procedures of a kind of forced arbitration; i.e., whenever conciliation failed, a court was able to make a decision in lieu of conciliation, prevailed throughout the entire civil justice system. Post-war reform led by the American adversarial style of litigation bred confusion. As for a certain period after the war commercial arbitration by business associations was banned as a way to revive the old cartel system. It was interpreted as a relic of the past mouldering in democratisation of the nation's judicial system. Accordingly, arbitration by the private sector was taken lightly during the government-led rapid economic growth. Thus, in the context of structural impediment talks between Japan and the US, Japanese practice was criticised as unfair commercial dispute processing, and this triggered a review of the arbitration law.

Until recently Japan has had little experience in arbitration, partly because the arbitration practice is regulated by the CCP. Thus, the particular emphasis in domestic arbitration has been on arriving at a settlement by strictly adhering to courtroom litigation procedure. However, in the existing global judicial environment for global business, Japan had to overhaul arbitration legislation to fit in the common law style; there must be a switch from traditional mixed dispute processing to the "combined" form of "med-arb" or "arb-med."

Conceptual philosophy in the new Law

For enactment of better law on arbitration, the author has proposed an article of philosophy, which reads, "This law maximises application of the party autonomy to the extent that it will not contradict public policy." Now the new Law (Article 26(1)) provides,

> The parties are free to agree on the procedure to be followed by the arbitral tribunal in conducting the arbitral proceedings. Provided, it shall not violate the provisions of this Law relating to public policy.

This provision expresses the principle of party autonomy subject to public policy along the line of my proposal although the new Law does not provide for any principle or purpose of the law. The provision will also help facilitate other Alternative Dispute Resolutions (ADR), in particular, hybrid dispute processing as the coverage. On the other hand, the issues on natural justice should have been articulated in the new Law since it is natural justice that justifies party autonomy. Enhancement of party autonomy is the key concept of English revised law (Arbitration Act 1996) that lies behind the revised Hong Kong Ordinance 1996 (Sato, 1998: 6–7).[7] Japan has also stepped forward to adjust herself to globalisation of the free market economy based on independent individuals by adopting the new Law addressing international dispute processing.

We shall now look into some of the issues through international comparison of hybrid dispute processing.

HYBRID DISPUTE PROCESSING: IS IT A COMBINATION OF AGREEMENT AND ENFORCEMENT OR SIMPLY A MIXTURE?

Background of hybrid dispute processing

Behind recent discussions of hybrid dispute processing, which combines such basic dispute processing elements as conciliation, arbitration, and

---

7 1996 revision of the Arbitration Ordinance of Hong Kong 2AA: "(1) The objective … is to facilitate the fair and speedy resolution of the dispute without unnecessary expense, (2) based on the principles that (a) subject to the observance of such safeguards as are necessary in the public interest, the parties to a dispute should be free to agree how the dispute should be resolved; and (b) the Court should interfere in the arbitration of a dispute only as expressly provided by this Ordinance."

litigation, lie two distinct issues: the evolution of ADR in the US and the need to cope with mounting evils brought about by the tendency of assimilation of international arbitration to litigation.

In the US, against the backdrop of post-modernism (generic scepticism regarding modern rationale), and influenced by a third wave of Access to Justice, an ADR movement[8] prevailed in the 1980s essentially in the form of mediation (Miki, 1995: 1048–1049). Apart from this, private enterprise was devising assorted ADR methods to avoid payment of rising legal costs by discovery and bolster predictability by precluding a jury verdict following the trial. On the other hand, arbitration becomes more prevalent in resolving international commercial disputes mainly among US lawyers. Thus, it became apparent that arbitration often took on the aspect of litigation, which technically positions the law as a source of objective criteria for judgment as well as procedural justice. As a result, arbitration shifted to a legal means virtually equal to litigation in terms of time and cost (Inomata, 1999: 57–59; Taniguchi, 1997: 6–8). In this context, devising ADR as an alternative to arbitration is ironic.

Examples of hybrid dispute processing

Hybrid dispute processing currently prevails in the US and England and influences not only areas where common-law convention prevails but also those in which continental legal convention carries sway. Asia and Oceania, including Japan, are no exceptions. This merits an overview of various types of ADR in the common law jurisdiction, followed by their comparison with Japanese hybrid dispute processing.

---

8 According to Cappelletti and Garth, it first refers to the provisions for legal aid to those who are economically vulnerable, secondly to representing dispersed benefits of a "group of persons" and, thirdly, to mounting interest in the dispute processing system or in the entire process (Cappelletti [ed.], translated by a group headed by Takeshi Kojima and Yasuhei Taniguchi, 205–207 n1). The origin of ADR may be ascribed to such issues as the US civil rights movement of the 1960s and the subsequent development of the study of law and society, such as found in CLS (Critical Legal Studies). Regarding this, Richard Abel and Owen Fiss have panned it as second-class justice representing paternalism and apt to sacrifice functions of litigation as creating law (Abel: 1982, 270–271, 275; Fiss: 1984, 1085–1086).

Types developing in the common law jurisdiction

Mediation using adversarial structures used by arbitration

a) Dispute Review Board / Disputes Adviser: Originally this was a dispute processing clause included in large-scale construction agreements. The dispute review board consisting of experts representing the client and the construction firm and a neutral party under the clause, issues a recommendation, which legally binds all the parties unless an objection is submitted within a specified period. Technically it is a combination of non-binding arbitration and mediation. The English Housing Grants Construction and Regeneration Act 1996 established it as "Adjudication" (non-binding arbitration that binds all parties concerned until the dispute is finally resolved by either arbitration or conciliation) (Newman, 1999: 49–54).

b) Mini-Trial (Executive Tribunal): This is a panel comprising management representatives of the parties in dispute and a neutral third party that hears the claims of lawyers representing each party. Based on the outcome of the hearing, the parties undertake conciliatory negotiations and hear the recommendation of the third party. This method has the form of either persuasive conciliation in the style of court procedure or non-binding negotiation and has been recognised since the 1980s as ADR attached to the court. It was formerly applied to resolve disputes between major corporate entities seeking to maintain relationships. But recent years have seen it frequently used to settle disputes related to international transactions or issues centring on technology (Miki, supra: 1188–1192).

c) Neutral Fact-finding Expert: As a neutral judge of such dispute components as fact verification and technical or legal issues, this specialist conducts investigations and, when necessary, engages in conciliation. When requested, he will also offer a non-binding arbitral award (Brown and Marriott, 1993: 20, 276–278).

d) Early Neutral Evaluation: To avoid dispute issues arising from discovery, the most costly facet of lawsuits, a neutral evaluator assigned by the court will, based on summary statements by the individual parties in the dispute, work to promote a settlement and carry out conciliation. Failing a viable agreement, all pertinent information will be kept secret unless the parties concerned consent to its disclosure (Miki, supra: 1192–1195).

e) Summary Jury Trial: As a form of mini-trial, in litigation, following discovery or a pre-trial discussion, leaning on the recommendation of a simulated jury, conciliation will be effected.

Arbitration preceded by mediation and its variation

a) Med-Arb: Technically, this process starts as mediation then turns to arbitration when the former fails. In the US it is widely used in labour and construction disputes, and in cases of parental custody. The fact that the mediator automatically becomes arbitrator may facilitate a quick settlement, but there is criticism that prejudice on the part of the arbitrator is counterproductive and can lead to narrowing the process of mediation.

b) Med-Arb-Opt-Out: To preclude the above form of criticism, in this scheme, when negotiations stalemate, if the mediator is to turn arbitrator, the parties concerned are given the right to veto.

c) Mediator-Adviser: Here, the mediator-adviser is limited to non-binding arbitration, that is, simply making recommendations.

d) MEDALOA: This is mediation combined with last-offer arbitration, a device to effect settlement by making the arbitrator choose one of a plurality of solutions submitted by the parties concerned, thereby resolving the Med-Arb matter according to American Arbitration Association (AAA) (Newman, supra: 66–67).

Hybrid processing at World Intellectual Property Organisation (WIPO)

Article 13 of the 1994 WIPO Mediation Rules stipulates that if mediation fails, the mediator can propose either an expert determination or arbitration, including MEDALOA. In the case of arbitration, the mediator can, with the expressed consent of the parties, act as sole arbitrator, whereby the mediator may, in the arbitral proceedings, take into account information received during the mediation.

Recent SMC-SIA Med-Arb service in Singapore

The Singapore Mediation Centre (SMC) has become independent of the Singapore International Arbitration Centre (SIAC), still the two engage in joint Med-Arb services. In special cases, the mediator can become an arbitrator if the parties agree and the mediator so consents, and he is of the opinion that any confidential information obtained during the mediation will not affect his decision as an arbitrator in the matter.[9]

Examples of the hybrid form in Japan

As already discussed, in Japan the basic practice in dispute processing has been conciliation, hence it was positioned at the centre of lawsuit practice following the nation's modernization. Even after the enactment of its modern statutes and judiciary system and until today, this particular tradition remains.

a) Settlement-in-court: Two legal stipulations refer to hybrid processing in the litigation procedure: settlement-in-litigation as a result of the attempt of settlement by the litigation court (the CCP, Article 98) and settlement prior to filing in the summary court (Article 275 of the Code). The former is a type of *de facto* conciliation by the judge in charge of the litigation case, with the resultant settlement as enforceable as a judgment. In actual practice there are many cases wherein a judge effects settlement at the request of the parties or by the judge's own initiative, and about half of the nation's lawsuits end in this sort of settlement.[10] Certain judges prefer to transfer cases to the Civil Conciliation Procedure instead of attempting settlement-in-litigation in order to ensure natural justice, as the same judge will render judgment when a settlement is not reached in the litigation process.[11] Moreover, as a result of the settlement provision (the CCP, Article 265, which was introduced in the 1996 reform of the CCP), if all the parties request in written form, the terms stipulated by the court or judge in charge of the settlement attempt for the litigation case will be deemed to be settlement-in-litigation. This can be interpreted as a form of arbitration following conciliation by the court. As for settlement prior to filing in the summary court (Article 275), the court settlement becomes enforceable as judgment.

9 The SMC-SIAC Med-Arb Procedure, 10, provides, "... A person appointed by the SMC to act as a mediator may, if all parties agree and if he consents, be appointed as an arbitrator or one of the arbitrators in the dispute if he is of the opinion that the conduct of any party or any confidential or privileged information that a party had earlier disclosed to him during the mediation will not affect his decision as an arbitrator in the matter."

10 According to 1997 judiciary statistics, settlement as a means of solving civil disputes in local courts occupies about 25% of all the completed cases; if including withdrawal, which technically can be interpreted as settlement, the figure would rise to all of 50%.

11 As per interviewing Judge Takashi Sonoh on 29 October 1998.

b) Conciliation under the Law on Civil Conciliation: In civil dispute, the parties concerned can apply to the court for the civil conciliation at any time. After receiving the request, the court, when deeming it appropriate, can transfer the case to civil conciliation procedure (Reference to conciliation: the Law on Civil Conciliation, Article 20). In principle, a different court will organise a conciliation committee to handle the case, while the litigation court may also handle the conciliation proceedings (called self-serving conciliation). The settlement reached as the conciliation is enforceable as judgment. Some hold the view that, technically, persuasive conciliation grounded on reason presided over by a conciliation committee, a member of which is a judge, is a sort of a court decision rather than an agreement by and between the parties affected (Ishikawa and Kajimura, 1996: 50).

Non-binding arbitration by a judge: Instead of effecting conciliation, a court may, within the limit that will not run counter to the objection of appeal by the parties in dispute, render a decision in lieu of conciliation terms on its own authority when the court considers it appropriate as the conciliation by the conciliation committee will not be successful (Article 17). If one of the parties files an objection within two weeks, the decision will become void, but in practice the ratio of cases where an objection is filed stands at only about 10 percent in recent years (Ishikawa, supra: 272–274).

Arbitration by conciliation committee: In commercial conciliation cases and other special conciliation cases, requested by the parties in written form, the conciliation committee decides on the terms of conciliation (same Article 24(3)), but there are few practical instances.

c) International Commercial Arbitration: Rule 47 of the Commercial Arbitration Rules of the International Commercial Arbitration Association, amended and effective on 1 March 2004, states, "The arbitral tribunal may attempt to settle the dispute in the arbitral proceedings if all of the parties consent, orally or in writing, thereto." Accordingly, there are cases wherein arbitrators indeed perform agency functions to realise conciliation as agreed to by the parties affected. The maritime arbitration rule, Article 32(2) of the Tokyo Maritime Commission under Tokyo Shipping Exchange, amended on 1 March 2004, states, "The Tribunal may, at any stage of the arbitral proceedings, attempt to settle the whole or a part of the dispute between the parties." In other words, conciliation by arbitration tribunal is possible without consent of the parties concerned.

However, taking natural justice assurance into account, it added Article 32(3), providing, "In case settlement conducted in accordance with the preceding paragraph fails, the Tribunal shall resume the arbitral proceedings, provided however that it must not issue an award based on any of the information it gained during the settlement proceedings."

d) Domestic arbitration by the bar associations, etc.: As discussed above, institutional arbitration service is available in the Construction Ministry, the bar associations, and the Industrial Property Arbitration Centre in Japan. Most of the cases processed there, however, begin and end as conciliation,[12] while those including arbitration awards based on an arbitration agreement made during the conciliation procedure are quite few. Most of the latter cases have the form of arbitration merely to more or less clothe them with legality or formal awards in spite of settlement via conciliation having been virtually reached in advance.[13] In these

---

12 Article 19 (Commencement of Arbitration or Conciliation Procedure) (1) of the Arbitration and Conciliation Procedural Rules (fully revised on June 9, 2000) of the Second Tokyo Bar Association Arbitration Centre provides that "The conciliation procedure commences with receipt of the application for conciliation or for arbitration which does not accompany an arbitration agreement." Its Article 36(2) provides, "The Arbitrator at any stage of arbitration proceedings may recommend settlement on the whole or a part of disputes." Article 25 (Commencement of Conciliation Procedure), the Conciliation and Arbitration Rules of Industrial Property Arbitration Centre provides, "In the event that there is no arbitration agreement, the conciliation procedure may be commenced" and its Article 38(2) is almost identical to Article 36(2) of the Bar Association rules.

13 Article 23(1) of the above Bar Association rules provides, "In the conciliation process, when a settlement is made by the parties, the conciliator may, except when it is considered to be inappropriate in terms of the stipulation of mandatory rules or against public policy, etc., after preparing an agreement acceptable to the parties, sign as a witness to the settlement." Its Article 23(3) further provides that, "Regarding the settlement specified in paragraph (1), after the parties agree to arbitration and submit an arbitration agreement, when they seek an arbitration award, the conclusion of which is identical to the content of the settlement, the conciliator shall become an arbitrator and render an award regarding its contents. In such a case, there is no need to provide reason in the document of the award." Rule 29 (Transition to arbitration) (3) of the Industrial Property Arbitration Centre has it that, "In the conciliation process, when a settlement agreement is reached and, with submitting an arbitration agreement signed by both parties, they request an arbitration award, the conclusion of which refers to the terms of settlement, the conciliation procedure shall be switched to that of arbitration." Article 41 (Resolution by settlement and preparing for an arbitration award) (1) of the rules stipulates, "When settlement is reached in the arbitration process, the parties shall effect a written agreement of settlement. Instead, should the parties so agree, the arbitrator shall make an arbitral award statement conclusion of which is totally or partially the terms of the settlement." Regarding the description of reasons for the award, applying the same rule of (2), *mutatis mutandis*, the provision of Article 40, as with the ordinary arbitration award, a description of the reasons is mandatory unless the parties expressly refuse it.

disputes, the conciliator in principle becomes the arbitrator.[14] But the parties, in the context of conciliation procedure, rely heavily on the conciliator and in practice are requested to apply arbitration on unsolved issues within certain bounds agreed upon by the parties when a settlement is not reached. Thus, in reality there is no surprise attack; the yoking of conciliation with arbitration is not regarded as posing a technical problem.[15] However, there are academic arguments on this natural justice issue. The Nagoya Bar Association Centre for Mediation and Arbitration amended its procedure rule in order to address the natural justice issues (see below).

Thus, in the common law countries, hybrid dispute processing has evolved mainly as agreements among parties concerned without court intervention and this practice has been introduced in court practice and arbitration procedure. In contrast, hybrid dispute processing in Japan has developed grounded primarily on court procedure, which, through intervention by judges, has been applied to resolving disputes outside

14 Article 24 (Transfer to arbitration) (2) of the Bar Association stipulates, "In the process of conciliation, when the parties agree to arbitration and submit a written agreement for same, the arbitration proceedings shall begin. In this case, the conciliator dealing with conciliation procedure shall become an arbitrator." Its Article 24(3) has it that, "In the case stated in the preceding paragraph, should one or both of the parties seek arbitration with different parson as an arbitrator, in accordance with the provision of Rule 6, another person shall be appointed as arbitrator." Article 29(2) of the Industrial Property Arbitration Centre's rules provides, "during the conciliation process, should the parties agree to arbitration and submit an arbitration agreement, the conciliation procedure shall be converted to that of arbitration." Its Article 29(4) contains the provision, "In the case provided in the preceding two paragraphs, separately submitting a request for arbitration shall not be necessary, in which instance all records of the conciliation proceedings shall automatically be transferred to arbitration ones." In its paragraph (5), "In the case of paragraphs (2) and (3), the conciliator shall become the arbitrator, except as in the case of paragraph (2), if both parties, after reaching an agreement, request entirely or in part dismissal of the conciliator, the management committee of the Arbitration Centre shall relieve the conciliator and assign a new arbitrator for the arbitration proceedings."

15 The 10 July 1999, interview with Attorney Sanji Harago, who established the Arbitration Centre of the Second Tokyo Bar Association, refers to the application of decision in lieu of conciliation in civil conciliation procedure in their dispute processing. Article 79 (6–2) of Law on Security Exchange, which was recently amended as part of financial institutional revision, enforced on 1 December 1998, provides a stipulation on intervention by the Japan Securities and Exchange Association that it shall conciliate securities related disputes. Based on this, the Association's rules for informal conciliation were revised to the effect that, when an investor who accepted an informal conciliation proposal drafted by the *Assen* (informal conciliation) committee, if the securities firm as the counter party does not agree to the proposal, it is required to initiate a lawsuit for seeking confirmation of the non-existence of debt. It is noteworthy that this scheme, as a whole, represents a kind of non-binding unilateral arbitration.

the court by practising lawyers. In the common law jurisdiction, when third party recommendation is sought for facilitating settlement by furnishing relevant information for compromise, it should be given as a result of adversarial procedure and it should be separated from the process of decision to bind the parties. Compared with this, in Japan, when conciliation by a third party fails, they tend to rely on the third party, who is given the authority to make a binding decision. In this, the same person serves as both conciliator and umpire, resulting in paternalistic dispute processing, which often is the target of criticism. Using negotiation for settlement and conciliation as the basic tools of dispute processing supported by forced solution by the third party satisfies the needs of dispute resolution. But from the aspect of promoting party autonomy in dispute processing, and taking into account international orientation, natural justice issues must be duly addressed.

NATURAL JUSTICE ASSURANCE FOR HYBRID DISPUTE PROCESSING AND THE NEW LAW

The central issue of hybrid dispute processing is how to strike a balance between speed/economy (time/cost) and assurance of natural justice or procedural fairness, which in principle must be judged by the parties concerned. That is, the basic viewpoint of natural justice assurance is to specify minimal obligation in order to deliver as many alternatives as possible from among which they can choose at their own responsibility. The author proposes of the following text of the legal stipulation based on this viewpoint.

Article X: (Settlement recommendation in arbitration and linkage between arbitration and conciliation)

(1) The arbitrator may recommend settlement or conciliation for the settlement at any time during arbitration proceedings except when it contradicts obligation.
(2) Based on a written agreement by the parties and within its limitations, the arbitrator may suspend the arbitration proceedings anytime and as conciliator, conciliate the dispute for settlement. However, to obtain the written consent, the arbitrator must explain to the parties in advance that when conciliation fails and an arbitral award is made, the assurance of natural justice may be difficult.

(3) The arbitrator who becomes conciliator as described in the preceding paragraph must not use the information obtained in the process of conciliation, without the consent of the party, for other than the conciliation and must keep it confidential.

(4) Should the conciliation as cited in the preceding paragraphs fail and the arbitration resumes, the arbitrator who became the conciliator, if deeming the information material to rendering an arbitral award, shall disclose it to the opposing party after obtaining the consent of the party who submitted it, and identify individual issues of the arbitration proceedings with all the parties. When the consent to the information disclosure is not obtained, the arbitrator (turned conciliator) may avoid acting as arbitrator for the resumed arbitration proceedings. Should the arbitrator resume the arbitration proceedings as arbitrator by notifying the opposing party of the existence of undisclosable material information, said party shall have the right to challenge the appointment of the arbitrator.

(5) If the parties have the conciliator continue to serve as arbitrator for the subsequent arbitration proceedings with an arbitration agreement, the paragraphs of (2) and (4) above shall apply *mutatis mutandis*.

Unfortunately, the New Law does not provide for such a comprehensive article on linking between arbitration and conciliation. However, there are some significant provisions along with my proposal.

Link between arbitration and conciliation (Arbitrator's attempt of settlement)

The New Law provides in Article 38(4) and (5), as follows:

> (4) An arbitral tribunal or one or more arbitrators designated by it may attempt to settle the civil dispute subject to the arbitral proceedings, if consented to by the parties.
>
> (5) Unless otherwise agreed by the parties, the consent provided for in the preceding paragraph or its withdrawal shall be made in writing.

In instances of settlement attempt by the arbitrator, it can be a mere recommendation of settlement between the disputing parties by themselves, or for practical conciliation by the arbitrator, in which an amicable settlement may be sought through persuasion by the arbitrator. In the first case, as paragraph (1) of my proposed article provides, such a mere proposal can be made by the arbitrator without the parties' consents unless it contradicts the arbitrator's duty even under the New Law. Article 38(4) above deals with the latter case of practical conciliation by the arbitrator like paragraph (2) of my proposal that conciliation is possible based on agreement by the parties to the extent of the agreement. Article 38(5) intends to ensure the parties' will. This regulation is different from the court practice under the Code of Civil Procedure. But owing to the fact that arbitration is a process grounded on agreement by the parties, when compared with a court judge, that a person not necessarily proficient regarding natural justice can become an arbitrator. The recent procedure in litigation cases tends to take on the form of civil conciliation under the Law on Civil Conciliation in order to separate litigation procedure from settlement procedure. Thus, the author considers Article 38(4) and (5) does not provide for natural justice assurance since it does not separate conciliation procedure from arbitration procedure like my proposal.

Party autonomy and natural justice in cases where the arbitrator becomes conciliator and vice versa

Let us assume that an arbitrator, based on agreement by the parties can suspend arbitration and conduct conciliation within the scope of the agreement. Two issues will surface if efforts to seek settlement fail and the arbitrator resumes the arbitration process: the avoidance of prejudice grounded on the information revealed during the conciliation process (for assurance of the right of rebut), and the impact on conciliation to prevent frankness from fear of referring to unfavourable comments made during the process. The stipulation in paragraphs (3), (4) and (5) of the article the author proposed above intends to provide measures to resolve these issues.

First of all, the New Law does not have any provision for the arbitrator's duty on confidentiality like the author's paragraph (3). However, in case the arbitrator use confidential information obtained in the conciliation proceedings, the arbitrator can be challenged due to a ground listed in Article 18(1)(ii):

> (ii) if circumstances exist that give rise to justifiable doubts as to its impartiality or independence.

The author's paragraphs (4) and (5) intend safeguard measures for ensuring the paragraph (3). Regarding the use of confidential information obtained during the conciliation process during arbitration proceedings, there is a distinction among nations. China, for instance unilaterally prohibits their application (as stipulated by the China International Economic and Trade Arbitration Commission's Arbitration Rule Article 51, the so-called Chinese method). In contrast, Hong Kong, for example makes it compulsory to disclose material confidential information to the opposing party (the so-called Hong Kong method, as mentioned in the Hong Kong Arbitration Ordinance, Article 2B(3), and a similar provision in Article 17(3) of the Singapore International Arbitration Law). Since banning the unwarranted application of confidential information cannot effectively prevent doing so, the latter would be better (Matsuura and Aoyama, 1999: 305–306). In addition, making the arbitrator specify issues before resuming arbitration proceedings prevents a surprise attack and ensures the right to rebut. The stipulation to require the consent of the parties concerned was included to protect their interests. Accordingly, without this consent, the information cannot be used as ground for an arbitration award.

However, even though the information cannot be legally used for the arbitration award, in practice there is no denying its effect on the arbitrator's evaluation of the case. In this context, the party should reserve the right to refuse the conciliator's re-appointment as the arbitrator in the subsequent arbitral proceedings, if the opposition party refuses to disclose confidential information. Also if appointed as arbitrator, he or she has the right to waive becoming such, contending there is a fear of prejudice arising from the fact that material information that may affect his or her award will not be disclosed to the opponent. Further, the conciliator is obliged to let the opposition party decide if he or she is competent as an arbitrator by stating to have confidential material information. In this manner, the opposition party can either choose to dismiss the person or to ask him or her to arbitrate at his/her risk with forfeiting the right to object.

Although the New Law does not provide for such detailed measures, Article 18(4) provides for the arbitrator's duty to disclose any fact which may give rise to doubts over the arbitrator's own impartiality or independence, as seen below.

(4) An arbitrator, during the course of arbitral proceedings, shall without delay disclose any circumstances likely to give rise to

> justifiable doubts as to its impartiality or independence (unless the parties have already been informed of them by the arbitrator).

Thus, when the arbitrator obtains during conciliation process such confidential information as material to decision making for arbitration, he/she must disclose such a fact subject to this paragraph. Although it is not clear from the New Law since it does not contain any provision for the arbitrator's duty on confidentiality, the arbitrator should first seek consent of the party who gave the confidential information to do so. Otherwise, the arbitrator loses credibility and thus the conciliation process will not be productive since the parties hesitate to be open and frank in their communication with the arbitrator. Thus, the author considers that a provision on arbitrator's duty on confidentiality should be added.

If such consent on disclosure cannot be obtained, the arbitrator should resign or inform the opposing party of the fact since the opposing party might loose an opportunity to cross-examine and rebut such harmful information. Again there is no clear provision in the New Law. Nevertheless, the arbitrator's such action must be justified by Article 25 on equal treatment to both parties, which follows as below.

> (1) The parties shall be treated with equality in the arbitral proceedings.
> (2) Each party shall be given a full opportunity of presenting its case in the arbitral proceedings.

If the arbitrator does not have self-confidence to fulfil his/her duty underlined in the article, he/she should resign as arbitrator (resignation releases his/her duty pursuant to Article 21(1)(ii) of the New Law). Thus, natural justice as to combining arbitration with conciliation can be safeguarded under the New Law. However, it fails to provide for clear and detailed mechanism for it. Now the New Law is enacted, the proposed article should be reflected in procedure rules to be amended by arbitration institutions in accordance with the New Law.

Furthermore, even with these measures articulated in the article, if the parties should make an unfavourable statement by themselves during conciliation process, there is no denying that it may negatively affect the arbitrator's evaluation of the case. With respect to the procedure to disclose material confidential information (checking fairness in judging the importance of the information), the issue of the opposition party being kept in the dark cannot be avoided. Thus, such procedural risk should be duly explained to both parties before they agree to the arbitrator's becoming a conciliator (so-called "informed consent") (Elliott, 1996: 117). By following this alone, waiving the right of questioning (to prohibit dismissal of an arbitrator on ground of having been a conciliator) will be justified.

IMPACT ON DISPUTE PROCESSING PRACTICE IN JAPAN

The New Law entered into force on 1 March 2004. It will significantly change dispute processing practice in Japan. Even before it, the attitude of practising lawyers was changed quite significantly. In fact in 2002, along the line of the article the author proposed, the Nagoya Bar Association Centre for Mediation and Arbitration revised its Procedural Rule and adopted natural justice safeguards given in the article. First, it distinguishes mediation procedure from arbitration procedure by making respective chapters for both procedures. Second, modelled on the article I proposed above, it creates provisions for shifting from mediation process to arbitration proceedings and *vice versa* i.e.; Articles 32 and 41, as follows.

Article 32

(1) The mediator may, at any stage of mediation process, confirm both parties' will whether they want to agree on arbitration and thus shift to the arbitration proceedings.

(2) When the parties agree on arbitration and request arbitration by submitting an arbitration agreement in the written form during mediation process, the mediation process is terminated and replaced by arbitration proceedings provided under Chapter 3. On this occasion, the mediator conducting mediation may be appointed as arbitrator.

(3) In the event of the previous paragraph, the mediator, who obtained from one party information and the like material to an arbitration award and confidential to the opposing party, shall disclose it to the opposing party with a consent of the providing party prior to appointment of arbitrator and confirm with the parties outstanding issues for the arbitration proceedings at the first hearing. ....

(4) Where the providing party do not consent, the mediator shall inform the opposing party that there is material information and the like which cannot be disclosed. In this event, the mediator may refuse to be appointed as arbitrator.

(5) ....

Article 41

(1) Both parties may settle a dispute by amicable settlement at any stage of arbitration proceedings.

(2) The arbitrator may, despite the extent of arbitration proceedings unless it contradicts the arbitrator's duty, recommend that the parties by themselves should settle the whole or part of a dispute or that if necessary for settlement, the arbitration proceedings should be suspended and enter into mediation process provided under Chapter 2.

(3) One of the parties may, during the arbitration proceedings, apply for mediation and if the opposing party consent on it, the arbitration proceedings is suspended and transferred to mediation process provided under Chapter 2. On this occasion, the parties may appoint the arbitrator conducting the arbitration proceedings as mediator.

(4) Where the mediation of the previous paragraph fails and the mediator declares the termination of the mediation process, the suspended arbitration proceedings resume. On this occasion, when the arbitrator of the suspended arbitration became the mediator, Article 31(3)–(5) shall be applicable mutatis mutandis as for the arbitrator.

(5) ....

Other bar associations are expected to follow this initiative. However, it is not yet known if their practices are really changing. This must be carefully examined by themselves and practising lawyers and other candidates for arbitrators must be duly trained. In fact on 16 October 2003, an Arbitration Association was established for promoting arbitration in Japan. In this process, Japan's arbitration enhances the quality of arbitration currently practised by the bar associations, so rapidly moving into professional arbitration treating financial and construction disputes,[16] and it will be competent in handling international arbitration by a review of existing international arbitration rules and practices.

Thus, the New Law is now a baseline of law and practice of dispute processing in Japan. The training for the New Law has been held by the Arbitration Association in order to make it work in practice. Japan has pursued international cooperation for activating arbitration in Asia-

16 Commission by the Tokyo Bankers Association of dispute processing to the Tokyo Bar Association was started. Apart from this, the bar associations were specified as an authorised dispute processing institute based on the Law on Housing Quality Warranty.

Oceania region.[17] These Japanese new initiatives will bring a positive impact on cross-border dispute processing not only in this region, but also in the world. The new Japanese model will contribute to harmonization of dispute processing based on individual dispute cultures across the world.

REFERENCES

Abel, R. L. (1982) Contradictions of Informal Justice. In Abel, R. L. (ed.) *The Politics of Informal Justice: The American Experience.* Vol. 1. New York: Academic Press, 267–320.

Brown, H. and Marriott, A. (1993) *ADR Principles and Practice.* London: Sweet and Maxwell.

Elliott, D. C. (1996) Med/arb: Fraught with Danger or Ripe with Opportunity? *Arbitration,* vol. 62, no. 3, 175–183.

Fiss, O. M. (1984) Against Settlement. *Yale Law Journal,* no. 93, 1073–1090.

Hayakawa, Y. (1999) Japanese ADR as Viewed by American Eyes and Issues Requiring Further Clarification (Nos. 1–5). *JCA Journal,* vol. 46, nos. 8–12 (Japanese).

Inomata, Takashi (1999) Admissibility of Linkage between Arbitration and Conciliation and Its Limit (1). *Tôin Law Study,* vol. 5, no. 2, 57–59 (Japanese).

Ishikawa, A. and Kajimura, T. (eds.) (1996) Commentary on Civil Conciliation Law (Revised). *Seirin Shoin* (Japanese).

Kawashima, T. (1967) Legal Consciousness of the Japanese. *Shoten I.* (Japanese).

Matsuura, K. and Aoyama, Y. (1999) "Issues on Modern Arbitration Law" (Japanese).

Miki, K. (1995) ADR Accompanying Lawsuits of U.S. Federal Regional Courts Vol.1. *International Commercial Law Practice*, vol. 23, no. 10, 1048–1049 (Japanese).

Neumann, R. (March 1998) The Role of Arbitrator as Mediator in International Arbitration Cases in Japan. *JCA Newsletter,* no. 3.

Newman, P. (1999) *Alternative Dispute Resolution.* Hertfordshire: CLT Professional Publishing, Ltd.

Ohkawa, H. (1990) Second Tokyo Lawyers Association Arbitration Centre, 728, Hanrei Taimusu, 181–182 (Japanese).

17 Professor Matsuura's *Meijo* project, in which ten jurisdictions has participated into comprehensive join research on this topic since 1999. The Tokyo conference on 11–13 September 2003 discussed furtherance of such an international cooperation in this region.

Ragan, C. (1991) Arbitration in Japan: Caveat Foreign Drafter and Other Lessons. *Journal of International Arbitration,* no. 2, 93–119.

Sato, Y. (1998) Privatisation of Dispute Processing: A Practitioners' Guide and an Interpretation of the Idea of the 1996 English Arbitration Law (1). *JCA Journal,* vol. 45, no. 6, 6–7 (Japanese).

Taniguchi, Y. (1997) International Commercial Arbitration Becoming Similar to Litigation under Globalisation, *Study of Law Series,* vol. 140, no. 5, 6–8 (Japanese).

Taniguchi, Y. (1985) Procedural Justice, Basic Law No. 8. *Dispute*, Shoten I. (Japanese).

Tashiro, K. (1995) Conciliation or Mediation during the Arbitral Process: A Japanese View. *Journal of International Arbitration,* no. 12, 119–133.

4

Confidentiality in Arbitrations

Christopher To[1]

INTRODUCTION

Confidentiality, like privacy, has long been perceived as one of the prime advantages of arbitration[2] and the very reason why parties opt for arbitration as opposed to public Court proceedings to resolve disputes. Until the recent decade or so, confidentiality was taken for granted and widely assumed as the fundamental feature of arbitration in the international arbitral regime.[3] This assumption cannot be whole-heartedly assumed today as the scope of arbitral confidentiality is "far from a settled issue".[4]

Eight years on from the dramatic decision by the High Court of Australia in *Esso Australia Res. Ltd v. Plowman*,[5] there is still no international consensus on the existence and ambit of confidentiality in arbitration. Relevant institutional rules, national legislations and case laws vary from legal system to legal system and nation to nation. Crucial divergence in judicial opinion remains even among the common law jurisdictions such as England and Australia.

---

1 Written with the assistance of Ms. Elizabeth Wong, a second year LLB (Hons) student in the City University of Hong Kong.

2 Confidentiality was listed as the most important perceived benefit in the statistical survey of US/European users conducted in 1992 for the LCIA by the London Business School.

3 *Hassneh Insurance Co. of Israel v. Stuart J. Mew* [1993] 2 Lloyd's Rep 243.

4 Fulvio Fracassi, Confidentiality and NAFTA, Chapter 11 Arbitrations, 2 CHI.J.INT'L. 213 (2001). See also Alexis C. Brown, Presumption Meets Reality: An Exploration of the Confidentiality Obligation in International Commercial Arbitration, 16 AM. U. INT'L. REV. 69 (2001).

5 (1995) 128 A.L.R. 391.

CONCEPT OF CONFIDENTIALITY

According to the Oxford Advanced Learner's Dictionary, "confidentiality" is defined as a situation in which one party expects another party to keep information secret. To be more precise, confidentiality, in the arbitral context, relates to the rights and obligations of the parties to arbitration in respect of the documents and other materials produced in, or discovered by, the arbitral process.[6]

Many may consider confidentiality, coupled with other facilitative features like cost-effectiveness and flexibility, the principal attribute of arbitration that parties look for when they decide whether to refer the dispute to arbitration rather than litigation. Despite the international differences on the existence and scope of the duty of confidentiality and the relative low ranking of privacy as the most important attribute of arbitration in a recent analysis,[7] it remains true that there is a collateral expectation of parties to arbitration that the proceedings will be conducted in the absence of strangers to the arbitration and their business and personal confidences will be kept in strict confidence. This can be particularly important when the issues in dispute are highly sensitive financial and technological matters. However, disputants must be aware that certain aspects of the outcome of an arbitral process may need to be notified to other authorities such as creditors, investors, company receivers and liquidators.

In saying this, arbitration is generally deemed to be a private matter unless the agreements provide otherwise. The fact that arbitration is even underway is not necessarily a matter of public knowledge, as is the conduct of arbitral proceedings and arbitral awards. It is assumed that any sensitive evidence, documentation or matters raised in the proceedings will not be made public. In other words, contrary to the situation in court proceedings, personal confidences, trade secrets, business processes and reputations are effectively safeguarded.

The confidential and informal nature of arbitration not only protects parties from potentially inconsistent jury awards, settlements and punitive damages that carry large liability, but also from public scrutiny and

6 Peter Sheridan, Privacy and Confidentiality — Recent Developments; The Divergence between English and Australian Law Confirmed, 1998 *International Arbitration Law Review*.

7 Richard W. Naimark and Stephanie E. Keer, International Private Commercial Arbitration: Expectations and Perceptions of Attorneys and Business People, *International Business Lawyer* (May 2002).

embarrassing criticism. In the case of labor disputes, arbitration is much preferred, since this allows the preserving of a solid employer-employee relationship and the creating of a greater possibility of employee reinstatement. The American Arbitration Association, which resolves some 14,500 labor-management disputes annually, has established a new specialised labour panel of arbitrators to accommodate the growing need.

Although confidentiality is invariably seen by the parties in dispute as a positive factor, nevertheless some legal practitioners feel that it has a negative impact on the development of the standardization of commercial practices. Confidentiality, in this view, prevents the dissemination of details of reasons and rulings. Without such precedent or legal principle in place, the issue of certainty and consistency would be factors which legal counsel will find difficult, if not impossible to justify to their clients in advising them to adopt arbitration as a possible means of resolving business disputes. It seems in practice to come down to the practical experience and degree of exposure of that particular legal counsel and his/her ability to negotiate and to draft appropriate provisions which will ensure that the arbitration process maintains the essence of confidentiality.

LEGAL PRIVILEGE AND CONFIDENTIALITY

Confidentiality and privilege are different concepts and although either one can exist in relation to material without the other being present, nevertheless sometimes they overlap and confusion arises. "Privilege" has been defined as

> a legally recognized right to withhold certain testimonial or documentary evidence from a legal proceeding, including the right to prevent another from disclosing such information.[8]

In England, the Law Reform Committee defined "privilege" as

> the right of a person to insist on there being withheld from judicial tribunal information which might assist it to ascertain certain facts relevant to an issue upon which it is adjudicating.[9]

---

8 Richard M. Mosk and Tom Ginsburg, Evidentiary Privileges in International Arbitration, I.C.L.Q. 50, 2, p. 345 at 346.

9 Law Reform Committee, 16th report (Privilege in Civil proceedings), Cmnd 3472 (1967), paragraph 1.

In arbitrations, the applied evidentiary rules are more flexible compared with those for litigation. For example in Hong Kong under both, the domestic and international arbitration regime, the arbitrator can proceed without regard to the strict rules of evidence:

> When conducting arbitration proceedings, an arbitral tribunal is not bound by the rules of evidence and can receive any evidence that it considers relevant to the proceedings, but must give such weight to the evidence adduced in the proceedings as it considers appropriate.[10]

In the case of *S. D. Meyers and Canada,*[11] the general view held by the arbitral tribunal is that an international tribunal will determine the appropriate rules of evidence based on the particular circumstances of each case. The tribunal is ready to protect certain confidential business documents from disclosure by considering the facts of the case and the nature of the involved information as noted by the Court in *Pope and Talbot and Canada.*[12]

As a general rule in the legal profession, lawyers owe their clients a duty of confidentiality. Such privileged communications between lawyers and clients have to be made in confidence, especially when the client is obtaining legal advice from the lawyer and where subsequently the information relates to pending legal proceedings.[13] However, such professional privilege could be overridden, for example in Hong Kong by court order or by law, e.g. through the Prevention of Bribery Ordinance[14] or where the communication was not made before the lawyer during his course of employment, or where the consultation was made to a friend who happens to be a lawyer but who later refused to act as such.[15] As a creature of the common law, legal professional privilege can be abrogated by statutes. In other common law jurisdictions such as Australia and the United Kingdom, the legislature has left the privilege "untouched" so far as it applies to legal proceedings. Conversely, the privileged right can be preserved by express statutory provision. The Independent Commission

10 Arbitration Ordinance, Laws of Hong Kong, Chapter 341 section 2GA(2).

11 Decision of 13 November 2000. See www.naftaclaims.com.

12 Noral Gallagher, Legal Privilege in International Arbitration, 2003 *International Arbitration Law Review.*

13 Johnson Stokes and Master, *In-house Counsel and the Attorney-Client Privilege,* Lex Mundi, 2002.

14 S13 of the Prevention of Bribery Ordinance.

15 Ibid n11.

Against Corruption Ordinance, Chapter 204, Laws of Hong Kong expressly preserves the full force of the common law doctrine of legal professional privilege by providing that nothing in the Ordinance will prejudice any claim to privilege which any person may have at common law.

In *Canadian Transit Co v Girdhar,*[16] a recent Canadian case involving professional privilege, an engineer's obligation to keep confidential information that has been given to him and the legal relationship that may exist or develop between him and the client, is sharply distinguished by the Court. It was held that

> the fiduciary obligation that professional owes to the client arises based on the factual context of their particular relationship and not merely because there is a statutory relationship.[17]

Despite the universal recognition they have gained, the rules of privilege differ from country to country, and there is no uniform approach to the question of privilege. The American Arbitration Association's (AAA) International Rules[18] provides expressly that the tribunal shall take into account applicable principles of legal privilege:

> The tribunal shall determine the admissibility, relevance, materiality and weight of the evidence offered by any party. The tribunal shall take into account applicable principles of legal privilege, such as those involving the confidentiality of communications between a lawyer and client.

However, the International Chamber of Commerce (ICC), London Court of International Arbitration (LCIA), International Centre for Settlement of Investment Disputes (ICSID) and the United Nations Commission on International Trade Law (UNCITRAL) rules are silent on the issue.[19] Nevertheless, some jurisdictions that have adopted the UNCITRAL Model Law have included provisions which deal with the issue. For example in Hong Kong, a party may object to the disclosure of certain documents or

16 Ontario Superior Court of Justice Divisional Court.

17 *per* Day J.

18 Article 20(6) of the International Arbitration Rules of the American Arbitration Association, as amended on 1 July 2003.

19 Hans Bagner, Confidentiality: A Fundamental Principle in International Commercial Arbitration? *Journal of International Arbitration* 2 (2001):18.

categories of document to the tribunal and/or his opponent on the ground that they are covered by legal privilege:

> A person cannot be required to produce in arbitration proceedings any document or other material evidence that the person could not be required to produce in civil proceedings before a court.[20]

CONFIDENTIALITY IN MEDIATION AND LITIGATION

Before examining the position of various jurisdictions and the precise extent to which confidentiality can be relied upon in international arbitration, it is worth taking a look at the development of confidentiality in two other dispute resolution procedures, namely mediation and litigation.

The importance of confidentiality to mediation will not be less, indeed it may well be more, paramount than it would be to arbitration. In mediation, all information and communications are to be kept within the confines of a private hearing and will not be disclosed to the public at large. The Hong Kong International Arbitration Centre Mediation Rules[21] section 12(i) states that

> Mediation is a private and confidential process. Every document, communication or information disclosed, made or produced by any party for the purposes of or related to the mediation process shall be disclosed on a privileged and without prejudice basis and no privilege or confidentiality shall be waived by such disclosure. Confidentiality also extends to the settlement agreement except where its disclosure is necessary for implementation or enforcement.

Whereas under the laws of Hong Kong there are provisions[22] to allow an arbitrator to act as a conciliator[23] this procedure is wholly consensual. The arbitrator's role as a conciliator may be brought to an end when one party withdraws his consent to the procedure. The confidentiality provision in section 2B(3) of the Arbitration Ordinance is of course pivotal to this procedure. The phrase at the end of section 2B(3) of the Arbitration

20 Arbitration Ordinance, Laws of Hong Kong, Chapter 341 section 2GB(8).

21 Effective 1 August 1999.

22 Arbitration Ordinance, Laws of Hong Kong, Chapter 341 section 2B.

23 Under the Arbitration Ordinance, Laws of Hong Kong, Chapter 341 section 2 *Conciliation include mediation.*

Ordinance "as much of that information as is material to the arbitration proceedings" enables the conciliator/arbitrator to identify whether the information disclosed to him during the conciliation is material to the arbitration proceedings. The success of this section will depend upon the respect and confidence that the parties have in the individual arbitrator/conciliator. No one is forced to use this procedure against their will but it is thought to be a useful addition to the armoury in dispute resolution. The rationale behind this section is best explained by the Law Reform Commission Report, which suggested it. It reads as follows:

> The [conciliation provisions] should ... provide that the parties may agree in writing after the commencement of an arbitration that any arbitrator or umpire may act as a conciliator. During the time he acts as conciliator, he should be permitted to see the parties separately or together, and unless a party giving information agrees otherwise he should treat information given to him by either party as confidential while he continues to act as conciliator, the arbitrator should disclose any material information given him in confidence during the period of conciliation. The purpose of these proposals is to provide a statutory framework within which an arbitrator can conciliate without committing misconduct by breaching the rules of natural justice. He is permitted access to the parties alone subject to the two important safeguards of:
>
> (i) over continuing consent, and
> (ii) post failure disclosure of material facts.
>
> We accept that (ii) may inhibit frankness, but we think this is better than compelling an arbitrator to try to ignore material information. We do not anticipate procedural difficulty. If the arbitrator were to send to each party a list of the information he regarded as material and disclosable, and then consider that party's views before acting, the chances of error should be slight. We therefore think that this framework should enable an arbitrator fairly and effectively to conciliate, if and so long as that is what the parties want, without misconduct, and without impairing his capacity to make an award thereafter. Finally an agreement reached under conciliation should be able to be treated as an award on the arbitration agreement. We have taken the opportunity to suggest some minor modifications to s.2A. These simplify the procedure, but do not affect its substance.[24]

24 The Law Reform Commission of Hong Kong Report on the adoption of the UNCITRAL Model Law of Arbitration [Topic 17], April 1987.

Many people have reservations about the wisdom of an arbitrator acting first as mediator as they feel that people will be less frank with a mediator knowing that he may subsequently have the authority to adjudicate on the issues. Others believe that no one is better qualified to sit as an arbitrator than a person who is already familiar with the issues having acted as a mediator, and that to appoint someone else, at this stage, would be an unnecessary waste of time and money. Parties and arbitrators must decide for themselves whether or not they feel the two processes should be kept separate or may be combined.[25]

Owing to this private and confidential nature of mediation, more and more parties are now resorting to the use of mediation to solve disputes relating to information technology and intellectual property matters.[26]

In Scotland, the Scottish Law Commission published a discussion paper in 1991 on the subject of "Confidentiality in Family Mediation"[27] which contains a very useful summary of the law on the subject in Scotland, England and Wales and other jurisdictions. It outlines those areas where reservations or uncertainties exist and presents the issues and options for reform. A paper published in 1992 entitled "Evidence in Family Mediation" followed.[28]

Despite the key role of confidentiality in mediation, neither the Courts nor the academy are able to provide any absolute answer to the issue of confidentiality, considering the fundamental difficulties surrounding the precise definition of such a rule and all the possible attendant exceptions. Three recent United States mediation cases, *Olam v Congress Mortgage Company,*[29] *Rinaker v Superior Court*[30] *and Foxgate Homeowners' Association, Inc v Bramalea California and Bramalea Ltd,*[31] confirm a substantially accepted view that the duty of confidentiality is no longer ironclad and is subject to exceptions and qualifications.

The United States litigation regime, here taken as an example to illustrate the development of confidentiality in litigation, entitles each

25 Michael Thomas, CMG, QC, Mediation at Work in Hong Kong, *Arbitration: The Journal of the Chartered Institute of Arbitrators* 58, 1 (February 1992):29.

26 Michele Zamboni, Confidentiality in Mediation, 2003 *International Arbitration Law Review*.

27 Discussion Paper No. 92, published by the Scottish Law Commission of 140 Causewayside, Edinburgh, EH 1PR.

28 SLC-136. It was also followed by the Civil Evidence (Family Mediation) (Scotland) Act 1995, which provides for a family mediation privilege.

29 Ibid.

30 Ibid.

31 Ibid.

party to know what information the other party may hold in the litigation by participating in discovery, in which each party is allowed to ask the other to answer written questions which usually cover trade secrets and other confidential business information.[32]

In order to protect a party or person from annoyance, embarrassment, oppression, or undue burden or expense, the Courts are vested with power to either block the production of confidential information altogether or to permit its production in a designated manner.[33] The extent to which the confidential information is protected is left up to the Court's full discretion. Evidently, confidential commercial information is not entitled to any automatic or absolute immunity from discovery in civil litigation in the United States. Given the discovery rules applicable in United States Courts, the prevention of confidential materials relating to the lawsuit at hand from production in Court is highly unlikely.[34] Most often, the Court will grant extensive protection to these types of materials by issuing a protective order to limit access to the confidential information.

INTERNATIONAL DIFFERENCES IN CASE LAW

The English perspective

It is a central principle of English law that privacy and confidentiality are inherent characteristics of arbitration. Irrespective of the fact that the nature and ambit of the confidentiality obligation has not fully been delineated in case law, the prevailing English judicial view is that an implied duty of confidentiality, derived from the private nature of arbitration, exists in the arbitral model. Generally, English Courts allow parties to an arbitration substantial protection against divulgence of materials produced in the course of proceedings, albeit subject to a number of exceptions and qualifications.

In *Dolling-Baker v Merrett*,[35] the English Court of Appeal held that the very nature of arbitration dictates that there must be some implied obligation attached to both parties not to disclose, or use for any other

32 Peter Sullivan, Protection of Confidential Information in Private Antitrust Litigation, *International Business Lawyer* (August 2003).

33 OJ 2000 C 365 E/284.

34 Ibid n30.

35 [1991] 2 Al E.R. 890.

purpose, information arising from the arbitral proceedings. By issuing an injunction restraining one party from disclosing documents relating to an arbitration in any subsequent proceedings, which was not linked to any earlier proceedings, the Court unambiguously acknowledged the existence of the duty of confidentiality. As the Court noted, the duty of confidentiality arises from the essentially private nature of arbitration, coupled with the implied obligation of a party who obtains documents on discovery not to use them for any purpose other than the dispute at hand, notwithstanding the consensual and wholly voluntary nature of the proceedings.

Nevertheless, the principle of confidentiality is not absolute and could be overruled, for example by the consent of the parties or pursuant to an order or with leave of the Court. To determine whether to order disclosure, the Court must consider the confidentiality obligation relating to that arbitration and whether the same outcome could be reached by other less costly ways, which do not involve any breach of the implied undertaking.

In *Hasseneh Insurance Co of Israel v Stuart J. Mew,*[36] Mr. Justice Coleman reaffirmed the ruling in *Dolling-Baker v Merrett* and established some exceptions to the fundamental principle of confidentiality. In this case, an arbitrating party intended to disclose the recently published arbitral award in a subsequent action against the third party. However, the court banned the party from doing on the ground that this "release of the subject documents would amount to a breach of confidence."[37]

The Court accepted the implied term basis for the confidentiality presumption and concluded that in the case of documents produced in the course of, or for the purpose of, the arbitration, the confidentiality obligation is implied as a matter of business efficacy in the parties' agreement to arbitrate. However, this only applies to documents or information revealed during the proceedings. As to the arbitral award itself and the reasons of the award, the confidentiality obligation applies. If it is reasonably necessary to advance or protect a party's legal rights against a third party, it is possible for a party to disclose the award and its reasons without breaching the duty of confidentiality.

The question before the Court in *Insurance Co v Lloyd's Syndicate*[38] was "How necessary does disclosure of the award have to be for the

36 [1993] 2 Lloyd's Rep. 243.
37 *per* Colman J. at 249.
38 [1995] 1 Lloyd's Rep. 272.

protection of the party's legal rights before he is entitled to disclose it as of right?"[39] Mr. Justice Coleman further discussed the meaning of "reasonably necessary" and confirmed an agreement to arbitrate contains an implied term imposing a duty of confidentiality on both parties. His Lordship in that instance concluded that the duty would only cease to exist if it were necessary for one party to establish legal rights vis-à-vis a third party, merely for the reason that it may have a persuasive effect in a related action would be insufficient to override the undertaking.

Another exception to the duty of confidentiality was identified in *London and Leeds Estates Limited v Paribas Limited.*[40] In this case, a party to arbitration wished to obtain statements provided by the other party's witness in earlier arbitrations. The Court ruled that a party to litigation was entitled to obtain the proof of a witness, where it demonstrates that the witness expresses himself in a materially different sense when representing different sides, for the public interest and for the interest of individual litigants.

The ruling in *Ali Shipping Corporation v Shipyard Trogir*[41] helped dispel doubts in relation to arbitral confidentiality. In this case, the Court held that the duty of confidentiality on the documentation prepared during the arbitration proceedings was deemed to arise from private nature of arbitration. By ruling that arbitral confidentiality was implied by operation of law as opposed to business efficacy, the Court once again cemented the existence of a duty of confidentiality. The implied term was brought to a more reasonable position and furthermore, exceptions to the duty were identified. Potter L. J., in his judgment, provided some

1. Consent of the other arbitrating party to disclosure the confidential information
2. Court's order to disclose the confidential documents
3. Where disclosure is reasonably necessary for the protection of the legitimate interests of an arbitrating party vis-à-vis a third party, as illustrated in *Insurance Co v Lloyd's Syndicate.*[42]
4. Where disclosure is sought for the interests of justice/ public interest, as set out in *London and Leeds Estates Limited v Paribas Limited.*[43]

39 [1995] 1 Lloyd's Rep. 273.
40 [1995] E.G. 134.
41 [1998] 2 All E.R. 136.
42 Ibid n36.
43 Ibid n38.

The most recent significant English authority is that of *Associated Electric and Gas Insurance Services Limited v the European Reinsurance Company of Zurich*,[44] in which the Privy Council examined the scope of the principle of privacy, a detailed confidentiality agreement between parties to two separate arbitration proceedings and issue estoppel in arbitral context being at odds with the prevailing English judicial views that a duty of confidentiality is implied in an arbitration agreement, this decision is perceived by many as a curtailment of the arbitral confidentiality obligation.

The case involved two insurance companies, *Aegis* and *European Re*, who had entered into a reinsurance agreement with a particularly detailed confidentiality clause. Later, two separate disputes were referred to arbitration. The tribunal issued an award regarding the first dispute, and in the second arbitration in respect of the second dispute, *European Re* sought to rely on the first arbitration award but *Aegis* obtained an injunction to restrain *European Re* from doing so. The injunction was subsequently lifted and *Aegis* appealed to the Privy Council against the decision. It was held that *European Re* was not precluded from raising a plea of issue estoppel in the second arbitration. The action was dismissed accordingly.

The Privy Council acknowledged the existence of confidentiality of arbitration proceedings in the decision. However, *Ali Shipping* case, in which confidentiality was affirmed as an implied term of an agreement, was distinguished from the present case for the reason that the latter involved a detailed confidentiality clause, contrary to the rather general one in *Ali Shipping* case. The Privy Council was of the view that the approach adopted in *Ali Shipping* case fails to distinguish between different types of confidentiality that attach to different types of documents, blurring the distinction of the concept of privacy and confidentiality.[45]

Having agreed with *Aegis* that the confidentiality agreement expressly stated that the arbitration result would not be communicated to any non-arbitrating party, the Privy Council noted that the provisions were required

> to be evaluated having regard to the surrounding circumstances in which this confidentiality agreement was made and the basic principles and purpose of arbitration.[46]

---

44 [2003] UK PC 11 (29 January 2003).

45 John P. Gaffney, Confidentiality in International Arbitration; A Recent English Decision, 18 *Mealey's International Arbitration Report*, 5(2003).

46 Ibid n43.

The Privy Council recognized that the essential purpose of arbitration is to determine disputes whereas the enforcement rests with the courts. As set out in the Bermuda International Conciliation and Arbitration Act 1993 and the UNCITRAL Model Law, which the arbitration was based on, the parties were bound to recognize and respect the rights which the award declared. In other words, the confidentiality agreement

> should not be construed so as to prevent one party from relying upon an award as having given him rights against the other. But that is what the application of injunction sought to achieve.[47]

Regarding the issue of estoppel, the argument of *Aegis* that estoppel was merely an evidential or procedural matter for the arbitrators was rejected by the Privy Council on the basis that the way to look at it was how estoppels are given effect to, and not at what is the nature of the private law right which the estoppel recognizes and protects. Hence, it could be concluded that issue of estoppel could possibly create substantial rights, which could be regarded as a kind of enforcement of rights conferred by the arbitral award.

The Australian perspective

In the *Esso Australia Res. Ltd v. Plowman* case,[48] in which public authorities were involved, the court had to decide whether the implied duty of confidentiality is rooted in privacy that all documents and information disclosed in the arbitral proceedings are confidential simply because of the private nature of arbitration.

By concluding that

> confidentiality is not an essential attribute of private arbitration imposing an obligation on each party not to disclose the proceedings or documents and information provided in and for the purpose of the arbitration[49]

47 Ibid n43.

48 Ibid n3.

49 *per* Mason C.J.

the case profoundly impacted on the international arbitration regime.[50] In the court's view, confidentiality obligation could not be justified by the privacy of the proceedings, custom and practice or an intention to provide arbitration with business efficacy.

As the present case concerned two public authorities, public interest became the core issue to be examined by the Court,

> while private arbitration will often have the advantage of securing for parties a high level of confidentiality or their dealings, where one of those parties is government, or an organ of a government, neither the arbitral agreement nor the general procedural powers of the arbitrator will extend so far as to stamp on the government litigant a regime of confidentiality or secrecy which effectively destroys all limits of general governmental duty to pursue the public interest.[51]

In other words, the obligation of confidence in arbitration is similar to that in litigation, which applies only to documents produced in arbitral proceedings and is subject to public interest in Australian law.

As held in a later decision, the Commonwealth of *Australia v. Cockatoo Dockyard Pvt. Ltd*,[52] where a public authority was involved in an arbitration, the confidentiality obligation could possibly be restricted or even discharged albeit that the parties might have clearly agreed on specific provisions relating to confidentiality.

The American perspective

In *United States v. Panhandle Eastern Corp*,[53] another landmark case on confidentiality, the *United States Government* requested *Panhandle*, an American company, to produce documents relating to an International Chamber of Commerce (ICC) arbitration. The documents requested by the *United States Government* comprised

---

50 L. Yves Forties, The Occasionally Unwarranted Assumption of Confidentiality, 15 ARB. INT'L 131, 134 (1999).

51 *per* Mason C.J.

52 Andrew Rogers QC and Duncan Miller, Non-confidential Arbitration Proceedings, *Arbitration International* 12, 3(1996).

53 (D,Del 1988) 118 F.R.D. 346.

> All documents relating to Sonatrach Arbitration, including, but not limited to: briefs, correspondence and other papers filed with or submitted to the arbitrators, or their delegates; communications between any and all of the defendant, depositions or other witness statements; transcripts of all hearings before the arbitrators, or their delegates; proposals to settle the arbitration; and, inter-or-intra company documents.

By relying upon the Internal Rules of the ICC Court which, as then in force, provided that participants in the work of the ICC Court must respect the "the work of the Court of Arbitration is of a confidential character which must be respected by everyone who participates in that work in whatever capacity" of that work, *Panhandle* sought to resist the demanded recovery by reasoning that arbitration is confidential by nature and that disclosure in question would clash with the expectations of the parties that documents would be kept in confidence.

However, the Court rejected the argument and held that the rules governing the internal functioning of the Court of Arbitration were inapplicable to parties to the arbitration or to the arbitral tribunal. In other words, no obligation of confidentiality was imposed on the arbitrating parties and *Panhandle* had to make the production of the relevant documents to the *United States Government*. Being the first instance to judicially attack confidentiality, this American decision is of critical significance in the development of the principle of confidentiality worldwide.

In a recent mediation case,[54] the Court ruled that confidential information from a separate mediation is admissible in Court to prevent a gross manifest injustice. The case centres on the parents of Emily C. B. Shortly after Emily C. B. was born, she was left in the custody of her father (David B.). More than a year later, the parties entered into a stipulated judgment of paternity. The agreement provided for joint legal custody, with father having primary custody. Seven months later, mother (Stephanie C. S.) filed a motion to modify the placement and paternity stipulation. After a ten-day hearing, the trial court granted primary custody to the mother. The Court determined that the father was not fostering a healthy relationship between Emily C. B. and her mother. The father appealed claiming the trial Court erred when it admitted a tape of an unrelated mediation session, the father had with his older daughter. The

54 *Re the Paternity of Emily C. B., 2004 WL 240227 (Wis. App., February 11, 2004).*

older daughter testified at the custody trial and revealed the existence of the tape in her testimony. The father argued that the tape should not have been admitted since it was part of a confidential mediation session. However, the father supplied the tape to a Court-appointed psychologist and the Court would not allow selective disclosure. The issue in the case was the mental instability of the parents and the tape was relevant to that issue. Nevertheless the Court of Appeal held otherwise that confidential information from a separate mediation may be admitted at trial to prevent a manifest injustice "the importance of which outweighs the principle of confidentiality".

The Singaporean perspective

A recent Singaporean decision on arbitral confidentiality confirms that Singapore, like many other common law jurisdictions, strictly adheres to the English view that there is a general implied duty of confidentiality imposed on arbitrating parties. In *Myanma Yang Chi Oo Co Ltd v Win Win Nu and Anor*,[55] the Singapore High Court upheld the existence of an implied duty of confidentiality in arbitration by referring to the leading English authorities, namely *Dolling-Baker*, *Hassneh Insurance* and *Ali Shipping*.

It was ruled that the general principles of confidentiality and privacy in English law apply to arbitration in Singapore. While the duty of confidence could extend to "any documents prepared for and used in the arbitration, or disclosed or produced in the course of the arbitration, transcripts or notes or the evidence in the arbitration or the award", the Singapore High Court followed the English position that this obligation was subject to limitations by the Court. As affirmed by the Court, disclosure is permissible where it is made by order or leave of the Court, with the consent of the other party, in the interests of justice or deemed reasonably necessary for the protection of the legitimate interest of an arbitrating party. Beyond doubt, the English judicial views on confidentiality prevail as opposed to the Australian position in Singapore.

55 [2003] SGHC 124.

The Swedish perspective

The principle of confidentiality receives a different treatment in the Swedish jurisdiction as illustrated in the *A.I. Trade Finance Inc v Bulgarian Foreign Trade Bank Ltd*[56] case decided by the Swedish Supreme Court. There, *Bulkbank*, a party to an arbitration, applied to Court to set aside the award on the basis that the other party to the arbitration breached the confidentiality obligation by disclosing certain information relating to the dispute early in the course of the proceedings. The Swedish Supreme Court upheld the arbitration award and ruled that there is no legal duty of confidentiality implied in both the Swedish law and the applicable arbitration rules of the United Nations Economic Commission For Europe (UN-ECE) nor was it inherent in the arbitration agreement. Parties to arbitration proceedings should not be deemed to be bound by the duty, unless the parties have specifically agreed the confidentiality obligation within their contract or adopted arbitration rules that expressly provide for such a provision.

It was decided that the private nature of arbitration will exclude outsiders from the hearings and deny access to any document produced during the arbitral proceedings. Although the Court acknowledged that arbitrators have to uphold confidentiality in performing their duties, it denied any contradiction between this and the right of arbitrating parties to disclose information about the proceedings to a third party. As noted by the Court, the possibility that the parties normally recognise the duty of confidentiality and a legal duty of confidentiality attached with legal sanctions exists are fundamentally distinct, even the Swedish Arbitration Act 1999 remains silent on the subject.

The Hong Kong perspective[57]

Arbitration in Hong Kong is governed by the Arbitration Ordinance. This Ordinance sets out a framework for the two distinct regimes in the territory — a domestic regime derived from English law and an international regime, which includes the UNCITRAL (United Nations

56 Olivier Oakley-White, Confidentiality Revisited: Is International Arbitration Losing One of Its Major Benefits? 2003 *International Arbitration Law Review*.

57 *Arbitration in Hong Kong: A Practical Guide*, Sweet and Maxwell, 2003, pp. 730–731.

Commission on International Trade Law) Model Law.[58] Hong Kong, like many other common law jurisdictions, acknowledges the duty of arbitral confidentiality in their arbitration system. Specific provisions like section 2D and section 2E are included in the Ordinance to safeguard this prime advantage of arbitration. This view is supported in New Zealand. Section 14 of the New Zealand Arbitration Act 1996 provides

> An arbitral agreement, unless otherwise agreed by the parties, is deemed to provide that the parties shall not publish, disclose or communicate any information relating to arbitral proceedings under the agreement or to an award made in those proceedings.

In essence the confidentiality obligation is enshrined within the legislation.

Privacy has always been put forward as a key benefit of arbitration. It is the decision of the parties, not that of the Court, as to whether they wish their arbitration proceedings to be held in open Court or not. Nevertheless as stated in section 2D of the Arbitration Ordinance, a party can always apply to the High Court of Hong Kong to have "the proceedings be heard otherwise than in open court". In other words, applications under the Ordinance are allowed for an in camera hearing so as to maintain privacy of the arbitral process.[59] Furthermore, reporting restrictions are imposed on proceedings which are heard otherwise than in open Court.

Under section 2E[60] of the Arbitration Ordinance, a Court is allowed to provide directions as to what information concerning the proceedings may be published, unless all parties to the proceedings agree otherwise or the Court opines that the information in question would not disclose any matter that the party deems confidential even if published.

> A court in which proceedings to which this section applies are being heard shall, on the application of any party to the proceedings, give directions as to what information, if any, relating to the proceedings may be published.[61]

58 Michael J. Moser, *Dispute Resolution in Asia,* 2nd ed., Kluwer Law International, 2002, pp. 101–121.

59 Robert Morgan, *The Arbitration Ordinance of Hong Kong: A Commentary,* Butterworths Asia, 1997.

60 Provisions under s2E bring judgments pursuant to proceedings under Rules of High Court Order 73 within the scope of the Judicial Proceedings (Regulation of Reports) Ordinance.

61 Article 2E(2) of the Arbitration Ordinance.

> A court shall not give a direction under subsection (2) permitting information to be published unless —
> (a) all parties to the proceedings agree that such information may be published; or
> (b) the court is satisfied that the information, if published in accordance with such directions as it may give, would not reveal any matter, including the identity of any party to the proceedings, that any party to the proceedings reasonably wishes to remain confidential.[62]

Where a Court gives a judgment, which is of major legal interest, the court may direct that the reports of the judgment may be published in law reports or professional publications. However, directions and restrictions will be provided upon reporting if any arbitral party reasonably wishes to keep the matter confidential. Whether the wish is reasonable or not is to be determined by the fact that the applicant can demonstrate legitimate interest in protecting his identity, or trade secrets or other sensitive information as to that party's trading position which would be of interest to a competitor or a hostile bidder.[63]

> Notwithstanding subsection (3), where a Court gives a judgment in respect of proceedings to which this section applies and considers that judgment to be of major legal interest, it shall direct that reports of the judgment may be published in law reports and professional publications but, if any party to the proceedings reasonably wishes to conceal any matter, including the fact that he was such a party, the court shall —
> (a) give directions as to the action that shall be taken to conceal that matter in those reports; and
> (b) if it considers that a report published in accordance with directions given under paragraph (a) would be likely to reveal that matter, direct that no report shall be published until after the end of such period, not exceeding 10 years, as it considers appropriate.[64]

Under the Hong Kong International Arbitration Centre Code of Ethical Conduct for arbitrators,[65] arbitrators are required to "keep any

62 Article 2E(3) of the Arbitration Ordinance.
63 Ibid n56.
64 Article 2E(4) of the Arbitration Ordinance.
65 Effective 1 January 2001.

correspondence private and confidential and shall not copy to anyone other than the parties to the dispute" unless with the agreement of the parties.[66] Moreover, they should be "faithful to the relationship of trust and confidentiality inherent in that office".[67]

The duty of confidentiality also extends to an arbitrator who acts as conciliator in the proceedings. Under the Arbitration Ordinance, information obtained by the arbitrator or umpire from a party to the reference shall be treated in confidence unless the parties otherwise agrees or unless:[68]

> Where confidential information is obtained by an arbitrator or umpire from a party to the reference during conciliation proceedings and those proceedings terminate without the parties reaching agreement in settlement of their dispute, the arbitrator or umpire shall, before resuming the arbitration proceedings, disclose to all other parties to the reference as much of that information as he considers is material to the arbitration proceedings.[69]

The Mainland China perspective

As one of the prime characteristics of arbitration, confidentiality is well recognized in the Arbitration Law of the People's Republic of China 1994. This cornerstone piece of legislation governing arbitration in China expressly provides that the arbitral proceedings will be held in private. By implication, there is a duty for any party participating in an arbitration, including arbitrators, arbitration tribunal and arbitral parties, to keep the process and documents in strict confidence.

> Arbitrations shall be conducted in camera. If the parties agree to public arbitration, the arbitration may be public unless state secrets are involved.[70]

The China International Economic and Trade Arbitration Commission (CIETAC) Arbitration Rules 2000 aim at enhancing the level of

66 Rule 2 of the HKIAC Code of Ethical Conduct for Arbitrators.
67 Rule 4 of the HKIAC Code of Ethical Conduct for Arbitrators.
68 Article 2B(2)(b) of the Arbitration Ordinance.
69 Article 2B(3) of the Arbitration Ordinance.
70 Article 40 of Arbitration Law of the People's Republic of China 1994.

internationalization of CIETAC arbitral services, while expanding the jurisdiction to cover purely domestic arbitration cases, thus providing users more choice. Arbitration before CIETAC is conducted in accordance with statutory law and judicial interpretations issued by the Supreme People's Court, international treaties and the procedural rules of CIETAC.[71] Guidelines for conciliation, a key feature in arbitration in the mainland of China, are included in the rules[72] in great detail. Regulations to govern the confidentiality of arbitration are developed to impose duty of confidentiality upon anyone involved in an arbitration. Private hearings are ensured and disclosure of confidential materials relating to arbitral proceedings (including the process of conciliation) is prohibited.

> The arbitration tribunal shall not hear cases in open session. However, if both parties request that an open session hearing be held, the arbitration tribunal shall decide whether to do so or not.[73]
>
> For cases heard in closed session, the parties, their arbitration agents, witnesses, arbitrators, experts consulted by the arbitration tribunal and appraisers appointed by the arbitration tribunal and the relevant staff-members of the secretariat of the Arbitration Commission shall not disclose to outsiders the substantive or procedural matters of the case.[74]
>
> Should conciliation fail, any statement, opinion, view or proposal which has been made, raised, put forward, acknowledged, accepted or rejected by either party or by the arbitration tribunal in the process of conciliation shall not be invoked as grounds for any claim, defense and/or counterclaim in the subsequent arbitration proceedings, judicial proceedings or any other proceedings.[75]

A similar position is taken by the Beijing Arbitration Commission which holds that detailed rules are there to safeguard arbitral confidentiality. As expressly stipulated, "Arbitration shall be conducted in private" unless "so agreed to by the parties, except for cases that involve state secrets."[76] Where a case is heard in private, the parties, witnesses, arbitrators, relevant personnel of the Commission or anyone taking part in the proceedings

---

71 Michael J. Moser, *Dispute Resolution in Asia,* 2nd ed., Kluwer Law International, 2002, pp. 79–99.

72 Effective 1 October 2002.

73 Article 36 of the CIETAC Arbitration Rules.

74 Article 37 of the CIETAC Arbitration Rules.

75 Article 50 of the CIETAC Arbitration Rules.

76 Article 35 of the Rules of Arbitration of the Beijing Arbitration Commission.

shall maintain confidentiality of the proceedings.[77] This duty of confidentiality also covers a failed process of mediation so that:

> no statement, comment, opinion or proposal which was raised by either party or the Tribunal during the process of mediation shall be cited as grounds for any claim, defense and/or counterclaim in subsequent arbitration, judicial procedure or other proceedings.[78]

In line with the general arbitration rules, the Rules for Arbitrators of the Beijing Arbitration Commission demand that arbitrators shall neither disclose any information linking to the proceedings, "including details of the dispute, the process of the hearings, or any trade secrets involved in the case", nor reveal to "any of the parties their own opinions about the case or information about private sittings of the Tribunal."[79] Similar provision can be found in the Ethical Rules of CIETAC to uphold the obligation of confidentiality imposed on arbitrators:

> Arbitrators shall strictly maintain the privacy and confidentiality of arbitration. They shall not divulge to the outsiders any substantial or procedural matters of cases, nor shall they divulge to the parties the details of the discussions of the arbitration tribunal or their own personal views.[80]

NATIONAL LEGISLATION — NEW ZEALAND ARBITRATION ACT OF 1996

Other than the case of New Zealand, there is little national legislation that caters specifically for arbitral confidentiality. In many cases the issue of confidentiality is considered to be too complicated to be included in legislation. The United Kingdom Arbitration Act 1996 remains silent on the subject as English law recognizes a number of exceptions to the general duty of confidentiality. For instance, disclosure is permitted not only by the consent of the parties, but also in confirmation and enforcement proceedings, either by Court order or in a later action by

77 Article 37 of the Rules of Arbitration of the Beijing Arbitration Commission.
78 Article 56 of the Rules of Arbitration of the Beijing Arbitration Commission.
79 Article 19 of the Rules for Arbitrators of the Beijing Arbitration Commission.
80 Article 13 of the Ethical Rules of CIETAC.

leave of Court where "*reasonably necessary*"[81] to protect or pursue a legal right. Colman J. expanded on this in *Insurance Co v. Lloyd's Syndicate*[82] stating:

> ... For the purpose of coming within the qualification to the duty of confidence which attaches to an arbitration award, it is sufficiently necessary to disclose an arbitration award in order to enforce or protect the legal rights of a party to an arbitration agreement only if the rights in question cannot be enforced or protected unless the award and reasons are disclosed to a stranger to the arbitration agreement. The making of the award must therefore be a necessary element in the establishment of the party's legal right against the stranger, this is the furthest boundary to the qualification which business efficacy will support.

On this basis it was felt that to try and attempt to develop a comprehensive statutory definition of confidentiality would be difficult and it was of the view that the matter should be left to the Courts to develop in the light of actual cases.

The New Zealand Arbitration Act of 1996, based upon the UNCITRAL Model Law, was enacted to provide statutory support for confidentiality in arbitration proceedings. Section 14 of the Act provides that

> an arbitration agreement, unless otherwise agreed by the parties, is deemed to provide that the parties shall not publish, disclose, or communicate any information relating to arbitral proceedings under the agreement or to an award made in those proceedings. This is subject to the exception that in respect of publication, disclosure, or communication is contemplated by the Act or publication, disclosure or communication of information to a professional or other adviser of any of the parties.

In saying this, section 14 of the New Zealand Arbitration Act 1996 is not perfect, as pointed out in the New Zealand Law Commission Report 83 entitled "Improving the Arbitration Act 1996" (2003), paragraph 5:

---

81 Ibid n34.

82 [1995] 1 Lloyds Rep 272, [1994] CLC 1303, [1995] 4 Re LR 37, (1994) The Times, 11 November, (1994) The Independent, 8 November, (1995) Lloyd's List, 1 February.

1. The exceptions to the implied term seem insufficiently wide to deal with many everyday situations where disclosure may be necessary.
2. It is arguable that no statutory implied term can ever set out exhaustively all the exceptions that may arise and these need to be determined on a case-by-case basis.

The new Croatian Law on Arbitration only provides in Art 23 (5) that "unless otherwise agreed by the parties, the arbitral proceedings are not public". In France, the New Code of Civil Procedure provides that the deliberation of arbitrators shall be in camera[83] but there are no provisions on the conduct of the parties relating to information and documents exchanged in the course of the arbitral proceedings. Nevertheless in *Aita v. Ojjeh*[84] French law does appear to provide more stringent protection for the confidentiality of arbitral proceedings and awards. As summarized by Paulsson and Rawding:[85]

> In the case of Aita v. Ojjeh, the Court of Appeal of Paris — perhaps the most important jurisdiction in France in the context of international arbitration given the fact that it reviews almost all challenges to awards — rendered a judgment against a party which rather bizarrely was seeking the annulment in France of an award rendered in London (by Lord Wilberforce acting an umpire). The Court of Appeal not only dismissed the challenge, but ruled that the very bringing of the proceedings violated the principle of confidentiality and therefore ordered the challenging party to pay a significant penalty to the party which had won the arbitration, noting that the action had "caused a public debate of facts which should remain confidential," and that it is in "the very nature of arbitral proceedings that they ensure the highest degree of discretion in the resolution of private disputes, as the two parties had agreed."

83 Article 1469 of New Code of Civil Procedure.

84 1986 *Revue de L'Arbitrage* 583 (Cour d'Appel de Paris, 18 February 1986).

85 "The Trouble with Confidentiality", *Arbitration International* 11(1995):303 at 312.

DIVERGENCE IN INSTITUTIONAL ARBITRAL RULES

The Arbitration Rules of the London Court of International Arbitration[86]

The Arbitration Rules of the London Court of International Arbitration (LCIA) offers confidentiality with extensive protection. Other than providing for privacy of the hearings, it expressly states that there is a duty of the parties to keep all awards and relevant materials in the proceedings confidential, except where the disclosure may be required by legal duty or to protect a legal right. Also, the deliberations of the Arbitral Tribunal are likewise confidential to its members and no award will be published without the consent of all the arbitrating parties.

> Unless the parties expressly agree in writing to the contrary, the parties undertake as a general principle to keep confidential all awards in their arbitration, together with all materials in the proceedings created for the purpose of the arbitration and all other documents produced by another party in the proceedings not otherwise in the public domain — save and to the extent that disclosure may be required of a party by legal duty, to protect or pursue a legal right or to enforce or challenge an award in bona fide legal proceedings before a state court or other judicial authority.
>
> The deliberations of the Arbitral Tribunal are likewise confidential to its members, save and to the extent that disclosure of an arbitrator's refusal to participate in the arbitration is required of the other members of the Arbitral Tribunal under Articles 10, 12 and 26.
>
> The LCIA Court does not publish any award or any part of an award without the prior written consent of all parties and the Arbitral Tribunal.[87]

International Court of Arbitration Rules of Arbitration[88]

Confidentiality is provided only to a limited degree. The International Court of Arbitration (ICC) Rules of Arbitration contain a provision stipulating that the tribunal may take measures to protect trade secrets

86 Effective 1 January 1998.
87 Article 30 of the London Court of International Arbitration, effective 1 January 1998.
88 Effective 1 January 1998.

and confidential information.[89] Confidentiality of the award[90] and the privacy of the hearings[91] are also provided.

> The Arbitral Tribunal may take measures for protecting trade secrets and confidential information.[92]
>
> The Arbitral Tribunal shall be in full charge of the hearings, at which all the parties shall be entitled to be present. Save with the approval of the Arbitral Tribunal and the parties, persons not involved in the proceedings shall not be admitted.[93]
>
> Additional copies certified true by the Secretary General shall be made available on request and at the time to the parties, but to no one else.[94]

The United Nations Commission on International Trade Law Arbitration Rules[95]

The United Nations Commission on International Trade Law (UNCITRAL) Arbitration Rules provides for private hearings.[96] Parties will be blocked from making the award public unless the parties consent to the disclosure,[97] suggesting that parties to arbitration should enter into an express confidentiality agreement at the outset.

> Hearings shall be held in camera unless the parties agree otherwise. The arbitral tribunal may require the retirement of any witness or witnesses during the testimony of other witnesses. The arbitral tribunal is free to determine the manner in which witnesses are examined.[98]

89 Article 20 of the ICC Rules of Arbitration.
90 Article 28 of the ICC Rules of Arbitration.
91 Article 21 of the ICC Rules of Arbitration.
92 Article 20(7) of the ICC Rules of Arbitration.
93 Article 21(3) of the ICC Rules of Arbitration.
94 Article 28(2) of the ICC Rules of Arbitration.
95 Adopted by UNCITRAL 28 April 1976 and UN General Assembly 15 December 1976.
96 Article 25(4) of the UNCITRAL Arbitration Rules.
97 Article 32(5) of the UNCITRAL Arbitration Rules.
98 Ibid, n95.

The American Arbitration Association International Arbitration Rules 2003[99]

Limited protection for confidentiality is found in the American Arbitration Association (AAA) International Arbitration Rules 2003. It is provided that the hearings shall be private, the award may not be made public and that confidential information disclosed during the arbitration may not be divulged by the tribunal, which, prima facie, is not imposed on the parties.

> Confidential information disclosed during the proceedings by the parties or by witnesses shall not be divulged by an arbitrator or by the administrator. Except as provided in Article 27, unless otherwise agreed by the parties, or required by applicable law, the members of the tribunal and the administrator shall keep confidential all matters relating to the arbitration or the award.[100]

Singapore International Arbitration Centre International and Domestic Arbitration Rules

The Singapore International Arbitration Centre (SIAC) international arbitration rules are based largely on the UNCITRAL Arbitration Rules and the Arbitration Rules of the LCIA with some modifications. As expressly stipulated in the International Rules, "all meetings and hearings shall be in private unless the parties agree otherwise".[101] The International Rules,[102] as well as the Domestic Rules,[103] contain detailed provisions regarding confidentiality of documents on proceedings and the arbitral award:

> The parties and the Tribunal shall at all time treat all matters relating to the proceedings (including the existence of the proceedings) and the award as confidential. A party or any arbitrator shall not, without the prior written consent of the other party or the parties, as the case may be, disclose to a third party any such matter except:

---

99 Effective 1 July 2003.
100 Article 34 of the American Arbitration Association International Arbitration Rules.
101 Rule 22.5 of the SIAC International Arbitration Rules.
102 Second Edition, 22 October 1997.
103 First Edition, 1 May 2001.

(a) for the purpose of making an application to any competent court;
(b) for the purpose of making an application to the courts of any State to enforce the award;
(c) pursuant to the order of a court of competent jurisdiction;
(d) in compliance with the provisions of the laws of any State which is binding on the party making the disclosure; or
(e) in compliance with the request or requirement of any regulatory body or other authority which, if not binding, nonetheless would be observed customarily by the party making the disclosure.[104]

Hong Kong International Arbitration Centre Domestic Arbitration Rules[105]

As stated earlier, law-governing arbitration in Hong Kong is the Arbitration Ordinance Chapter 341 (Ordinance). The Arbitration Ordinance is divided into two parts, one for domestic arbitrations and the other for international arbitrations. International Arbitrations implement the UNCITRAL Model Law on International Commercial Arbitration of 1986, which is set out in the Fifth Schedule of the Arbitration Ordinance. The Arbitration Ordinance does not provide a complete procedural code. This is a matter for arbitration rules. For international cases the UNCITRAL Arbitration Rules are commonly used whereas for domestic cases the Hong Kong International Arbitration Centre (HKIAC) Domestic Arbitration Rules 1993 are used. Under the HKIAC Domestic Arbitration Rules, private hearings are guaranteed. Disclosure requires a written consent, failing which matters discussed in arbitrations proceedings are confidential.

> All meetings and hearings shall be in private unless the parties agree otherwise.[106]
>
> No information relating to the arbitration shall be disclosed by any person without the written consent of each and every party to the arbitration.[107]

---

104 Rules 34.6 of the SIAC International Arbitration Rules and Rule 41 of the SIAC Domestic Arbitration Rules.

105 1993 Edition.

106 Article 8.6 of HKIAC Domestic Arbitration Rules.

107 Article 26 of HKIAC Domestic Arbitration Rules.

World Intellectual Property Organisation Arbitration Rules[108]

The World Intellectual Property Organisation (WIPO) provides extensive provisions on confidentiality, in which confidential information is defined and private hearings are guaranteed.

Confidentiality

<u>Confidentiality of the Existence of the Arbitration</u>

Article 73

(a) Except to the extent necessary in connection with a court challenge to the arbitration or an action for enforcement of an award, no information concerning the existence of an arbitration may be unilaterally disclosed by a party to any third party unless it is required to do so by law or by a competent regulatory body, and then only:

(i) by disclosing no more than what is legally required; and

(ii) by furnishing to the Tribunal and to the other party, if the disclosure takes place during the arbitration, or to the other party alone, if the disclosure takes place after the termination of the arbitration, details of the disclosure and an explanation of the reason for it.

(b) Notwithstanding paragraph (a), a party may disclose to a third party the names of the parties to the arbitration and the relief requested for the purpose of satisfying any obligation of good faith or candor owed to that third party.

<u>Confidentiality of Disclosures Made During the Arbitration</u>

Article 74

(a) In addition to any specific measures that may be available under Article 52, any documentary or other evidence given by a party or a witness in the arbitration shall be treated as confidential and, to the extent that such evidence describes information that is not in the public domain, shall not be used or disclosed to any third party by a party whose access to that information arises exclusively as a result of its participation in the arbitration for any purpose without the consent of the parties or order of a court having jurisdiction.

(b) For the purpose of this Article, a witness called by a party shall not be considered to be a third party. To the extent that a witness

108 Effective 1 October 2002.

if given access to evidence or other information obtained in the arbitration in order to prepare the witness's testimony, the party calling such witness shall be responsible for the maintenance by the witness of the same degree of confidentiality as that required of the party.

Confidentiality of the Awards

Article 75

The award shall be treated as confidential by the parties and may only be disclosed to a third party if and to the extent that:
(i) the parties consent; or
(ii) it falls into the public domain as a result of an action before a national court or other competent authority; or
(iii) it must be disclosed in order to comply with a legal requirement imposed on a party or in order to establish or protect a party's legal rights against a third party.

Maintenance of Confidentiality by the Center and Arbitrator

Article 76

(a) Unless the parties agree otherwise, the Center and the arbitrator shall maintain the confidentiality of the arbitration, the award and, to the extent that they describe information that is not in the public domain, any documentary or other evidence disclosed during the arbitration, except to the extent necessary in connection with a court action relating to the award, or as otherwise required by law.
(b) Notwithstanding paragraph (a), the Center may include information concerning the arbitration in any aggregate statistical data that it publishes concerning its activities, provided that such information does not enable the parties or the particular circumstances of the dispute to be identified.

Stockholm Chamber of Commerce Rules

The Rules of the Arbitration Institute of the Stockholm Chamber of Commerce (SCC) only provide that the SCC Institute and the Arbitral Tribunal, rather than the parties, must maintain the confidentiality in arbitration.[109]

109 Article 9 and 20(3) of the SCC Arbitration Rules.

Article 9
The SCC Institute shall maintain the confidentiality of the arbitration and shall deal with the arbitration in an impartial practical and expeditious manner.

Article 20.3
The arbitral tribunal shall maintain the confidentiality of the arbitration and conduct each case in an impartial practical and expeditious manner, giving each party sufficient opportunity to present its case.

International Bar Association Rules

The International Bar Association (IBA) has promulgated rules on "The Taking of Evidence in International Commercial Arbitration"[110] and "Ethics for International Arbitrators".[111] Both sets of rules contain limited provisions on the issue of confidentiality and can only apply to arbitrations upon party's agreement to adopt such rules or provisions.

Article 9 of the Rules of Ethics
The deliberations of the arbitral tribunal, and the contents of the award itself, remain confidential in perpetuity unless the parties release the arbitrators from this obligation. An arbitrator should not participate in, or give any information for the purpose of assistance in, any proceedings to consider the award unless, exceptionally, he considers it his duty to disclose any material misconduct or fraud on the part of his fellow arbitrators.

Article 3(12) of the Rules of Taking of Evidence in International Commercial Arbitration
All documents produced by a Party pursuant to the IBA Rules of Evidence (or by a non-Party pursuant to Article 3.8) shall be kept confidential by the Arbitral Tribunal and by the other parties and they shall be used only in connection with the arbitration. The Arbitral Tribunal may issue orders to set forth the terms of this confidentiality. This requirement is without prejudice to all other obligations of confidentiality in arbitration.

110 Issued in 1999.
111 Issued in 1987.

CONCLUSION

Concerning the private nature of proceedings, the English Courts deem it as the foundation of an implied term in the arbitration agreement, whereas the High Court of Australia regard it as inhering in the subject matter of an agreement to arbitrate. Concerning the implied confidentiality of documents produced on discovery, the duty applies to all documents generated upon discovery, whereas the duty in Australia is restricted to those produced in accordance with the direction of the arbitrator. While English law upholds the implied term of privacy that there is a duty of confidentiality covering the award and reasons and the documents generated relating to, and during the arbitration, Australia takes a wholly different stance on the subject.

This wide divergence between the English and Australian position on the issue of arbitral confidentiality will not diminish, unfortunately, unless new Court rulings are handed down, statutory protections are offered, and consistent institutional rules are established as times go on. To guarantee the existence of duty of confidentiality that the confidential information produced in the arbitral proceedings will not be divulged for unassailable reasons, arbitrating parties are encouraged to seek legal advice with the view to carefully devising appropriate confidentiality provisions at the appropriate stage of their contract negotiation. As institutionally recommended, "generic" arbitration clauses rarely mention the issue of confidentiality. Only when a consensus is achieved internationally on the existence and scope of a duty of confidentiality, continuing uncertainty in the area can breed only distrust of the arbitral process.

In saying this some practitioners have advocated the use of Uniform Default Rules:

> not only to resolve a conflict over the duty of confidentiality in international arbitration, but also to foster stability and predictability, two paramount requirements of most participants in international transactions.[112]

112 Jeffrey W. Sarles, *Solving the Arbitral Confidentiality Conundrum in International Arbitration. ADR and the Law*, 18th Edition, A Report of the American Arbitration Association, the Fordham International Law Journal and the Fordham Urban Law Journal, 2001, pp. 428–439.

Only time will tell whether this philosophy is achievable but in the mean time the issue of confidentiality in arbitration proceedings is a concern of which every practitioner or user of arbitral services should be aware. Only by addressing this matter thoughtfully and carefully would we be in a position to gain worldwide acceptance as well as to build confidence in the usage of arbitration as the means of dispute resolution across all facets of contractual arrangements.

5

International Commercial Arbitration in India: A Study of Discursive Practices

Kusum Dhanania

INTRODUCTION

This chapter undertakes a critical discourse analysis of arbitration proceedings in International Commercial Arbitration in India in the context of globalisation. The study demonstrates the differences in the discourses of Commercial Arbitration proceedings in India, whether domestic or international, when influenced by (a) the adversarial legal practice typical of litigation and (b) by arbitration practices undertaken by non-legal participants, especially in commercial arbitration cases. The chapter seeks to identify the patterns of discourse in dispute resolution mechanisms: legal practice, arbitration, and Alternative Dispute Resolution (ADR). From the point of view of the disputant ADR like *negotiation* and *conciliation* are seen as essentially dialogic in nature while the adversarial model litigation practice is seen as monologic. Discourse of arbitration takes on and displays the qualities of the actors involved in the proceedings. Given that dispute sites such as those within the commercial world are intensely dialogic and dynamic, these require an equally dialogic dispute settlement mechanism. It becomes even more significant in the context of two different commercial cultures in a globalising economy. In other words, whenever arbitration fails in commercial disputes, domestic or international, it is because of the preponderance of the monologic discursive practices in its proceedings over the dialogic commercial procedures and processes involved in the dispute. In order to reinforce the conceptual framework used in the study interviews with arbitrators and lawyers, observations of live arbitration proceedings were studied.

PERSPECTIVES

The environment within which a person is located is integral to framing his perspective towards what one studies. The author hails from the Marwari community, traditionally a trading community from the north west of India. Although there exists a particular region in the North West of India known as Marwar, the term is multivalent. It is used to identify the trading community of the traditional Aggrawal and Maheshwai caste from that part of the country. The term became popular as a means of identifying this trading community much later in the 1900s. The community is now spread all over the world in pursuit of trade. As a result of their scrupulous business practices, this trading community prospered, and with colonization, many of these traders also became industrialists.

For a 'bania' or a trader of the Marwari community, trade and commerce is a way of life. Business relations and business associates are integral to his way of life. Conflict is accepted as inevitable in trade. Since commercial relationships are always more important than the disputed issue at hand, interestingly, attitudes to dispute resolution are not at all adversarial. *Punch,* the amicable method of dispute resolution traditionally followed by the Marwari business community, does not allow conflict to take over the business relationship, and facilitates its fair and consensual resolution. Parties approach a trusted person from the community, usually a community elder. Trust in the person who would help in dispute resolution is essential to *acceptable* dispute resolution. The fact that the person who is helping the parties in dispute resolution is known to both the parties or even related to them is only an added advantage because then the intricacies of the problem could be well appreciated.[1] This helps in maintaining business relationships. Further, this informal procedure does not take a long time.[2] Sometimes, even private meetings with the person helping in resolving the dispute are helpful if some sensitive issue has to be addressed. The elder plays a proactive role in such procedures. There is no imposition from above in such procedures; there is no hierarchy. The meetings are informal. The privacy of the parties is always maintained. This aspect of privacy helps in the optimum solution of the conflict, which might not have been possible in a court of law. There is

1 Such a case in a court of law would have been a fit case for bias.

2 In such processes the clear distinctions between formal and informal did not exist.

no appeal from the agreement which the parties arrive at since this settlement is essentially consensual. This process of dispute resolution is not guided by any specific or exact rules of law; it is often guided by rules of viability and accepted business practices. The formal courts of law were never usually resorted to by the 'bania' for the resolution of his commercial disputes. The law courts were resorted to only when business relationships were damaged beyond repair and when there was no mutual trust among the parties. Thus the conflicting identities of the author, one as a member of the Marwari community where dispute resolution is essentially amicable, and the other as a student of law in a country that follows the common law and the adversarial mode, have been significant in framing this perspective on the issue of discursive practices in arbitration practice.

DISCOURSE SITUATIONS IN COMMERCIAL DISPUTE RESOLUTION

The world of commerce is vibrant with interaction, activity and variety. Business activity, commercial transactions and contracts for various business activities are the main constituents of this world. These transactions and contracts are formulated through the human agency. Formulations of these contracts and conclusions of these transactions necessarily involve exchange of ideas and views as a necessary requirement for decisions to be taken. Conflict is inevitable to any such process of decision making. Interestingly there have never been strict processes or defined rules for the settlement of these conflicts in the world of commerce. There are various options before a person in the world of commerce for the settlement of these conflicts. One may choose to litigate, arbitrate, mediate, conciliate or negotiate this conflict. However it is interesting to note that each of mechanisms of dispute settlement has its own discourse situations, patterns and experiential meanings. The judicial process in the common law countries is adversarial and power laden.[3] This is mainly due to the fact that power hierarchies are integral to the adversarial process. Here communication patterns are dictated and choices

3 Yon Maley in "The Language of the Law" examines how the generic structure, interactive strategies, witness strategies and experiential meanings of the court room discourse are power laden (Maley 1994: 32–41).

are often limited. It demands an unconditional allegiance to its choice of meanings through the sole authority of the law. This authoritative discourse has to be accepted in totality; there is no scope for partial acceptance or exercise of the choice of a litigant. Consequently influences of authority and absence of choice make the discourse in the adversarial system monologic.[4] Alternative dispute resolution mechanisms on the contrary are devoid of the imperatives of adversarial process. Mediation and conciliation, for instance, are 'dialogic' methods of dispute resolution. They are designed to encourage parties to settle their differences through dialogue and to facilitate option generation or choices by the parties themselves.

Arbitration interestingly treads the border between the monologic character of the adversarial process and the dialogic nature of negotiation and conciliation. It comes with an inherent potential either to permit dialogue or to succumb to tropes of authority. What ultimately determines the dialogic or monologic nature of the discourse pattern of arbitration seems to be the participants who operate in a given discourse situation. In litigation the actors are the parties, the lawyers who represent the litigants and the judge or judges who decide on the dispute. Negotiation has as its actors, the disputants who themselves resolve the dispute. Mediation has the parties along with the mediator who helps them to resolve their dispute. In arbitration the actors in the particular discourse situation are parties, lawyers/ legal representatives and arbitrators.[5] However all these actors operate within certain social contexts, the 'reality' perceptions of which give dispute resolution its character.

---

4 Monologue is where the characters become mouthpieces for the author. They do not develop on their own. Bakhtin makes a distinction between Tolstoy's monologism and Dostoevsky's dialogism in fiction. In the former, the characters become mouthpieces of the author — "There is nothing like an ongoing process of interchange of suggestion or exploratory creative encounter between Tolstoy and his characters." But in the latter, the characters possess "extraordinary independence in the structure of the work …" (Bakhtin 1984: 7).

5 These actors are quintessential to arbitration though there may be involvement of others depending upon the facts and circumstances of the case. For example in institutional arbitration the registrar of the institution who oversees the administrative aspect of the disputes. Sometimes certain claims require expert opinions relating to various technical matters involved. In such cases the various personnel appointed by the parties also have a major influence on the case.

Actual reality

Perception is the essence of construction or existence of any reality. The different realities which exist in the social sphere are representations of what we may choose to call 'actual reality'. Actual reality as a frame of reference is the core reality within which perceived realities exist. It includes perceptions of occurrences in both the dispute site and the non-dispute site. It is akin to core standards of morality which all of us would agree exist but where each one's perception of it would be different. Commercial reality, factual reality and legal reality are perceptions of occurrences in each of these respective worlds in this actual reality.

ACTUAL REALITY:
Realities with the actual reality

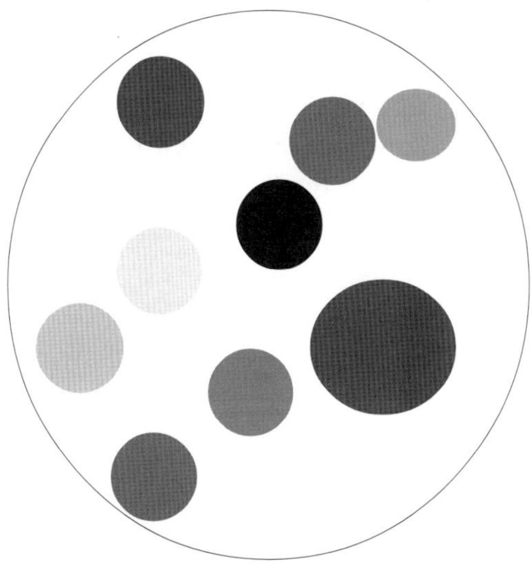

Factual reality

The process of adjudication in the adversarial system requires the construction of perspectives of an event or events under dispute. Factual reality is the first level. For a judge to adjudicate, the events constituting a dispute or leading to dispute have first to be enumerated. Very simply put, it is the presentation of events or event constituting a dispute (actual reality) after it has passed through the filter of the rules of evidence. There are certain rules or norms which guide the construction of this reality. The rules of evidence are one of the main norms. The common law rules of evidence are exclusionary, that is, all that is said or done is not admissible but only those that are mandated or allowed by these rules.[6] Though adversarial practices are not yet part of this reality, they very much influence the processes in use.

Legal reality

This is the representation of factual reality after it has passed through a further filter of legal rules and norms. The rules of interpretation and the rules of procedure are an essential part of the process of the construction of this reality. Language plays a very important role in the creation of this disputed reality because the events can be enumerated and recounted only with the help of language.[7] Adversarial discursive practices are an essential part of this reality. Lawyers can create minute distinctions in perceptions of reality, which only exist in law and thus can give a sense of alienation to those outside the framework of this reality. They strengthen the perception of the 'other' as an adversary and sharpen monologic communication dictated by mandates of law.

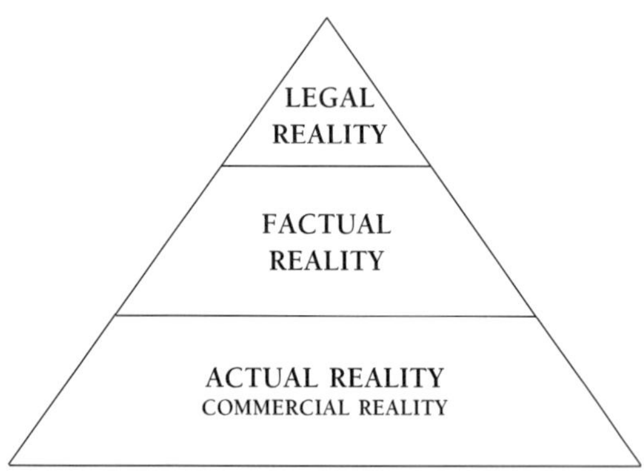

6 Though *The Indian Evidence Act 1857* does not follow the exclusionary rules of evidence, the lawyers practicing law often seem to forget this.

7 This is why the written records of the event becomes important and it helps the Judge gauge the various events involved which are legally relevant.

This process of creating factual and legal reality is essential however to adjudication. Adjudication is meant to be a neutral exercise for resolution of 'disputes' in the legal reality. A judge adjudicating on a particular event resulting in a dispute would first try to establish whether the event or the act complained of is one that is legally defined and only then apply further rules. For example, the judge will prove how a 'transaction' resulted in a 'formal contract' according to common law principles of contract, and then prove how the 'terms' were 'violated' and thus the 'relief' sought would be usually 'compensation'.

To cite another example, certain acts are defined by law as "criminal" and accordingly, law provides for punishing those acts under the Penal Code. Therefore, a judge adjudicating would first have to see whether the act complained of is actually criminal and then only punish the culprit. The decision of the judge whether the act complained of actually is criminal or not would mainly depend upon the 'act' actually committed fitting into the definition of criminal act as defined by law. This seems to be a fairly reasonable way of judging criminality of the act. But all cases may not be as simplistic as the given example. What if the culprit accused of the criminal act was stealing bread to feed her children. This adds an *external factor*, that is, the 'motive' behind the criminal act might mitigate the apparent criminality of the act.[8] But criminal law does not take 'motive' into account, it takes 'intention'. This is basically the rule of expediency. But the problem here is that legal reality very often does not take into account some of these particularities or real issues of the act and merely addresses 'intention' and punishment. This reality often does not take into account the other realities which exist. This process of the construction of reality may finally be represented in such a manner that it may be very different from the actual reality of things.

Commercial reality

Commercial reality may be defined as the perception of reality shared by the world of commerce. Commercial reality consists of understood and accepted trade practices and transactions in the commercial world. These

8 The role of sentence hearing in a criminal case to a great extent may represent the appreciation of the other realities. But it takes place only after the criminality of the act is established. Hence the only thing it might influence is the sentencing and in no way the guilt.

are guided by the requirements of *viability* of transactions and dealings. Commercial viability precludes any definition although it may be said to be the means and ends of all doings in the world of commerce. Business relationships based on mutual trust and sound practices are integral to commercial viability. The 'other' is always the trusted trade associate. Components of commercial viability are known to all in the world of commerce and are the guiding principles of this reality, which are accepted as desirable in the world of commerce. These aspects contribute to vibrancy and dialogism in business discourse.

However, these realities do not exist in water-tight compartments. The perceptions of each of these realities intensely interact with one another, particularly if there is any disagreement regarding a commercial transaction. The actors in the commercial reality have various options to choose from as far as the methods of settling the matter are concerned. Very often the actors would choose internal mechanisms to get over this impasse. Guided by concerns of viability actors would usually negotiate or mediate a settlement as opposed to any other adversarial settlement and would ideally try to reach such a mediated settlement. Here communication between the parties ensures that the business relationships between them remain intact. The actors are very well aware of the limitations of the litigation process.[9] The adversarial process damages relationships because the 'other' is always an adversary and not a business associate as is the case in commercial reality. The interface between these two realities in dispute resolution invariably results in the legal reality overtaking the commercial reality. Thus the vibrancy and dialogism of the commercial reality loses out to the authoritative and monologic adversarial process in the legal reality.

PRACTICE OF INTERNATIONAL COMMERCIAL ARBITRATION IN INDIA

As a result of globalisation, the role of arbitration as a method of dispute resolution has become quite pronounced in India. Arbitration has the

9 Reinforcing the concept of process pluralism which recognises the fact that the process we choose influences the outcome in a major way. The litigative process has only limited outcomes because of insufficiency of legal remedies. An aggrieved person has to choose from already existing ones; he would not have the option of creating one. Carrie-Menkel-Meadow. *Raising the Bar*.www.aals.org/am 2003/booklet.pdf.visited on 11 Sept. 2003.

potential of addressing and balancing both commercial viability concerns as well as legal concerns, as a consequence of which parties should opt for arbitration; however, in practice this is hardly recognised. Even though there may be a policy decision to resolve disputes through arbitration, the mindset of the parties is not geared towards it. The persons involved in the arbitral process are very often drawn from the world of legal reality. These actors, consciously or unconsciously, do not depart from their adversarial and judicial mindset. Legal reality thus overtakes commercial reality. It is this that I refer to as 'judicialised' arbitration. In judicialised arbitration, the interpolations of actors from the legal reality and the discursive practices based on the adversarial process dominate arbitration proceedings. As soon as the parties face a problem in the world of commercial reality they choose the actors from the world of legal reality to address their legal concerns and help them to extricate themselves from this impasse. The lawyers, true to their legal training, start with a representation of the conflict as a *dispute* according to the rules of the legal reality. But all conflicts or problems in the commercial reality are not *disputes* as we legally understand them. Instead, all efforts are geared towards showing that the elements constituting the disputes are illegal or a violation of law. Such an attitude is adversarial. The proceedings are no different from those before a court of law. The procedural laws may not be followed on paper but are adhered to in spirit. This representation of commercial conflict within the context of legal reality may solve the problem at hand but it does not further the cause of commercial reality i.e., commercial viability. The experience of adversity spoils commercial relationships and does not satisfy the commercial viability concerns of the parties. Paradoxically, an unsatisfactory resolution of the dispute through this method gives the parties added grounds to challenge the award in the legal reality later, on various legal grounds.[10]

Judicialised arbitration

International commercial transactions enable an interface between two different business cultures. Although commercial viability concerns may be common irrespective of cultural differences, they do not exist independent of the cultural context within which they are practiced.

10 The UNCITRAL model law requires the award to be a reasoned award almost along the lines of a judgement, which obviously furthers challenge of the award on legal grounds.

Cultural differences also play a role in the cause of a conflict, choice of a conflict resolution method and the choice of arbitrators.[11]

The arbitrator in judicialised arbitration is the passive listener like the judge in a court of law. His role is limited to ensuring strict adherence to law and only giving relief in terms of what is sought for in the claims. He does not try to be innovative while settling the dispute; in fact what he does is merely to *decide* in favour of or against a particular party instead of *settling* the dispute. A major reason for this is that the arbitrators in India are retired Judges of the High Courts, the Supreme Court, or the Constitutional Courts of India. They are addressed by the lawyers as they would be in a court of law with the only difference being that they address them from their chairs. 'Justice' concerns remain constant. The proceedings fail to recognise that in the case of a commercial conflict mainly arising from problems of commercial viability or the lack of understanding of another business culture, the only resolution would be the restoration of this commercial viability. As an example from an arbitration proceeding I happened to observe, one of the issues concerned the clubbing together of certain bills. The lawyers representing the claimants were contending that the clubbing together of the bills was a common business practice, whereas the lawyers representing the respondents were obviously disputing this interpretation. The lawyers for the claimants wanted to be recorded in an affidavit whether this was the ultimate position of the respondents regarding the issue at hand. The fact that this would be recorded as part of the minutes of the meeting was not enough for them. They demanded a tangible documentary record of this. The retired judges who were acting as arbitrators for the particular matter found it perfectly reasonable. This is mainly due to the fact that the lawyers and the arbitrators were so embedded in legal reality that they could not draw a distinction between an arbitral proceeding and a court room proceeding where minutes are not recorded but only orders given.

As opposed to this, we also have good examples of interaction and the maintenance of a fine balance between the legal reality and commercial reality in what I choose to call '*Punch*-style' arbitration. This is arbitration that imbibes the true spirit of commercial reality. Here there are no formalized rules, but the actors, including the arbitrator, share the experiential meanings of commercial reality, particularly, the goal of

11 As a subtext I would like to mention that international transactions are not independent of the social, political and economic factors related to the commercial transactions and investments.

commercial viability. The party is one who does not detach the problem from commercial reality. This is unlike the trained legal minds who tend to convert commercial reality into legal reality. The arbitrators are also persons drawn from the commercial reality. They do not merely *decide* on the dispute but help the parties to come to a settlement. The parties appoint such a person not because of his or her reputation in the world of law but because of his deftness at arriving at the most commercially viable solution. He is guided by the ideals of commercial viability. There are usually no fixed rules of law applicable but the method of resolution is one which would best settle the problem at hand.

To give an example of *Punch*-style arbitration, Mr. J. P. Sil[12] who I interviewed for this chapter told me that the Bengal Chamber of Commerce in case of jute arbitrations did not permit lawyers to represent the parties. The parties could either represent themselves or bring any one else from the commercial reality whom they trusted could represent them. The arbitrators were also persons from the commercial world and never retired judges from the High Courts or the Supreme Court.[13] He also pointed out that whenever there was any dispute regarding no delivery or delay in delivery and considerable costs were incurred to the buyer or the seller, the arbitrators examined the market conditions in particular whether it was the buyer's market or the seller's market, and decided the dispute accordingly. This ensured the commercial viability of the transaction.

Lex Mercatoria is also a rule of law sensitive to concerns of commercial viability. The UNCITRAL model laws also provide that "the arbitration tribunal shall take into account the usages of the trade applicable to the transaction", but this is very rarely followed.[14] One major reason for this is that commercial reality has been totally overtaken by the legal reality. The application of *Lex Mercatoria* would be a good example of interaction between the legal and the commercial reality. Goldman (1986) coined this term. According to him, the Roman concept of *uis gentium* was a

12 Former Head of the Department for Tribunal of Arbitration, Bengal Chamber of Commerce, Kolkata, India.

13 This is not to generalize that judges and lawyers are not sensitive to commercial viability concerns. But usually the person from the commercial reality would be in a better position to appreciate the problem and the persons in the commercial reality presume that viability concerns are more appreciated by the persons situated in commercial reality than persons from legal reality.

14 Article 33(3) of the UNCITRAL model law on Arbitration. Even the Indian Arbitration and Conciliation Act, 1996, is based on the UNCITRAL model law.

precursor of this term, which was an autonomous source of law proper to the economic relations (*commercium*) between citizens and foreigners (*peregrine*). The modern concept of the *lex mercatoria* is that of the rule of law which has been developed by the international business community so as to regulate commercial activities within that community (Hunter and Redfern 1999: 118). Another definition of this concept is "spontaneous law consisting of usages of arbitral awards and of the reoccurring solutions concerning international trade which are found in conventions on uniform laws and in national laws as in the Czechoslovakian Code of International Trade and in the precedents in the various legal systems" (Sammartano 1990: 273). Yet another definition is that of a set of general principles and customary rules spontaneously referred to, or elaborated upon, in the framework of international trade without reference to a particular national system of law (Julian 1986: 116).

Lex Mercatoria is an acceptance of the requirement of commercial viability in commercial relations. The application of *Lex Mercatoria* is meant to particularize the problem and settle the problem at hand only.[15] However, application of *Lex Mercatoria* is not without problems. It has very often been challenged in the national courts. For example, in *Fougerolle v. Banque de Proche Orient*, the case regarded the challenge of an arbitral award in a court of law (Goldman 1986: 121). The dispute was regarding the termination of agency of the intermediary before completion of its mission. The intermediary had already been granted partial remuneration for services already rendered. The arbitration tribunal decided in favour of the intermediary basing its decision on general principles of obligation applicable in international trade. The principal (that is the losing party) challenged on the ground that the tribunal had assumed powers which it had not been granted. But the final court of appeal decided in favour of the tribunal. It held that the tribunal had the power to define the law applicable to the agreement by virtue of the terms of reference of Article 8 in terms of reference.

THE COMMON SENSE METHOD

The common sense method is the method adopted by the arbitrator in dispute resolution. It is an attitude which an arbitrator who is sensitive

15 Unlike laying down precedents in case of disputes resolved in the court of law.

to commercial reality develops. Mr. D. C. Singhania, a prominent lawyer who has a commercial background and is an experienced arbitrator, says that the method of resolving commercial disputes is 'common sense'.

This method of dispute resolution helps the arbitrator to arrive at the most commercially viable decision. The standard of reasonableness applied in legal reality may not be applicable in commercial reality. Therefore arbitration guided by the common sense method is a more desirable method of dispute resolution in commercial contexts. But it may be difficult for someone not situated in the commercial reality to appreciate the practicality of applying the common sense method of dispute resolution. An experienced arbitrator from the judiciary may not be in a position to appreciate these viability concerns. For him the common law standard of "the reasonable man on the Clapham omnibus" may be a more practical method of judging a particular issue at hand, little realizing that this man on the omnibus may not be sensitive to requirements of viability, because he is not from the commercial reality. The questions of importance of business relationships and trust as essential ingredients of commonsense would hardly be appreciated by him.

This method of dispute resolution is an essential ingredient of the *Punch* style of dispute resolution. The arbitrator is guided by viability concerns rather than abstract legal standards. But this common sense method of dispute resolution is *not* the same as the concept of commercial viability that guides commercial reality. The common sense method of dispute resolution comes into the picture only in the case of *resolution* of commercial disputes. The role of the arbitrator is *proactive*[16] like the social engineer balancing conflicting interests. The arbitrator in this process of balancing takes account of the whole picture and not as filtered through legal reality. This makes the *Punch*-style arbitration a dialogic exercise.

To give an example, Mr. M. L. Daga, a qualified Chartered Financial Secretary who also arbitrates, said that to him in arbitration it was not important to establish the disputed event but to remedy it. He said it was important for him to engage himself "*not* in the *discovery* of facts but the *recovery* of facts". Therefore for him it was not important to prove the factuality or the legality of breach but to remedy the loss caused by the loss. For example, if there is a case arising out of a commercial transaction, he would not first try to establish whether the transaction is a contract

16 This is different from the *reactive* role of a common law judge whose decisions are reactions to the pleadings of the parties before him.

under law but would remedy the problem arising out of the transaction. In commercial context, the requirement to make the claim under the law would not have been felt in the absence of a problem.

CONCLUSION

In India, the new Arbitration and Conciliation Act, 1996, was enacted with reference to the UNCITRAL model law to facilitate international trade and commerce post-liberalisation policy. The provisions of the act as such do not bind international commercial arbitration but are intended to facilitate international arbitration in India. This is especially the case in section 11 which deals with the appointment of arbitrators and the section dealing with foreign awards. Laws of the land are very important for a potential foreign investor while deciding on investment, for example the law applicable to the transaction like those of contract and taxation and the law that takes into account potential dispute situations like procedural laws and the arbitration law. However, in practice, the way arbitration proceedings are generally conducted do not seem to further the commercial viability concerns of a foreign investor. The law was enacted to promote foreign trade and investment, however in practice it does not seem to further that purpose due to the fact that arbitration proceedings are increasingly becoming mere replicas of the judicial process in private settings. Adversarial resolution of disputes is not designed for the resolution of commercial conflicts.

REFERENCES

Arbitration Rules of the Bengal National Chamber of Commerce.

The Arbitration and Conciliation Act, 1996.

Bakhtin, M. M. (1984) *Problems of Dostoevsky's Poetics*. Ed. and Trans. Caryl Emerson. *Theory and History of Literature*. 8th vol. Manchester: Manchester University Press.

Goldman, B. (1986) The Applicable Law: General Principles of Law — the *lex mercatoria*. In Lew, Julian D. M (ed.), *Contemporary Problems in International Arbitration*. School of International Arbitration, Centre for Commercial Studies, University of London.

Hunter, M. and Redfern, A. (1999) *Law and Practice of International Commercial Arbitration*. London: Sweet & Maxwell.

Maley, Y. 1994. The language of the law. In J. Gibbons (ed.) *Language and the Law*. New York: Longman.

Meadow, C. M. (2003) Raising the Bar. In *Legal Disputes to Conflict Resolution and Human Problem Solving: An Introduction to Dispute Processing and Conflict Resolution: Theory, Practice and Policy*. Ashgate: Dartmouth Press. Available at www.aals.org/am2003/booklet.pdf/, accessed on 11 September 2003.

Sammartano, M. R. (1990) *International Arbitration Law*. Boston: Kluwer Law & Taxation Publishers.

UNCITRAL Model Law for Arbitration.

INTERVIEWS

Interview with Mr. J. J. Reddy, retired Supreme Court Judge, presently doing arbitrations, in April 2003.

Interview with Professor H. E. Chodosh, Professor of Law, and Director (1998–2003) of the Frederick K. Cox International Law Centre, Cleveland, Ohio, in April 2003.

Telephone interview with Mr. Justice M. M. Dutt, retired Supreme Court Judge, presently doing arbitrations, on 5 June 2003.

Interview with Mr. R. N. JhunJhunwala, Attorney-at Law, Calcutta High Court and a prominent member of the Marwari Community in Calcutta, on 13 May 2003.

Interview with Mr. Vyas, Senior Advocate Calcutta High Court, 25 May 2003.

Interview with Mr. M. L. Daga., Financial Controller and Secretary, Calcutta, on 4 June 2003.

Interview with Mr. D. Sengupta, Deputy Secretary, Indian Chamber of Commerce, on 10 June 2003 and 12 September 2003.

Telephone conversation with Mr. J. P. Sil, former Head of the Tribunal of Arbitration, Bengal Chamber of Commerce, 13 June 2003.

Interview with Mr. D. Dhanania, a member of the Marawari Community, on 6 September 2003.

Interview with Mr. P. K. Ghosh, Partner, Singhania and Co. L.L.P., Kolkata, 9 September 2003.

Comparative Analysis and Interpretation

6

Interpretation across Legal Systems and Cultures: A Critical Perspective

Vijay K. Bhatia and Christopher N. Candlin

INTRODUCTION

Recent trends in global trade and commerce have made international commercial arbitration an increasingly important area of development. With this new development it has become more likely than ever before that laws written in one specific context are being interpreted in another or several other contexts at the same time. In the context of such developments, especially where economic, trade, financial, and commercial interests of individual countries are at stake, laws are carefully written with two somewhat conflicting objectives in mind: firstly, to make them look internationally competitive, fair and transparent, and secondly, to make them serve national interests, not simply commercial, but also socio-political and cultural. In order to achieve these dual objectives, national laws are often adopted from a reputed international source but are rewritten in a way that best serves national interests. International commercial arbitration is one such area where most national laws are based on UNCITRAL model recommended by the United Nations, but modified in different ways to serve these specific national interests (See Bhatia, Candlin and Gotti, 2003; Bhatia and Engberg, 2004). Variations in construction and interpretation of international commercial arbitration laws and practices in different countries have been studied by an international project, led by the authors, entitled "Generic Integrity in Legal Discourse in Multilingual and Multicultural Contexts".[1]

1 An RGC funded CERG project (Ref. 9040474) entitled "Generic Integrity in Legal Discourse in Multilingual and Multicultural Contexts" in which more than 12 countries participated. For details, visit the web-site: http://gild.mmc.cityu.edu.hk/.

In this chapter we specifically focus on the construction and interpretation of international arbitration laws from the perspective of critical genre analysis (Bhatia, 1993). Based on the analysis of specific sections of a sample of these laws from a number of diverse legal systems and varied socio-political as well as cultural contexts, we suggest that just as the constraints on construction of these legislative statements is not simply a matter of selecting particular linguistic features as a means of communicating legislative intentions in an attempt to control the behaviour of those who are governed by such statements, similarly the interpretation of these intentions does not entirely rely on such linguistic data alone. Both these processes, i.e., construction as well as interpretation, draw upon and assume a number of other factors underpinning these textualisations, for example, important features of the socio-political system and the cultural background of the country and also the legal system(s) within which they are written and interpreted (Bhatia, Engberg, Gotti, and Heller, 2005). Such factors, in our view, often emphasise asymmetries where power and control are often accorded to one party over the other.

Moreover, analysis of these laws, we believe, allows us to claim that the fundamental issues underlying these legal interpretations extend well beyond even these linguistic, socio-political, and cultural considerations (Maley: 1987, 1994). In essence, the substantive issues, those of transparency and the lack of adequate specification within the legislation, are themselves indices of asymmetrical distributions of power. Here a number of key questions suggest themselves:

1. Who determines the interpretation of the legislation in question?
2. Who is given the authority to interpret, and execute decisions based on such interpretations?

   and, conversely,
3. Who is impoverished by the denial of such power and rights to interpretation?'

These are important issues from the point of view of critical genre analysis more generally, not merely in our field here of international commercial arbitration. They play an important role in the construction and interpretation of legal discourse in a more general sense, especially where two different legal systems interact within a specific territory. One such example is the case of the Basic Law of Hong Kong, which was written by the National People's Congress of the People's Republic of China within its Civil Code legal system and is subject to interpretation and application in Hong Kong in the context of its Common Law system (Bhatia, 2000, Candlin and Bhatia, 1998).

The main argument of the chapter is set out in two main sections. The first focuses on the issue of the adequacy of specification of the legal scope of legislative provisions, and is based on our analysis of the linguistic options available in international arbitration laws from specific contexts. Our claims are supported by the study of syntactic features that make a significant difference in the construction and interpretation of arbitration processes and practices. We draw additional evidence from a consideration of what Scollon and others have referred to as 'critical sites of engagement' (Scollon, 1998), i.e., from arbitration cases. The second section extends the argument by incorporating socio-pragmatic factors by adducing an example that illustrates how legal interpretation draws on instances of intertextuality, suggesting the need to take into account interdiscursivity and conventions beyond a strict consideration of the text itself (Bhatia, 2004).

LINGUISTIC DETERMINANTS OF LEGAL MEANING

We consider here specific sections of International Arbitration Laws from two different legal systems, that is, the Arbitration and Conciliation Ordinance (1996) of India (ACOI), which follows a Common Law system, and the Arbitration Law of the People's Republic of China (ALPRC), which follows a Civil Law system. Both these laws have been largely based on the UNCITRAL Model Law (UNML)(1985), proposed by the United Nations. We focus our analysis on specific sections of these laws from various perspectives: lexico-grammatical, rhetorical and discoursal, and consider their implication by reference to the socio-cultural conventions and the political, economical, and legal systems that underpin the construction and interpretation of these laws.

So far as matters of content and style are concerned, the two sets of laws are very different from each other. The Arbitration and Conciliation Ordinance (1996) of India (ACOI) is largely an adaptation of the UNCITRAL Model, and highlights three main principles: 'party autonomy', 'freedom for arbitrators', and 'finality of arbitral award'. The Arbitration Law of the People's Republic of China (ALPRC), on the other hand, emphasizes somewhat different principles: 'to ensure fair and timely arbitration of economic disputes', 'safeguarding of legitimate rights and interests of the litigants', and 'guaranteeing the sound development of the socialist market economy'. Obviously, the concerns expressed and implied in the two versions are different, even given that the laws were based on the same UNCITRAL Model Law. What distinguishes the construction and interpretation of these two sets of laws, and how may the implications of such differences be explained?

SPECIFICATION OF LEGAL OPTIONS

To substantiate the issue of specification of legal options (Bhatia, 1982) in these two sets of laws, we focus initially on the section legislating what constitutes an arbitration agreement in the two countries. The PRC article 4 clearly states:

> Where the litigants choose to settle their dispute through arbitration, they should reach an arbitration agreement of their own accord. When, in the absence of an arbitration agreement, a litigant applies for arbitration, the arbitration commission shall not accept it.

Although there is here a clear provision for the requirement of an arbitration agreement for settling disputes, there is no further specification of any kind, either of the nature of agreement, or concerning the communication of such an agreement. Further specification is found in Article 16 of the ALPRC:

> An Arbitration agreement refers to an arbitration clause provided in the contract or other written agreements requesting arbitration concluded prior or subsequent to the occurrence of disputes. An arbitration agreement shall have the following contents:
> 1. An expressed intent to request arbitration;
> 2. Items for arbitration; and
> 3. The chosen arbitration commission.

Through this clause the Act makes it mandatory for the parties to have the agreement in writing. There is, however, no further specification of the form in which it is reached and communicated. To look for any further information on this aspect, one needs to go to other laws in use in the PRC. For example, Article 7 of the 'Law of Foreign-related Contracts', 1985 provides:

> If an agreement is reached by means of letters, telegrams or telex and one party requests a signed letter of confirmation, the contract shall be formed only after the letter of confirmation is signed.

The three separate sections go on to provide some of the essential details about the nature of what is understood by 'agreement'. Although these sections mention a number of means through which agreements can be reached, it interesting to note that fax, which is one of the most commonly used means of communication today, is not mentioned at all. The issue became a major point of contention in a recent China International Economic and Trade Arbitration Commission (CIETAC) Shenzhen Commission case, in which the legitimacy of a contract/agreement reached by means of fax was questioned. The two parties had entered into a contract of the sale by means of fax. After the contract had been signed, some amendments were made to the contract in the form of an annex, and as such, the annex was intended to form part of the contract. Counsel for the respondent referred to the 'Law of Foreign-related Contracts, 1985' of the PRC and 'Convention on Contracts for the International Sale of Goods' of the UN and argued that fax could not be recognized as a means of written agreement because it was not considered a reliable means of serving as evidence of written contract. A contract, according to the counsel, is held to be in writing only if it is contained in an exchange of letters, telex, or other means of telecommunication, but excluding fax. Notwithstanding this argument, the arbitration tribunal held that, "fax is only a means through which the stamped and signed contract was transmitted between the two parties." The arbitration tribunal perceived 'fax' as a legitimate means of communication between the parties. The decision of the arbitration tribunal therefore rejected the allegation of the respondent that the faxed copy of the contract shall not be viewed as a valid agreement.

How are such circumstances taken care of in other arbitration laws? An example is provided by a comparison with Article 7 of the Arbitration and Conciliation Ordinance of India (1996), which provides:

(1) In this Part, 'arbitration agreement' means an agreement by the parties to submit to arbitration all or certain disputes which have arisen or which may arise between them in respect of a defined legal relationship, whether contractual or not.
(2) An arbitration agreement may be in the form of an arbitration clause in a contract or in the form of a separate agreement.
(3) An arbitration agreement shall be in writing.
(4) An arbitration agreement is in writing if it is contained in —
    (a) a document signed by the parties;
    (b) an exchange of letters, telex, telegrams, or other means of telecommunication which provides a record of the agreement; or

(c) an exchange of statements of claim and defence in which the existence of the agreement is alleged by one party and not denied by the other.

(5) The reference in a contract to a document containing an arbitration clause constitutes an arbitration agreement if the contract is in writing and the reference is such as to make that arbitration clause part of the contract.

Like Article 16 of ALPRC, Article 7 of ACOI also makes it mandatory to have the written agreement, but it further specifies a number of other conditions such as the signatures of both the parties, means of communication, etc with an all-inclusive option such as 'other means of communication' which is meant to cover yet unspecified options such as fax or indeed any other means. The two sections thus differ from each other, as one is more restrictive in terms of all-inclusiveness than the other. Taking the issue of specification further, we can point out that ALPRC specifies only two ways to go for arbitration, i.e., by reaching an agreement (which we are also told can be an agreement clause) provided in the contract or other written agreement. ACOI, on the other hand, provides at least eighty (80) different ways in which arbitration can take effect. This kind of all-inclusiveness is generally achieved through the use of binomials and multinomials (Bhatia, 1993). Consider the following options:

Submitting to arbitration all or certain disputes (2)
Legal relationship can be contractual or not (2)
Disputes may have arisen or may arise (2)
Arbitration in the form of a clause in a contract or a agreement (2)

Arbitration can be in the form of a letter, telex, telegram, or other means or an exchange of statement claim (5)

Total options: 2 x 2 x 2 x 2 x 5 = 80

Other significant aspects which may require detailed specification in such documents deal with those sections that are concerned with legal process or action, both likely to contribute to matters of transparency in legal construction and interpretation. In the appointment of arbitrators, for instance, ALPRC Article 32 gives the power for direct appointment of arbitrators to the arbitration commission:

ALPRC Article 32 *(Direct Appointment of the Arbitrators)*

> In the event the litigants fail to reach an agreement on the form of an arbitration tribunal, or fail to select their arbitrators within the period prescribed in the arbitration rules, the arbitration commission director shall make the decision for them.

In the case of ACOI, on the other hand, if the parties fail to agree on the arbitrators within thirty days, the appointment is made by the Chief Justice, but only upon the request of the party. ACOI also provides an explicit indication of the procedure that is required to be followed in individual cases, and stipulates at each stage the constraints operating on individual actions of each of the player, whether it is any of the parties at dispute, or the members of the arbitration commission, or, indeed, the judiciary:

ACOI Article 11

(5) Failing any agreement referred to in sub-section (2), in an arbitration with a sole arbitrator, if the parties fail to agree on the arbitrator within thirty days from receipt of a request by one party from the other party to so agree the appointment shall be made, upon request of a party, by the Chief Justice or any person or institution designated by him.

(6) Where, under an appointment procedure agreed upon by the parties, —
   (a) a party fails to act as required under that procedure; or
   (b) the parties, or the two appointed arbitrators, fail to reach an agreement expected of them under that procedure; or
   (c) a person, including an institution, fails to perform any function entrusted to him or it under that procedure, a party may request the Chief Justice, or any person or institution designated by him to take the necessary measure, unless the agreement on the appointment procedure provides other means for securing the appointment.

We can readily see then, that whereas ALPRC lacks adequate specification, ACOI attempts to make each step detailed and transparent. Our argument is that these two different ways of legal specification are largely constrained by the system in which they are constructed. What is interesting are the implications one may draw, namely that one way of specifying displays greater transparency of information in respect of individual rights and obligations, while the other concentrates power of interpretation in the executive bodies of the administration, that is the arbitration commission.

Challenge procedures offer further evidence of similar differences. Consider first ALPRC (Article 35):

ALPRC Article 35 (Challenge Procedure)

Where one litigant submits a withdrawal request, he shall state the reasons, and the reasons shall be submitted prior to the opening of the first court session. When a cause of the withdrawal is not known until the first court session has been held, the cause may be submitted prior the closure of the last court session.

On the other hand, ACOI section 13 is detailed in terms of the specification of scope.

ACOI Article 13 — Challenge Procedure

(1) Subject to the sub-section (4), the parties are free to agree on a procedure for challenging an arbitrator.
(2) Failing any agreement referred in sub-section (1), a party who intends to challenge an arbitrator shall, within fifteen days after becoming aware of the constitution of the arbitral tribunal or after becoming aware of any circumstances referred to in sub-section (3) of section 12, send a written statement of the reasons for the challenge to the arbitral tribunal.
(3) Unless the arbitrator challenged under sub-section (2) withdraws from his office or the other party agrees to the challenge, the arbitral tribunal shall decide on the challenge.
(4) If a challenge under any procedure agreed upon by the parties or under the procedure under sub-section (2) is not successful, the arbitral tribunal shall continue the arbitral proceedings and make an arbitral award.
(5) Where an arbitral award is made under sub-section (4), the party challenging the arbitrator may make an application for setting aside such an arbitral award in accordance with section 34.

Where an arbitral award is set aside on an application made under sub-section (5), the court may decide as to whether the arbitrator who is challenged is entitled to any fees.

Comparing these two provisions, we find them very different both in terms of the length of the article and in terms of the depth of coverage. ALPRC has a single article of 57 words, whereas ACOI has 6 different sections totalling 206 words. In terms of the depth of coverage, ALPRC incorporates information primarily on the ‘freedom of parties’ to challenge arbitration procedures, but incorporates very limited options for them. ACOI, on the other hand is extremely detailed incorporating clarificatory information on at least 7 different aspects of the arbitration challenge procedures.

ISSUES	ALPRC	ACOI
Freedom of parties	Yes	Yes
Specification of procedure	No	Yes
Agreement of parties	No	Yes
Specification of constraints of time period	No	Yes
Specification of form	No	Written
Power of Arbitration Tribunal on Challenge	No mention	Yes
Appeal process against challenge	No mention	Yes

As we suggest above, specification of legal scope may be associated with the distribution of power within the legal process. If a particular law is specified in detail, it follows that the information incorporated is seen to make the law transparent, in the sense that readers or interpreters, including not only the lawyers and judges but also members of the executive arms of the government and the general public, may thereby have access to the necessary detailed information. In consequence, this affords less room for multiple interpretations by users with particular interests. Unlike ACOI Article 11, ALPRC article 32, for instance, does not include information on the exact procedures that the Arbitration Council is required to follow. This raises a number of relevant questions.

- How does one conclude that the parties have 'failed' to make the appointments?
- Can the parties avoid making appointments indefinitely?
- Who in the arbitration Council is authorized to make the appointments?

Questions like these and doubtless others, may achieve relevance in specific situations. One consequence is that in such circumstances the power to make decisions one way or the other is assigned to the Arbitration Council. Although not stated explicitly, it is clear in such circumstances that executive bodies are assigned more power than the parties in the arbitration process. This is quite different from the situation in the ACOI, where the stated principle of 'party autonomy' and 'freedom to arbitrators' is signalled through the use of more transparent detailed specification of scope at various points in the arbitration process.

The two sets of arbitration laws thus differ in terms of the freedom they give to the parties concerned. ACOI treats 'party autonomy' as one of the prime objectives, whereas ALPRC makes 'safeguarding of legitimate rights and interests of the litigants' as its main objective. This is also reflected in the use of modals in the two sections we have just discussed. ALPRC overwhelmingly uses the legally mandatory 'shall' in most sections, and relatively fewer uses of 'may'. On the other hand, ACOI makes use of a much wider choice of modality with a more differentiated use of modals. This indicates lexico-grammatically and semantically the greater freedom of interpretive choice accorded to parties or to the executives. Any mandatory use of 'shall' assigns power to the legal subject, which in most cases is the executive or the judiciary, at the cost of other parties, and conversely 'may' offers a 'right to choose' (Bhatia, 1982) most often in this section for the parties concerned to determine, rather than to the executive or the judiciary.

These two different styles of drafting may be regarded as a function of the specific legal traditions from which they derive. In the common law tradition of legislative construction, detailed specification is always considered a desirable virtue because it is used as a means to keep the interpreters of legislative discourse in courts under the firm control of the legislative community, who are constitutionally empowered to control public behaviour through legislation. This is seen as one of the most powerful instruments in western democracies to uphold the view that it is the role of judiciary to interpret faithfully the wishes of the legislature, although the judiciary is always considered independent of the legislature as well as of the government (Bhatia, 1993, 2004). In the civil code system, on the other hand, laws are often under-specified, and are written in the form of general principles. The interpretation and application of such laws is left to the judiciary. The judiciary therefore enjoys much wider scope for interpretation than in the common law system. We may say that the two systems are in consequence equally valid within their own respective legal systems. However, if we consider the section on 'Grounds for challenge' it appears that the two arbitration laws are exceptions to that which we have seen in other sections. Contrary to our expectations, Article 34 of ALPRC is reasonable detailed, whereas ACOI section 12 is less so. This aspect of all-inclusiveness is measured in terms of the use of binomials and multinomials:

ALPRC Article 34 — Grounds for Challenge

An arbitrator shall withdraw from serving in the tribunal when his case is one of the following, and the litigants also have the right to present a withdrawal request:

(1) where he is { one of the litigants in the arbitration,
or he is a close relative of any one litigant,
or a relative of the attorney; }

(2) where he has a vital interest in the arbitration;

(3) where he is related to { the litigants, or their attorneys, }
in other respects in the case
and the relationship may affect an impartial arbitration;
or where he has had private meetings { with the litigants
or
with their
attorneys, }

or when he has { accepted the invitation of the litigants
of the attorneys, to dine, or accepted
their gifts. }

IACO Article 12 — Grounds for Challenge

(1) When a person is approached in connection with his possible appointment as an arbitrator, he shall disclose in writing any circumstances likely to give rise to justifiable doubts as to his { independence or impartiality. }

(2) An arbitrator, from the time of his appointment and throughout the arbitral proceedings, shall, without delay, disclose to the parties in writing any circumstances referred to in sub-section (1) unless they have already been informed of them by him.

(3) An arbitrator may be challenged only if —
(a) circumstances exist that give rise to justifiable doubts as to his independence or impartiality, or —
(b) he does not possess the qualifications agreed to by the parties.

A party may challenge an arbitrator { appointed by him, or in whose appointment he has participated, }

only for reasons of which he becomes aware after the appointment has been made.

The issue here is not simply the number of options provided in the ALPRC, but also the kind of options it includes. The section specifies explicitly no fewer than 28 different possibilities for challenging the appointment of arbitrators. We note, however, that most of these possibilities rest on the basis of some relationship existing between the parties at dispute. There is also a detailed attempt to define such relationships in terms of specifics. Here the danger is that the more one specifies in a case like this, the more eventualities one is likely to exclude as possibilities. On the other hand, ACOI mentions only 8 possibilities, but each one of them are quite open-ended, allowing by extension and implication for the incorporation of a number of others.

SOCIO-PRAGMATIC FACTORS IN LEGAL INTERPRETATION

Our argument here is that legal interpretation based on purely syntactic information can be misleading, and that the achieving of such interpretation often relies on a consideration of socio-pragmatic factors lying outside specific linguistic textualisation. As Bhatia (1998) claims, legal writing is highly intertextual and its interpretation interdiscursive, requiring for the interpreting of any piece of legislative provision the need to take into account the socio-political objectives that the document is written to achieve. As an illustration of this argument we consider a recent arbitration case from India — *Lohia v. Lohia* (2002) AIR SCW 898 (from India) (See Appendix 1 for the material facts and the arguments of the case). This case brings into focus section 10 of ACOI, which states:

> **Article 10 —**
>
> (1) The parties are free to determine the number of arbitrators, provided that such number shall not be an even number;

So far as the lexico-grammar is concerned, there appears to be no scope for ambiguity in Article 10. It clearly establishes the free will of the parties to agree on any number of arbitrators, provided this number is not an even number. However, as the material facts of the case point out, the parties decided to have only two arbitrators. The question then was whether this determination was contrary to the provision in Article 10. On linguistic grounds there seems to be no doubt that such an agreement contravened the provision in question. However, if we move beyond the linguistic textualisation of the provision and consider the main objectives of the arbitration practice as alternative to litigation, we find a number of relevant factors (including the basic assumptions, aim and objectives of arbitration, expectations, and bases of arbitration process, etc.) that allows us to assign a somewhat different interpretation to the same provision.

Arbitration is meant to provide an economic, expeditious and informal remedy for the settlement of commercial disputes. This process has been preferred as alternative to litigation, chiefly because of the financial costs of the latter, both for the parties at dispute and for the government. The arbitration process is meant to legitimise and respect the party's autonomy and free will, and it is to this end that mutual agreement is legislated to be the pre-requisite to arbitration. That is the reason why the judge highlights arbitration as the creature of agreement. To emphasise this aspect of party autonomy, the arbitration rules give unprecedented freedom to parties to choose arbitration procedures. It is obvious that the spirit of arbitration lies within the arbitration agreement, which in turn represents the free will of the parties to settle commercial disputes through arbitration rather than litigation. However, it is a feature of human nature that, faced with arbitration award against one's interest, the affected party will not hesitate to go for litigation. This seems to be the situation in this case. The parties initially agreed to go for arbitration by two arbitrators, but when the award was not as advantageous as they had expected, they decided to opt for litigation on the grounds that the constitution of the arbitration commission did not accord with Article 10. The Supreme Court of India's decision rejected the claim and upheld that the two-member arbitration commission was still legal and valid, notwithstanding the mandatory requirement in Article 10 that the number of arbitrators be odd and not even. Here the interpretation of the judge is clearly not based on a simple reading of the text, but takes into account the other intertextual as well as interdiscursive information and assumptions.

In fact, the interpretation of the Court highlights an important tension between two legal documents, Article 10 of the ACOI and the arbitration agreement. A possible explanation could be that before the constitution of the arbitration commission the two parties had full freedom to appoint a mutually agreed number of arbitrators. At that point, Article 10 should have been the determining force, and any violation of the said article would have made the constitution of the arbitration commission null and void. The Court's opinion would seem to depend on the decision by the two parties to opt for a two-member arbitration commission and their failure to object to such an arrangement within the given period of time, implied that they accepted such a commission. In short, they were taken to have waived their right to object to such appointment. However, when the parties did not find the award to their liking and decided to go for litigation, this was interpreted by the judge as going against the spirit of arbitration which clearly considers 'arbitration as a creature of agreement'. Here we can see that after the arbitration process is complete, agreement becomes a more dominant force rather than the other way round. So, in spite of the fact that the case seems to rest on a violation of an interpretation based on a strict interpretation of the text of Article 10, the judge goes beyond such a purely linguistic interpretation. He takes into account what we are referring to here as socio-pragmatic factors such as the tension existing between the agreement between the parties and the arbitration law, and the underlying assumptions, aim and objectives, and the spirit of arbitration practice, in order to rule against the purely textual interpretation of Article 10.

CONCLUSIONS

The analysis and discussion above brings into focus two main conclusions. The first one suggests that although law has traditionally been considered jurisdictional in nature, it is increasingly being constructed, interpreted, used and exploited in settings across jurisdictional boundaries. Moreover, the perception that legislative discourse is impersonal and highly formal, and hence differences in linguistic, socio-political, economic, and cultural factors across national and ideological boundaries have no significant influence in its construction and interpretation, is no longer entirely valid. With the increasing dismantling of international trade barriers, laws are often being written and interpreted across geographical and socio-political borders in different ways. This makes one wonder whether one can take anything for granted in these contexts when one crosses such boundaries.

The second conclusion concerns social action in the context of law. The analysis supports the view that legal action depends not simply on semantically or logically accurate interpretation, but also on socio-pragmatically appropriate interpretations, keeping in mind the socio-political, economical and cultural constraints. This view is often preferred by institutions that hold executive powers. The institutions with executive responsibilities would like to exercise maximum control and power to implement administrative and social policies, and would like to have under their control a measure of flexibility in interpretation, which is often lost through detailed specification in legislative instruments. It is hardly surprising that a high degree of transparency in legislative intention is often negatively viewed by autocratic executive organisations and institutions.

REFERENCES

Bhatia, V. K. (1982) *An Investigation into Formal and Functional Characteristics of Qualifications in Legislative Writing and Its Application to English for Academic Legal Purposes*. Ph.D. thesis, University of Aston in Birmingham.

Bhatia, V. K. (1993) *Analysing Genre — Language Use in Professional Settings*. London: Longman.

Bhatia, V. K. (2000) Genres in Conflict. In Anna Trosborg (ed), *Analysing Professional Genres*. Amsterdam: John Benjamins Publishing Company, 147–162.

Bhatia, V. K. (2004) *Worlds of Written Discourse*. London/New York: Continuum.

Bhatia, V. K., Candlin, C. N. and Gotti, M. (eds.) (2003) *Legal Discourse in Multilingual and Multicultural Contexts: Arbitration Texts in Europe*. Bern: Peter Lang.

Bhatia, V. K., and Engberg, J. (2004) Special Issue of *Hermes, Journal of Linguistics*, Volume 32.

Bhatia, V. K., Engberg, J., Gotti, M. and Heller, D. (eds.) (2005) *Vagueness in Normative Texts*. Bern: Peter Lang.

Candlin, C. N. and Bhatia, V. K. (1998) The Project Report on *Strategies and Competencies in Legal Communication: A Study to Investigate the Communicative Needs of Legal Professionals*. The Law Society of Hong Kong.

Maley, Y. (1987) The language of legislation, in *Language and Society* 16: 25–48.

Maley, Y. (1994) The language of the law. In Gibbons (ed.), *Language and the Law*. London: Longman.

Scollon, R. (1998) *Mediated Discourse as Social Interaction — A Study of News Discourse*. London: Longman.

APPENDIX 1

2002 AIR SCW 898

Appellant: Narayan Prasad Lohia Respondent: Nikunj K Lohia

The appellant and the respondents are family members, who had disputes and differences in respect of family business and properties. All the parties agreed to resolve their disputes through one Mr Khaitan. Subsequently they agreed that Mr Khaitan and one Mr Jain resolve their disputes. For the purpose of this appeal, the judges presumed that the parties had agreed to the arbitration of these two persons. ... The parties made their claims before these two persons, and all the parties participated in the proceedings. On 6th of October 1996 an award came to be passed by the two persons.

On 22nd December 1997 the first respondent filed an application in the Calcutta High Court for setting aside this award. Later on the second respondent also filed an application for setting aside this award. One of the grounds, in both these applications was that the Arbitration was by two Arbitrators whereas under the Arbitration and Conciliation Act, 1996 there cannot be an even number of Arbitrators. It was contended that arbitration by two arbitrators was against the statutory provision of the said Act, and therefore void and invalid. These contentions found favour with a single Judge of the Calcutta High Court, who set aside the award on 17th Nov. 1998. On the 18th May 2000 the Appeal was also dismissed. Hence this Appeal to this Court.

Mr Venugopal, the counsel for the respondents, submits that section 10 is a mandatory provision which cannot be derogated. He points out that even though the parties are free to determine the number of arbitrators, such number cannot be an even number. Any agreement which permits the parties to appoint an even number of arbitrators would be contrary to this mandatory provision. He submits that such an agreement would be invalid and void as the Arbitral Tribunal would not have been validly constituted. He submits that composition of the arbitral tribunal itself being invalid, the proceedings and the award, even if one be passed, would be invalid and unenforceable.

On the other hand, Mr Dwivedi, the counsel for the appellant, submits that Sections 4, 10, and 16 are part of the integrated scheme provided in the said act ... the provisions have to be read in a manner whereby there is no conflict between any of them ... He submits that undoubtedly Section 10 provides that there should not be an even number of arbitrators. He points out that Section 10 starts with words. "The parties are free to determine the number of arbitrators".

He submits that arbitration is a matter of agreement between the parties. He submits that generally, in an arbitration, the parties are free to determine the number of arbitrators and the procedure. Parties could agree upon an even number of arbitrators. He submits that even after a party has agreed to an even number of arbitrators he can still object to the composition of the arbitral tribunal. He submits that such objection must be taken before the arbitral tribunal no later than the date of the submission of the statement of defence … .

We have heard the parties at length … Undoubtedly, Section 10 provides that the number of arbitrators shall not be an even number. The question still remains whether Section 10 is a non-derogable provision. In our view the answer to this question would depend on question as to whether, under the said Act, a party has a right to object to the composition of the arbitral tribunal, if such composition is not in accordance with the said Act and if so at what stage. It must be remembered that arbitration is a creature of an agreement. There can be no arbitration unless there is an arbitration agreement in writing between the parties.

In the said Act, provisions have been made in Sections 12, 13 and 16 for challenging the competence, impartiality and jurisdiction. Such challenges must however be before the arbitral tribunal itself … A party is free to object within the time prescribed in section 16(2). If a party chooses not to so object there will be a deemed waiver under section 4. Thus we are unable to accept the submission that Section 10 is a non-derogable provision. In our view Section 10 has to be read along with Section 16 and is, therefore, derogable provision.

Respondent 1 and 2 not having raised any objection to the composition of the arbitral tribunal, as provided in Section 16, they must be deemed to have waived their right to object.

For the reasons aforesaid, the Judgments of the learned Judge and the Division Bench on the question of law discussed cannot be sustained. They are accordingly set aside.

7

Vagueness and Indeterminacy in Law

Jan Engberg and Dorothee Heller

VAGUENESS — A COMMON GROUND FOR LAWYERS AND LINGUISTS[1]

Introduction

Everyday experience with language in practice shows that it is not always clear what a sender means when he or she employs language for communication. This is especially true in the area of law.[2] Stated informally, the main reason for this lack of clarity is that it is not possible for the receiver of a message to determine exactly what the sender is referring to in the world. However, this observation covers a wide variety of different phenomena. Some examples are:

a. The use of context-dependent deictic expressions like *this Act*, where the receiver needs to access knowledge about the situation in which an expression is uttered in order to understand what the sender means.
b. Expressions like *give me the document*, when a judge addresses a lawyer in court but a number of different documents may be referred to and the receiver cannot decide which one, relying on the information contained in the utterance.

---

1 In this co-authored chapter, Jan Engberg is responsible for "Vagueness — A Common Ground for Lawyers and Linguists", whereas Dorothee Heller is responsible for "The Negotiation of Scope in Legislative Provisions".

2 For other examples of vagueness and indeterminacy in specialised communication, see Hahn 1998.

c. Expressions like *a sufficient cause*, where the receiver does not know what criterion or scale is applied, apart from the fact the sender considers the cause to be sufficient.

This pre-theoretical concept (i.e. when the receiver does not know exactly what a word refers to) is the point of departure for the issues addressed in this paper. Terminologically, the concept is generally known as 'vagueness' and 'indeterminacy'. Our interest lies in the description of such phenomena in statutory texts, that is within specialised settings. However, in order to proceed from the aforesaid pre-theoretical concept of indeterminate/vague language use to a more theoretically-based concept, we shall first introduce the taxonomy suggested by the German linguist Manfred Pinkal. Subsequently, the special relevance of this concept of vagueness in the law will be discussed in the light of prototypical examples of theoretical approaches to vagueness contributed by legal philosophy and the analysis legal argumentation. The second part of this paper describes the results of an analysis of German and Swiss statutory rules on international commercial arbitration. Its aim is to identify indeterminacy triggered by linguistic items at different levels within such statutes and the extent of culture-bound differences linked to the expression of indeterminacy in the drafting procedures reflected by the two statutes.

Vagueness in general — Pinkal's classification

Pinkal primarily distinguishes between two possible objects when examining lack of determinacy (Pinkal 1981: 4): *communicative underdeterminacy* (when the receiver gets less information than expected in a given situation) and *semantic indeterminacy* (see below). The two kinds of object are not mutually exclusive because they function at different descriptive levels of description, and should rather be seen as two different perspectives on the same problem. This paper concentrates on semantic indeterminacy, reflecting our interest in the contribution of linguistic resources to the understanding and interpreting of legal texts, rather than on the communicative process of statutory interpretation. Pinkal defines semantic indeterminacy as follows:

> Ein Ausdruck ist *semantisch unbestimmt* genau dann, wenn er in Sätzen vorkommt, denen in bestimmten Situationen keiner der

> Wahrheitswerte ‚wahr' oder ‚falsch' eindeutig zugeordnet werden kann, … (Pinkal 1981: 4).[3]

The central point in Pinkal's definition is thus the impossibility of determining unequivocally whether a sentence is true or false. As additional criteria, the definition requires that (1) it must be at least theoretically possible to make the utterance more precise, and (2) that indeterminacy must arise from the linguistic expression (Pinkal 1981: 5). In line with this definition, our focus will be on semantic indeterminacy and on how specific textual expressions make it more or less difficult to determine whether an utterance is true or false. In so doing so, we have restricted the theoretical scope of this paper.

A further point taken into account is Pinkal's distinction between *ambiguity* and *vagueness* as types of semantic indeterminacy:

> Ein semantisch unbestimmter Ausdruck ist *mehrdeutig*, wenn seine Verwendung (in der Regel) zu kommunikativer Unterbestimmtheit führt, falls er nicht durch Situation, sprachlichen Kontext oder explizite Erläuterung präzisiert wird.
>
> Ein semantisch unbestimmter Ausdruck ist *vage*, wenn er (in der Regel) unpräzisiert oder unvollständig präzisiert verwendet werden kann, ohne zu kommunikativer Unterbestimmtheit zu führen. (Pinkal 1981: 10)[4]

The difference between these two types of semantic indeterminacy lies in the fact that **ambiguous** expressions call for precision. Normally speaking, more precision is expected when the receiver knows that the utterance refers to a limited number of alternatives but does not know specifically what these are, as in the cited deictic expression (*this Act*) or in the request to hand over a document; the receiver requires this knowledge for an adequate understanding of the sentence. **Vague** expressions, on the other hand, do not necessarily require precision to be adequately understood by the receiver (as in the example *a sufficient cause*).

---

3 An expression is *semantically indeterminate* only when it occurs in sentences to which, in a given situation, none of the 'true' or 'false' values may be attributed unequivocally.

4 A semantically indeterminate expression is *ambiguous* if its use (as a rule) leads to communicative underdeterminacy and it is not made more precise by the situation, the linguistic context or an explicit explanation. It is *vague* if (as a rule) it may be used without being made more precise or only partially precise, without its use leading to communicative underdeterminacy.

This paper will concentrate on the use of vague expressions, which (as we shall see below) are an accepted, necessary element of legal drafting arising from the communicative purpose of statutory texts. The same may not be said of ambiguity, which in communicative terms is a rather undesirable feature. This is confirmed also by the guidelines for clear legal drafting developed by The Australian Centre for Plain Legal Language, which highlight the need to avoid ambiguous words but make no reference to vagueness as an issue for clear drafting.[5] The following section attempts to account for this apparent inconsistency.

Vagueness in statutory texts

The key feature of vagueness is that it leaves room for interpretation and communicative negotiation of the exact meaning of a word or expression. An example of a vague expression may be seen in the following statutory sentence:

> a. If without showing *sufficient* cause a party fails to comply with any order or directions of the tribunal, the tribunal may make a peremptory order to the same effect, prescribing such time for compliance with it as the tribunal considers appropriate. (Arbitration Act of England 1996, section 41, 5; our emphasis)

This sentence is inherently vague in that a reader, on the basis of the statute's wording, will be unable to decide or describe what amount of justification will be adequate in concrete cases. This difficulty is due to the use of the word *sufficient*. Being one of key words in the sentence, it leaves it up to the recipient (here the tribunal) to decide whether in a concrete case the cause is sufficient or not; there is no single answer to be found, without knowledge about the case in question or subjective interpretation of the utterance through knowledge of previous uses of the expression. The example is perfectly consistent with the definition given earlier: an expression (*sufficient cause*) within a sentence cannot be objectively classified as true or not and is therefore responsible for the lack of truth value.

As will be seen in the following section, this linguistic description of the phenomenon agrees with an ongoing debate among legal scholars.

5 http://www.lawfoundation.net.au/information/pll/cpllchecklist.html#plain/.

We may safely claim, therefore, that vagueness is a prototypical example of convergence between the interests of linguists and lawyers. Later in the paper, we shall explain how publications in linguistics and the law tend to overlap, thereby constituting an area of investigation that is interesting linguistically but may also allow academic cooperation between applied linguistics and legal scholars. For this reason, the status of indeterminacy will be assessed both as a local/global characteristic of legal communication and as reflecting the ideal of the rule of law.

Indeterminacy — local or global?

Much of the legal debate connected with vagueness and the law may be subsumed, from a linguistic standpoint, under the question of whether vagueness is a global or local characteristic of legal writing. If global, then all legal texts are vague and indeterminate; if local, only parts of such texts and only some of them are vague. The latter approach makes the existence of determinate legal texts highly possible.

Endicott (2000, 2005) is among those who argue that indeterminacy is a local characteristic. His definition of *legal indeterminacy* and *linguistic indeterminacy* is very similar to that given above by Pinkal:

> Legal theorists say that the law is indeterminate when a question of law, or of how the law applies to facts, has no single right answer. I will call such indeterminacy 'legal indeterminacy' and I will use 'linguistic indeterminacy' to refer to unclarity in the application of linguistic expressions that could lead to legal indeterminacy. (Endicott 2000: 9)

Endicott's basic assumption is that not all texts are legally indeterminate, but only those connected to so-called *borderline cases* (Endicott 2000: 9). Apart from these, there are many cases that allow a single right answer as to whether a statutory rule applies to a specific situation or not. At the same time, there are cases that require interpretation (i.e. an active, subjective decision by an individual as to the applicability or non-applicability of a rule) and others where it is not. A distinction is therefore possible between legally clear and legally indeterminate cases (Endicott 2000: 29).

The opposite view, which views indeterminacy as a global characteristic, is represented by James Boyd White:

> Instead of each term having a meaning of the sort necessary for deductive operations to go on in the first place, each term in a legal rule has a range of possible meanings, among which choices will have to be made. … the intellectual process of law is one of arguing and reasoning about which of them is to be preferred. (White 1982: 427)

This quotation makes two claims that are relevant to our discussion:

a. The meaning of all legal terms is indeterminate (and therefore contestable and vague) because we have no foreknowledge of what choices lawyers will make in the process of interpreting the statutes.
b. Consequently, interpreting the law (i.e. its *intellectual process*) implies providing arguments for a given choice among a number of possible meanings.

This view results in a high degree of scepticism, as to the role of texts in legal interpretation:

> To sum up my point in a phrase, what characterizes legal discourse is that it is in a double sense (both substantively and procedurally) constitutive in nature: it creates a set of questions that define a world of thought and action, a set of roles and voices by which experience will be ordered and meanings established and shared; a set of occasions and methods for public speech that constitute us as a community and as a polity. *In all of this it has its own ways of working, which are to be found not in the rules that are at the centre of the structure, but in the culture which determines how these rules are to be read and talked about.* (White 1982: 433; our emphasis)

According to White and others (cf. Christensen/Sokolowski 2002), the meaning of legal rules cannot be retrieved from the rules themselves but only in the (professional) culture working with those texts. In this sense, all legal texts may be considered inherently vague or indeterminate because nothing entirely determinate can be said about a text's meaning.

This postmodern approach has interesting repercussions on how we conceptualise legal argumentation[6] and legal translation.[7] However, in terms of linguistic description it takes the concepts of indeterminacy and vagueness to an even higher level of abstraction, making it impossible to

6 See e.g. Christensen/Sokolowski (2002) and Solan (1993).
7 See e.g. Joseph (1995) and Engberg (2002).

describe the aspects of semantic indeterminacy presented earlier in this chapter. Taking this argument to the extreme, one might say that if indeterminacy is a feature of all words, then expressions like *a sufficient interest in the matter* do not differ basically from any other expression in legal statutes. Such extreme readings deprive us of the opportunity to investigate different degrees of explicitness in indeterminacy. Moreover, the outcome would have the disadvantage of being counterintuitive, at least for a linguist.

The search for common ground between linguists interested in semantic vagueness and lawyers interested in vagueness in the law requires an alternative decision, i.e. the view that vagueness is a local characteristic, as suggested by Endicott. However, it is important to acknowledge also the common ground between linguistic approaches and the postmodern view exemplified here by White. Linguistic meanings should generally be seen within their socio-pragmatic context, especially where the interpretation of legal statutes is concerned. We would add that such studies should not target semantic vagueness but a specific kind of (pragmatic) indeterminacy that may be investigated scientifically also in linguistic terms. What we have, therefore, is a case where it would be useful to distinguish between (linguistically triggered) semantic vagueness and (pragmatically triggered) indeterminacy.[8]

The legal issue: rule of law as an ideal

Why then is the description of vagueness and indeterminacy interesting from the perspective of both linguistics and legal scholars? The main reason is that vagueness and indeterminacy in statutory texts pose a substantial dilemma to legal theory, which works on the assumption (built on Locke as well as Aristotle) that a good legal system should be governed by "the rule of laws, not of men" (Endicott 2000: 198). This is countered by the fact that indeterminacy and vagueness are seen as inherent in law for reasons of efficiency, so that the language of statutes cannot avoid elements — like the ones mentioned above — conducive to semantic indeterminacy. Interpretation is necessarily part of the rule of law and necessarily implies *someone* (albeit vested with proper authority) who interprets in the context of a specific case — hence our dilemma. This

8 For a more detailed discussion of the issue, see Engberg (2004).

issue also involves the linguistically important relationship between interpreted texts and the law (in terms of textual meaning). How can 'the rule of law' exist if law is communicated only through texts containing language that is at least partly vague?

There are a number of answers to this philosophically oriented problem, but we shall focus on Endicott's solution, since his approach to vagueness and indeterminacy fits in nicely with the linguistic approach chosen here.

Endicott first observes that the law is necessarily vague:

> Vagueness is ineliminable from a legal system, if a legal system must do such things as to regulate the use of violence among citizens, and commercial agreements between citizens. (Endicott 2000: 190)

In his example, only legal systems that do not list every specific type of unlawful violence can be sure to achieve the rule of law, i.e. to prevent the use of violence among citizens. If such a list were provided, any use of violence not mentioned in the list would be lawful.[9] In linguistic terms, a statute must contain elements of semantic indeterminacy in order to be efficient.

On the other hand, if laws must be inherently vague in order to work, then the rule of law can become arbitrary because it does not necessarily treat similar cases equally and the outcome of judicial decisions may not be entirely predictable (Endicott 2000: 186). The rule of law depends on human agents whose insight is inevitably limited at all times whose decisions rely on experience that is necessarily subjective. Endicott solves this paradox by relativising the ideal definition of the rule of law, which implies not that the law alone rules (an impossible condition) but that there is "a commitment to *minimize* vagueness" (Endicott 2000: 191; his emphasis) and thus to minimize the degree of arbitrariness in the rule of law.

This inevitable vagueness means that every legal system should have an institution (i.e. a court) with the authority to remove vagueness: an institution capable of acting creatively by providing solutions to vague rules (i.e. those whose sentences cannot be unequivocally assigned as 'true' or 'false' truth values, as in Pinkal above). The ideal of the rule of law is only attainable, therefore, if we accept that it implies to a certain extent

9 This is how Bhatia (1983: 3) labels the ideal of all-inclusiveness in legal writing. See Bhatia (1993: 106–113) for a discussion of the consequences of this ideal.

the rule of human agents. Otherwise vagueness cannot be eliminated and no rule of law is achieved. The greatest tension between vagueness and the ideal of the rule of law occurs when vagueness diverges from *the reason of the law* (Endicott 2000: 203), but this concept is itself interestingly vague and requires interpretation!

A general collaborative effort between lawyers and linguists is therefore needed, to establish whether this ideal is actually followed by the institutions that interpret the law. The contribution to semantic indeterminacy made by different linguistic elements will help to identify textual *highlights*, i.e. statutory points where the receivers (courts and lawyers) are expected to apply their socio-legal creative competence. The use of linguistic methods may provide a basis for more specific knowledge regarding the type of interpretations necessary in statutory texts.

Thus the linguistic and legal insights to the phenomenon show that vagueness is a necessary prerequisite of any efficient legal system. Far from being a flaw in statutory provisions (though Endicott argues that this may also occur) it serves as a device for all-inclusiveness.[10] Following on from here, the next part of our paper looks more specifically at vague expressions that add an element of discretion to qualifications, which makes them textual *highlights* of the kind described above.

THE NEGOTIATION OF SCOPE IN LEGISLATIVE PROVISIONS

A topical example

The field of international commercial arbitration was chosen as an example because it is inherently less formalised and more negotiable than standard procedural law.[11] Arbitration is an alternative for companies looking for a smoother, quicker option for settling disputes across borders and legal systems. Moreover, it does not necessarily follow the rules of a single country but allows the parties considerable freedom (depending on the place and the rules chosen) to agree on the procedure themselves. This suggests, at least hypothetically, that the rules for international commercial arbitration contain a high degree of vague expressions, resulting from negotiation between the parties and the arbitrators.

---

10 See also Bhatia (2005) and Bhatia et al. (2005b) in Bhatia et al. (2005a).

11 Bhatia and Candlin (2004), however, show that this characteristic is not equally dominant across different cultures and political systems.

Every legal system — and not only its authorities concerned with international commercial arbitration — includes a traditional repertoire of inherently vague concepts, as the English "without undue delay" or the German "Treu und Glauben". These items, which pertain to the field of semantic vagueness, may be described as a class of crystallised vague elements with their own interpretive history and have been (and still are) discussed in much detail by legal scholars. As our empirical investigation is linguistically oriented, our focus is not on these standardised elements, however, but on more generally vagueness-related linguistic devices and in particular on those indicating negotiation of scope. The findings are presented below, drawing on two national statutory texts (one German and the other Swiss) with consideration for the use of vagueness and indeterminacy within the argumentative structures of normative provisions.

Data on information loading

Despite similarities in macrostructure and topic (see Appendix), there are substantial differences between the two arbitration statutes considered. The German Arbitration Law (1998), belonging to the Code of Civil Procedure, was completely revised after national implementation of the UNCITRAL Model Law (1985).[12] The new version (Zivilprozessordnung §§ 1025–1066, henceforth: ZPO) follows the UNCITRAL Model faithfully, in its general structure as well as in the wording of most articles, which partly accounts for its syntactic complexity and high information load. The Swiss Arbitration Law (1989), belonging to the Federal Statute on International Private Law (Arts. 176–199, henceforth: IPRG), makes no reference to the UNCITRAL Model Law; compared to the German statute, its sentence structure is rather simple with low density of information.

A quantitative overview is necessary to appreciate the above-mentioned differences. ZPO tends to be highly explicit, with details provided in sections comprising 2 to 6 subsections; IPRG does not exceed 3 subsections. Both statutes differ in sentence length and information load, as shown by the peak value of 246 words in only a single sentence/ subsection of ZPO (§ 1059.2), as compared to a peak of 77 words in the

12 Compared to previous German statutes on arbitration (see Heller 2003), the present version is more accessible thanks to the introduction of headings and subheadings guiding the reader to relevant information. This 'reader-friendly' approach is particularly helpful given the high information load typical of most sections in the new version of the statute.

same IPRG provision (Art. 190.2). These differences will be taken up again below in the next section.

Table 7.1 Subdivision into sections/subsections and word range in ZPO and IPRG

	ZPO 42 sections 5121 words 186 sentences	IPRG 19 sections 1177 words 43 sentences
Sections without subsections	16.66%	21.05%
Sections with 2–3 subsections	52.38%	78.95%
Sections with more than 3 subsections	30.95%	–
Subsections consisting of 1 sentence	60.5%	94.74%
Subsections consisting of 2–3 sentences	38.65%	5.26%
Subsections with more than 3 sentences	0.84%	–
Subsection length (min.)	7 words (§ 1039.2)	7 words (Art. 184.1)
Subsection length (max.)	246 words (§ 1059.2)	77 words (Art. 190.2)
Sentence length (min.)	6 words (§ 1034.2)	6 words (Art. 189.2)
Sentence length (max.)	246 words (§ 1059.2)	77 words (Art. 190.2)

A closer examination of argumentative structures and micro-structural details of individual sections points to the use of various strategies for qualifying normative provisions and shows that increased explicitness does not automatically eliminate vagueness or indeterminacy (see also Hahn 1998: 384; Pinkal 1985: 48).

Argumentative structures in legislative provisions: qualifications

The argumentative structure of normative texts such as statutes is closely connected to the use of (linguistic) qualifications. The openness of a legal provision depends on interaction between the main provisional clause and various qualifying inserts. A typology of such textual features has been offered by Bhatia (1993: 113–118), who describes them as strategies whereby legal draftsmen achieve clarity and precision, on the one hand, and all-inclusiveness on the other. This dual nature of qualifications points to elements of both vagueness and indeterminacy. ZPO provisions are qualified chiefly by (premodifying, postmodifying or inserted) conditional clauses such as the following:

Table 7.2 Conditional qualification of legislative argumentation

A (gilt) ➔ wenn / falls / sofern B	'A (applies) ➔ if B'
A (gilt) ➔ wenn nicht / falls nicht / sofern nicht B	'A (applies) ➔ unless B'
A (gilt) ➔ wenn / falls B ← sofern nicht C / es sei denn C	'A (applies) ➔ if B ← unless C'

Conditional argumentation is deeply rooted in legal drafting traditions (Crystal/Davy 1969; cf. also Bhatia 1993 and Soffritti 1999) and is typical of provisions with a high amount of detailed information. While such cases are very frequent in ZPO (see Heller 2003), the IPRG provisions are generally written in a more simple style with only a few instances of exception clauses (*sofern nicht / es sei denn* ...).

Such differences are closely associated with different drafting traditions. Most IPRG sections appear to reflect the basic principles of Swiss legislative writing, known as *Eugen-Huber-Regel*: no section should exceed 3 subsections; each subsection should contain only one sentence; each sentence should express only one idea (Nussbaumer 2000: 205).

Balancing precision and indeterminacy

Because of the dual nature of qualifications, mentioned earlier, it is advisable to analyse such pragmatic features by looking at subordinate clauses and such embedded qualifying elements as adjectives, adverbs, noun phrases and verb phrases with a degree of semantic fuzziness (Lakoff 1972). The following ZPO examples illustrate how these 'internal' qualifiers interact with conditional argumentation, leaving room for interpretation.

Section 1040 of ZPO regulates the arbitral tribunal's competence and jurisdiction; under subsection 2, recourses concerning the tribunal's jurisdiction (or claiming that it exceeded the bounds of its authority) shall be made no later than the submission of a defence statement or as soon as the matter is raised during proceedings. The last sentence in this subsection states that the tribunal may admit recourse also at a later time, <u>if it considers that the party has justified its delay</u>:

(2) Das Schiedsgericht kann [...] eine spätere Rüge zulassen, wenn die Partei die Verspätung *genügend* entschuldigt. (ZPO § 1040.2; our emphasis)[13]

The authorisation expressed in the main provision (*das Schiedsgericht kann* ...) is restricted by an operational qualification (*wenn die Partei* ...) specifying competence of the tribunal. The adverb *genügend* ('sufficient') acts as internal qualifier, thus reducing the generic nature of the conditional restriction; as an adverb of degree and evaluation, however, it introduces an additional element of discretion and vagueness. Similar wordings may be found in the following provision:

(3) Haben die Parteien nichts anderes vereinbart, so kann jede Partei im Laufe des schiedsrichterlichen Verfahrens ihre Klage oder ihre Angriffs- und Verteidigungsmittel ändern oder ergänzen, es sei denn, das Schiedsgericht läßt dies wegen Verspätung, die nicht *genügend* entschuldigt wird, nicht zu.(ZPO § 1046.2; our emphasis)[14]

Legal commentaries admit that vagueness and indeterminacy are pervasive at various levels, affecting provisions as well as interpretative practices. The only clues given for interpreting *sufficient justification* (*sollte* ... *sein*) are the use of intertextual devices (*in Anlehnung an* § 282 ...), indeterminate adjectives and nominal groups (*einer sorgfältigen und auf Förderung des Verfahrens bedachten Prozessführung*) that do not allow a clear-cut decision (i.e. true or not true) about the accuracy of procedures:

> Kriterium für die genügende Entschuldigung *sollte* in Anlehnung an § 282 Abs. 1 *sein*, ob der Zeitpunkt der Klageänderung nach der Prozesslage einer *sorgfältigen und auf Förderung des Verfahrens bedachten* Prozessführung entspricht. (Thomas/Putzo et al. 1999: 1573; our emphasis)[15]

---

13 ZPO § 1040.2 (English version): The arbitral tribunal may, in either case, admit a later plea if it considers that the party has justified the delay.

14 ZPO § 1046.2 (English version): Unless otherwise agreed by the parties, either party may amend or supplement his claim or defence during the course of the arbitral proceedings, unless the arbitral tribunal considers it inappropriate to allow such amendment having regard to the delay in making it without sufficient justification.

15 According to Art. 282.1, sufficient justification *should* take into account congruency between the time of the claim's emendation, the stage reached by the process and its conduction, which should be *accurate and bring a greater clarity to the proceedings without added delay*.

Endicott (2000: 49) points out that expressions that imply a standard without setting it can be considered as *dummy standards*, which are closely related to those expressing 'grants of discretion'. This kind of device is also found in the operational qualification from a provision for Termination of Proceedings (*Beendigung eines schiedsrichterlichen Verfahrens*):

(4a) Das Schiedsgericht stellt durch Beschluß die Beendigung des schiedsrichterlichen Verfahrens fest, wenn

1. der Kläger a) es versäumt, seine Klage nach § 1046 Abs. 1 einzureichen und kein Fall des § 1048 Abs. 4 vorliegt, oder b) seine Klage zurücknimmt, es sei denn, daß der Beklagte dem widerspricht und das Schiedsgericht *ein berechtigtes Interesse* des Beklagten an der endgültigen Beilegung der Streitigkeit *anerkennt*; oder
2. die Parteien die Beendigung des Verfahrens vereinbaren; oder
3. die Parteien das schiedsrichterliche Verfahren trotz Aufforderung des Schiedsgerichts nicht weiter betreiben oder die Fortsetzung des Verfahrens aus einem anderen Grund unmöglich geworden ist. (ZPO § 1056.2; our emphasis)[16]

The main provision in this subsection contains several conditional specifications (1–3). Notably, one of these contains the preparatory qualification *wenn der Kläger [...]* ('when the claimant ...'), which restricts general applications and is followed by an operational qualification introduced by *es sei denn, daß* ... ('unless ...') indicating an exception in contrast to the given pre-condition. Besides the negotiation of scope and application through preparatory/operational qualifications, the collocation *ein berechtigtes Interesse anerkennen* ('to recognise a legitimate interest') implies pragmatic vagueness and — according to Pinkal's view of vague language — a lack of truth value.

Legal commentaries point out that the definition of 'legitimacy' is not always clear-cut and requires evaluation. They refer explicitly to the

16 ZPO § 1056.2 (English version; our emphasis): The arbitral tribunal shall issue an order for the termination of the arbitral proceedings when 1. the claimant a) fails to state his claim according to section 1046 subs. 1 and section 1048 subs. 4 does not apply, or b) withdraws his claim unless the respondent objects thereto and the arbitral tribunal *recognizes a legitimate interest* on his part in obtaining a final settlement of the dispute; or 2. the parties agree on the termination of the proceedings, or 3. the parties fail to pursue the arbitral proceedings in spite of being so requested by the arbitral tribunal or when the continuation of the proceedings has for any other reason become impossible.

discretion of the arbitral tribunal in recognising whether an interest is legitimate or not (Thomas/Putzo et al. 1999: 1586). Owing to juridical conventions, the criteria for such evaluations are context bound (cf. Creifelds 2000: 420):

(4b) … es sei denn, daß der Beklagte dem widerspricht und das Schiedsgericht *ein berechtigtes Interesse* des Beklagten an der endgültigen Beilegung der Streitigkeit *anerkennt* (ZPO § 1056.2; our emphasis)
("unless the respondent objects thereto and the arbitral tribunal *recognizes a legitimate interest* on his part in obtaining a final settlement of the dispute")

berechtigtes Interesse: ➔ … was das Gericht *nach pflichtgemäßem Ermessen* zu beurteilen hat (Thomas/Putzo 1999: 1586; our emphasis)
("*legitimate interest* ➔ … which shall be evaluated by the tribunal at its discretion")

nach pflichtgemäßem Ermessen: ➔ … d.h. in einer dem *Sinn und Zweck* der Ermächtigung *entsprechenden* Weise (Creifelds 2000: 420; our emphasis)
("*at its discretion* ➔ … i.e. in accordance with the spirit and purpose of the authorisation")

A comparison of provisions on the same topic in ZPO (1059.2) and IPRG (190.2) confirms the aforesaid differences between the two statutes in terms of hypotactic complexity as well as the strategies for balancing precision and indeterminacy.

According to both statutes, the right to appeal and apply for setting aside is subordinated to preconditions involving irregularities in arbitral proceedings or the composition of the arbitral tribunal. The five different cases described in IPRG (Art. 190.2, *Endgültigkeit, Anfechtung* / "Definiteness, Appeal") cover incompatibility with various rights and obligations (*vorschriftswidrig ernennen / zusammensetzen, sich zu Unrecht für zuständig erklären, Rechtsbegehren unbeurteilt lassen, Grundsätze verletzen, unvereinbar sein*) without providing details or grants of discretion. They are listed sequentially, from the tribunal's composition to the award's incompatibility with law and order). The rather simple paratactic structures ease comprehension, although in terms of word range and number of subordinates this is the most extensive subsection in IPRG:

(5) Der Entscheid kann nur angefochten werden,
a. wenn ein Einzelschiedsrichter vorschriftswidrig ernannt oder das Schiedsgericht vorschriftswidrig zusammengesetzt wurde;
b. wenn sich das Schiedsgericht zu Unrecht für zuständig oder unzuständig erklärt hat;
c. wenn das Schiedsgericht über Streitpunkte entschieden hat, die ihm nicht unterbreitet wurden oder wenn es Rechtsbegehren unbeurteilt gelassen hat;
d. wenn der Grundsatz der Gleichbehandlung der Parteien oder der Grundsatz des rechtlichen Gehör verletzt wurde;
e. wenn der Entscheid mit dem Ordre public unvereinbar ist. (IPRG Art. 190.2)[17]

The equivalent subsection in ZPO (§ 1059.2: Aufhebungsantrag / "Application for setting aside") has the main provisional clause qualified by two highly complex conditional clauses (cf. underlined connectors for hypotactic and paratactic subordination). More specifically, the first connector (*1. wenn der Antragsteller begründet geltend macht …*) is remarkably dense, with detailed information on alternative reasons for applying (a, b, c or d).

(6) (2) Ein Schiedsspruch kann nur aufgehoben werden,
1. wenn der Antragsteller begründet geltend macht, daß
a) eine der Parteien, die eine Schiedsvereinbarung nach §§ 1029, 1031 geschlossen haben, nach dem Recht, das für sie persönlich maßgebend ist, hierzu nicht fähig war, oder daß die Schiedsvereinbarung nach dem Recht, dem die Parteien sie unterstellt haben oder, falls die Parteien hierüber nichts bestimmt haben, nach deutschem Recht ungültig ist; oder
b) er von der Bestellung eines Schiedsrichters oder von dem schiedsrichterlichen Verfahren nicht gehörig in Kenntnis gesetzt worden ist oder daß er aus einem anderen Grund seine Angriffs- oder Verteidigungsmittel nicht hat geltend machen können; oder
c) der Schiedsspruch eine Streitigkeit betrifft, die in der Schiedsabrede nicht erwähnt ist oder nicht unter die Bestimmungen der Schiedsklausel fällt, oder daß er

17 "An award may be impugned only a) if the appointment of an arbitrator or the composition of the tribunal was contrary to regulations; b) if the tribunal has wrongly declared its competence or incompetence; c) if the tribunal has decided on matters which have not been submitted or if legal claims have not been considered; d) if the principle of equal treatment of the parties or their right to have full opportunity of presenting their cases have been infringed; e) if the award is in conflict with public policy (*ordre public*)".

Entscheidungen enthält, welche die Grenzen der Schiedsvereinbarung überschreiten; kann jedoch der Teil des Schiedsspruchs, der sich auf Streitpunkte bezieht, die dem schiedsrichterlichen Verfahren unterworfen waren, von dem Teil, der Streitpunkte betrifft, die ihm nicht unterworfen waren, getrennt werden, so kann nur der letztgenannte Teil des Schiedsspruchs aufgehoben werden; oder

d) die Bildung des Schiedsgerichts oder das schiedsrichterliche Verfahren einer Bestimmung dieses Buches oder einer zulässigen Vereinbarung der Parteien nicht entsprochen hat und *anzunehmen ist*, daß sich dies auf den Schiedsspruch ausgewirkt hat; oder

2. wenn das Gericht feststellt, daß

a) der Gegenstand des Streites nach deutschem Recht nicht schiedsfähig ist; oder

b) die Anerkennung oder Vollstreckung des Schiedsspruchs zu einem Ergebnis führt, das der öffentlichen Ordnung (ordre public) widerspricht. (ZPO § 1059.2; our emphasis)[18]

Operational qualifications often contribute to the all-inclusiveness of a provision, particularly in one of the alternative conditions for application (d) dealing with the possible consequences of irregularities in the tribunal's composition tribunal or in the arbitral procedure itself:

> wenn [...] die Bildung des Schiedsgerichts oder das schiedsrichterliche Verfahren einer Bestimmung dieses Buches oder einer zulässigen Vereinbarung der Parteien nicht entsprochen hat

18 ZPO §1059.2 (English version): An arbitral award may be set aside only if: 1. the applicant shows sufficient cause that: a) a party to the arbitration agreement referred to in sections 1029 and 1031 was under some incapacity pursuant to the law applicable to him; or the said agreement is not valid under the law to which the parties have subjected it or, failing any indication thereon, under German law; or b) he was not given proper notice of the appointment of an arbitrator or of the arbitral proceedings or was otherwise unable to present his case; or c) the award deals with a dispute not contemplated by or not falling within the terms of the submission to arbitration, or contains decisions on matters beyond the scope of the submission to arbitration; provided that, if the decisions on matters submitted to arbitration can be separated from those not so submitted, only that part of the award which contains decisions on matters not submitted to arbitration may be set aside; or d) the composition of the arbitral tribunal or the arbitral procedure was not in accordance with a provision of this Book or with an admissible agreement of the parties and this presumably affected the award; or 2. the court finds that the subject-matter of the dispute is not capable of settlement by arbitration under German law; or recognition or enforcement of the award leads to a result which is in conflict with public policy (*ordre public*).

> und *anzunehmen ist*, daß sich dies auf den Schiedsspruch ausgewirkt hat.
> ("if the composition of the arbitral tribunal or the arbitral procedure was not in accordance with a provision of this Book or with an admissible agreement of the parties and this *presumably* affected the award".)

Operational qualification here is an interesting case of vagueness, both from a legal and from a linguistic standpoint. For legal scholars, this provision makes it difficult to establish whether and to what extent a procedural error has influenced the award:

> … , weil nie gesagt werden kann, ob sich der Fehler auf den Inhalt des Spruchs ausgewirkt hat oder nicht. Spekulationen darüber, ob ‚anzunehmen' ist, ein richtig besetztes Schiedsgericht hätte einen inhaltsgleichen Spruch gefällt, sind nicht gestattet. (Stein/Jonas 2003: 596)[19]

No information is given as to the nature and seriousness of potential consequences arising from such irregularities, or their possible impact on the award. The conditional qualification (which goes beyond the analogous provision in the UNCITRAL Model Law) is extremely vague. No single right answer (true or false) can be given when the reasoning is only hypothetical: this pragmatic value distinguishes point (d) from the other reasons (a, b, c) for application:

> Der Aufhebungsgrund *wirkt relativ*, nicht absolut, so wie es die anderen tun. Potentielle Kausalität genügt allerdings. […] Beweispflichtig für die Ursächlichkeit ist allgemein aber derjenige, welcher Aufhebung gewährt; ihm hilft *uU* [= unter Umständen] indes die tatsächliche Vermutung eventuellen Einflusses; der Kausalverlauf ist allemal ein hypothetischer. Kausalität *dürfte etwa anzunehmen sein* bei Konstituierungsmängeln und auch bei Fehlen von allgemeinen Prozessvoraussetzungen; unwesentliche Verfahrensfehler […] werden *idR* [= in der Regel] jedoch den Schiedsspruch *wohl* selten beeinflussen. (Lüke/Wax 2001: 1389; our emphasis)[20]

---

19 …, because it may never be decided whether the error has had an impact on the content of the decision of the tribunal or not. Speculations concerning whether a correctly composed tribunal would presumably have reached the same decision are not allowed.

20 The reason for setting aside the award *has relative*, not absolute, *effect*. Potential causality, however, is enough. […] The evidence for causality normally has to be presented by the

The cited studies (Stein/Jonas 2003; Lüke/Wax 2001) both mention the vague expression *und anzunehmen ist* and the hypothetical framework related to the interpretation of this modalised infinitive. The indeterminacy of a modal value is due not only to its gradience (from possibility to necessity), but results chiefly from its combination with the verb *annehmen* ('to presume') which — being a lexical marker of epistemic modality — expresses an inferential process. Endicott (2000: 4) observes that "whether interpretative considerations are part of the law or not, there is no reason to think that they tend to eliminate indeterminacy." Hedges and mitigators (*Aufhebungsgrund wirkt relativ …uU [= unter Umständen] … dürfte etwa anzunehmen sein … idR [= in der Regel] … wohl selten*) in the aforesaid quotation signal that the interpreter of this provision intends to avoid exact, unequivocal attribution of truth values, thus suggesting that indeterminacy is both "pervasive and obdurate" (Endicott 2000: 7).

Vague qualifiers

The meaning of context-bound adjectives and adverbs in such collocations as *in* ***angemessener*** *Frist* ('without undue delay'), *in* ***geeigneten*** *Fällen* ('where appropriate') is intrinsically vague; these items sometimes co-occur with lexical markers in the semantic field of 'evaluation' (e.g. *nach* ***pflichtgemäßen*** *Ermessen* / 'at its discretion'). Verbal phrases like *berücksichtigen* / *Rechnung tragen* ('have regard' / 'have due regard') or *in Erwägung ziehen* ('take into account') also belong to these "weighing and balancing markers" (Fjeld 2001: 648). While the former occur rather frequently in ZPO, the latter and the above-mentioned discretion markers (see Section 2.4) were not found in IPRG.

A clear hedging function is played by qualifying inserts signalling possible exceptions or alternatives — e.g. *in der Regel* ('in general'), *aus einem anderen Grund* / *aus anderen Gründen* ('for any other reason' / 'otherwise') — which, however, only occur infrequently in both statutes.[21]

Time phrases such as *unverzüglich* ('without undue delay') and *rechtzeitig* ('in good time /with sufficient advance') are also linked to

party that wants to set aside the award, who *may possibly* find help in the concrete presumption of possible influence; the causal chain is only hypothetical. Causality *presumably exists* for example in the case of errors in the composition of the tribunal or if general procedural requirements are not met; unimportant procedural errors […] *would normally hardly* influence the award.

21 For hedging in academic discourse and discipline-specific writing, see Hyland (e.g. 1998).

vagueness and indeterminacy. Insofar as they pertain to the field of vague legal concepts (*unbestimmte Rechtsbegriffe*), their interpretation depends upon specialised knowledge of conventional norms in the relevant jurisdiction. At the same time, the definitions themselves (which may appear the Code or in commentaries) confirm the intrinsic vagueness of such terms and phrases. An example of this is the definition of *unverzüglich* ('without undue delay'), which makes it clear how in legal terms the evaluation of time limits depends on individual factors and is therefore necessarily context-bound:

> Unverzüglich
> ➔ ohne schuldhaftes Zögern; Entscheidend ist also, wo das Gesetz diesen Ausdruck gebraucht, nicht das (objektive) Sofort, sondern die (subjektive) Zumutbarkeit alsbaldigen Handelns. (Creifelds 2000: 1383, see also German Civil Code: BGB § 121 I) [22]

Conclusions and perspectives of further research

As argued by Channell (1994: 196–197), "vague expressions [...] are part of the linguistic repertoire of the competent language user, who uses them to accomplish particular communicative goals." This is particularly true for discretion markers in legislative writing and especially in contexts like arbitration, where the flexible nature of proceedings depends on room for interpretation.

Qualifying inserts are integral features of argumentative structures in legislative provisions but they do not necessarily eliminate vagueness, chiefly because of 'internal' qualifiers which contribute significantly to the negotiation of scope and application. In the corpus investigated here, such items occurred mainly within operational qualifications.

Culturally bound drafting traditions like those illustrated above call for further research. In particular, the use of hedges and discretion markers as well as interpretative practices related to the pragmatic features of legislative writing seem to yield useful insights into the interaction between legal and linguistic indeterminacy but also into the issue of whether, and to what extent, German-speaking countries do or do not employ similar strategies for dealing with vagueness and indeterminacy in normative provisions.

---

22 As for the socio-cultural influence on legal discourse and the interpretation of rules, also cf. White (1982: 433).

REFERENCES

Bhatia, V. K. (1983) *An Applied Discourse Analysis of English Legislative Writing* (Ph.D. Thesis). University of Aston, Birmingham.

Bhatia, V. K. (1993) *Analysing Genre: Language Use in Professional Settings*. London: Longman.

Bhatia, V. K. (2005) Specificity and Generality in Legislative Expression: Two Sides of the Coin. In Bhatia, V. K., Engberg, J., Gotti, M. and Heller, D. (eds.), *Vagueness in Normative Texts*. Bern: Peter Lang.

Bhatia, V. K. and Candlin, C. N. (2004) Analysing Arbitration Laws across Legal System. *Hermes* 32, 13–43.

Bhatia, V. K., Engberg, J., Gotti, M. and Heller, D. (2005a) *Vagueness in Normative Texts*. Bern: Peter Lang.

Bhatia, V. K., Engberg, J., Gotti, M. and Heller, D. (2005b) Introduction. In Bhatia, Engberg, Gotti, and Heller (eds.), (2005a).

Channell, J. M. (1994) *Vague Language*, Oxford: Oxford University Press.

Christensen, R. and Sokolowski, M. (2002) Wie normativ ist Sprache? Der Richter zwischen Sprechautomat und Sprachgesetzgeber. In *Sprache und Recht*, Ulrike Haß-Zumkehr (ed.), 64–79. Berlin / New York: de Gruyter.

Creifelds, C. (2000) *Rechtswörterbuch*, begründet von Carl Creifelds, herausgegeben v. Klaus Weber, 16., neubearbeitete Auflage, München: Beck.

Crystal, D. and Davy, D. (1969) *Investigating English Style*. London: Longman.

Endicott, T. A. O. (2000) *Vagueness in Law*, Oxford: Oxford University Press.

Endicott, T. A. O. (2005) "The Value of Vagueness." In Bhatia, Engberg, Gotti, and Heller (eds.), (2005a).

Engberg, J. (2002) Legal meaning assumptions — what are the consequences for legal interpretation and legal translation? *International Journal of the Semiotics of Law* 15–4: 375–388.

Engberg, J. (2004) Statutory Texts as Instances of Language(s) — Consequences and Limitations on Interpretation. *Brooklyn Journal of International Law* 29–3: 1135–1166.

Fjeld, R. V. (2001) Interpretation of Indefinite Adjectives in Legislative Language. In F. Mayer (ed.), *Language for Special Purposes: Perspectives for the New Millennium*, 643–650. Tübingen: G. Narr.

Hahn, W. V. (1998) Vagheit bei der Verwendung von Fachsprachen. In Hoffmann, L., Kalverkämper, H. and Wiegand, H. E. (eds.), *Fachsprachen. Languages for Special Purposes*. 378–383. Berlin / New York: de Gruyter.

Heller, D. (2003) Prinzipien der Textgestaltung und der Gebrauch von Konditionalsätzen im deutschen Schiedsverfahrensrecht. In Bhatia, V. K., Candlin, C. N. and Gotti, M. (eds.), *Legal Discourse in Multilingual and Multicultural Contexts*, 287–312. Bern: Peter Lang.

Hyland, K. (1998) *Hedging in Scientific Research Articles*. Amsterdam: Benjamins.

Joseph, J. E. (1995): Indeterminacy, Translation and the Law. In M. Marshall (ed.), *Translation and the Law*, 13–36. American Translators Association Scholarly Monograph Series, vol. VIII. Amsterdam/Philadelphia: Benjamins.

Lakoff, G. (1972) Hedges: A Study in Meaning Criteria and the Logic of Fuzzy Concepts. In *Papers from the 8th Regional Meeting*, 183–228. Chicago Linguistic Society.

Lüke, G. and Wax, P. (ed.) (2001) *Münchener Kommentar zur Zivilprozessordnung*, Bd. 3, 2. Auflage: München Beck.

Nussbaumer, M. (2000) Textlinguistik für die Gesetzgebung. In Veronesi, D. (ed.), *Linguistica giuridica italiana e tedesca. Rechtslinguistik des Deutschen und des Italienischen*, 195–208. Padova: Unipress.

Pinkal, M. (1981) Semantische Vagheit: Phänomene und Theorien, Teil I. *Linguistische Berichte* 70: 1–26.

Pinkal, M. (1985) *Logik und Lexikon — die Semantik des Unbestimmten*, Berlin/New York: De Gruyter.

Solan, L. M. (1993) *The Language of Judges*. Chicago and London: University of Chicago Press.

Soffritti. M. (1999) Textmerkmale deutscher und italienischer Gesetzesbücher: Übersetzung und kontrastive Analyse. In P. Sandrini (ed.), *Übersetzen von Rechtstexten: Fachkommunikation im Spannungsfeld zwischen Rechtsordnung und Sprache*, 119–135. Tübingen: Gunter Narr.

Stein / Jonas (2003) *Kommentar zur Zivilprozessordnung*, 22. Aufl. bearbeitet von Christian Berger, Reinhard Bork, Peter Schlosser et al., Tübingen: Mohr Siebeck.

Thomas, H. and Putzo, H. et al. (1999) [Erläuterung zu] *Zivilprozeßordnung mit Gerichtsverfassungsgesetzen, dem Brüsseler EWG-Übereinkommen und dem Luganer Übereinkommen über die gerichtlicher Entscheidungen in Zivil- und Handelssachen sowie dem Anerkennungs- mund Vollstreckungsgesetz*, 22. neubearbeitete Auflage, München: Beck.

White, J. B. (1982) The Invisible Discourse of the Law: Reflections on Legal Literacy and General Education. *Michigan Quarterly Review*: 420–438.

Materials: Arbitration Laws of Germany (ZPO) and Switzerland (IPRG)

ZPO: Zivilprozessordnung, 10. Buch: Schiedsrichterliches Verfahren: §§ 1025–1066 (1998).

IPRG: Bundesgesetz über das Internationale Privatrecht, 12. Kapitel: Internationale Schiedsgerichtsbarkeit: Art. 176–199 (1989).

APPENDIX

National statutes on arbitration (German ZPO and Swiss IPRG) in comparison to the UNCITRAL Model Law on Commercial Arbitration

UNCITRAL Model Law	**ZPO 1998 §§ 1025–66 English**	**ZPO 1998 §§ 1025–66 German**	**IPRG Art. 176–194**
Chapter I: General Provisions (Art. 1–6)	Chapter I: General provisions (section 1025–28)	1. Abschnitt: Allgemeine Vorschriften (§§ 1025–28)	I. Art. 176 Geltungsbereich. Sitz des Schiedsgerichtes II. Art. 177 Schiedsfähigkeit
Chapter II: Arbitration Agreement (Art. 7–9)	Chapter II: Arbitration agreement (section 1029–33)	2. Abschnitt: Schiedsvereinbarung (§§ 1029–33)	III. Art. 178 Schiedsvereinbarung
Chapter III: Composition of Arbitral Tribunal (Art. 10–15)	Chapter III: Constitution of arbitral tribunal (section 1034–39)	3. Abschnitt: Bildung des Schiedsgerichts (§§ 1034–39)	IV. Art. 179 Schiedsgericht 1. Bestellung Art. 180 2. Ablehnung eines Schiedsrichters
Chapter IV: Jurisdiction of Arbitral Tribunal (Art. 16–17)	Chapter IV: Jurisdiction of arbitral tribunal (section 1040–41)	4. Abschnitt: Zuständigkeit des Schiedsgerichts (§§ 1040–41)	
			V. Art. 181 Rechtshängigkeit
Chapter V: Conduct of Arbitral Proceedings (Art. 18–27)	Chapter V: Conduct of arbitral proceedings (section 1042–50)	5. Abschnitt: Durchführung des schiedsrichterlichen Verfahrens (§§ 1042–50)	VI. Art. 182 Verfahren 1. Grundsatz Art. 183 2. Vorsorgliche und sichernde Maßnahmen Art. 183 3. Beweisaufnahme Art. 184 4. Weitere Mitwirkung des staatlichen Richters
			VII. Art. 186 Zuständigkeit
Chapter VI: Making of Award and Termination of Proceedings (Art. 28–33)	Chapter VI: Making of award and termination of proceedings (section 1051–58)	6. Abschnitt: Schiedsspruch und Beendigung des Verfahrens (§§ 1051–58)	VIII. Sachentscheid Art. 187 1. Anwendbares Recht Art. 188 2. Teilentscheid Art. 189 3. Schiedsentscheid

Chapter VII: Recourse against Award (Art. 34)	Chapter VII: Recourse against award (section 1059)	7. Abschnitt: Rechtsbehelf gegen den Schiedsspruch (§ 1059)	IX. Endgültigkeit, Anfechtung Art. 190 1. Grundsatz Art. 191 2. Beschwerdeinstanz X. Art. 192 Verzicht auf Rechtsmittel
Chapter VIII: Recognition and Enforcement of Awards (Art. 35–36)	Chapter VIII: Recognition and enforcement of awards (section 1060–61)	8. Abschnitt: Voraussetzungen der Anerkennung und Vollstreckung von Schiedssprüchen (§§ 1060–61)	XI. Art. 193 Vollstreckbarkeits-bescheinigung XII. Art. 194 Ausländische Schiedssprüche
—	Chapter IX: Court proceedings (section 1062–65)	9. Abschnitt: Gerichtliches Verfahren (§§ 1062–65)	—
—	Chapter X: Arbitral tribunals not established by agreement (section 1066)	10. Abschnitt: Außervertragliche Schiedsgerichte (§ 1066)	—

8

Powers of the Court in the Malaysian Arbitration Act

Azirah Hashim

INTRODUCTION

This chapter focuses on the general powers of the High Court in the Malaysian Arbitration Act to ascertain similarities and differences that exist between the UNCITRAL Model Law of 1985 and the Arbitration Act of Malaysia of 1952 ("the Act"), respectively. It also examines some of the linguistic features found in the relevant sections of the Act. References to related cases are included to illustrate the judicial interpretation of the language in the Act in the different sections involving powers of the High Court and the implications of the language used.

The High Court has a vast range of powers under the different sections of the Malaysian Arbitration Act 1952 covering different aspects of arbitration. In general, the High Court has powers with respect to the appointment of arbitrators and umpires, revocation of their authority, granting of extension of time for the making of an award by the arbitrator, or commencement of arbitration proceedings under an arbitration agreement which has a time limit clause, or mandatorily requiring any special case to be stated by the arbitrator or umpire for its decision.

The High Court also has powers to enforce, remit back to the arbitrator or set aside an award under some circumstances. It also has the power to give relief where the arbitrator is not impartial or the dispute between the parties involves a question of fraud. Furthermore, the High Court is also given the power to deal with and make orders in respect of costs, fees and interest in arbitration matters. Lastly, the High Court is empowered to make rules for giving effect to the provisions of the Arbitration Act and to delegate all or any of its jurisdiction on the Registrar or other officer of the Court. Almost all the powers are discretionary, and the court is at liberty to exercise its power in any way based on the facts and circumstances of each case as the cases included will illustrate.

The arrangement of sections in the Act is as follows:

Preliminary
Section

1. Short title
2. Interpretation

Effect of arbitration agreement, etc.

3. Authority of arbitrators and umpires to be irrevocable
4. Death of party
5. Bankruptcy
6. Power to stay proceedings where there is submission to arbitration
7. Reference of interpleader issues to arbitration

Arbitrators and Umpires

8. When reference is to a single arbitrator
9. Power of parties in certain cases to supply vacancy
10. Umpires
11. Agreement for reference to three arbitrators
12. Power of High Court in certain cases to appoint an arbitrator or umpire

Conduct of proceedings, witnesses, etc.

13. Conduct of proceedings, witnesses, etc.

Provisions as to awards

14. Time for making award
15. Interim awards
16. Specific performance
17. Awards to be final
18. Power to correct slips

Costs, fees and interest

19. Costs
20. Taxation of arbitrator's or umpire's fees
21. Interest on awards

Special cases, remission and setting aside of awards, etc.

22. Statement of case

23. Power to remit award
24. Removal of arbitrator and setting aside of award
25. Power of High Court to give relief where arbitrator is not impartial or the dispute involves question of fraud
26. Power of high Court where arbitrator is removed or authority of arbitrator is revoked.

Enforcement of award

27. Enforcement of award
28. Power of High Court to extend time for commencing arbitration proceedings
29. Terms as to costs, etc.
30. Government to be bound
31. Rules of court
32. Application of Act to statutory arbitrations
33. Application of Act
34. Act not to apply to certain arbitrations

Compared to the UNCITRAL Model Law which has few references to 'court', the Malaysian Arbitration Act has references to 'the High Court' several times as section headings. The High Court is also referred to in many of the sections in the Act, for example, with regard to stay of proceedings, appointment of arbitrators and enforcement of award. References to 'court' in the Model Law is found in Article 6.

> Article 6. Court or other authority for certain functions of arbitration assistance and supervision
> The functions referred to in articles 11(3), 11(4), 13(3), 14, 16(3) and 34(2) shall be performed by ... [Each State enacting this model law specifies the court, courts or, where referred to therein, other authority competent to perform these functions.]

On the other hand, 'the High Court' is mentioned in section headings in the Malaysian Arbitration Act:

Section 12. Power of High Court in certain cases to appoint an arbitrator or umpire

Section 25. Power of High Court to give relief where arbitrator is not impartial or the dispute involves question of fraud

Section 26. Power of High Court where arbitrator is removed or authority of arbitrator is revoked.

Section 28. Power of High Court to extend time for commencing arbitration proceedings

The 'High Court' has been defined in Section 2 of the Act as "the High Court in Malaya or the High Court in Borneo, as the case may be". This is because of the two High Courts which are in existence in Malaysia, in Malaysia and in Borneo. The qualification 'as the case may be' indicates that the case may be brought up to either of the two High Courts in Malaysia, the High Court in Malaya or the High Court in Borneo, depending on the place of the proceedings.

GENERAL POWERS OF THE HIGH COURT: ANALYSIS OF CONTENT AND LANGUAGE

In this section, the relevant sections of the Malaysian Arbitration Act are examined to determine the extent of the general powers of the High Court in arbitration proceedings in Malaysia. This entails an analysis of the contents and language of the Act and references to related cases.

Court's powers to stay proceedings where there is submission to arbitration

Section 6 of the Arbitration Act 1952 enables the High Court to grant stay of all proceedings before it in any action initiated by a party to arbitration on an application by a party seeking to have the disputes or differences resolved through arbitration.

> Section 6. Power to stay proceedings where there is submission to arbitration
> If any party to an arbitration agreement or any person claiming through or under him commences any legal proceedings against any other party to the arbitration, or any person claiming through or under him, in respect of any matter agreed to be referred to arbitration, any party to the legal proceedings may before taking any other steps in the proceedings, apply to the court to stay the proceedings, and the court, if satisfied that there is no sufficient reason why the matter should not be referred in accordance with the arbitration agreement, and the applicant was at the time when the proceedings were commenced and still remains ready and willing to do all things necessary to the proper conduct of the arbitration, may make an order staying the proceedings.

The language of section 6 of the Act is such that if the party which opposes the application for stay can show sufficient reason why the matter should not go to arbitration, the court should not normally grant stay. (This is shown in the qualification "if satisfied that there is no sufficient reason why the matter should not be referred in accordance with the arbitration agreement and the applicant was at the time when the proceedings were commenced and still remains ready and willing to do all things necessary to the proper conduct of the arbitration"). It is of course the court that must be satisfied that there is sufficient reason for the arbitration provision not to be complied with.

Section 6 makes it clear that for considering the application for grant of stay, the proceedings commenced by any party to an arbitration agreement must be "in respect of any matter agreed to arbitration". One of the requirements of section 6 is that there must be a dispute or difference falling within an arbitration clause. In the absence of any dispute or difference between the parties, no question of stay can arise.

Despite all the conditions stated, the use of the word 'may' indicates the discretionary power of the High Court to stay all proceedings. The High Court makes the decision as to whether a certain issue is to be decided by the court or by arbitration by looking at each case. The following cases illustrate the interpretation of the qualifications "in respect of" and "if satisfied that there is no sufficient reason why the matter should not be referred to arbitration". In *Seloga Jaya Sdn. Bhd. v Pembenaan Keng Ting* 1994, the judge stated that

> It is well known that if a party can satisfy the court that the conditions for the grant of a stay under section 6 of the Act are satisfied, it does not ipso facto follow that he will be entitled as of right, for the court still retains a discretion to refuse it … We consider that in this case, an arbitrator with the necessary expertise might well be better able to deal with the issues which will arise for decision — and they would be mainly issues of fact — than a judge. (2MLJ, 1994: 99, 113)

In *Perbadanan Kemajuan Negeri Perak v Asean Security Paper Mill Sdn Bhd.* 1991, it was stated that:

> it is also a well-settled principle that where parties have agreed to refer disputes to arbitration and the court is satisfied that a dispute exists, but one of the parties to the contract commences an action to have the matter determined by the court the prima facie stand of

> the court is to stay the action and allow the parties to go to the tribunal to which they have agreed. In other words once the party applies for a stay and there is dispute within the meaning of a valid and subsisting arbitration clause the inclination of the court is that effect should be given to the arbitration clause …
>
> Once it is established that there has arisen a dispute, difference or question, the language of section 6 of the Act places on the plaintiff the burden to show that it ought not to be referred to arbitration … the fact that there is apparent weakness in the respondent's case should not be taken as an excuse to brush aside an arbitration clause to which the appellant was a party and which was being insisted on by the respondent. (3MLJ, 1991: 312)

Stay of court proceedings is not provided for in the Model Law.

Powers of the High Court in the appointment of arbitrators

Section 12 of the Act reads as follows:

> In any of the following cases:
>
> (a) where an arbitration agreement provides that the reference shall be to a single arbitrator, and all the parties do not, after differences have arisen, concur in the appointment of an arbitrator;
>
> (b) if an appointed arbitrator refuses to act, or is incapable of acting, or dies, and the arbitration agreement does not show that it was intended that the vacancy should not be supplied and the parties do not supply the vacancy;
>
> (c) where the parties or two arbitrators are at liberty to appoint an umpire or third arbitrator and do not appoint him, or where two arbitrators are required to appoint an umpire and do not appoint him;
>
> (d) where an appointed umpire or third arbitrator refuses to act, or is incapable of acting, or dies, and the arbitration agreement does not show that it was intended that the vacancy should not be supplied, and the parties or arbitrators do not supply the vacancy, …

Conditions specifying when the High Court can intervene in the appointment of an arbitrator or umpire are provided as qualifications in Section 12 of the Act:

- if all parties do not concur with the appointment of a single arbitrator
- if an arbitrator is unable to act for reasons such as death
- when a third arbitrator is required but not appointed by the parties
- when an appointed arbitrator or third arbitrator is incapable of acting

The use of binomial and multinomial expressions such as "refuses to act or is incapable of acting" make the section all-inclusive and precise.

Thus, when any of the above has occurred and it is not possible to proceed with the arbitration agreement, any of the parties

> may serve the other parties or the arbitrators, as the case may be, with a written notice to appoint or, as the case may be, concur in appointing, an arbitrator, umpire or third arbitrator, and if the appointment is not made within twenty-one days after the service of the notice, the High Court may, on application by the party who gave the notice, appoint an arbitrator, umpire or third arbitrator, who shall have the like powers to act in the reference and make the award as if he had been appointed by consent of all parties.

In some cases it has been found that an arbitrator, especially one who has to deal with issues which are technical in nature, is better able than the courts to resolve the differences between the parties. In *Seloga Jaya Sdn. Bhd. v Pembenaan Keng Ting (Sabah) Sdn. Bhd.* (2MLJ, 1994), it was found that none of the above conditions applied and the judge stated that an arbitrator with the necessary expertise might well be able to deal with the issues which will arise for decision than a judge. On the other hand, there are also instances when the court would prefer to determine the question of law in a dispute rather than to refer it to an arbitrator. For example, in *Hashim bin Majid v Param Cumaraswamy* (2MLJ, 1993), in the dispute regarding the validity of a notice of termination given to a partner of a firm, it was decided that the question of law was to be determined by the court. According to the judge:

> In this case, the plaintiff has alleged that the defendants' 'notice of termination' is in truth and fact a wrongful and unlawful expulsion of the plaintiff as a partner … What is being alleged by the plaintiff is 'a fraud upon a power'. … The plaintiff has set out in his claim the various grounds for the allegation of fraud …
>
> In my view, this is a dispute which is outside the arbitrator's power to decide. It is therefore not the type of dispute that should be referred to an arbitrator …

> An arbitrator derives his authority from the agreement between the parties and that consequently, his powers and duties are those and only those that the parties have agreed to place upon him. Accordingly, if an arbitrator has no authority at the time of his original appointment to do any act, then he has no greater authority later to agree to waive objection to that act having been done. (2MLJ, 1993: 25)

Thus it is clear that the perimeters of the arbitrator's jurisdiction must be determined with regard to the interpretation of the particular agreement in each case. This is also illustrated in *State Government of Sarawak v Chin Hwa Engineering Development Co.* whereby the judge stated:

> It is obvious that the perimeters of the arbitrator's jurisdiction must be determined having regard to the interpretation of the particular agreement in each case … Nevertheless, where the agreement provides for disputes or differences which have arisen 'in respect of', or 'with regard to' or 'under' … or 'out of' … the contract, or where similar words are used, then, taken at their full face value, it will give the arbitrator jurisdiction to decide all allegations of breach of contract by either party … (3MLJ, 1995: 245)

There are other sections in the Act which state the Court's powers with regard to the appointment or removal of an arbitrator. Section 14(3) of the Act states

> The High Court may, on the application of any party to a reference, remove an arbitrator or umpire who fails to use all reasonable dispatch in entering on and proceeding with the reference and making an award, and an arbitrator or umpire who is removed by the High Court under this subsection shall not be entitled to receive any remuneration in respect of his services.

The use of modals 'may' and the qualification 'on the application of any party to a reference' indicates that the High Court has at its discretion the power to remove an arbitrator by examining each case. The word 'shall' however stipulates clearly that an arbitrator who is removed by the High Court will not be given any remuneration for his services.

Enforcement of award

An arbitrator's award is a final and binding document and enforceable as a judgement of the High Court. This is provided for in Section 17 of the Act:

> Unless a contrary intention is expressed therein, every arbitration agreement shall, where such a provision is applicable to the reference, be deemed to contain a provision that the award to be made by the arbitrator or umpire shall be final and binding on the parties and the persons claiming under them respectively.

However, the award can be challenged and the court has held that an arbitrator's award, unlike an order of judgment and court, does not immediately allow the party to levy execution against the assets of the losing party. The award, until it is converted into a judgment or order of the court is not final and binding on the parties and may be challenged by the parties.

An arbitrator's award that did not comply with the said requirements may be set aside or remitted by the court according to sections 23 and 24 of the Act. Only when an arbitrator has committed a clear error of law may the court set aside or remit the award to the arbitrator for further consideration. This can be seen in the sections below and the interpretation of the sections by the judge in the following case, *Ong Guan Teck and Ors v Hijjas*.

> Section 23: Power to remit award
> (1) In all cases of reference to arbitration, the High Court may from time to time remit the matters referred, or any of them, to the reconsideration of the arbitrator or umpire.
> (2) Where an award is remitted, the arbitrator or umpire shall, unless the order otherwise directs, make his award within three months after the date of the order.
>
> Section 24: Removal of arbitrator and setting aside of award
> (1) Where an arbitrator or umpire has misconducted himself or the proceedings, the High Court may remove him.
> (2) Where an arbitrator or umpire has misconducted himself or the proceedings, or an arbitration or award has been improperly procured, the High Court may set the award aside.
> (3) Where an application is made to set aside an award, the High Court may order that any money made payable by the award

> shall be brought into court or otherwise secured pending the determination of the application.

Section 23 (2) states that the High Court may remit the matters to the reconsideration of the arbitrator or umpire. However, Order 69 rule 4(1) of the Rules of the High Court provides that an application to remit an award under section 23 may be made within six weeks after the award has been made and published. In this case there was a delay of four months after expiry of the period required by Order 69 rule 4. Given this limitation to section 23, the applicants would have to satisfy the court that there were good grounds for the delay and sufficient merit for the award to be remitted to the arbitrator. In considering the matter, the judge was not able to grant the extension of time to the applicants.

The interpretation of the section 24 of the adverbial "where an arbitrator or umpire has conducted himself wrongly or the proceedings or the award has been improperly procured" can be seen in *Ong Guan Teck and Ors v Hijjas*, the judge stated:

> As referred to earlier in the judgment section 23 of the Arbitration Act 1952 seems to confer a wide discretion for the court to remit an award. However, the power of the court to set aside an award is not unlimited and section 24(2) of the Act provides that the High Court may set aside an award only where an arbitrator or umpire has misconducted himself or the proceedings or the award had been improperly procured. The language of section 24(2) would seem to be rather narrow and limited. In other words, the power of the High Court to set aside an award is restricted to cases where some form of dishonesty or bias is shown …
>
> It has also been held as settled law as early as 1897 in Montgomery Jones & Co. v. Liebenthal & Co. that the following grounds would constitute good grounds for the court to remit an award, namely:-
>
> (1) that the award is bad on the face of it;
> (2) that there has been misconduct on the part of the arbitrator;
> (3) that there has been an admitted mistake and the arbitrator asks that the matter be remitted; and
>
> where additional evidence has been discovered after the making of the award …

The judge concluded that:

> there is nothing to show that the award or any part of it, contains any error on the face of it. The applicants having "doubts", however

> genuine, could not constitute sufficient ground to remit the award. In my opinion therefore there was no merit in the application for remission. (1 MLJ, 1982: 106–107)

CONCLUSION

This paper has focussed on the powers of the High Court in the Malaysian Arbitration Act. The contents and language of the relevant sections have been examined and the interpretation of aspects of language of the Arbitration Act discussed. It appears that the High Court has a fairly extensive role in arbitration proceedings in order to ensure that the proceedings are conducted properly, with the aim of ensuring a fair and just award. The analysis reveals the extent of the general powers of the High Court and the important role of language in the Act. The influence of the High Court was seen to be a detriment to foreign parties and this led to the amendment in the Act in 1980 with the insertion of section 34.

> Section 34
>
> (1) Notwithstanding anything to the contrary in this Act or in any other written law but subject to subsection (2) in so far as it relates to the enforcement of an award, the provisions of this Act or other written law shall not apply to any arbitration held under the Convention on the Settlement of Investment Disputes Between States and National of Other States 1965 or under the United Nations Commission on International Trade Law arbitration Rules 1976 and the Rules of the Regional Centre for Arbitration at Kuala Lumpur.
>
> (2) Where an award made in an Arbitration held in conformity with the Convention or the Rules specified in sub-section (1) is sought to be enforced in Malaysia, the enforcement proceedings in respect thereof shall be taken in accordance with the provisions of the Convention on the Recognition and Enforcement of Foreign Arbitral Awards 1958, as may be appropriate.
>
> (3) The competent court for the purpose of such enforcement shall be the High Court.

This section shows that the court's supervisory jurisdiction does not govern all arbitration proceedings. Before this section was included, the Act stipulated that the court has the power to exercise supervisory functions to ensure that the arbitration proceedings are conducted properly thus ensuring the provision of fair and just awards. This stipulation led to the reluctance of foreign parties who did not want to be subjected to the jurisdiction of the courts in Malaysia to hold their arbitrations in Malaysia. Hence, international arbitrations in Malaysia are held at the Regional Centre for Arbitration which was set up in 1978 for this purpose. The Centre functions as an independent international institution. With the amendment to the Act, all arbitrations administered by the Centre, including those held under the UNCITRAL Arbitration Rules and Rules of the Centre are excluded from the supervision of the Malaysian Courts, except with regard to the enforcement of arbitral awards. The reason for section 34 is to ensure that foreign investors have an attractive venue for arbitrating their disputes.

REFERENCES

Arbitration Act 1952 (1999) Kuala Lumpur: International Book Services.

Hashim bin Majid v Param Cumaraswamy (1993) *Malayan Law Journal* 2: 20–25.

Ong Guan Teck and Ors v Hijjas (1982) *Malayan Law Journal* 1: 105–107.

Perbadanan Kemajuan Perak, v ASEAN Security Paper Mill Sdn. Bhd. (1991) *Malayan Law Journal* 3: 309–314.

UNCITRAL Model Law. (1985).

Seloga Jaya Sdn. Bhd. v Pembenaan Keng Ting (1994) *Malaysian Law Journal* 2: 97–113.

State Government of Sarawak v Chin Hwa Engineering Development Co. (1995). *Malayan Law Journal* 3: 237–246.

9

Discourse Systems in English Arbitration Awards

Girolamo Tessuto

This chapter provides a descriptive and critical analysis of a recent specimen of an English arbitral award relative to consumer disputes which I obtained from the Chartered Institute of Arbitrators in London. The analysis will be twofold: firstly, I will examine the drafting format of the final award based on the Arbitration Scheme for the Travel Industry Rules, which focuses on a claim for compensation arising from a breach of contract in the travel industry. Secondly, I will describe and comment on the lexical, syntactic and modality realizations in this discourse type seen as language in use and social interaction, and an assessment of the understandability of the award.

THE DRAFTING SYSTEM OF AN ENGLISH AWARD

In the English practice, the drafting of an arbitral award comes at the end of dealings when the hearing is over and the arbitrator[1] is in his/her office with several notebooks full of evidence, the parties' submissions, their pleadings, and the advocates' closing submissions. At this stage the arbitrator has to decide the issues in the reference by writing the award. There is no doubt about awards enjoying their own status in English jurisdiction. Section 48 of Arbitration Act 1996 defines that, in the absence of party agreement to the contrary, an arbitrator may, in an award, make

1 In the present text, this is a sole arbitrator rather than an arbitral tribunal (collective term) as under the AA 1996.

a declaration, order payment of money, order a party to do or refrain from doing something, order specific performance of a contract, etc. Nothing here changes the *status quo ante* as regards the essence of arbitration awards. There are, however, statutory requirements as to the form of an award. Whereas under the old law there was no requirement for an award even to be in writing, s. 52 of the Arbitration Act 1996 changes that, according to which an award has to be written, signed, reasoned and dated. Despite the specificity of the English statute to lay down the essentials of a valid award, no mention is made in Practice Directions or other relevant literature about the drafting format of the award itself, i.e. in terms of the specific rules and techniques to produce an award which is more than a mechanical process of recording the terms of a transaction in writing. The fact that there are still no fixed rules or guidelines covering this process, has not changed the attitude of English jurisdiction towards emphasising the need for arbitral awards to rely more on content rather than the formal features of writing. Incidentally, this accounts for the fact that arbitrators, like lawyers, are not always drafters. The effect of this is that the modern drafting of English and international awards as conventional text types or genres associated with a specific communicative function will not only vary from one another in both format and style to take account of the sociocultural environment, but, by implication, will also determine other elements in the systemic framework. The first of these is the issue of register which includes an element of individuality as part of discourse semantics of the reasoned award, which I will discuss in detail in the next section.

Looking at the format of the award from the perspective of its structural elements (with the exclusion of the statement of reasons), three sections can be identified (see Appendix):

(a) The recitals appearing on the cover page make a continuous flowing text and emphasise that descriptive words or phrases are used to carry a particular meaning; for example, the conventional citation **IN THE MATTER OF THE ARBITRATION ACT 1996** meaning 'as regards' specifies the procedural basis of the arbitration, and the case title **AND IN THE MATTER OF AN ARBITRATION UNDER THE RULES … BETWEEN** identifies that it is an arbitration under the specified rules for the travel industry; the parties are identified using the plain English terminology Claimant/Respondents in line with the 1999 Woolf reform of civil procedure. At this point, it should be pointed out that in common with international awards it is a rule of policy not to indicate the names of the parties in the excerpts of the award and to leave out any data which might reveal identity. In this section the use of standard options is to improve the presentation of the award. For example, the use of capitals, bold print and underlining for printing awards are a feature of the house style of the Chartered Institute of Arbitrators. Moreover, capitals are used for complete words, to break up blocks of text into manageable chunks being displayed in subsequent sections.

(b) The list of the documentation of the award, that is the precedents, is placed on the cover page under the heading of **GENERAL**, these precedents being given short numbered headings with the underlined words Booking/Reference to Arbitration/Reasons for Award etc. While they are intended to describe the course of the arbitration process from its inception up to the final award in simple, ordinary language usage, these precedents not only assist the parties to understand their contents for reference but also introduce the dispositive section of the award in (c).

(c) This section contains the disposition, that is, the decisions of the arbitrator and the directions for disposing of the reference. This section is introduced by the formal, capitalised bold-typed proposition NOW, I MARCUS WILLIAM, HAVING CAREFULLY **CONSIDERED THE EVIDENCE** ..., the function of which being to signal the final and binding decisions as textualised in points 2.1 to 2.4 down to the formal, capitalised bold-typed phrase **MADE AND PUBLISHED** by me ... which then closes the award (for details see the award in the appendix).

Section (c) follows traditional English drafting practice which is to use the words "I hereby award and direct as follows" to introduce the sentences from 2.1 to 2.4, which have the advantage of being unambiguous and capable of performance by the parties to whom they refer. More specifically, this is achieved in three sentences out of four (2.2, 2.3, 2.4) using deontic "shall" in the verbal group (i.e. the standard deontic/performative form of statute, rule and regulation formats), and clearly expressing a binding obligation on recipients of the rule, as well as necessarily implying an element of futurity (the "shall" provision relates only to the period after the document's date). The fact that "shall" is avoided in sentence 2.1, in which the present indicative forms "succeeds/fails" are used instead also with a performative value, should not by reason be justified as to imply a lower level of formality and weaker deontic force than the corresponding expressions "shall succeed/shall fail". It should instead be justified in terms of the temporal configuration: *shall* provisions imply an element of futurity which is absent in the simple present forms of the lexical verbs "succeeds/fails", these verbs are not modalised and as such qualify a state of fact resulting from the arbitrator's authoritative role and decisions (cf. Šarčević this volume). Such decisions are not hedged by indications of the arbitrator's point of view of the type "In my opinion" or "According to the arbitrator"; indeed, the arbitrator objectifies his decisions by way of highly performative lexical verbs. The formal and binding use of *shall* intruding in the dispositive section of the award to import an obligation is avoided in the statement of reasons and replaced with something less harsh or heavy-handed, namely "must" in the statement of reasons. "Must" is a pointer to the linguistic reality that is common in ordinary speech like the statement of reasons (*shall* is now used only rarely). Moreover, the sentences referred to above are made concise and are limited to a single core concept which aims at being factually and legally accurate and relevant to the parties. By contrast, variously lexicalised structures appear in other English award specimens, such as "I hereby make and notify this my first award .../ And accordingly I make and publish this my final award — save as to costs — and I award and direct that ..." etc, the difference being that the type of award, whether final or interim, is fully specified. Along similar lines, international awards found in the Yearbook of the International Council for Commercial Arbitration use other combinations of the type "For the reasons set forth, it is ordered that the defendant shall ... ," as well as instances of archaic, legal jargon terms or even heavy-handed phrases of the type "having taken upon myself the burden of this reference," unlike the award under analysis which is expressed in modern and standard language.

The linguistic and structural elements of the award under examination are also supplemented by a user-friendly layout and design in which the following features emerge: the words and lines used in it are spaced so that the text does not look as if words have been squeezed into it in order to save paper, and the printing is in the same style throughout. It therefore becomes clear that central to the plain drafting format is the assumption that the parties to the document are the audience — and not the lawyers — who are being guided through a functionally structured award. It is also clear in this case that the production of a simple, well organised and neatly bound award which reads logically will encourage the parties to move forward. This will have a positive effect on costs in that it does not require attaching any supplementary explanatory award by the London Chartered Institute arbitrator. This, in turn, avoids any possible request for clarification of ambiguities in the drafting format by the parties concerned, as this specimen well illustrates.

THE STATEMENT OF 'REASONS': LINGUISTIC AND DISCOURSAL ANALYSIS

Referring back to the second point mentioned in the introduction, the approach taken in this analysis is one in which the researchers into discourse and interaction have shown great interest (Goffman 1981; Halliday 1994; Thomas 1995), with a focus on the communicative function of the statement of reasons. This approach views meaning in the arbitrator's linguistic choices and systematically relates these choices to the sociocultural framework. In this chapter it is argued that the statement of reasons as a conventionalized text type associated with a specific discourse communicative function or "speech act" in Searle's terms (Searle 1979), should be formulated primarily in terms of a consistently personal tenor of discourse, involving a great deal of reasoning (Stein and Wright 1995).

This approach raises the question: what is the proper perception of 'reasons', and of a 'reasoned award'? While the Arbitration Act does not provide a definition of reasons, s. 52(4) requires all awards to contain reasons unless the parties have agreed otherwise. The award specimen clearly illustrates that 'reasons' implies a broad notion, not only capable of alluding to the reasoning of an arbitrator strictly perceived as a cognition process, but also extending to the entire findings (issues of fact) and holdings (issues of law) on which the award is made. This notion includes the conclusions based upon those findings and holdings, the latter further including what is otherwise known in legal jargon to amount to the reasons for "an" and the reasons for "quantum". From this point of view, and as illustrated in <u>REASONS</u> of the sample text (points 3–4), 'reasons' are the means to establish the 'how', 'why', 'what' and 'where' of issues of fact (for example, stating terms of contract, facts and complaints) which are material to issues of law. Here, to use Searle's own examples of "declaratives" and "performatives" in the first person singular active simple present (Searle 1979: 12–29),[2] the statement of reasons (the arbitrator's "speech act") culminates in the declarative syntax statement

2 For details of performatives cf. Garzone (2001: 153–162).

in capitalised bold-print with the use of explicit performatives "find/hold" followed by "that"-clause as in the performative formula **I FIND AND HOLD THAT**. This formula, in its occurrence as a formal pronouncement from an authoritative source and located appropriately to break up the text of the statement of reasons, includes both the declarative force and the propositional content, the latter being textualized as "the Respondents are in breach of contract", which opens the dispositive section of the award in (c). While this performative formula can be said to carry a constitutive (thetic) value, the formula is repeated in different wording (in point 2 of the sample text) with the use of directive verbs in the performative formula **I ... HEREBY AWARD AND DIRECT** ... also in the first person active simple present, in which the illocutionary force refers to the kind of utterance being intended, that is ordering, since in sentences 2.2 to 2.4 the arbitrator disposes of the questions of success or failure and costs. Thus the grammatical patterns of the performative formulas change from a simple construction (beginning with the subjective personal pronoun *I* plus two verbal forms "find" and "hold" plus one "that"-complementary clause) to a more conventional construction (beginning with deictic function of *Now* expressing the speaker attitude towards interaction, followed by the subject pronoun *I* which is further qualified by the full name of the arbitrator). The main clause is broken by a subordinate clause introduced by the participle form "having". This positioning of the subordinate clause immediately after the subject with the mid-positioned adverb "carefully" emphasises the fundamental duty of the arbitrator to give his/her decision based on objective standards. This does not subtract from the legal impact and weight of the broken main adverb clause which is expressed in terms of archaic language "hereby award and direct" and which adds more legal authority to the award. Thus, the difference in wording between the two patterns of realization changes the tone from ordinary, everyday language as in "I find and hold" to a formal legal statement with the use of "hereby award and direct as follows". This change in tone, which maintains specificity and generic integrity of the award (as a legal document), makes it operative in the context of the award.

The above illustration of the performative functions of speech acts is in line with what Benveniste (1966: 264–65) calls "la subjectivité du discourse" to specify the authoritative source performing the action which, at the same time, allows for the award to rely on other requirements found in the 1996 statute. These are: finality — the award must not leave any point undecided — and absolute certainty — the parties must know what the arbitrator's decision is, for example, if a sum of money has to be paid, who has to pay it, and to whom.

The personal tenor underlying the statement of reasons (points 4 to 5) is realised by an expository sequence of propositions and evaluative elements and focuses on utterances as social interaction which construct meaning. In this text, however, some of the lexical, syntactic and modality realisations should be analysed.

From the point of view of lexicon and style, and in line with the tendency to draw attention to content rather than the formal features of writing I have referred to before, the statement of reasons evidences a type of language which is stripped of vocabulary and truncated in form. Plain English is achieved by the use of words and phrases in a way in which their common or natural meaning is intended to prevail over any technical meaning they may have. While lexical redundancy, legalese, Latin terms and gender bias are avoided in favour of good straightforward and concrete language, the use of words in their ordinary meaning ensures that the concepts are readable, relevant and accurately conveyed to the intended audiences. These are likely to include the client, lawyers, other professional advisers and laymen.[3] However, an exception to the prevalence of ordinary, natural language over technical language occurs in the text with seven instances of lexical technicality. These are: "pleadings" / "compensation" / "balance of probabilities" / "breach of contract" / "duty of care" / "consideration" / "admission of liability". These technical terms assure that the audience comprehends the legal meaning, not only because they are in general use, but because they are also inevitable lexical items characterising the nature and purpose of similar texts. These features are complemented by two instances of colloquial usage of "get" in 4.1.9 and 4.2.3 which are part of the common language: for example, "you get what you pay for" instead of "you receive". This choice of code adds an informal tone in the present award. In 4.1.2 the code of choice is reflected in the use of the idiomatic collocation "make something good" in place of the expressions "compensate for loss, damage, or expense". The examples of phrases in fact are found at different levels of formality, ranging from official and legal documents to casual conversation.

Clarity of language is also achieved through the use of short paragraphs and sentences, each numbered paragraph containing only one

3 For an overview of the AA 96 including the corpus under investigation cf. Tessuto (2003: 340–41).

idea. The use of paragraphs for one idea is an example of what Bhatia (1983), in legislative writing, calls "easification". In my case this is achieved by reducing information load in the overall statement of reasons, therefore aiding assimilation of content as well as being precise and all-inclusive. This process is reinforced by the frequent repetition of S + V + *that* sentence structures as in "I must prove that" / "I bear in mind that" / "it is apparent that"; this repetition in which *that* is not left out given the formal style of the writing, accelerates and plays an important role in the absorption of content. The effect is that the audience is not distracted from the content by a more varied, complex sentence structure. On average, the subject is not widely separated from the predicate in the various paragraphs throughout the text. Sentences range from a minimum of 16 to a maximum of 65 words within one single paragraph. By way of example:

> 4.1.1 In order to succeed in a claim for compensation against a tour operator, the Claimant must prove on a balance of probabilities that the Respondents have broken some term express or implied of the contract which existed between them, or failed in the duty of care which they owed to the Claimant <u>and</u> that as a result of this breach the Claimant has suffered loss.

Although the example above is not an instance of clarity of language achieved by short sentences, since the 65 word sentence exceeds the safe maximum of 22 words, as suggested in much plain English literature (Kimble 1992; Rylance 1994), it is however easy to absorb on account of conciseness of information. In this case, it is worth noticing that conciseness of the sentence runs parallel to the various ideas being expressed in the paragraph which is formulated as a compound conditional statement, which reads very much like a statutory rule, which is reported indirectly by the speaker to give rise to a successful claim for compensation. This complexity is further enhanced by the use of the underlined conjunction <u>and</u> stressing the need to unite in continuous flow rather than separate with a full stop the words or clauses which precede and follow it. The conjunctive effect is to set out the two conditions introduced by disjunctives "or" expressing two alternative types of behaviour ("breach of contract" and "failure of the duty of care") which must be fulfilled so that the claimant can successfully claim for compensation. Conciseness of information then proceeds in the second concluding sentence of 25 words with the use of the determiner "such" in the protasis. This avoids the need to refer again to antecedent conditions which are expressed in the present indicative regardless of whether they are conditions precedent, and the use of uninterrupted clause made up of subject and verbal phrase "… respondents will not be liable to pay compensation" in the apodosis. Though this sentence succinctly states the rule to be applied, it is completed with a subjective adjunct clause introduced by "however" which expresses the speaker's sympathetic attitude to the holiday makers (see the complete award in the appendix for details).

As mentioned previously, the non-neutral individual tenor and evaluative elements can be seen to establish a dynamic of different forms of meaning (interpersonal meaning) through the patterns of modality, that is, modal verbs and evaluative lexis. First of all, the first person speech role orientates the statement of reasons from the arbitrator's point of view and attitude towards the entities and propositions that he is talking about. His attitude is displayed towards the ideas expressed, towards the interaction and in the relationship among ideas in the discourse. This can, first of all, be observed in the various paragraphs where the arbitrator assesses the relevant principles and duties in which modal verbs are variously used to express the theme underlying the award, that is, the need for the claimant to prove his case. Thus in 4.1.1 "In order to succeed … the claimant must prove on the balance of probabilities that …", he reports an obligation arising from the statutory rule enshrined in the arbitration act, this being the standard of proof required of the claimant to win in a civil case (actually the arbitrator does so by connecting word-order and pronouns of the original statutory sentence more closely to his own sentence by using "that" in the first sentence and "If" to initialise the second sentence). This obligation, however objective it is legally speaking, explains how the discourse communicative function fully comes into play in the statement of reasons, in which "must" instead of "shall" is used to imply that 'the speaker shares' what he is saying and which is a pointer to a lower degree of formality in tone and more individualised content of the text compared to the previous dispositive section where "shall" is used instead. The obligation imported in "must" then moves to a subjective obligation in 4.1.2 "The parties must understand how an Arbitrator …" This use of "must" indicates that the arbitrator himself feels it is necessary for the parties to understand how disputes are usually conducted by arbitrators. This modality proceeds in the same sentence to the hypothetical "would" form of the predication as in "would adopt". In this paragraph, the obligation for the claimant to prove his case on the balance of the evidence is expressed by the arbitrator from a subjective point of view as in 4.1.2 with the use of the impersonal modality marker "It is for" in the sentence "It is for the claimant to prove ..." followed by the epistemic possibility of the predication "may not be enough to make good the case". The same attitudinal stance towards subjective obligation applies in 4.1.8 to the modal expression "I have to take into account such matters ..." It may be interesting to note that the move from "must" to the more neutral and de-personalized "It is for" modalisation (the latter being an alternative now quite acceptable as a means of creating compulsion) is a device of the arbitrator perhaps not wishing to introduce an unnecessarily adversarial attitude in the overall reasoned award which regulates the parties' relationship. The arbitrator's commitment towards the ideas expressed (epistemic modality / evidentiality) can also be observed in the use of adjectives and adverbs as in "it is apparent that" / "it is almost inevitable" / "which is most certainly" / "undoubtedly"; the use of adjectival modifiers such as "disgusting" / "offensive" / "acceptable"; and, as regards his attitude towards interaction, the choice of code "you get what you pay for" / "in my view" as referred to before. Moreover, his attitude towards the ideas expressed is also signalled in 4.2.2 by the emphatic use of auxiliary verbs "do/does" in the proposition "I do believe that the relatively disappointing facilities for children does amount to a breach of contract" to express in this context a contrastive rather than emotive emphasis on the subject of facilities. In other words, the speaker expresses a value judgment about facilities being regarded as "truly" rather than "falsely" disappointing for the children just as the claimant intended to prove his case. Similarly, the use of mid-positioned adverbs in emphatic sentences in 4.1.3 as "I simply balance the evidence" and in 4.1.5 as "I can quickly dispose of some of the complaints", exemplify the speaker's attitude to what he is saying. In 4.1.4. it is also interesting to note that the use of inverted commas for the word "lying" visually reinforces the arbitrator's value-indicating comment to emphasise that the word forms the subject of the cause of action. Finally, in 5.1 the same holds good for the word "Success" which, though being applied to a different line of argumentation, presupposes inter-textually the principle included in sub-section 61(2) of the Arbitration Act 1996 that costs follow the event when awarding costs. While the statutory phrase "costs follow the event" may raise semantic ambiguity in temporal terms, for the "cognoscenti" however it implies that a successful party should be entitled to recover his reasonable costs from the unsuccessful party. However, the statutory wording "cost follow the event" is ambiguous in that it offers no guidance to the lay client as to the specified time. However clear and unambiguous the language in the reasons for "quantum", no reference is made to the specified time in this text.

CONCLUSION

This analysis has attempted to show that the modern English arbitral award as a professional genre relies more on content than on the formal features of writing, especially the non-neutral and evaluative elements of discourse semantics. The interpersonal metafunction realised by lexico-grammatical features does indeed enhance our understanding of the role in arbitration practice of the private document, which is presented and expressed in modern, plain and effective English and is readily comprehensible for the lay or specialist audience.

While the main purpose behind linguistic and discoursal realisations of the award is to provide simple, cost effective ways of resolving *inter-partes* disputes, central to the arbitrator's attitude is his socioculturally institutionalised judgment in contexts where social behaviour needs to be controlled, and justificatory language needs to be attributed value relative to their social significance. This is also evidenced by the referential nature of the award which is coherent with the essential intertextual nature of the 1996 statutory framework.

An important aspect of the professional genre is that it is sufficiently standardized by the members of the professional community and, therefore, has "recognizable generic integrity" (Bhatia 1993; 2004). It epitomises a typically national English genre constrained to *locally relevant* aspects of communication in terms of linguistic resources, content, and discourse realisations, while nonetheless dynamically evidencing variations in practice in a global context. Future analysis should look at the way in which English for Specific Purposes (ESP) practitioners can participate more actively in the concerns of specialist (legal) communities in order to provide end users with a deeper understanding of the functional use of language in professional domains, bearing in mind local contraints.

REFERENCES

Arbitration Act 1996 (AA 1996). Available at: www.hmso.gov.uk (Legislation — United Kingdom — Acts of the UK Parliament — full text: Public Acts — 1996).

Benveniste, É. (1966) De la subjectivité dans le langage. In *Problèms de linguistique générale*. Paris : Gallimard, 1: 258–266.

Bhatia, V. K. (1983) "Simplification v. Easification: The Case of Legal Texts". *Applied Linguistics* 4, 1: 42–54.

Bhatia, V. K. (1993) *Analysing Genre: Language Use in Professional Settings*. London: Longman.

Bhatia, V. K. (2004) *Worlds of Written Discourse*. London: Continuum.

Garzone G. (2001) Deontic Modality and Performativity in English Legal Texts. In Gotti and Dossena (eds.), *Modality in Specialized Texts. Selected Papers of the 1st CERLIS*, 153–170.

Goffmann, E. (1981) *Forms of Talk*. Philadelphia: University of Pensylvania Press.

Halliday, M. A. K. (1994) *An Introduction to Functional Grammar* (2nd ed). Melbourne and Auckland: Arnold.

Kimble, J. (1992) Plain English: A Charter for Clear Writing, 9 *Thomas M. Cooley Law Review*, 25ff.

The London Chartered Institute of Arbitrators (2001) "Rules: Reasoned Award", in *Arbitration Scheme for the Travel Industry*. London.

Rylance, P. (1994) *Legal Writing and Drafting*. London: Blackstone Press.

Searle, J. R. (1979) *Expression and Meaning*. Cambridge: Cambridge University Press, 12–29.

Stein, D. and Wright, S. (eds.) (1995) *Subjectivity and Subjectivisation: Linguistic Perspectives*. Cambridge: Cambridge University Press.

Thomas, J. (1995) *Meaning in Interaction*. London and New York: Longman.

APPENDIX

PRECEDENT FOR ABTA ARBITRATION AWARD
Case Reference: ___________
IN THE MATTER OF THE ARBITRATION ACT 1996

AND IN THE MATTER OF AN ARBITRATION UNDER THE RULES OF THE ARBITRATION SCHEME FOR THE TRAVEL INDUSTRY (1994 EDITION)

BETWEEN

____

Claimant
-and-

____

Respondents

1. GENERAL

1.1 Booking On or about [**date of booking**] the Claimant entered into a contract with the Respondents for a holiday to [**where**] departing on [_______________] and returning on [_____________] at a total cost of [£_________] for [__] adults and [__] children, including return flights from [__________], transfers to and from the overseas airport, accommodation in the [_________] and the services of the Respondents' representative in the resort.

1.2 Reference to Arbitration Disputes and differences have arisen between the parties over the terms of the contract which, being unable to resolve amicably, they have agreed to refer to arbitration under the Rules of the Arbitration Scheme for the Travel Industry (the ABTA Scheme Rules).

1.3 Resolution by documents only The parties have agreed that the Arbitrator should decide the case solely on the documents which have been submitted by them.

1.4 Appointment of Arbitrator In accordance with the ABTA Scheme Rules I was appointed Arbitrator by the Vice President of the Chartered Institute of Arbitrators on [_________] and on [_________] I accepted that appointment.

1.5 Pleadings [**Set out timetable and special directions given**]

1.6 Reasons for Award The reasons upon which this Award is based are set out and annexed to this Award and form part of the Award.

2. NOW I, MARCUS WILLIAM REID RUTHERFORD, HAVING CAREFULLY CONSIDERED THE EVIDENCE AND WRITTEN SUBMISSIONS OF THE PARTIES HEREBY AWARD AND DIRECT AS FOLLOWS

2.1 The Claimant's Claim [succeeds] [in part] [fails] against the Respondents [and is dismissed].

2.2 The Respondents shall pay to the Claimant the sum of £________ and no more in respect of his claim.

2.3 The Respondents shall pay to the Claimant the sum of £______ in respect of his costs.

Or

2.4 The Claimant shall however pay to the Respondents the sum of £____ in respect of their costs.

MADE AND PUBLISHED by me, MARCUS WILLIAM REID RUTHERFORD, at 12 Bloomsbury Square, London WC1A 2LP on [__] day of [___________] 2001

....

M W R Rutherford

Case Reference:________________

[______________] –v- [_____________]

<u>REASONS</u>

These reasons are given with and form part of this Award

3. FACTS AND ISSUES

3.1 The Claimant has set out his claim fully on the Claim form and in the correspondence to which he refers. Although I have of course read all the documents submitted by both parties, I do not need to deal with each and every dispute of fact in this Award. ABTA arbitrations are intended to be simple, cost effective ways of resolving disputes.

3.2 [**Set out relevant terms of the contract and the facts**]

3.3 The Claimant makes a number of complaints which are fully set out in the correspondence and particularly his letter of [___________]. [**Set out complaints**].

3.4 The Claimant asks for a full refund of the cost of the holiday in the sum of [£________], plus [£__________] compensation in respect of the emotional upset and distress experienced.

3.5 The Respondents say that everything has been provided which was promised in the brochure and that there has been no breach of contract. They deal with each and every allegation made by the Claimant. [**Set out the defence in brief**]

3.6 The Respondents made an offer of compensation of £______ to settle the matter, but this was rejected by the Claimant.

4. I FIND AND HOLD THAT

4.1 The Respondents are in breach of contract, [but only in relation to part of the holiday].

Reasons

4.1.1 In order to succeed in a claim for compensation against a tour operator, the Claimant must prove on a balance of probabilities that the Respondents have broken some term express or implied of the contract which existed between them, or failed in the duty of care which they owed to the Claimant and that as a result of this breach the Claimant has suffered loss. If no such breach or loss is proved, the Respondents will not be liable to pay compensation however disappointed or upset the holiday-makers are.

4.1.2 The parties must understand how an Arbitrator approaches this type of dispute, which is no different in its essential elements from the approach which a judge would adopt in a Court of Law. It is for the Claimant to "prove" his case on the balance of the evidence, and mere assertion, no matter how strongly expressed, may not be enough to make good the case. ABTA arbitrations are not however intended to be dealt with as strictly as if they were High Court or County Court litigation.

4.1.3 It is apparent that the Claimant misunderstands the role of the Arbitrator in such a dispute. I simply balance the evidence which is presented to me, and it is no part of my function to carry out an independent investigation of the facts by for instance, contacting witnesses. If their evidence is said to be relevant, then it should have been brought into this dispute.

4.1.4 It is almost inevitable in such an arbitration that conflicts of evidence arise, and the mere fact that the Arbitrator finds in favour of one party on a particular issue does not mean that the other is deliberately telling an untruth. Generally, it is not helpful to accuse one side or the other of "lying", and it is unnecessary for me to do so.

4.1.5 The starting point is to look at what the Respondents have contractually agreed to provide, which is why I set out parts of the relevant terms of the contract earlier in this Award. I can quickly dispose of some of the complaints made where the Claimant has failed to prove his case.

4.1.6 [**Set out reasons in detail**]

4.1.7 Complaints about food are very difficult to assess objectively, because what may for one guest be disgusting and offensive, may for another be perfectly acceptable. Whether food is acceptable is largely a cultural issue, and it is not helpful to import English standards into the food and culture of a different society.

4.1.8 The correct approach in relation to such complaints, is to start by looking at what was offered as part of the contract. The next step is to try to assess whether the standard of what was on offer actually came up to its contractual promise. The fact that the Claimant did not like the food is not enough for compensation to be payable, and I have to take into account such matters as the standard of the hotel, the price paid for the holiday, what other guests said about the food, the menus which were offered over the period in question, and complaints made at the time.

4.1.9 I bear in mind that the hotel was rated "Three Globes" in the Respondents' brochure, which is most certainly not at the luxury end of the scale. The total cost of the holiday was [£______] for a family of four for 7 nights on a half board basis. When one takes into account the cost of the flights, the fact that transfers to and from the foreign resort were included, as was the accommodation, this was not an expensive holiday. It is as true to say of a holiday as it is with any other purchase, that you get what you pay for, and in my view the Claimant's expectations were too high.

4.1.10 [**Set out mitigation if this is an issue**]

4.2 <u>The appropriate compensation payable is [£] and no more</u>.

Reasons

4.2.1 The Claimant asks for the full cost of the holiday to be reimbursed. A full refund is only justified if there has been a total failure of consideration — that is, if the Claimant did not receive anything for the price he paid. Plainly this is not the case, and the Claimant is only entitled to damages for the relatively minor breach of contract I have identified.

4.2.2 However, I do believe that the relatively disappointing facilities for children does amount to a breach of contract for which the Claimant must be compensated. Undoubtedly this detracted from the enjoyment of the holiday, which should have been an occasion for the Claimant and his party to relax. Since his children are of an age also to have had their enjoyment spoiled, my assessment is that each member of the family is entitled to the sum of [£______], or [£______] in total.

4.2.3 The Respondents offered the Claimant [£_______] to settle the matter, but he chose not to accept the offer. That of course is entirely a matter for him, but it does affect the order for costs which I am obliged to make. The fact that the offer was made is not to be taken as an admission of liability on the part of the Respondents. It is costly and time consuming for a tour operator to become involved in a dispute which leads to arbitration, and it is often cheaper for them to pay something simply to get rid of it. It is also a fact that an early offer to settle may help to preserve a client relationship which would otherwise be destroyed in the course of an arbitration or litigation.

5. COSTS

5.1 The normal rule in litigation and arbitration is that the losing party pays the costs of the successful party. "Success" means obtaining an award greater than would have been available by compromise or offer from the other side. In this case, the Claimant's claim has succeeded but not to the extent of the sum offered by the pondents to settle the matter without recourse to arbitration, and the Claimant must pay the Respondents' costs.

5.2 The ABTA Scheme Rules limit the Arbitrator's discretion to order costs and provide that "the Arbitrator may, at his discretion, direct the reimbursement by one party of the other's registration fee".

5.3 It is therefore appropriate for the Claimant to pay the Respondents' costs limited to the amount of the registration fee, and I so order.

Source: The London Chartered Institute of Arbitrators (2001) "Rules," in *Arbitration Scheme for the Travel Industry*. London.

10

Rhetorical Strategies in Arbitration Law

Anna Trosborg

INTRODUCTION

The two primary functions of law are the ordering of human relations and the restoration of social order when it breaks down. With regard to the latter, we are concerned with the way in which language is used to maintain justice in cases of conflict, either between citizens in the case of civil law or between the individual and the state in the case of criminal law. Arbitration law is a particular case of resolving conflict within civil law.

With regard to text type, the contextual focus of arbitration law is the instructional text type. Two subtypes have been specified by Hatim and Mason (1990: 156): instruction with option and instruction without option. Whereas, for example, advertising is of the former kind leaving compliance to the addressee, arbitration law is an instance of instruction without option.

Although the language of the law is primarily in the written mode, the statute is distinguished from other modes of written discourse in that it is written later to be printed as a public document relating to the members of society. The mode of a statute is to be universal, not esoteric, and, in principle, accessible to all members of a society. As a statute, arbitration law is a highly serious document of ultimate authority, which needs careful expression. The language used in "the ordering of human relations" is concerned with a particular style used for the specific purpose of laying down the law. As it has been stated in a number of previous studies, the language of the law is renowned for its syntactic complexity, such as sentence length and use of nominalizations, a high frequency of passive sentences, the use of complex conditionals and a high incidence of prepositional phrases (see Trosborg 1997: 14 for references). Lexical complexity is also evident. Characteristic of the legal register are technical terms, common terms with uncommon meanings, archaic expressions, and formal items (see Danet 1985: 279–80).

Generally, written legal texts demand great effort on the reader's part. For example, the meaning of a statute can be extremely difficult to grasp due to the abstract nature of statutory expression. This stems from complex content and future hypothetical reference, is often described in complex syntax, in impersonal style, and in vocabulary peculiar to the legal register (as mentioned above). It is no wonder then that many studies of legal language have been concerned with syntactic and lexical features. For a very recent study of these aspects in arbitration law, see Engberg and Rasmussen (2003).

However, another area which has been of growing interest in the study of legal genres is pragmatics (see e.g. Gunnarsson 1984; Kurzon 1986; Bowers 1989). One aspect of particular salience is communicative acts (or rhetorical functions to use Trimble's 1985 term) of legal English. Bowers (1989) has described the field of a statute as follows:

> The field of a statute is that of a real social action which carries the whole weight of law in that it is constitutionally authorized. A public statute, whether it is declaratory, remedial, codifying, enabling, or penal is concerned with the conduct of social affairs and the granting of permissions or the imposing of obligations on members of the society. (Bowers 1989: 53, also quoted in Trosborg 1997: 27)

As pointed out by Kurzon (1989: 288), very little work has been done in this field. To fill this gap, Trosborg (1997) undertook a study of the genres of statutes and contracts in the domain of contract law focussing on communicative acts (speech acts) intended to modify/regulate social behaviour.

In the present chapter, this approach is extended to the domain of arbitration law. It analyses the regulative acts in the UNCITRAL Model Law on International Commercial Arbitration and in the Arbitration Law of the People's Republic of China. The purpose is to identify rhetorical strategies fundamental to laying down the law in the domain of international arbitration and to establish their relative frequencies in Chinese Law in comparison with UNCITRAL Model Law. The focus is on the functional tenor in order to analyse communicative functions pertaining to "laying down arbitration law", i.e. regulative acts and their realisation patterns as they appear under the conditions of field, tenor and mode. Particular attention is paid to focalisation/defocalisation of the regulated party. Finally, the results are compared to those obtained for contract law (cf. Trosborg 1997).

REGULATIVE ACTS IN ARBITRATION LAW

The laying down of the law is a declaration. In national law, each statute is preceded by an enacting formula, for example, the so-called promulgation formula found in British statutes:

> BE IT ENACTED by the Queen's most Excellent Majesty, by and with the advice and consent of the Lords Spiritual and Temporal, and Commons, in this present Parliament assembled, and by the authority of the same, as follows ... (Minors' Contract Law, quoted in Trosborg 1997: 34)

In the arbitration laws in question, no such enacting formula was observed. Neither was there any use of performative verbs, such as *declare* (British English) or *authorize, entitle* and *amend* as (to be) found in American statutes (Kurzon 1989: 24). Instead, we are informed that the UNCITRAL Model Law on International Commercial Arbitration was adopted by the United Nations Commission on International Trade Law (UNCITRAL) on 21 June 1985, at the close of the Commission's annual session. In its resolution 40/72 of 11 December 1985, the General Assembly recommended

> that all States give due consideration to the Model Law of International Commercial Arbitration, in view of the desirability of uniformity of the law of arbitral procedures and the specific needs of international commercial arbitration practice. (UNCITRAL p. 14)

The model law is

> designed to meet concerns relating to the current state of national laws on arbitration. The need for improvement and harmonization is based on findings that domestic laws are often inappropriate for international cases and that considerable disparity exists between them. (UNCITRAL p. 14)

The Arbitration Law of the People's Republic of China (ALPRC) was adopted at the Ninth Standing Committee Session of the Eighth National People's Congress on 31 August 1994.

The regulation of behaviour in the laws examined was carried out by means of conferring rights, imposing obligations, stating prohibitions and outlining constitutive rules. The results appear in Table 10.1 for UNCITRAL and ALPRC in comparison with my results from English Contract Law. The rhetorical strategies used to express these communicative functions are described and exemplified in the following. The strategies comprise *action rules, definition rules* and *stipulation rules.* Action rules are "mainly meant to impose duties and obligations, to give rights, to prohibit actions, to assign power to certain members of bodies of the executive or other parties", *definition rules,* are applicable to the entire Act and are primarily meant to provide terminological explanation, and, finally, *stipulation rules* define "the domain of application of a particular act or any section of it" (cf. Gunnarsson 1984: 84, quoted in Bhatia 1994: 138–139).

The account to follow in this section is based on Trosborg 2004: 102–108, which exemplifies regulative strategies used in UNCITRAL and ALPRC. For further details, the reader is referred to this paper. When nothing else is mentioned, the examples are from UNCITRAL. In section 4, these findings are discussed in comparison to the observations for English Contract Law.

Table 10.1 Regulative Act in UNCITRAL, ALPRC and Contract Law

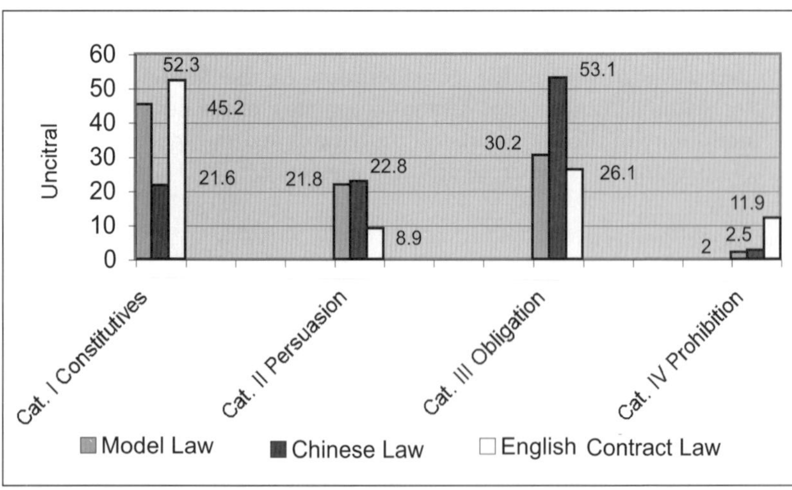

Permission

In legislation, permission issues from authority. The legislature grants permission to the body in question to perform certain acts; it does not order the body to do so, as is the case of statements of obligation. In arbitration law, statements of permission serve to establish the rights of the arbitral tribunal and the parties of the conflict. A typical rhetorical strategy is the use of the modal *may*:

> The arbitral tribunal **may** rule on its own jurisdiction, including any objection with respect to the existence in validity of the arbitration agreement. (p. 7)
>
> The arbitral tribunal **may** require any party to provide appropriate security in connection with such measure. (p. 7)
>
> If the arbitral tribunal rules as a preliminary question that it has jurisdiction, any party **may** request, within thirty days after having received notice of that ruling, the court specified in article 6 to decide the matter, which decision shall be subject to no appeal. (p. 7)

May is the predominant illocutionary device used when conferring rights. A few examples made use of the expression *be free to*:

> The parties **are free to** determine the number of arbitrators. (p. 5)
>
> The parties **are free to** agree on a procedure of appointing the arbitrator or arbitrators, subject to the provisions of paragraph (4) and (5) of this article. (p. 5)

Furthermore, *may* also occurred in examples where the act of permission is dubious:

> An arbitration agreement **may** be in the form of an arbitration clause in a contract or in the form of a separate agreement. (p. 4)

Such statements belong to the category of stipulation rules and are better classified as constitutive rules.

The verbs *could* and *need not* were each observed only once in the UNCITRAL data. In ALPRC there was one instance in which the modal *can* was used to express possibility:

> If ... , a ruling **can** be made by default. (p. 7)

Can was not used to regulate behaviour in UNCITRAL. Strategies classified as permission statements amounted to 21.8% for UNCITRAL and to 22.8% for ALPRC.

Obligation

Statements of obligation used to regulate behaviour have the illocutionary force of orders. Only one instance employing the performative verb *oblige* was found:

> Modelled on article II(3) of the 1958 New York Convention, article 8(1) of the Model Law **obliges** any court to refer the parties to arbitration if seized with a claim on the subject matter unless it finds that the arbitration agreement is null and void, inoperative or incapable of being performed. (p. 17)

Typically the modal *shall* expresses obligation in legal acts. This use of *shall*, referred to as "mandatory *shall*" is not only endowed with the meaning that the subject shall do X, it also carries the implication that if he/she doesn't, there will be sanctions. Examples of *shall* to impose obligation are:

> The arbitral tribunal **shall** decide the dispute in accordance with such rules of law as are chosen by the parties as applicable to the substance of the dispute. (p. 10)
>
> If, during arbitral proceedings, the parties settle the dispute, the arbitral tribunal **shall** terminate the proceedings, and, if requested by the parties and not objected to by the arbitral tribunal, record the settlement in the form of an arbitral award on agreed terms. (p. 10)

A number of statements employing the modal *shall* were not used to impose obligation but rather had the function of stipulation rules. These are counted and exemplified under constitutive rules.

The modals *must* and *have to* are typically used to express obligation in conversational English, but in legal contexts they are rarely observed. *Must* did not occur in ALPRC at all, and it was observed only three times in UNCITRAL:

> The award **must** be in writing and state its date. It **must** also state the reasons on which it is based, unless the parties have agreed otherwise or the award is an award on agreed terms, … (p. 20)

The verb *have to* occurred in neither.

Other modals expressing obligation are *should, ought to* and *need.* Whereas *ought to* was not observed at all, the modal *should* occurred three times in UNCITRAL and three times in ALPRC:

> These instances are listed in article 6 as functions which **should** be entrusted ... to a specially designed court or ... (p. 16)
>
> The arbitration commission director shall decide whether an arbitrator **should** withdraw ... (p. 6)

The modals *should* and *ought to* are "weak" indicators of obligation, which explains their infrequent use in arbitration law.

The modals *will* and *would* were not observed in ALPRC, whereas *will* occurred three times and *would* four times in UNCITRAL, both with the function of stipulation or prediction:

> The vast majority of situations commonly regarded as international **will** fall under this criterion. (p. 15)
>
> According to article 1(2), the Model Law as enacted in a given State **would** apply only if the place of arbitration is in the territory of that State. (p. 16)

Altogether 30.6% of the strategies classified fell in the category of statements of obligation for UNCITRAL; for ALPRC no less than 53.1% did.

So far, it appears that the modal *shall* is used to impose obligations on people; when the other modals with regulative meaning occur, they are mainly used to express stipulation rules. With regard to the use of legal *shall*, the predominant function was regulation in action rules. There were, however, a substantial number of *shall*'s which were used to define domain of application or even to provide terminological explanations. These are analysed as a separate category of constitutive rules.

Prohibition

The regulation of behaviour can also take place by issuing prohibitions, but this device is infrequent in use compared with statements of obligation. Prohibition is used in examples like "No person shall ..."; "No court shall ...". Additionally, *shall* + negation is used to state rules according to which a given law operates:

> In matters governed by this Law, **no court** shall intervene except where so provided in this Law. (p. 4)
>
> This law **shall not** affect any other law of this State by virtue of which certain disputes may not be submitted to arbitration or may be submitted to arbitration only according to provisions other than those of this Law. (p. 3)

Both laws showed a low percentage on this category (2.0% for UNCITRAL and 2.5% for ALPRC).

Constitutive rules

Statements which do not include performative verbs, or modals which function as implicit performatives, may still serve the purpose of regulating behaviour. This applies to English legislative texts as well as conversational English. Sentences used to explain or define expressions and words in the statute or to supply information concerning the application of the statute, or part of it, are constitutive rules (Kurzon 1986: 23). In UNCITRAL and ALPRC, unmarked statements outlined constitutive rules concerning definition rules and stipulation rules. A typical indicator of definition rules is the verb *mean*, but also words such as *define, constitute*, and *be* are found:

> "arbitration" **means** any arbitration whether or not administered by a permanent arbitral institution;
>
> "arbitral tribunal" **means** a sole arbitrator or a panel of arbitrators; ... (p. 3)
>
> The reference in a contract to a document containing an arbitration clause **constitutes** an arbitration agreement provided that ... (p. 5)

A typical indicator of stipulation rules is the verb *apply*; other indicators are *have, include, be deemed to, be intended to, ensure*:

> This Law **applies** to international commercial arbitration, subject to any agreement in force between this State and any other State or States. (p. 2)
>
> Such an award **has** the same status and effect as any other award on the merits of the case. (p. 10)

> ... such agreement **includes** any arbitration rules referred to in that agreement; ... (p. 3)
>
> Any written document **is deemed to** have been received if it is delivered to the addressee personally or it is delivered at his place of business, habitual residence or mailing address. (p. 4)
>
> ... his mandate **terminates**, if he withdraws from his office or if the parties agree on the termination. (p. 6)

Other verbs observed in constitutive statements are: *is given, exists, envisages, is stated, guarantees, deals with, follows closely, recognizes, expresses*, etc. There is no sharply defined distinction between definition rules and stipulation rules. Furthermore, many rules classified as constitutive rules go far beyond definition and stipulation and are part of the law *per se* regulating people's behaviour.

For constitutive rules, the observed strategies amounted to 45.2% for UNCITRAL and 21.6% for ALPRC.

A special category of constitutive rules are those involving the modal *shall*:

> The award **shall** be deemed to have been made at that place. (p. 10)
>
> The interpretation **shall** form part of the award. (p. 11)
>
> The provisions of article 31 **shall** apply to a correction or interpretation of the award or to an additional award. (p. 11)

Here we find that the typical indicator of obligation in action rules is in fact also used in stipulation rules (6.5% for UNCITRAL, 9.5% for ALPRC).

SENDER/RECEIVER REFERENCES IN ARBITRATION LAW

In legislation, the sender is the legislative body and the receivers are the citizens. In English statutes, laws passed through Parliament are preceded by the promulgation formula and signed by the sovereign. This formula, which functions as an explicit performative, contains the performative verb *enact* and has, currently, *the Queen's Most Excellent Majesty* as the expressed agent. In UNCITRAL, there is no promulgation formula, but we learn that the law was adopted by the United Nations Commission on International Trade Law (UNCITRAL) on 21 June 1985, at the close of the Commission's annual session, as mentioned in the introduction.

For ALPRC, we learn that it was adopted at the Ninth Standing Committee Session of the Eighth National People's Congress on 31 August 1994.

The relationship between sender and receiver in statutes has been described as asymmetrical (see Trosborg 1997: 30ff), in that the legislative body as regulator has an authoritative position in relation to the citizens. Legislative writing is highly impersonal and decontextualised, in the sense that its illocutionary force holds independently of who is the sender (originator) or the receiver of the document (cf. Bhatia 1993: 102). Even though the drafter, in principle, may choose to address the citizens directly, a third person point of view addressing the whole speech community of a jurisdiction is more likely to be chosen. This view reduces the immediacy of the illocution, and adds to the generality of the message. Besides, it serves the purpose of creating social distance between sender and receiver.

In face-to-face interaction, when the speaker issues a directive, the hearer is generally the intended receiver of the directive. In writing, however, a high level of explicitness is often necessary. If the writer wants to downtone the impact of the directive on the receiver, s/he may avoid mentioning the addressee as the agent of the desired act. This leaves the directive as potentially ambiguous with regard to receiver. Defocalising reference to the receiver is no problem as long as the act extends to all citizens, but if this is not the case, it must be explicitly stated to whom the act extends (see Trosborg, 1997: 105).

Focalising/defocalising reference to the regulated party

In focalising reference to the addressee, the regulator explicitly establishes the addressee as the agent of the desired act. Alternatively, reference to the addressee can be defocalised. Defocalising reference to the addressee is concerned with implicit or non-specific reference to the agent of the directive. In principle, any person may be the intended referent. For this reason, this kind of reference is useful in situations where the writer wants to suppress the identity of the agent of the desired state of affairs mentioned in the proposition. This may be done for several reasons. First of all the agent may be unknown to the writer and therefore cannot be mentioned, or establishing an agent may be of little importance. More likely, though, when we are concerned with regulatives is it that the identity of the agent is suppressed for the strategic purpose of avoiding direct ordering of the addressee. A further possibility is that the identity of the agent is supposed to be known to both parties. If this presupposition holds true, the regulative is directed at the addressee even though no explicit reference to him/her has been made.

In order to gain insight into the regulation of parties in arbitration law, an analysis was made first of all "agents" of *shall*, and thereafter, all subjects in regulating acts were subjected to analysis in order to determine the writer's focus of attention and his way of organising the content of regulation.

Agents of "shall" in arbitration law

Interest centres on the regulated part, and the crucial question to be addressed is that of focalising/defocalising reference to the citizen as addressee of the regulated act. The actants in question are referred to as "Agents", as structures with mandatory *shall* are expected to be either active sentences with human agents as subjects or passive sentences with human agents, though not in subject position. However, as shown in Trosborg (1997) agents may be suppressed from the text and subject positions may be taken by non-human agents. In Table 10.2, the analysis of Agents of *shall* is presented for both UNCITRAL and ALPRC. The results obtained for contract law are added for comparative discussion in the 'Discussion' section.

Table 10.2 Agents of "shall" in Regulative Acts

	Human actants	Agent suppressed	Non-human actants
UNCITRAL	55.6	29.6	14.8
ALPRC	69.1	21.8	9.0
Contract law	15.3	18.6	65.1

The following categories were observed. Active sentences with human agents as subjects; passive sentences with agents mentioned; passive sentences in which the human agent was "suppressed" from the text, and finally, active sentences with non-human "agents" in subject position.

In regulatives with human agents, nouns referring to individuals as well as collective nouns were used with a frequency of 55.6% for UNCITRAL and 69.1% for ALPRC. A variety of different actants occurred, such as *each party, any party, the parties, an arbitrator, the two arbitrators, the claimant, the respondent, the expert*. For collective nouns, the agents were typically *the court, the people's court*, or *the arbitral tribunal*. The agent would typically occur in subject position (49.4% for UNCITRAL and 60.8% for ALPRC):

> ... **a party** who intends to challenge an arbitrator shall, within fifteen days ... send a written statement of the reasons for the challenge to the arbitrary tribunal. (p. 6)
>
> **The court or other authority**, in appointing an arbitrator, shall have due regard to any qualifications ... (p. 6)
>
> Failing such agreement, **the arbitrary tribunal** shall determine the language or languages to be used in the proceedings. (p. 8)

The agent could also be specified in object position in passive sentences, where the subject was either a human actant (0.0% for UNCITRAL and 3.1% for ALPRC) or a non-human actant (6.2% for UNCITRAL and 5.2% for ALPRC):

> The third arbitrator shall be selected by **the litigants**, or by **the arbitration commission director** at their request. (ALPRC p. 6)
>
> The director, deputy directors, and members of the arbitration commission shall be held by **legal, economic or trade experts and persons with working experience**. (ALPRC p. 3)
>
> Failing such agreement, the place of arbitration shall be determined by **the arbitral tribunal** having regard to the circumstances of the case, including the convenience of the parties. (p. 8)

Instances of agent suppression amounted to 29.6% for UNCITRAL and 21.8% for ALPRC. Agents would either be recoverable from the context of the situation or altogether unspecified:

> ... a plea that the arbitral tribunal do not have jurisdiction shall be raised no later than the submission of the statement of the defence. (p. 7)
>
> After the award is made, a copy signed by the arbitrator in accordance with paragraph (1) of this article shall be delivered to each party. (p. 11)
>
> Any designation of the law or legal system of a given State shall be construed ... as directly referring to the substantive law of the State and not to its conflict of laws rules. (p. 10)

In the first example, the agent is recoverable from the context; in the second and third, the agent is unspecified, as interest does not centre on who delivers the copy or who construes the designation.

Alternatively, non-human "agents" would occur as subject in an active sentence, typically one in which the subject could not be given orders or assigned obligations. Consider the following examples:

> **This law** shall not affect any other law of this State by virtue of which certain disputes ... (p. 3)
>
> ... **the signatures** of the majority of all members of the arbitral tribunal shall suffice, provided that the reason for any omitted signature is stated. (p. 10)
>
> **The interpretation** shall form part of the award. (p. 11)
>
> **The provisions of article 31** shall apply to a correction or interpretation of the award or to an additional award. (p. 11)

Non-human "agents" as subjects occurred with a frequency of 14.8% in UNCITRAL and 9.3% in ALPRC.

Subjects in regulative acts in arbitration law

In order to throw further light on the use of human/non-human actants as subjects in regulative acts and their role as potential agents for the proposition identified as having illocutionary force, all subjects of regulative acts were analysed. The categorisation involved 'Human Nouns'; and non-human nouns subcategorised as 'Legal Abstract', 'Legal Concrete', 'Conditions of the Law' and finally 'Pronominal Reference'. Table 10.3 shows the proportion of each category for the two laws under investigation. The results obtained for Contract Law are added for comparison in the 'Discussion' section.

Table 10.3 Subjects in Regulative Acts (% in Arbitration Law)

Pronoun	Human Noun	Legal Abstract	Legal Concrete	Condition of the Law
UNCITRAL 6.8	36.4	4.2	35.6	16.9
ALPRC 12.8	59.0	0.6	8.3	19.2
Contract law 1.2	13.9	27.8	44.3	12.8

For UNCITRAL, the category Human Nouns amounted to 36.4%, whereas ALPRC had human subjects in no less than 59% of the cases analysed. This category involved a variety of different actants:

> Failing such agreement, **a party who intends to challenge an arbitrator** shall, within fifteen days ... send a written statement of the reasons for the challenge to the arbitral tribunal. (p. 6)
>
> **The parties** are free to agree on the language or languages to be used in the arbitral proceedings. (p. 8)
>
> ... **the arbitral tribunal** may, unless otherwise agreed by the parties, meet at any place it considers appropriate for consultation among its members ... (p. 8)

These subjects occurred in the so-called action rules.

The category Legal Abstracts extends to abstract legal concepts which are thematised in subject position:

> **The Model Law** defines an arbitration as international if "the parties to an arbitration agreement have, at the time of the conclusion of that agreement, their places of business in different States" (article 1(3)). (p. 15)
>
> **The vast majority of situations** commonly regarded as international will fall under this criterion. (p. 15)
>
> As regards the term "commercial", **no hard and fast definition** could be provided. (p. 15)
>
> It should be noted that "**recourse**" means actively "attacking" the award; a party is, of course, not precluded. From seeking court control by way of defence in enforcement proceedings (article 36). Furthermore "recourse" means resort to as court, i.e. an organ of judicial system of a State ... (p. 20)

Typically, this category involves definition rules meant to provide terminological explanation. Only 4.2% of the strategies in UNCITRAL and 0.6% in ALPRC fell in this category.

The category Legal Concrete referred to the law, or part of it. A number of constitutive statements with the law as focalised subject occurred:

> According to article 1(2), **the Model Law** as enacted in a given State would apply only if the place of arbitration is in the territory of that State. (p 16)

> **Chapter II of the Model Law deals** with the arbitration agreement, including its recognitions by courts. The provisions follow closely article II of the Convention on the Recognition and Enforcement of Foreign Arbitral Awards ... (p. 16)

Other typical actants of active sentences with non-human subjects were constitutive elements such as provision, article, arbitration clause, application, agreement, etc.:

> **The provisions of article 31** shall apply to a correction or interpretation of the award or to an additional award. (p. 11)
>
> **Article 7(1)** recognizes the validity and effect of a commitment by the parties to submit to arbitration an existing dispute ("compromise") or a future dispute ("clause compromissoire"). (p. 17)
>
> For that purpose, **an arbitration clause** which forms part of a contract shall be treated as an agreement independent of the terms in the contract. (p. 7)
>
> **An application for setting aside under article 34** must be made within three months of receipt of the reward. (p. 20)
>
> **This agreement or determination** ... shall apply to any written statement by a party, any hearing and any award, decision or other communication by the arbitral tribunal. (p. 8)

This category involved stipulation rules which define the domain of application of a particular act or any section of it (Article 8 and 9 deals with ... ; Article 26(2) obliges the expert ... , etc.).

The strategies classified as Legal Concrete amounted to 35.6% for UNCITRAL and 8.3% for ALPRC.

The category Conditions of the Law occurred in examples like the following:

> **The conditions set forth is this paragraph** are intended to set maximum standards. (p. 13)
>
> **A plea that the arbitral tribunal does not have jurisdiction** shall be raised not later than the submission of the statement of defence. (p. 7)
>
> **The majority principle** applies also to the signing of the award, provided that the reason for any omitted signature is stated. (p. 20)
>
> **The interpretation** shall form part of the award. (p. 11)

> **The award** shall state the reasons upon which it is based, unless the parties have agreed that no reasons are given or the award is an award on agreed terms under article 30. (p. 10)
>
> **The award** shall state its date and place of arbitration as determined in accordance with article 20(1). **The award** shall be deemed to have been made at that place. (p. 10)
>
> Unless otherwise agreed by the parties, **the arbitral proceedings** in respect of a particular dispute commence on the date on which a request for that dispute to be referred to arbitration is received by the respondent. (p. 8)
>
> **The majority principle** applies also to the signing of the award, provided that the reason for any omitted signature is stated. (p. 20)

Grounds for 'setting aside' were formulated as follows:

> Although the ground for setting aside are almost identical to those for refusing recognition or enforcement, two practical differences should be noted: Firstly, the ground relating to public policy, including non-arbitrability, may be different in substance, depending on the State in question (i.e. State of setting aside or State of enforcement). Secondly, and more importantly, the grounds for refusal or recognition are valid and effective only in the State (or States) where the parties seek recognition and enforcement … (p. 21)

The proportion of non-human nouns specified as Condition of the Law amounted to 16.9% for UNCITRAL and 19.2% for ALPRC. The categories Legal Concrete and Conditions of the Law state the law and the principles on which it is based. There was no sharp distinction between the two categories.

The category Pronominal Reference was used as anaphoric reference to actants already mentioned. Interest centres on personal pronouns. References could be to persons, to collectives, or to non-human actants:

> When a person is approached in connection with his possible appointment as an arbitrator, **he** shall disclose any circumstances likely to give rise to justifiable doubts as to his impartiality or independence. (p. 6)
>
> If the arbitral tribunal considers the request to be justified, **it** shall make the correction or give the interpretation within thirty days of receipt of the request. (p. 11)

> This provision is significant in two respects. **It** grants the parties the freedom to choose the applicable substantive law, which is important in view of the fact that a number of national laws do not clearly recognize that right. (p. 19)
>
> Autonomy of the parties to determine the rules of procedure is of special importance in international cases since **it** allows the parties to select or tailor the rules according to their specific wishes and needs, unimpeded by traditional domestic concepts and without the earlier mentioned risk of frustration. (p. 19)

Reference could also be to a preceding sentence:

> If … an arbitrator withdraws from his office or a party agrees to the termination of the mandate of the arbitrator, **this** does not imply acceptance of the validity of any ground referred to in this article or article 12(2). (7)

In the present study, pronominal reference to the focalised subject occurred with a frequency of 6.8% in UNCITRAL and 12.8% in ALPRC. When reading the two laws, pronominal reference did not generally lead to problems. Reference is less clear, though, in the following example:

> Provisions which empower the arbitral tribunal to carry out its task even if one of the parties does not participate are of considerable practical importance since, as experience shows, it is not uncommon that one of the parties has little interest in co-operating and in expediting matters. **They** would, thus, give international commercial arbitration its necessary effectiveness, within the limits of fundamental requirements of procedural justice. (p. 19)

Reference here must be to "provisions" and not to "the parties", even though the latter referent is closer to the pronoun. Compare the following examples, in which *they* clearly do refer to "the parties":

> When parties anticipate an uncertainty in this respect, **they** may wish to provide a clarification in the arbitration agreement by a more specific authorization to the arbitral tribunal. (p. 20)
>
> The Model Law gives the parties a wider range of options as regards the designation of the law applicable to the substance of the dispute in that **they** may, for example, agree on rules of law that have been elaborated by an international forum but have not yet been incorporated into any national legal system. (p. 20)

DISCUSSION

The study focused on the interpersonal function, realised through communicative acts (speech acts).

In the section "Regulative Acts in Arbitration Law", the regulative acts observed in the two laws under investigation were classified and compared. As Table 10.1 shows, the findings for the two laws are very similar on Cat. II Permission statements (21.8% vs. 22.8%), amounting to little above 1/5 of all strategies employed. The results are also very similar for Cat. IV Prohibition, which was very low on both laws (2.0% vs. 2.5%). However, when looking at Cat. III Obligation, it is apparent that strategies imposing obligation are the most frequent strategy used in ALPRC amounting to more than half the strategies used (53.1%). In comparison, UNCITRAL only has 30.2% strategies in this category. For Cat. I Constitutive rules, it was the other way round. These strategies were used in UNCITRAL with a frequency of 45.2% compared with only 21.6% in ALPRC. These findings need to be explained.

As regards Cat. III Obligation, UNCITRAL employed the widest range of modals (*shall, must, will, would, should*) even though it had the lowest score on this category, whereas ALPRC mainly employed mandatory *shall* (51.2%) (see Trosborg 2004: 109 for details). This points to a predominance of the use of *shall* in ALPRC. This tendency is also evident in Cat. I Constitutive rules, where ALPRC employs *shall* in 9.9% of the strategies used in comparison with 6.5% in UNCITRAL. This finding is observed despite the fact that as a total UNCITRAL has the double number of constitutives compared with ALPRC.

There is then less variety in the use of strategies (modals as well as constitutive rules) in ALPRC compared with UNCITRAL. This points to a 'playing-it-safe' strategy used in ALPRC with the modal *shall* as the predominant marker in regulative acts.

When comparing the results obtained on regulative strategies for UNCITRAL and ALPRC to those obtained in contract law, the predominance of constitutive rules is even greater here. In contract law, this category amounts to 60.9% compared with 45.2% in UNCITRAL and only 21.6% in ALPRC. Mandatory *shall* is used only with a frequency of 6.9% against 25.3% in UNCITRAL and 51.2% in ALPRC. This points towards an increase of the use of mandatory *shall* across the three kinds of law (contract law, UNCITRAL and ALPRC) counterbalanced by a decrease in the use of constitutive rules. Thus the findings point towards a shift away from a predominance of constitutive rules observed in contract law and UNCITRAL to a predominance of legal *shall* in ALPRC.

With regard to legal *shall* in constitutive rules, a decrease was observed from contract law to UNCITRAL (14.5% vs. 6.5%). There was, however, a slight increase on this category when the findings of ALPRC were compared to those of UNCITRAL (9.5% vs. 6.5%). The use of *shall* in constitutive rules needs to be commented on, as it has been criticised by a number of researchers. Bowers (1989) finds that *shall* is inappropriate in expressions where there is no agent. Stipulations of the kind *it shall be lawful* and *it shall de deemed* should be in the modal-less form of statements — simply *it is lawful* and *it is deemed.* Thus legal *shall* should be avoided in constitutive rules and in regulatives where no agent is present in explicit form or recoverable from context. The use of *shall* as the appropriate expression of a regulative with agent (explicit or recoverable) is recommended by Child (1992). At the same time she warns against the use of *shall* to express constitutive rules (referred to by her as "future tense"). She has emphasized the importance of "saving" *shall* for orders, and warns against the misuse of *shall* referred to as the "false imperative".

> *Shall* is the most powerful word in the legislative arsenal. It must not be squandered by misuse. *Shall* must not be wasted by being used to put verbs in the future tense. The future tense is seldom needed in statutes for a legislative act applies to the ever present present. (Child 1992: 205, quoted in Trosborg 1997: 137)

As an example of a false imperative, she mentions "It shall be a felony to commit murder". Assuming that the law is presently in effect, the accurate phrasing is: "It is a felony to commit murder". According to Child, overuse of *shall* is a common error among novice drafters. They find it unnatural to write in the present tense while thinking of the future. The drafter must learn to think in terms of the time when the statute is read. If this is done, the present tense comes easily and "those invaluable *shall*'s are saved for their proper use" (to give an order).

A comment is needed regarding the use of the modal *must*. In 1989, Eagleson writes that some lawyers are now moving to replace *shall* with *must* in their documents when an obligation is being imposed or mandatory conduct is prescribed (p. 76). This claim is made to avoid confusion for the clients (not familiar with "legal *shall*") who would be likely to interpret *shall* as expressing mere futurity. The urge to use *must* is supported by e.g. Bennet (1989) and Elliott (1990), whereas, for example, Child (1992) argues against the use of *must* to impose obligation.

The use of *must* to express obligation was not observed in contract law, neither was it found in ALPRC, and it was only used with a low frequency in UNCITRAL (1.1%). Thus the recommendation to use *must* to the exclusion of mandatory *shall* has not gained ground in the laws investigated. When the "agents" of *shall* were analysed, there was an increase of human subjects across the three laws: from 15.3% in contract law to 55.6% in UNCITRAL and 69.1% in ALPRC. The same tendency was observed when all subjects in regulative acts were analysed. Here, the increase was from 13.9% in contract law to 36.4% and 59.0% in UNCITRAL and ALPRC, respectively. Instead contract law envisaged a higher percentage of Legal Abstracts (27.8%) against 4.2% in UNCITRAL and 0.6% in ALPRC, and for Legal Concretes, the differences amounted to 44.3% against 35.6% and 8.3%, respectively. This increase in focalised human subjects was counterbalanced by a decrease both in Legal Abstracts (from 27.8% in contract law to 4.2% in UNCITRAL and 0.6% in ALPRC) and in Legal Concretes (from 44.3% in contract law to 35.6% in UNCITRAL and 8.3% in ALPRC).

The category Conditions of the Law did not vary greatly across the three laws.

For Pronominal Reference, a marked increase was observed across the three laws. The most common reference markers in English and in a large number of other languages are pronouns (Baker: 1992: 181). In narrative texts, anaphoric reference utilizing pronouns is a frequent cohesive device. In news reporting and investigative journalism frequent iteration of a concept is undesirable. Instead, variation is favoured. In contrast, legal writing has sought to achieve clarity and avoid ambiguity by repeating a concept. Thus excessive use of repetition was found in contract law and pronominal reference was only used with a frequency of 1.2%. In contrast, pronominal reference in the regulative strategies amounted to 6.8% in UNCITRAL and 12.8% in ALPCR.

The corpus of contract law included laws written between 1960 and 1987, whereas UNCITRAL dates from 1985 and ALPRC from 1994. The time factor may have played a role in the selection and realisation of regulative strategies. Besides, the observed differences to contract law, in particular the higher frequency of constitutive rules and the low involvement of human agents, may be due partly to the two types of law: contract vs. arbitration. It seems that arbitration law focuses on the regulation of humans, whereas for contract law, the regulation takes to a greater extent place through formulation of constitutive rules (to a greater extent). Selective references to individual human actants, realised through a variety of human nouns such as *the party, the arbitrator, the arbitral tribunal, the claimant, the expert*, etc., are chosen to make explicit to whom the act extends. In contract law, the only human referents were *the court*, and *people*.

This does not explain the differences between the two kinds of arbitration law, however. Here the most notable differences were the increase in ALPRC compared with UNCITRAL in the use of legal *shall* to the exclusion of other modals, and of unmarked constitutive rules, in particular. As mentioned, this can be explained as a strategy of "playing it safe". Drafters adhere to the powerful force of legal *shall* and still tend to overuse it even in constitutive rules.

Summing up, an increase was observed in the use of obligation strategies: from 17.5% in contract law to 30.2% in UNCITRAL and 53.1% in ALPRC. This increase was counterbalanced by a decrease in constitutive rules, from 60.9% in contract law to 45.5% in UNCITRAL and 21.6% in ALPRC. This tendency towards regulation through action rules with direct mention of the human agent was corroborated by the increase in the use of human agents of *shall* and focalised human actants as subjects in regulative acts across the three laws. A further increase was in the use of pronouns.

The analysis of focalised/defocalised reference to the regulated party helps explain differences between contract law and arbitration law. The need to specify the agent of the regulating act was urgent in UNCITRAL and ALPRC, in that acts were addressed to specific people and not to members of a jurisdiction as a whole. This also explains the wider spread of human actants in UNCITRAL and ALPRC compared with contract law.

Furthermore, the observed differences seem to point towards a legal writing style, which increasingly addresses the regulated party through action rules with human agents of *shall* and focalised human subjects of regulative acts as a strategy of 'playing-it-safe'. The increase in the use of pronominal reference also shows an approximation to prose writing in non-legal texts.

REFERENCES

Baker, M. (1992) *In Other Words: A Casebook on Translation*. New York: Routledge.

Bennet, J. M. (1989) In defence of "shall". *The Australian Law Journal* 63: 522–525.

Bhatia, V. K. (1993) *Analysing Genre: Language Use in Professional Settings*. London: Longman, 102.

Bhatia, V. K. (1994) Cognitive structuring in legislative provisions. In John Gibbons (ed.), *Language and the Law*. Harlow: Longman, 136–155.

Bowers, F. (1989) *Linguistic Aspects of Legislative Expression*. Vancouver: University of British Columbia Press.

Child, B. (1992) *Drafting Legal Documents: Principles and Practices*. American Casebook Series. St. Paul, MN: West Publishing Co.

Danet, B. (1985) Legal discourse. In Tuen A. van Dijk (ed.), *Handbook of Discourse Analysis*. Vol. 1, *The Discipline of Discourse Analysis*, 273–291. London: Academic Press.

Eagleson, R. D. and Asprey, M. M. (1989) Must we continue with "shall"? *The Australian Law Journal* 63: 75–78.

Elliott, D. (1990) *Legal Drafting: Language and the Law*. Canadian Institute for the Administration of Justice, Ottawa.

Engberg, J. and Rasmussen, K. W. (2003) Danish legal language in international commercial arbitration: A comparison of the Geneva Convention and the Danish Statutory Text incorporating its rules in Danish law. In Bhatia, V. K., Candlin, C. N. and Gotti, M (eds.), *Legal Discourse in Multilingual and Multicultural Contexts: Arbitration Texts in Europe*. Bern: Peter Lang.

Gunnarsson, B.-L. (1984) Functional comprehensibility of legislative texts. *Text* 4–1/3: 71–105.

Hatim, B. and Mason, I. (1990) *Discourse and the Translator*. London: Longman.

Kurzon, D. (1986) *It Is Hereby Performed ... Explorations in Legal Speech Acts*. Pragmatics and Beyond, v. VII: 6. Amsterdam/Philadelphia: John Benjamins Publishing Company.

Kurzon, D. (1989) Language of the law and legal language. In C. Laurén and N. Marianne (eds.), *Special Language: From Humans Thinking to Thinking Machines*. Multilingual Matters: Clevedon/Philadelphia, 283–290.

Trimble, L. (1985) The rhetoric of EST discourse. In Louis Trimble, *English for Science and Technology: A Discourse Approach*. Cambridge: Cambridge University Press, 10–21.

Trosborg, A. (1997) *Rhetorical Strategies in Legal Language: Discourse Analysis of Statutes and Contracts*. Tübingen: Gunter Narr Verlag.

Trosborg, A. (2004) Regulative strategies in arbitration law. Uncitral Model Law on International Commercial Arbitration (UNCITRAL) compared with Arbitration Law of the People's Republic of China. Aarhus: *Hermes*, 99–115.

11

Cultural Constraints on Arbitration Discourse

Maurizio Gotti

In recent years, the dismantling of cultural, disciplinary and national barriers, especially in the context of co-operation and collaboration in international trade, has accelerated moves towards the globalisation of socio-cultural, business and communication issues. In this context, law is fast assuming an international perspective rather than remaining a purely domestic concern. A case in point is international commercial arbitration. This paper aims to investigate the means whereby normative discourse (statutes and regulations) is employed in different cultural, linguistic and legal environments; to illustrate this phenomenon, it targets legislation on international arbitration from the 'Model Law on International Commercial Arbitration' issued by the United Nations in 1985 and later integrated into the laws of several countries with varying constitutional, sociocultural and economic conditions.

In particular, the chapter will take into consideration the extent to which cultural elements influence the differentiation of the texts concerning legislation on arbitration in various countries. As has been amply demonstrated (cf, among others, Kuper 1999), 'culture' is a notoriously polysemic term. In the context of this paper, the term 'culture' is used mainly to refer to the complex set of traditions and standardised social practices peculiar to a specific professional group — in this case that of legal practitioners involved in the use of arbitration discourse — and its dependence on norms, whether those of social behaviour or those accepted in language usage (Vermeer 1986: 33). The specific elements taken into consideration here belong to the social context determining the conditions of production within which legal texts are framed and the actual situations in which such texts are to be employed. The theoretical presupposition adopted is that as language is strictly tied to the sociocultural context in which it is used, the interpretation of discourse relies to a large extent on the contextual constraints of the event in which it is expressed and/or received, cultural elements representing an essential part of these contextual elements. As Merry aptly remarks:

> Discourses are aspects of culture, interconnected vocabularies and systems of meaning located in the social world. A discourse is not individual and idiosyncratic but part of a shared cultural world. Discourses are rooted in particular institutions and embody their culture. (Merry 1990: 110)

CULTURAL CONSTRAINTS ON ARBITRATION PROCEDURES

Even from a very superficial analysis of arbitration practices, it is easy to realise that the cultural environment greatly influences the outcome of the arbitration procedure. Particularly in international contexts, this conditioning effect derives from several kinds of differences existing at various levels: differences in legal systems, differences in the nature of proceedings, differences in terms of participants, etc. Some of the factors that most commonly affect the outcome of the arbitration procedure are examined below.

Local customs and traditions

Conditioning factors are clearly visible in those cases in which the national legislation imposes specific obligations in compliance with local customs and traditions: for example, some countries such as Korea and Saudi Arabia uphold requirements of nationality and/or residence for a person to serve as arbitrator (Jarvin 1999: 60); Saudi Arabia also requires arbitrators to be male and of the Islamic faith (Saleh 1992: 549). These criteria impose serious restrictions on the choice of arbitration to resolve international disputes. It is usually preferred by foreigners when they have to fix the site of an arbitration case with a party residing in one of those countries. But even when cultural differences are not so evident, it is impossible to guarantee a perfectly homogeneous process, as the various legal patterns of the countries involved will re-emerge in some of the procedures described or in a few of the principles set out. Such professional traits will not only characterise the written texts, but will be present in the minds of the arbitrators themselves, who — no matter how neutral and culturally open they wish to be — will be conditioned by their own specific legal philosophy. This emergence of the arbitrator's educational and professional background may create problems in the assessment of the parties' behaviour and generate negative consequences in relation to the outcome of the proceedings themselves, a risk international arbitrators are fully aware of:

> An arbitrator, without relinquishing impartiality, may nonetheless remain very distant in educational and cultural terms from the particular party or its counsel. In such a case, difficulties are likely to arise which have nothing to do with the probity of the arbitrator in question. They are due solely to the fact that the said arbitrator reveals a greater intellectual ability to grasp every detail of the arguments put forward by one party, while encountering objective and honest difficulties in understanding the submissions of the other(s) in the same way. Albeit unwillingly, the conduct of the arbitrator may thus adversely affect the equal treatment of the parties. (Bernini[1] 1998: 42)

A similar opinion is expressed by Lalive, who remarks:

> Participants in international arbitration have different origins or places of business, different educations, methods, reactions or *Weltanschauungen*. In short, what has perhaps struck me more than anything after many years of arbitral practice, either as advocate or as arbitrator, is the capital role played by what may best be called '*conflicts of cultures*' between the parties (as well as their respective counsel) and, as a result, by difficulties of 'communication' between them and arbitrators. (Lalive 1992: 80, italics in the original)

All these considerations explain the reason why at the beginning of the arbitration proceedings the parties devote such great attention to the choice of the arbitrator(s). This step constitutes a fundamental factor, as the proceedings will be determined by the arbitrator or arbitral tribunal selected. As Cremades remarks:

---

1 At the time when he made this remark, Giorgio Bernini was the President of the Association for the Teaching and Study of Arbitration (AISA) and a member of the Executive Committee of the Italian Arbitration Association.

> It is not the same to have an arbitral tribunal chairman or member who is an engineer or a jurist; or who comes from the common law or from the Continent; or who speaks well or passably well the language in which the arbitration proceeding is going to be conducted; or who is familiar or not with the normal practices of the professional sector in which the parties carry out their activities. (Cremades 1998: 169–170)

In spite of the growing international arbitration culture, national influences traceable in the arbitrators' behaviour may prove particularly harmful and may often derive from the arbitrators' unfamiliarity with one of the parties' site rules and practices. This is the reason why in recent legislation on arbitration there is a growing tendency to offer the parties a more comprehensive set of procedural rules rather than leaving the conduct of the proceedings completely to the discretion of the arbitral tribunal. This would be an approach in line with the UNCITRAL Model Law. This process of harmonization, however, is very hard to carry out, and even if all the procedures were to be unified some differences would still remain in their perception at a local level. The reason for this is to be found in the underlying professional background.

> Our own legal cultures remain, for the time being, in certain areas, an important limiting factor to harmonisation because [...] the application of the same rule may lead, despite all good intentions, to strikingly different results. (Lazareff 1999: 36)

Legal systems

Particularly in those cases in which the arbitrator is a professional judge, he or she may be influenced by the different roles that such a figure plays in common law and civil law proceedings (cf. David / Brierley 1985). He or she may be so deeply involved in his or her own system that those procedures tend to be followed which usually apply and are adopted in the system and environment that he or she is familiar with. The following testimony by Lalive confirms this type of experience:

> Many years ago I was acting as junior counsel to a distinguished New York lawyer for an American oil company before an international arbitral tribunal in Europe, presided over by a famous commercial lawyer, attorney and professor of Geneva University. Apparently following his usual New York practice, my 'leader' had

> submitted to the tribunal a very detailed set of rules and procedure, assuming doubtless that he would thereby protect himself and help the tribunal. Some time later, I was summoned by the chairman, my former professor, and received the mission to ask, as diplomatically as I could, my New York colleague whether he really believed the arbitrators to be idiots or untrustworthy, since the arbitral tribunal had neither the need nor the desire, the chairman told me, to be imprisoned by such a detailed code of procedure!

In another case, the arbitrators (all belonging to 'civil law' countries) became increasingly irritated during the proceedings by the practice — in their view quite unnecessary and burdensome — of English counsel of answering in detail every single letter of the other's side, presumably on the basis that, unless every point made, however marginal or irrelevant, was expressly refuted, it would be considered as conceded (Lalive 1992: 81).

With the common law 'adversarial' approach, the judge has a more passive role as the final decision is normally taken by a jury rather than the judge himself. In the civil law 'inquisitorial' procedure, on the other hand, the judge plays a more active role in the conduct of the proceedings as he or she is not only permitted but expected to take greater initiative in the assessment and evaluation of facts (cf. Borris 1994 and 1999). This differentiation in the judge's role also derives from the way in which the gathering of evidence is carried out in the two legal systems. In civil law procedure, the parties are required to state their case with all necessary detail and to present all documents and evidence relied on as early as possible. Instead, common law procedure is typically oriented towards the oral hearing, with great importance attributed to witness examination; all details of the case deemed relevant by the parties must be pleaded at the oral hearing even if such pleadings have already been made in the written statements. This depends on the fact that the jury is not involved in the proceedings prior to the oral hearing, but decides the facts of the case solely on the evidence presented at the trial. Therefore, in the common law procedure the judge generally leaves the examination of witnesses to the parties or their counsel and does not, on his or her own initiative, encourage the parties to settle the case. In contrast, the civil law judge usually examines witnesses himself and is more likely to encourage the parties to settle the case. This explains the parties' disappointed reaction when their expectations greatly differ from what actually happens in the case:

> The [civil law] model would have the judge do the questioning, with the lawyers making suggestions or filling in at the end, and some arbitrators modelled their role on that of the judge in their home country. I have seen [common law] counsel surprised and shocked that they were not expected to conduct the examination of their witnesses and the cross-examination of those of their opponents. (Lowenfeld 1999: 24)

The same reaction occurs when written evidence is used instead of oral testimony, which provokes a differentiation in cultural terms that is not easy to overcome:

> It remains, nevertheless, a fact [...] that the English and the American are more inclined to rely on the testimony of witnesses than their sceptical Continental colleagues who are more apt to rely on contemporary documentary evidence. This difference in underlying attitude explains why total harmonisation cannot be achieved by simply instituting a unified set of procedures. (Lazareff 1999: 35)

The more active role played by the arbitrator and his or her greater reliance on the written documentary evidence provided by the parties is due to a series of reasons: no jury is involved in the proceedings; the majority of the disputes in international commercial arbitration are of a technical and complicated nature; the purpose of the oral hearing (when effected) is limited to the clarification of any remaining questions and the examination of witnesses and experts. At the same time, there is more interaction between the parties and the arbitral tribunal in order to help them identify their positions more clearly and make the decision-making process more transparent. Moreover, the arbitrator often makes proposals for an amicable settlement of the dispute if he or she sees that any possible solutions are feasible.[2] The difficulties that might be encountered in the application of the latter policy in some countries are pointed out in the text of the UNCITRAL itself:

---

2 Over the last decades there has been a great change in this attitude, as is testified to by Cremades: "Traditionally, it was an agreed doctrine within the world of arbitration that an arbitrator's duty shall not be mixed with any mediating activity or intent to reconcile. This was one of the greatest dangers widely highlighted in arbitration seminars as it was stated outright that an arbitrator who initiated conciliation or mediation was exposed to the risk of an eventual challenge. Again, the participation in international commercial arbitration of jurists with such different origins has, in practice, caused such inflexible positions to be questioned. In fact, even in continental Europe, procedural law in countries of Germanic origin included an obligation for the judge to facilitate conciliation between the parties throughout the proceedings" (Cremades 1998: 162).

> Given the divergence of practices in this regard, the arbitral tribunal should only suggest settlement negotiation with caution. However, it may be opportune for the arbitral tribunal to schedule the proceedings in a way that might facilitate the continuation or initiation of settlement negotiations. (Section 12 of the UNCITRAL Notes on Organizing Arbitral Proceedings)

Nature of dispute resolution

The caution recommended by the UNCITRAL text also derives from the different cultural implications involved in dispute resolution. Indeed, the Western world is traditionally characterised, to varying degrees, by the litigation culture, while in Eastern countries the emphasis is on conciliation. The latter attitude is deeply embedded in Eastern traditions, mainly aiming at promoting amicable settlement of disputes and to suppress litigation. Although radical political and economic changes taking place in the last century have certainly affected this type of culture, it still persists in many noticeable forms. Here is Taniguchi's comment on the Chinese situation:

> In China, where this type of culture originated, a strong emphasis on conciliation was maintained even under the Maoist communist regime as the means to solve a so-called 'contradiction within the people'. The judge's primary obligation was said to be not to decide cases but to 'educate' the parties so that they would be willing to terminate their dispute. This is a good example of how a strong culture can survive even a very radical political, economic and social change. (Taniguchi 1998: 32)

The possibility of proposing an 'amiable composition' between the parties provides another instance of such cultural difference. Although this method of settling disputes is clearly stated in Article 28(3) of the Model Law, the arbitration provisions of some of the countries adhering to the common law system do not specifically state that arbitrators can be authorized to decide *ex aequo et bono* or as *amiable compositeurs*.[3] Civil

---

3 The two concepts are similar. The power to act as an *amiable compositeur* is the power to resolve a dispute without regard to express substantive rules of law and according to customary rules of equity and international commerce. The power to decide a case *ex aequo et bono* is the power to decide on the basis of fairness and good dealing.

law countries, on the other hand, generally have no difficulty in accepting 'amiable composition' together with arbitration, and explicitly state this possibility in their rules of law.

Procedural aspects

Another differentiation between common law and civil law practices consists in the possibility for a party to give evidence as a witness; this is acceptable in common law jurisdictions, while in the civil law tradition this is not generally the case, as it is considered unlikely that a party will give a testimony which may differ from the papers that they have previously submitted. The less formal situation of the arbitration case, however, enables the arbitrator to call a party to make any statement that may be in support of their own case. This testimony is made less binding also by the absence of putting the witnessing party under oath. A similar difference exists as regards written testimony; this is not accepted as evidence in civil law procedure, while it is in common law systems. In international arbitration — where the parties involved are often located in distant countries — written witness statements are admitted. However, in this case too, the arbitrator's cultural background will influence his attitude towards these statements: common law arbitrators will tend to give credence to signed testimony, particularly if it is sworn; civil law arbitrators, on the other hand, will be more cautious in the acceptance of a signed document, as they assume that it was prepared by someone other than the signatory, that is, his lawyers.

Further, as regards expert witnesses, there is a differentiation to be made between the two legal systems: in civil law procedure they are commonly appointed only by the court, while in the common law tradition they may be appointed either by the court or the parties. The latter possibility is also available in arbitration cases, which adhere to a more pragmatic approach: "What matters most are the facts" (Lowenfeld 1999: 24) and all the means considered the best way to establish the facts are adopted. However, even if the arbitrators have greater freedom and can take decisions according to a more pragmatic approach, their professional background will still surface. For example, in presenting international arbitration in France, Jarvin writes:

> The parties have great freedom to shape the procedure [...] and the procedure in international arbitration can be totally detached from

> French court practice. However, where the arbitrators are French-influenced they have a tendency to appoint experts to resolve technical issues and even conduct investigations into the facts, as is the practice in French court procedure. (Jarvin 1999: 44–45)

Interesting cultural differentiations may also emerge as regards the preparation of witnesses and experts with a view to their participation in hearings before the arbitral tribunal; these too may reflect profound ethical differences between the parties in conflict. In some countries it is considered the normal practice to prepare the parties for this process (including trial performances recorded on video), a procedure which may be regarded as shocking and even reproachable from an ethical and professional perspective by jurists from a different cultural background. For example, it is generally considered contrary to Italian professional ethical rules for lawyers to discuss a case in detail with a witness in private prior to calling him to give evidence; a legal representative who breaches this ethical code may expose himself or herself to a complaint to the law society and to disciplinary action (Cavasola / Paton 1994: 171). However, even in these contexts the situation is changing, in the sense that such procedure can be adopted in arbitration cases provided the parties expressly authorise it.

Linguistic issues

The choice of the language to be used in the arbitration case may have important consequences on the procedural approach adopted, as arbitrators themselves admit:

> Frequently the presence of American (or British) lawyers in a procedure normally leads to the de facto use of US (or English) procedures. Similarly, an American attorney, for example, would not object to applying Continental procedures in a French-speaking case. (Lazareff 1999: 37)

The fact that English is becoming so frequently used even in cases where no native English-speaking party is involved, is bound to have relevant consequences on the procedures adopted. Taniguchi comments on the use of the English language by Japanese companies:

> There are very many different arbitral practices associated with different legal and commercial cultures. However, the world has

> been unmistakingly proceeding toward a single commercial culture. Japanese businessmen, for example, are negotiating business in the English language not only with English speaking businessmen but also Korean, European and Middle Eastern businessmen. This is one of the realities of international trade today. (Taniguchi 1998: 39)

The language competence of the parties involved may also play a very influential role in the outcome of the arbitration proceedings, as can be seen from the following account by Borris of a dispute resolution case:

> I remember one case, where this was apparent: it involved a dispute between an American party (a distributor) and a German party (the manufacturer). The proceedings took place under Dutch procedural law in The Netherlands. The language of the proceedings was English. The American party was represented by a New York law firm with extensive experience in international arbitration. The German party was represented by German counsel with limited knowledge not only of the English language but also with little experience in international arbitration. Briefs of that party had been translated from German into English for submission to the arbitral tribunal. At the hearing, several witnesses had to be heard and the arbitral tribunal permitted their cross-examination. The American attorney questioned the witnesses in the typical way this would happen in an American court. With the questions he asked the witness (called by the American party), he had (or was given) the opportunity to tell the whole story from A to Z, not very surprisingly supporting his client's position. One sometimes wondered whether the dialogue between the attorney and 'his' witness was previously rehearsed. It took almost four hours before the questioning came to an end and it was then time for the German party to shake the credibility of this witness by asking further questions. The German party obviously did not expect this situation and was not prepared for it. Combined with language problems, the German party certainly did not leave the professional and self-assured impression the American attorney gave. Who would deny that this had some influence on the deliberation of the arbitral tribunal? (Borris 1994: 80)

> It is both customary and logical for the language of the arbitration to be the language of the contract. However, there may be special circumstances in which the parties wish to conduct the arbitration proceedings in one particular language. This is the case, for example, of contracts made in two languages, each of equal authenticity. In

> such cases, it is customary to adopt only one of the two languages in the arbitration proceedings to avoid any waste of time and money. The use of a single language, however, may create problems, as there is not perfect equivalence between the legal systems involved. For example, a certain legal concept or practice may not be in use in one of the two systems, which therefore will lack an appropriate term to denote it. In this case a direct translation of the concept involved will be impossible and may only be avoided by means of a periphrasis, which, however, will not render the original appropriately. An example of how the same term may be understood in different contexts is the interpretation of the word *commercial* in the expression 'international commercial arbitration'. Although this is commonly interpreted in its general sense in most countries, it may be submitted to strict delimitations of meaning in a few cultural contexts. This more limited semantic value of the term led, for example, an Indian party to contend that its agreement with Boeing, an American company, to provide consultancy services for the promotion of the sale of Boeing aircraft in India could not be regarded as a 'commercial' transaction. The dispute resolution judgment instead opted for the broader meaning of that expression. (Pathak 1998: 182)

In arbitration practice it is essential that an award — i.e. the final decision taken by the arbitrator(s) — should be unambiguous so as to avoid unnecessary interpretation by the arbitral tribunal or further litigation by application to a court. The award is normally rendered in the language of the arbitration although occasionally it may be made in the language which is most convenient for the parties. It is a condition of recognition and enforcement under the New York Convention (Art. IV. 2) that a foreign arbitral award must be accompanied by an officially certified translation into the language of the place in which recognition or enforcement of the award is sought, when this is not the language of the award. However, legal terminology is so culture-bound that a satisfactory translation of all the legal terms of one text from one context to another is at times impossible.[4]

4 This also applies to different contexts using the same language. As Nadelmann and von Mehren rightly exemplify, "Even in the same language the meaning of a legal term may differ from system to system. Thus, 'domicile' has one meaning in English law and quite different meanings in American jurisdictions" (1967: 195). As Nida aptly remarks, "competent translators are always aware that ultimately words only have meaning in terms of the corresponding culture" (Nida 2001: 13).

CULTURAL CONSTRAINTS ON ARBITRATION TEXTS

In this section specific samples taken from arbitration discourse in different languages will be analysed so as to point out how the linguistic choices adopted in them have been greatly influenced by the cultural environment in which these texts have been produced. In order to highlight the differentiations and adaptations to a particular context, the documents taken into consideration have been compared to the United Nations Model Law on International Commercial Arbitration (UML) and to the UNCITRAL Arbitration Rules (UAR), with the aim of offering a more detailed understanding of linguistic and textual phenomena closely linked to cross-cultural traits.[5]

Legal system

Legal constraints often play an interesting role in the construction of normative discourse. This is clearly visible also in the field of arbitration provisions. For example, many countries belonging to, or aiming to become members of the European Union pay special attention to the compatibility of their legislation with European law and with other documents passed by the EU institutions;[6] this is the case also where new provisions on international arbitration are elaborated (cf. Chroma 2003: 68 for the harmonization of Czech legislation with that of the European Union).

5 The texts taken into particular consideration are: articles 806–840 of the Code of Civil Procedure (CCP, avaliable at http://www.camera-arbitrale.com/codice.htm; an English translation, offered by the Milan Chamber of National and International Arbitration, is available from http://www.camera-arbitrale.com/eng/rifarb.htm; it is the version referred to in this article), UNCITRAL Arbitration Rules (UAR, available at http://www.uncitral.org/english/texts/arbitration/arbitrul.htm), the United Nations Model Law on International Commercial Arbitration (UML, available at http://www.uncitral.org/english/texts/arbitration/ml-arb.htm), the regulations enacted by the Milan Arbitration Chamber (CONAIAM, available at http://www.mi.camcom.it/eng/arbitration-chamber/reging.htm), the regulations enacted by the Bergamo Arbitration Chamber (ACOB, available at http://www.bg.camcom.it/camera_arbitrale), and the regulations enacted by the Venice Arbitration Chamber (VENCA, available at http://www.venca.it/rules.htm).

6 The European Court of Justice has recently stressed that besides regulations which have direct applicability, certain directives issued from time to time and normally implemented later by national governments also have direct applicability within the Member States; this means that not only EU regulations, but also EU directives, are now entering national legal systems.

The different legal system may determine the adoption of different textual strategies on the drafter's part. For example, common law legislation is usually associated with particular emphasis on precision and detail for action in specific circumstances (Campbell 1996). As regards arbitration legislation, this feature is confirmed by the frequent use of explicit textual schematization in UML, its major concern for clarity of expression and for conceptual and terminological clarity, and unambiguity. This explains why UML devotes various parts of its text to very detailed terminological explanations, particularly in Articles 2 and 7:

1) For the purposes of this Law:
   (a) 'arbitration' means any arbitration whether or not administered by a permanent arbitral institution;
   (b) 'arbitral tribunal' means a sole arbitrator or a panel of arbitrators;
   (c) 'court' means a body or organ of the judicial system of a State; (UML 2)
2) 'Arbitration agreement' is an agreement by the parties to submit to arbitration all or certain disputes which have arisen or which may arise between them in respect of a defined legal relationship, whether contractual or not. An arbitration agreement may be in the form of an arbitration clause in a contract or in the form of a separate agreement. (UML 7.1)

This concern for clarity can also be found in the many cases in which the UML reader is required to interpret the wider semantic value of a term by the verb *to include* or to understand an expression in the light of a given text by means of the verb phrase *refers to*:

3) For the purposes of this Law:
   [...]
   (d) where a provision of this Law, except article 28, leaves the parties free to determine a certain issue, such freedom *includes* the right of the parties to authorize a third party, *including* an institution, to make that determination;
   (e) where a provision of this Law *refers to* the fact that the parties have agreed or that they may agree or in any other way *refers to* an agreement of the parties, such agreement includes any arbitration rules *referred to* in that agreement;
   (f) where a provision of this Law, other than in articles 25 (a) and 32 (2)(a), *refers to* a claim, it also applies to a counter-claim, and where it *refers to* a defence, it also applies to a

> defence to such counter-claim. (UML 2; emphasis added, as in all quotations in this paper)

Another way of enhancing precision is the use of past-participle clauses to state clearly the source of the qualification of a term, as can be seen in the following quotations:

4) Where an action *referred to in paragraph (1) of this article* has been brought, arbitral proceedings may nevertheless be commenced or continued, and an award may be made, while the issue is pending before the court. (UML 8.2)
5) Any party may request the court or other authority *specified in article* 6 to take the necessary measure, unless the agreement on the appointment procedure provides other means for securing the appointment. (UML 11.4.c)

These forms also occur in civil law texts, but in general there is less marked emphasis on precision. In the Italian text, for example, there are also cases in which the link remains implicit or refers vaguely to law in general:

6) *Gli arbitri debbono pronunciare il lodo entro il termine stabilito* [...] ***dalla legge***; (CCP 813)
   [The arbitrators shall render their award within the time limit *set* [...] *by law*]
7) *se nel procedimento non sono state osservate le forme* ***prescritte per i giudizi sotto pena di nullità***. (CCP 829.7)
   [where the formalities *laid down for proceedings under penalty of nullity* have not been observed]

Different degrees of precision are also visible in the lexis found in the two texts, the Italian one employing a wider range of words. Indeed, types in CCP account for 20 percent of tokens, as compared to 14 percent in UML (Giannoni 2003: 229). Moreover, the great lexical variety of CCP also means a higher proportion of polysemous items in its specialized lexis. This evidence suggests that English legal discourse is more lexically restricted and specific than Italian, which results from the layering of the formal, specialized and bureaucratic registers (Petta 1994).

Important elements of a particular legal system are its drafting tradition and stylistic conventions. These too may influence arbitration discourse significantly, as can be seen in the differentiation between civil law and common law texts: the former being mainly characterised by generality, while the latter preferring particularity. Indeed, it is commonly asserted that civil law statutes are written in terms of principle, whereas common law statutes are written in detail as "the civil code draftsman is eager to be widely understood by the ordinary readership, whereas the common law draftsman seems to be more worried about not being misunderstood by the specialist community" (Bhatia 1993: 137). This difference may be observed also in contracts: the common law rules typically give almost absolute authority to the wording of the document, while the civil law systems put more emphasis on the actual intent of the parties at the time when the agreement was entered into. This stylistic difference derives from a basic conceptual differentiation underlying the two legal systems. In the civil law system the judiciary is entrusted with the task of construing, interpreting and applying the general principles outlined in the civil code to specific real-life situations. This requirement therefore privileges stylistic choices such as generality and simplicity of expression. The common law system, instead, is based on the principle of precedence, by means of which the decisions taken by one judge become binding on all subsequent similar cases. This system in consequence regards certainty of expression as the most valued quality in legal drafting. This conceptual differentiation is reflected in the drafters' stylistic choices. In common law legislation sentences are very long, consisting of three or more main clauses, each modified by many subordinate clauses. This remarkable sentence length depends on the great number of details to be inserted and the need that specifications should be precise and clear (Mellinkoff 1963, Gustafsson 1975, Tiersma 1999, Gotti 2003). Civil law sentences are shorter, with a less strict use of paragraphing. This makes the understanding of the sentences easier, but renders the reconstruction of the relationship between the various sentences more complex. The same stylistic difference may be seen as regards contract drafting techniques, as Borris points out:

> Parties with a Common Law background usually prefer long and detailed contracts, eager to mention and list expressly each and every contingency that could possibly become a subject of dispute under the agreement. This may be explained by their assumption and expectation that a contract can only be relied on to the extent it is expressly so worded. Parties with a Civil Law background, in contrast, find it often acceptable not to mention every detail because they expect that a court or an arbitral tribunal in interpreting the contract would not only look at the actual wording but also consider what the parties actually had intented to agree upon taking into account the circumstances surrounding the negotiations. (Borris 1994: 84)

The analysis of arbitration discourse has shown a great reliance of UML on the traditional features of common law legal discourse. A relevant aspect of this legal drafting tradition is the use of binomial expressions. These are frequently used in UML, with examples that include both crystallised forms such as *ex aequo et bono*, *null and void*, and free collocations such as *independent and impartial arbitrator*, *documents and other materials*.

A civil law text such as CCP uses similar expressions, but mainly with parallel coordination. Indeed, the two texts have a comparable amount of parallel coordination (with 55 *e(d)* in CCP, 59 *and* in UML), while alternative coordination is considerably more frequent in the UNCITRAL text, with 172 occurrences of *or* as compared to 70 of *o/oppure* (Giannoni 2003: 231). Garzone's (2003: 202) analysis of the set of rules of the London Court of International Arbitration shows a prevalent use of alternative coordination, with *or* being the fourth most frequent word in the text after *the*, *of* and *to*. The pervasiveness in UML of this second type of binomial is particularly evident inasmuch as it links whole paragraphs rather than single words. Alternative / complementary options with *or* are frequently used in the UNCITRAL text, and the way in which they are usually punctuated and paginated emphasizes their function of making the provisions both more inclusive and semantically transparent.[7] Here is a particularly striking example:

8) Grounds for refusing recognition *or* enforcement
  (1) Recognition *or* enforcement of an arbitral award, irrespective of the country in which it was made, may be refused only:
    a) at the request of the party against whom it is invoked, if that party furnishes to the competent court where recognition *or* enforcement is sought proof that:
      (i) a party to the arbitration agreement referred to in article 7 was under some incapacity; *or* the said agreement is not valid under the law to which the parties have subjected it *or*, failing any indication thereon, under the law of the country where the award was made; *or*

7 The advantages of good paragraphing is thus pointed out by Driedger: "[It] provides a visual aid to comprehension by breaking up solid blocks of type; it delivers the sentence in packages, so to speak, making it easier for the mind to grasp the whole. It does visually what the reader would do mentally without it" (Driedger 1982: 78).

(ii) the party against whom the award is invoked was not given proper notice of the appointment of an arbitrator *or* of the arbitral proceedings *or* was otherwise unable to present his case; *or*
(iii) the award deals with a dispute not contemplated by *or* not falling within the terms of the submission to arbitration, *or* it contains decisions on matters beyond the scope of the submission to arbitration, provided that, if the decisions on matters submitted to arbitration can be separated from those not so submitted, that part of the award which contains decisions on matters submitted to arbitration may be recognized and enforced; *or*
(iv) the composition of the arbitral tribunal *or* the arbitral procedure was not in accordance with the agreement of the parties *or*, failing such agreement, was not in accordance with the law of the country where the arbitration took place; *or*
(v) the award has not yet become binding on the parties *or* has been set aside *or* suspended by a court of the country in which, *or* under the law of which, that award was made; *or*

b) if the court finds that:
(i) the subject-matter of the dispute is not capable of settlement by arbitration under the law of this State; *or*
(ii) the recognition *or* enforcement of the award would be contrary to the public policy of this State. (UML 36)

By arranging content schematically, the drafter can construct a denser, more cognitively demanding text such as the one cited above. The prevailing pattern in Italian is simply coordination with *or* at word level:

9) *La parte che intende far eseguire il lodo nel territorio della Repubblica è tenuta a depositarlo in originale o in copia conforme, insieme con l'atto di compromesso o con l'atto contenente la clausola compromissoria o con documento equipollente, in originale o in copia conforme, nella cancelleria della pretura nella cui circoscrizione è la sede dell'arbitrato.* (CCP 825)
[The party intending to have the award enforced in the territory of the Republic shall file the original award *or* a certified copy thereof, together with the original arbitration agreement *or*

document containing the arbitration clause *or* an equivalent document, *or* a certified copy thereof, with the Registry of the Magistrate's Court [Pretura] of the district in which the arbitrator has its seat]

10) *Il lodo può esssere corretto, su istanza di parte, dagli stessi arbitri che lo hanno pronunziato, qualora questi siano incorsi in omissioni o in errori materiali o di calcolo.* (CCP 826)
[On the request of a party, the award may be corrected by the same arbitrators who have rendered it, where there have been omissions, material errors *or* miscalculations]

Another feature of the common law drafting tradition is its use of *shall*, signalling juridical obligation. This is confirmed by the frequent employment of this auxiliary in the UNCITRAL texts. The texts in English of the Italian arbitration chambers, on the other hand, make a limited use of this modal and more frequently recur to the present indicative tense. In doing so they emphasise the actuality and applicability of the legal provision and imply that the law draws its force from the natural order of things rather than an order imposed by human agents. This preference for the present tense is also part of the drafting tradition of France, another country belonging to the civil law system. As Garzone's (2003: 206) analysis shows, the simple present indicative — rather than the deontic modal *devoir* — is the form customarily used to convey both the prescriptive and the performative functions of normative and legislative texts. Here are some examples of this contrast:

11) An arbitral award, irrespective of the country in which it was made, *shall* be recognized as binding and, upon, application in writing to the competent court, *shall* be enforced subject to the provisions of this article and of article 36. (UML 35)
12) *Gli arbitri redigono il lodo in tanti originali quante sono le parti e ne danno comunicazione a ciascuna parte mediante consegna di un originale, anche con spedizione in plico raccomandato, entro dieci giorni dalla data dell'ultima sottoscrizione.* (CCP 825)
[The arbitrators *draft* the award in as many originals as the number of the parties and *give* notice of it to each party by handing over an original or sending it by registered mail within ten days of the date of the last signature]
13) The appointing authority *shall*, at the request of one of the parties, appoint the sole arbitrator as promptly as possible. In making the appointment the appointing authority *shall* use the following list-procedure, unless both parties agree that the list-

procedure should not be used or unless the appointing authority determines in its discretion that the use of the list-procedure is not appropriate for the case: (UAR 6.3)

14) In the event the Parties have not appointed the Arbitrator/s and not designated a different appointing authority within the applicable terms, the arbitrator/s *is/are appointed* by the Court within 30 (thirty) days from when the Court is noticed by the most diligent Party. (VENCA 10)

The adherence of the UNCITRAL texts to a more traditional common law style is also demonstrated by the lengthy and complex structure of most of its sentences, in line with the features of legal discourse (Gustaffson 1975, Bhatia 1994, Hiltunen 1984, 2001). As can be seen in Table 11.1, the average sentence length is greater in UAR than in three texts which — although written in English — are part of the civil law system:

Table 11.1 Average sentence length in the corpus analysed (From Belotti 2003: 33)

	Average sentence length
UAR	43.1
CONAIAM	37.0
ACOB	34.4
VENCA	29.8

The greater complexity of legal discourse in UAR is confirmed by the data concerning sentence types. As Table 11.2 shows, UAR has more complex sentences than the Italian texts; CONAIAM, ACOB and VENCA, on the contrary, contain more simple and compound sentences.

Table 11.2 Distribution of sentence types. (From Belotti 2003: 34)

	UAR		CONAIAM		ACOB		VENCA	
Simple	5	17%	9	19%	15	28%	4	33%
Compound	1	3%			2	4%	5	42%
Complex	24	80%	36	77%	37	68%	3	25%
Complex-compound			2	4%				

However, although sentences in the UNCITRAL text are long and complex, they are normally 'easified' (Bhatia 1983) by means of clear structuring and lettering, as illustrated in the example below:

15) An arbitral award may be set aside by the court specified in article 6 only if:
   (a) the party making the application furnishes proof that:
      (i) a party to the arbitartion agreement referred to in article 7 was under some incapacity; or the said agreement is not valid under the law to which the parties have subjected it to or, failing any indication thereon, under the law of this State; or
      (ii) the party making the application was not given proper notice of the appointment of an arbitrator or of the arbitral proceedings or was otherwise unable to present his case; or
      (iii) the award deals with a dispute not contemplated by or not falling within the terms of the submission to arbitration, or contains decisions on matters beyond the scope of the submission to arbitration, provided that, if the decisions on matters submitted to arbitration can be separated from those not so submitted, only that part of the award which contains decisions on matters not submitted to arbitration may be set aside; or
      (iv) the composition of the arbitral tribunal or the arbitral procedure was not in accordance with the agreement of the parties, unless such agreement was in conflict with a provision of this Law from which the parties cannot derogate, or, failing such agreement, was not in accordance with this Law; or
   (b) the court finds that:
      (i) the subject matter of the dispute is not capable of settlement by arbitration under the law of this State; or
      (ii) the award is in conflict with the public policy of this State. (UML 34.2)

Legal context

The different legal contexts in which two laws are embedded may also determine divergences in how their texts are encoded. This can be seen, for example, in the comparison of UML with the Italian legislative provisions on arbitration contained in articles 806–840 of the Code of Civil Procedure (CCP). Although the coverage of the contents of both UML and CCP is very similar — mainly following the chronological progression from the drafting of a commercial contract to the eventual recourse against the award — the Italian law is more comprehensive as it deals both with national and international arbitration while the Model Law does not apply to domestic controversies. Moreover, the Italian text displays a high degree of intertextual linking as this new law is embedded in the extant body of legislation, and therefore has to be interpreted in the light of hundreds of other texts of greater or equal authority. The sources of some of these references are explicitly mentioned in the text (cf. quotation 16), but in other cases the links to other documents remain implicit, as in quotation 17, where references to other parts of the Civil Code (c.c.) or Penal Code (c.p.) are given in brackets:

16) *La clausola compromissoria contenuta in condizioni generali di contratto oppure in moduli o formulari non è soggetta alla approvazione specifica prevista dagli* ***artt.1341 e 1342 del Codice civile***. (CCP 833)
[An arbitration clause contained in general conditions of contract or standard forms shall not be subject to the specific approval provided for in *Arts. 1341 and 1342 of the Civil Code*]
17) *Gli arbitri* **possono essere sia cittadini italiani sia stranieri. Non possono essere arbitri i minori** (*2 c.c.*), *gli interdetti* (***414 c.c.***; ***32 c.p.***), *gli inabilitati* (***415 c.c.***), *i falliti* (***50.1 fall.***), *e coloro che sono sottoposti a interdizione dai pubblici uffici* (***829 n. 3***; ***28, 23, 31 c.p.***). (CCP 812)
[The arbitrators may be Italian or foreign nationals. Minors (*2 c.c*), persons under a legal incapacity (*414 c.c.*; *32 c.p.*, *415 c.c.*), bankrupts (*50.1 fall.*) and those who have been disqualified from holding a public office (*829 n. 3*; *28, 23, 31 c.p.*) may not act as arbitrators]

In UML, instead, reference is usually internal and has the function of facilitating 'textual mapping' (Bhatia 1987). This is achieved mainly through the use of past-participle clauses and complex prepositional phrases, such as *under*, *in accordance with* or *according to*:

18) The functions *referred to in* articles 11 (3), 11 (4), 13 (3), 14, 16 (3) and 34 (2) shall be performed by … (UML 6)
19) in an arbitration with a sole arbitrator, if the parties are unable to agree on the arbitrator, he shall be appointed, upon request of a party, by the court or other authority *specified in* article 6. (UML 10.3.b)
20) If, *under* this article or article 13 (2), an arbitrator withdraws from his office or a party agrees to the termination of the mandate of an arbitrator, this does not imply acceptance of the

validity of any ground referred to in this article or article 12 (2). (UML 14.2)

21) The award shall state the reasons upon which it is based, unless the parties have agreed that no reasons are to be given or the award is an award on agreed terms *under* article 30. The award shall state its date and the place of arbitration as determined *in accordance with* article 20 (1). (UML 31.2–3)

Intra-textual links also occur in CCP, as can be seen in (22). However, these devices are less frequent in the Italian text, this being probably linked to the fact that this law is firmly embedded within the Code of Civil Procedure and its authority, whereas UML is a stand-alone law with no inherent intertextual linking.

22) *La clausola compromissoria deve risultare da atto avente la forma richiesta per il compromesso* ***ai sensi dell'articolo 807****, commi primo e secondo. Le controversie* ***di cui all'art. 409*** *possono essere decise da arbitri solo se ciò sia previsto nei contratti e accordi collettivi di lavoro purché ciò avvenga, a pena di nullità, senza pregiudizio della facoltà delle parti di adire l'autorità giudiziaria.* (CCP 808)
[The arbiration clause shall be contained in a document meeting the formal requirements for an arbitration agreement *according to Art. 807*, first and second paragraphs. Dispute *ex Art. 409* may be decided by arbitrators only if this is provided for in collective labour contracts and agreements and if, under penalty of nullity, the parties' right to have recourse to the courts is not affected.]

As seen above, one of the main features of arbitration procedures is the greater degree of autonomy enjoyed by the judge. It is important, therefore, that the decision-making process should be totally transparent and that the arbitrator should be impartial and independent. This need is particularly felt in the Italian context, where the custom of non-standard arbitration has often been regarded as too sensitive to the parties' interests and pressures (Ceccon 2000: 12). This reason provides an explanation for the specific rules that several Italian arbitration chambers have laid down to regulate the conduct of appointed arbitrators (cf. Bartolini/ Delconte 2001). In particular, CONAIAM and ACOB contain specific codes of conduct concerning such important issues as the arbitrator's competence, impartiality and independence, which are largely modelled on the Criteria of Arbitral Ethics *(Criteri di Deontologia Arbitrale)* enacted by AIA (the Italian Arbitration Association) in 1999 (cf. Bartolini/Delconte 2001). In UAR, on the other hand (instead), this issue is considered in very general terms:

> 23) In making the appointment, the appointing authority shall have regard to such considerations as are likely to secure the appointment of an independent and impartial arbitrator and shall take into account as well the advisability of appointing an arbitrator of a nationality other than the nationalities of the parties. (UAR 6.4)

The codes of conduct included in CONAIAM and ACOB, however consist of 15 articles covering various aspects connected with the issue of arbitrators' impartiality and independence. They regulate the conduct of arbitrators in a very detailed way, from the moment they accept the appointment throughout the entire arbitration procedure. Moreover, VENCA has a specific article (Art. 13) stating explicitly that the appointed arbitrator is expected to send a written statement expressing his independence and impartiality and declaring his freedom from any links with the parties involved in the arbitration process. ACOB also includes the need for a Roster of Arbitrators (Section 6) and outlines the characteristics of a potential arbitrator and of the application procedures in a very detailed way. The specification of a Roster of Arbitrators underlines the wish of this arbitration chamber to exercise strict control over the competence and reliability of prospective arbitrators. Concerning the procedure for challenging an arbitrator, UAR indicates the grounds for challenge in general terms, only mentioning "justifiable doubts as to his impartiality or independence" (Art.10). ACOB (Section 8.1), on the other hand, makes a clear reference to the reasons for challenging an arbitrator and refers to a precise external source of jurisdiction for their specification:

> 24) The party may reject the arbitrator *in the cases specified in Section 51 of the Italian Code of Civil Practice.* (ACOB 8.1.2)

In the Arbitration Law of the People's Republic of China the grounds for challenging the appointment of arbitrators are mentioned in very specific terms, offering as examples close relationships with any "one litigant" or "the attorney", "private meetings with the litigants or with their attorneys" or the acceptance of "invitation of the litigants or their attorneys to dine" or the acceptance of "gifts" (Bhatia/Candlin/Wei 2001: 10). This implication of possibilities of bribery or influence may be prompted by particular socio-cultural factors specific to that country, a hypothesis underscored by an expert on Chinese law, Professor Jerome Cohen from New York University, quoted by Jane Moir in an article in the *South China Morning Post* (5 October 2001):

> The longer my experience as either an advocate or an arbitrator in disputes presented to Cietac [China International Economic and Trade Arbitration Commission], the graver my doubts have become about its independence and impartiality. [...] At a minimum, I would surely no longer advise clients to accept Cietac jurisdiction unless the contract's arbitration clause required the appointment of a third country national as presiding arbitrator. (Quoted in Bhatia, Candlin and Wei 2001: 8)

Socio-economic context

The socio-economic environment also plays an important role in the construction and interpretation of legal texts relating to the field of international arbitration. A case in point is the wider applicability of the concept of 'international' according to the Scottish Law Reform. In specifying that " 'State', except in article 1(1), includes Scotland" (Dossena 2003: 91), this document indicates that even among parties that have their place of business within the United Kingdom, and where only one of them is based in Scotland, parties may refer to these 'international' arbitration provisions as long as the place of arbitration is Scotland.

The socio-economic environment in which legal provisions are issued may also influence the style adopted in drafting the normative texts. An example can be seen in the regulations enacted by the Milan, Bergamo and Venice Arbitration Chambers. These institutions are situated in one of the most industrialized areas in Northern Italy, where a large number of small enterprises operate successfully on foreign markets. Their sets of rules are intended for a number of business people running small and medium-sized companies and wanting clear indications on how to resolve commercial disputes without recourse to ordinary justice. This explains the higher degree of user-friendliness encountered in their texts. One instance is the fact that two of them (ACOB and CONAIAM) include standard arbitration clauses — such as the clauses for a sole arbitrator, for an arbitral tribunal and for a multi-party arbitration — which can be adopted verbatim and completed easily by the reader. This can be seen from the following examples:

25) *Arbitration agreement*[8]
The undersigned[9] .... and ....
considering that a dispute has arisen on the subject[10]
.... agree to defer this dispute to the decision of[11]
.... to be appointed in accordance with the Rules of the National and International Arbitration Chamber of Bergamo, which the parties expressly declare they know and which they accept in full.
The arbitrators / the sole arbitrator shall decide according to the rules and regulations .... / fairness (specify what is relevant).
The language of the arbitration shall be ....

26) *Clause for Sole Arbitrator*
All disputes arising out of the present contract,[12] including those concerning its validity, interpretation, performance and termination, shall be referred to a sole arbitrator according to the International Arbitration Rules of the Chamber of National and International Arbitration of Milan, which the parties declare that they know and accept in their entirety.
The sole arbitrator shall decide according to the norms ....[13]
The language of the arbitration shall be ....

The texts above take the form of ready-to-use specimens and are thus very easy to copy and complete. On the other hand, the UNCITRAL arbitration rules on which the Italian texts are modelled are mainly informative and imply some sort of adaptation on the part of the user of the clauses presented (cf. quotation 27). This is in line with the results of Salmi-Tolonen's (2003) analysis of the Finnish Arbitration Act compared with the UNCITRAL Model Law, confirming her hypothesis that the functions of the national law and the international law are slightly different: expository and descriptive in the case of international law, and directive in the case of national law.

8 The arbitration agreement is a document that is stipulated when the dispute has already arisen between the parties and in the absence of a precautionary arbitration clause.
9 Specification of the name and residence, or in the case of companies, the head offices of the parties.
10 Reference, also expressed in general terms, of the subject under dispute, with possible reference to the contract out of which the dispute originated.
11 Specification of the number of arbitrators (one or three) (ACOB, Arbitration agreement).
12 Where the arbitration clause is contained in a document other than the contract to which it pertains, the contract referred to shall be indicated.
13 The parties may indicate the norms applicable to the merits of the dispute; alternatively, they may provide that the arbitrator decide *ex aequo et bono* (CONAIAM, Clause for Sole Arbitrator).

27) *Model Arbitration Clause*
Any dispute, controversy or claim arising out of or relating to this contract, or the breach, termination or invalidity thereof, shall be settled by arbitration in accordance with the UNCITRAL Arbitration Rules as at present in force.

Notes
Parties may wish to consider adding:
a The appointing authority shall be ... (name of institution or person);
b The number of arbitrators shall be ... (one or three);
c The place of arbitration shall be ... (town or country);
d The language(s) to be used in the arbitral proceedings shall be ... (UAR 1)

The shorter sentence length and the higher average number of simple and compound sentences of the Italian texts (cf. Tables 11.1 and 11.2 in Section 2.1) enhance their level of readability and make them easier to process and more, user-friendly. This greater consideration of (attention to) readers' competence and expectations is further underpinned by the relative choice of lexical expressions. UAR contains many Latinate and French forms some of which already found in UML: for example, *ex aequo et bono, amiable compositeur, de iure, de facto, ipso iure, in camera.* Such terms do not occur at all in some of the Italian arbitration rules (such as ACOB) or only sparingly in others (in CONAIAM and VENCA). The same can be said for archaic words, as can be seen in Table 11.3:

Table 11.3 Type and number of occurences of archaic words (From Belotti 2002: 132)

	UAR	CONAIAM	ACOB	VENCA
Forthwith		1		
Hereinafter	1			
Such (used as adjective)				
Therefore	2	2		
Therefor	2	2		
Therein		1		
Thereof	2	3		3
Thereon	2			
Thereto	2			
Total	11	9	0	3

CONCLUSION

The analysis in this chapter has focused on the characteristics of a small set of arbitration documents issued at an international level and targeted to be implemented in specific national contexts. It has had the aim of detecting and explaining any significant variations which may be closely linked to cross-cultural traits. In spite of the growing efforts of the international arbitration community to guarantee even more harmonization in legislation and in procedures, local constraints and specific cultural aspects still represent relevant conditioning factors. Even in the case of the UNCITRAL Model Law and Arbitration Rules — which were conceived as to be fully international and not geographically conditioned — the influence of the common law legal system and drafting tradition is often detectable.

The comparisons drawn between the UNCITRAL Model Law and Arbitration Rules on the one hand, and a few national arbitration laws and regulations, on the other, have provided interesting insights into how normative discourse (statutes and regulations) varies in countries with different constitutional, sociocultural and economic conditions in response to different cultural, linguistic and legal environments. The study of such features as information spread, inter- and intra-textual linking, lexical choice, binomial/multinomial expressions and transparency has demonstrated that the UNCITRAL texts show great concern for conceptual or terminological clarity, unambiguity and explicit textual schematization, features which are indicative of the emphasis normally placed by common law legislation on precision and on detail in regard to action in specific circumstances. Concerning textual schematization, the civil law texts analysed present a divergent behaviour. The arbitration laws display fewer facilitating strategies for textual schematization, while the sets of rules provided by the arbitration chambers are simpler to decode thanks to the smaller number of words per sentence, the extensive use of simple and compound sentences and the adoption of common lexis. In addition, clear textual sequencing and organization combined with the provision of model clauses to be copied verbatim and simply completed with one's specific details make these texts much more user-friendly. The discrepancy between arbitration laws and arbitration rules can be attributed to difference in the target readership. Arbitration laws are exclusively aimed at legal experts while arbitration rules are intended for business people wanting clear indications on how to resolve commercial disputes without recourse to ordinary justice. The interpretation of this adaptation of the

UN Model Law to reflect different national realities is in line with the findings of other scholars (e.g. Vermeer 1996).

The textual, conceptual and stylistic discrepancies observed in this analysis present evidence of the problems that arise in the process of establishing closer harmonization in legal normative discourse at a global level. These problems become particularly evident when 'model' texts have to be adopted in various contexts, giving rise to interesting differentiations in the resulting texts. These variations are to be attributed not only to the languages in which the final texts are expressed but also to the different cultural traits and legal traditions of the communities for which they are meant. This can be seen, in particular, in the analysis of the degree of specificity of information included in the various texts. These may differ significantly, perhaps because of differences in socio-cultural expectations and practices that constrain social behaviour in local contexts. A relevant case in point was the comparison of the various clauses concerning the grounds for challenging the appointment of arbitrators: some being expressed in more general terms, while in others the constraints were re specified in greater detail.

This analysis has also emphasized an important matter of methodology. Although the main focus of the chapter was not on evaluating the degree of interlingual influence as a consequence of rendering legal discourse from one language into another, nonetheless, cultural constraints do exercise a significant influence where texts result from a translation or a re-writing process, such as those as here which concern international arbitration. These international documents have been shown to possess clear features of "hybrid" (Trosborg 1997: 146) discourse, deriving as they do from a process of adjustment and adaptation to the legal and socio-cultural traits of the various national target users. Differentiations among them result from conscious and deliberate decisions by local draftspersons, their final form showing that they "are arrived at as an outcome of negotiations between cultures and the norms and conventions involved" (Trosborg 1997: 146).

The choice of the UNCITRAL texts, in particular, has proved to be very useful. As a model law and model regulations are texts created with the purpose of achieving the highest degree of harmonization, individual countries are recommended to make as few changes as possible when incorporating them into their legal systems. As we have seen, however, this total harmonization is not yet realized, and may not yet be unanimously perceived as a final and attainable goal:

> It is necessary [...] to be pragmatic when measuring the significance of harmonisation which has undeniably taken place. [...] Our own legal cultures remain, for the time being, in certain areas, an important limiting factor to harmonisation. (Borris 1999: 11)

We may say that the current interpretation of the harmonization process implies a common understanding of the meaning of terms and practices, rather than any total adoption and blind acceptance of proposed models. This view is in line with the UNCITRAL approach which has carefully avoided the pitfalls that rendered the previous unification attempts inoperative, opting instead for flexibility and non-involvement in decreeing rules for domestic arbitration. In seeking to improve and harmonize national legislation, the Model Law places emphasis on the freedom of the single states and the discretion of the institutions involved. In this way, although the development towards harmonization and unification increasingly reduces the differences between the legal systems, it does not restrict arbitrators in conducting and structuring arbitration proceedings in the most appropriate and effective way. They still retain a high degree of flexibility in choosing and using the procedural techniques which best serve the purposes of the individual case.

Although this chapter has focused on the characteristics of only a few international documents targeting specific national contexts, its results may contribute to a wider understanding of how variations in legal texts may be closely linked to cross-cultural traits. Although governments relinquish increasing amounts of authority to foreign influence in their desire to make international arbitration procedures "unbound" (Paulsson 1981) by local constraints, the resulting 'harmonized' law texts still display considerable differences. These are the consequence of the important conditioning factor represented by cultural aspects in the construction and interpretation of legal discourse.

REFERENCES

Bartolini, F. and Delconte, R. C. (eds.) (2001) *Il codice dell'arbitrato* [The Arbitration Code]. Piacenza: La Tribuna.

Belotti, U. (2002) The Language of Italian Arbitration Rules in English: Some Measurable Aspects. *Linguistica e Filologia* 15: 113–141.

Belotti, U. (2003) Generic Integrity in Italian Arbitration Rules. In Bhatia, Candlin and Gotti (eds.), 19–40.

Bernini, G. (1998) Is There a Growing International Arbitration Culture? In ICCA, 41–46.

Bhatia, V. K. (1983) Simplification v. Easification: The Case of Legal Texts. *Applied Linguistics* 4 (1): 42 54.

Bhatia, V. K. (1987) Textual-Mapping in British Legislative Writing. *World Englishes* 1 (1): 1–10.

Bhatia, V. K. (1993) *Analysing Genre: Language Use in Professional Settings*. London: Longman.

Bhatia, V. K. (1994) Cognitive Structuring in Legislative Provisions. In John Gibbons (ed.), *Language and the Law*, 136–155. London: Longman.

Bhatia, V. K., Candlin, C. N. and Gotti, M. (eds.) (2003) *Legal Discourse in Multilingual and Multicultural Contexts: Arbitration Texts in Europe*. Bern: Peter Lang.

Bhatia, V. K., Candlin, C. N. and Wei, S. (2001) *Legal Discourse in Multilingual and Multicultural Contexts: A Preliminary Study*. Research Group Report. Hong Kong: City University of Hong Kong.

Borris, C. (1994) Common Law and Civil Law: Fundamental Differences and their Impact on Arbitration. *Arbitration* 60 (2): 78–85.

Borris, C. (1999) The Reconciliation of Conflicts Between Common Law and Civil Law Principles in the Arbitration Process. In Frommel and Rider (eds.), 1–18.

Campbell, L. (1996). Drafting Styles: Fuzzy or Fussy? *ELaw. Murdoch University Electronic Journal of Law* 3 (2). Available at http://www.murdoch.edu.au/elaw/issues/v3n2/campbell.html.

Cavasola, P. and Paton, A. G. (1994) Italy. In *Evidence in International Arbitration Proceedings*, Peter V. Eijsvoogel (ed.), 165–174. London: Graham & Trotman.

Ceccon, R. (2000) La Corte Arbitrale di Venezia, una nuova istituzione per attrarre l'arbitrato internazionale in Italia [The Venice Arbitration Chamber, a new institution to attract international arbitration to Italy]. In *Le prospettive dell'arbitrato interno ed internazionale: il Regolamento della Corte Arbitrale di Venezia*, 7–12. Turin: Giappichelli.

Chroma, M. (2003) The Language of Arbitration: From Intent to the Act. In Bhatia, Candlin and Gotti (eds.), 63–86.

Cremades, B. M. (1998) Overcoming the Clash of Legal Cultures: The Role of Interactive Arbitration. *Arbitration International* 14 (2): 157–172.

David, R. / Brierley, J. E. (1985) *Major Legal Systems in the World Today: An Introduction to the Study of Comparative Law*. London: Stevens and Sons.

Dossena, M. (2003) Arbitration in Scotland: Local Specificity and International Homogeneity. In Bhatia, Candlin and Gotti (eds.), 87–109.

Driedger, E. A. (1982) Legislative Drafting Style: Civil Law *versus* Common Law. In Jean-Claude Gémar (ed.), *Langage du droit et traduction / The Language of the Law and Translation*, 63–81. Montreal: Linguatech / Conseil de la Langue Française.

Frommel, S. N. and Rider, B. A. K. (eds.) (1999) *Conflicting Legal Cultures in Commercial Arbitration: Old Issues and New Trends*. The Hague: Kluwer Law International.

Garzone, G. (2003) Arbitration Rules across Legal Cultures: An Intercultural Approach. In Bhatia, Candlin and Gotti (eds.), 177–220.

Giannoni, D. S. (2003) The UNCITRAL Model and Italian Statute Law: A Linguistic and Topical Description. In Bhatia, Candlin and Gotti (eds.), 221–246.

Gotti, M. (2003) *Specialized Discourse: Linguistic Features and Changing Conventions*. Bern: Peter Lang.

Gustafsson, M. (1975) *Some Syntactic Properties of English Law Language*. Turku: University of Turku, Department of English.

Hiltunen, R. (1984) The Type and Structure of Clausal Embedding in Legal English. *Text* 4 (1–3): 107–121.

Hiltunen, R. (2001) Some Syntactic Properties of English Law Language: Twenty-five Years after Gustafsson (1975). In Hiltunen, Risto, Battarbee, Keith, Peikola, Matti, Tanskanen, Sanna-Kaisa (eds.) *English in Zigs and Zags*, 53–66. Turku: University of Turku.

ICCA (International Council for Commercial Arbitration) (1998) *International Dispute Resolution: Towards an International Arbitration Culture*. Albert Jan van den Berg (ed.). Dordrecht: Kluwer Law International.

Jarvin, S. (1999) Leading Arbitration Seats: A (Mostly European) Comparative View. In Frommel and Rider (eds.), 39– 61.

Kuper, A. (1999). *Culture: The Anthropologists' Account*. Cambridge: Cambridge University Press.

Lalive, P. (1992) On Communication in International Arbitration. *The American Review of International Arbitration* 3 (1–4): 79–82.

Lazareff, S. (1999) International Arbitration: Towards a Common Procedural Approach. In Frommel and Rider (eds.), 31–38.

Lowenfeld, A. F. (1999) International Arbitration as Omelette: What Goes into the Mix. In Frommel and Rider (eds.), 19–30.

Mellinkoff, D. (1963) *The Language of the Law*. Boston: Little, Brown & Co.

Merry, S. E. (1990) *Getting Justice and Getting Even*. Chicago and London: Longman.

Nadelmann, K. H. and von Mehren, A. T. (1967) Equivalences in Treaties in the Conflicts Field, *The American Journal of Comparative Law* 15: 195–203.

Nida, E. A. (2001) *Context in Translating*. Amsterdam: Benjamins.

Pathak, R. S. (1998) When and Where Do National Courts Reflect an International Culture When Deciding Issues Relating to International Arbitration? In ICCA, 173–186.

Paulsson, J. (1981) Arbitration Unbound: Award Detached from the Law of Its Country of Origin, *International and Comparative Law Quarterly* 30, 358–387.

Petta, P. (1994) Il linguaggio del legislatore [The legislator's language]. *Quaderni Regionali*, 1303–1316.

Saleh, S. (1992) La perception de l'arbitrage au Machrek et dans les pays du Golfe. *Revue de l'Arbitrage* 4, 549.

Salmi-Tolonen, T. (2003) Arbitration Law as Action: An Analysis of the Finnish Arbitration Act. In Bhatia, Candlin and Gotti (eds.), 313–332.

Taniguchi, Y. (1998) Is There a Growing International Arbitration Culture? An Observation from Asia. In ICCA, 31–40.

Tiersma, P. M. (1999) *Legal language*. Chicago: The University of Chicago Press.

Trosborg, A. (1997) Translating Hybrid Political Texts. In Anna Trosborg (ed.), *Text Typology and Translation*, 145–158. Amsterdam: Benjamins.

Vermeer, H. J. (1986) Übersetzen als kulturelle Transfer. In Mary Snell-Hornby (ed.), *Übersetzungswissenschaft — Eine Neuorientierung*, 30–53. Tübingen: Francke.

Vermeer, H. J. (1996) A Skopos Theory of Translation (Some Arguments For and Against). Heidelberg: Textcontext Wissenschaft.

Applications and Implications

12

Arbitration in Sport

Paola Evangelisti Allori

INTRODUCTION

The purpose of the study is to analyse from a cross cultural perspective some of the discursive practices of legal practitioners in the field of arbitration in sports. It will focus on some of the relevant rhetorical and textual features of the legal discourse exhibited by the *International Code of Arbitration for Sport*, issued by the International Council for Arbitration in Sport (ICAS), and the *Code for Conciliation and Arbitration for Sport*, recently issued by the Italian 'Camera di Conciliazione e Arbitrato per lo Sport' established within the Italian Olympic Committee (CONI).

Within the wider field of linguistic studies on arbitration (Bhatia, Candlin, Engberg and Trosborg 2003; Bhatia, Candlin and Gotti 2003; Gotti and Candlin 2004), sports-related arbitration is a new and interesting area of enquiry. This is in part because of the peculiarities of the field of sport which is a close, albeit worldwide, system with its own hierarchically structured internal organization, both at national and international level, of the bodies operating in it — associations, national and international federations, and national Olympic Committees. Arbitration practice in this field seems to constitute almost a system in its own, even though the basic mechanisms adopted for the arbitration procedure — as interpreted from the analysis of the regulations — would appear to be much in line with those of arbitration in commerce (Evangelisti Allori 2004). For one thing, in a manner different from arbitration in commerce, international arbitration for sports is regulated, worldwide, by one single code and by one single tribunal, that is, the Court for Arbitration in Sport (CAS; from now on 'the Court'), located in Lausanne, Switzerland, which is the only recognised seat for arbitration. Both ICAS and CAS are created and recognised by the International Olympic Committee (IOC). The ultimate authority behind the Court is, therefore, the IOC which regulates and coordinates sports activities worldwide. Regionally, on the other hand, arbitration is regulated by national codes created by the various National Olympic Committees (NOCs), the national authorities for any sports-related matters. Again, differently from the field of commerce, there seems to be only one national regulation and a single body qualified to carry out arbitration in each country.

The close ties linking the various NOCs to IOC would seem to imply evenness in arbitration practice in international and regional dispute settling. In practice, though, the national codes, while taking into account the international code and the workings of the international Court, are also influenced by the socio-political and legal context of the particular country, as seems also to be the case with the Italian regulation. In consequence, while the stated aim for the establishment of ICAS was to provide "a necessary harmonization of procedural rules by national and international sports federations …" much ground is still to be covered as stated in the Guide to the International Regulation (2000).

The aim of the comparison between national and international regulations is, thus, to identify the extent to which the country-specific socio-political and legal contexts may affect some aspects in of the practice of sports-related arbitration.

THE MATERIALS ANALYSED

The two regulations analysed were issued at different points in time. The international code was issued in 1994, when the ICAS was first created. The published edition dates from January 2000. The Italian code was first issued in 2002, when the 'Camera di Conciliazione e Arbitrato per lo Sport' (from now on 'CCAS'), was established.

The international code appears both in English and French, on facing pages in the published version. Rule S24 states that the English text and the French text are authentic, but "In the event of any divergence, the French text shall prevail". English and French are also the Court official languages. The code includes, as a first section, the 'Statutes of the Bodies working for the settlement of Sports-related issues' which includes both the ICAS and CAS statutory rules. No mention of the statute of the CCAS is made in the Italian code, this being included as article 12 within the

CONI Statute. In the analysis, therefore, only the rules dealing with the arbitration procedure proper were taken into consideration. These amount to 7,343 words in the international and 6,314 in the Italian code, both including the Schedule of Costs.

Both codes are based on civil law legal systems, the international Court's being based on the Swiss 'Federal Code on Private International Law' and the CCAS's on the Italian 'Code on Civil Procedure' and its further subdivisions into public and private law.

THE BACKGROUND CONTEXT OF PRACTICE

The issuing bodies

The ICAS is a supranational body established as the result of the 1994 Paris agreement between the International Olympic Committee, the National Olympic Committees and the International Federations to "settle, through arbitration, sports-related disputes". ICAS is, therefore, an independent international body, and, as such, is not called to respond to any specific state law system. Like many other supranational bodies, it has its seat in Switzerland, thus adopting the 'Swiss Code on Private International Law' as its working law.

The Italian Chamber for Conciliation and Arbitration for Sport (from now on 'the Chamber') was established by the Italian National Olympic Committee. The legal status of CONI is somewhat peculiar in that it can be regulated by either the public or private branch of the Italian Civil Code according to its multifaceted functions. In other words, CONI has a mixed area of legal competence; it acts as a public body, ruled by the public branch of the Italian civil law, in its function as a body coordinating, and ruling on, the sports activities of the national federations, military sport associations, sport clubs and non-profit associations, such as university and youth sport clubs. At the same time, it functions as a private limited company, ruled by the private branch of the Italian Civil Code, where commercial sports-related matters are concerned. Figure 12.2 shows the socio-political and legal context in which CONI operates.

Further, when acting as a public body with sports regulating functions, the regulations issued by CONI become part of public law. This means that there are close, and sometimes intertwined, ties between the public branch of the Civil Code and the CONI regulations. Thus, the

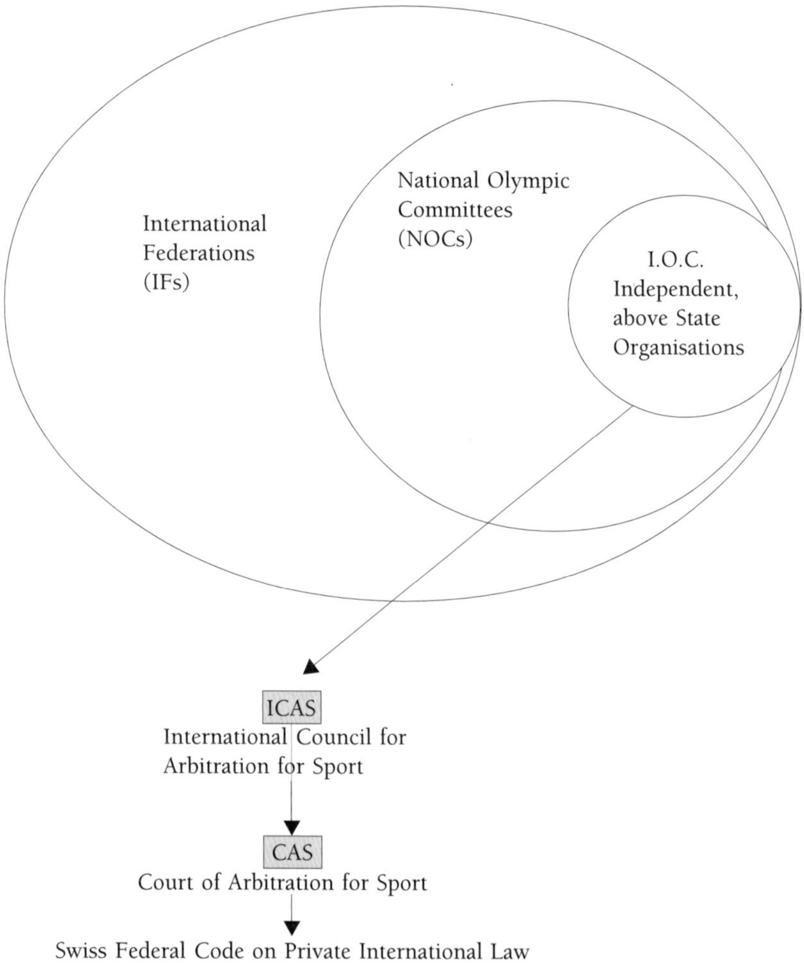

Fig. 12.1 The I.O.C. Areas of Competence and Legal System

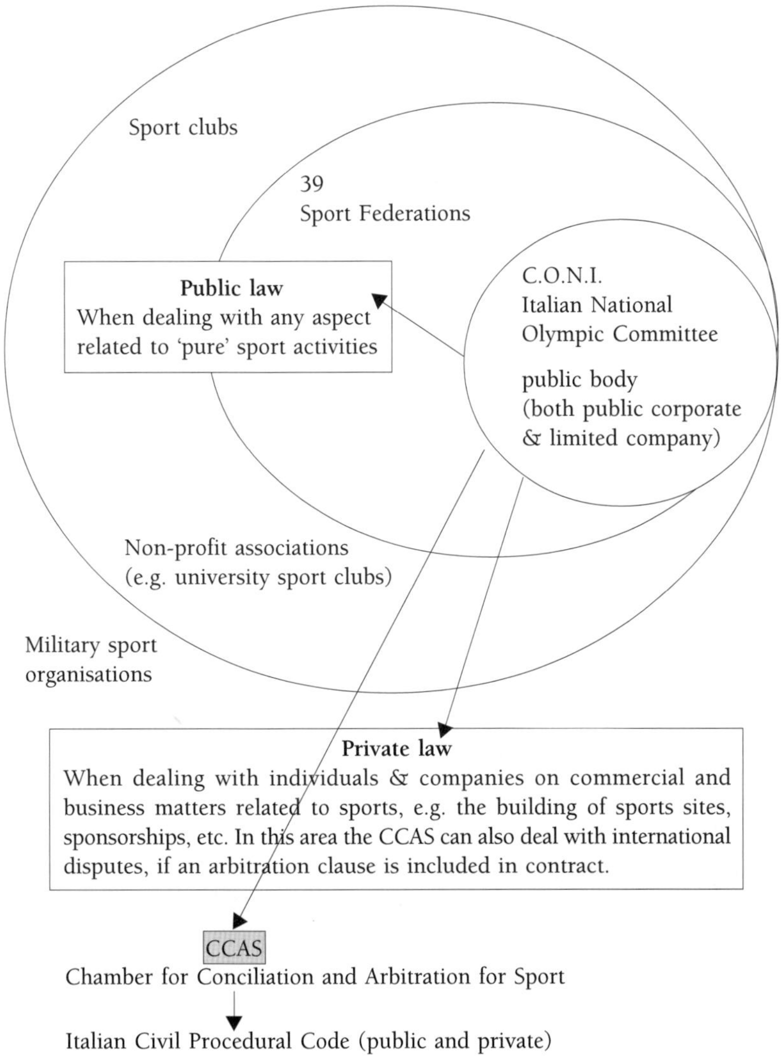

Fig. 12.2 The C.O.N.I. Areas of Competence and Legal System

Regulation of the Chamber for Conciliation and Arbitration for Sport, although pertaining to the private branch of the civil law, is also regulated in some way by the public branch through CONI, and is modelled on the standard public law procedure for regulation drafting, as specifically stated in Art. 20 (1) on the writing of the award.

The difference in the background legal context in which the two codes operate may, thus, explain some of the variation found in the analysis.

KEY ELEMENTS IN ARBITRATION REGULATIONS

A previous analysis carried out on the actions performed by the legislator in the process of laying out arbitration rules in two international regulations pertaining to the fields of sport and business (Evangelisti Allori, 2004) showed the presence in two of a common set of core actions seemingly relating to key aspects in the arbitration procedure. It was hypothesised that the common actions identified might be typical of any arbitration procedure, thus constituting the bare bones of, or the blueprint for, any regulation drafting in arbitration. The common actions related to such aspects of the drafting procedure as the definition of the scope of application and the field of action, the rules concerning the arbitral tribunal, its composition, the appointment of arbitrators and the qualification and behaviour requested of them, the identification of the seat or place of arbitration, the procedural rules and the rules about the Award, up to the indication of costs and directions about payments. The rules strictly relating to the arbitration procedure further specified the nature and form of the proceedings, the kind of action required of the various participants, the time-limits for different procedural actions, the law applicable and the language(s) to be used. Model arbitration clauses, to be included in contracts, were also provided in the two international codes.

Within this common conceptual frame (van Dijk 1977; Shank and Abelson 1977; van Dijk and Kintsch 1983), however, there appeared to be substantial variation in the sequence of sections and the distribution of information within the codes, as well as in the kind and amount of information given in rules bearing the same label. Such variation appeared to point to differences in the practice of arbitration in the two fields of action.

The same kind of "move analysis" (Swales 1990) previously applied (Bhatia and Candlin 2004) to the UNCITRAL and ICAS codes was therefore applied to ICAS and CCAS to identify the kind of pragmatic action(s) performed by the legal draftsperson in each rule/article in the writing of one or the other sports-related code. The comparison confirmed the substantial identity of steps to be found in what appears to be the common conceptual frame for the genre, notwithstanding place or headings under which the action is placed in the text. It would thus seem that provision about the following set of actions is necessary in the drafting of any arbitration regulation, independently of the field of action and of the scope of application:

1. (DEFINE) Scope of application;
2. (DEFINE) Field of action;
3. (PROVIDE) Standard arbitration clause(s) [to be inserted in contract] (*)
4. (ESTABLISH) Composition of arbitral tribunal/panel;
5. (QUALIFY) Arbitrators;
6. (ESTABLISH) Rules regarding arbitrators;
7. (IDENTIFY) Seat/place of arbitration
8. (ESTABLISH) Rules for arbitration procedure;
   - ➢ (DEFINE) Nature and form of proceedings [written, oral];
   - ➢ (DEFINE) Participants;
   - ➢ (ESTABLISH) Action required of participants;
   - ➢ (ESTABLISH) Time-limits [for different actions/aspects within procedure];
   - ➢ (STATE) Law applicable; (*)
   - ➢ (STATE) Rules about language(s) to be used; (*)
9. (ESTABLISH) Rules for award;
10. (ESTABLISH) Possibility of revision of award;
11. (ESTABLISH) Possibility of interpretation of award;
12. (ESTABLISH) Default rules;
13. (PROVIDE) Indications about costs +/- directions about payments.[1]

At the same time, however, variation was again found in the distribution of information, in the prominence and weight assigned to rules under the same headings, and in the provision made for some additional aspects rather than others. Such variation between the two sports-related regulations seems to be indicative of some kind of difference in the

---

1 The items marked with an asterisk in the list, which are common to the two international regulations previously analysed, do not appear in the Italian document — The reason for the absence of a model arbitration clause being its presence in Art. 12 in the CONI Stature which sets the basis for the creation of the Chamber; mention about the language to be used and the law applicable is, on the other hand, considered superfluous in a regulation for arbitration to be applied on a national scale.

approach to arbitration practice. Thus, while the previous hypothesis about a common frame for arbitration regulations still appears to hold true, we may also posit variation due to cultural factors.

VARIATION

Variation in section distribution and headings

Sections and section headings are indicative of the way the topic 'regulation' is subdivided and dealt with. Their distribution in the text indicates where in the code provisions about specific aspects are made. It also provides a first general idea of the prominence assigned to some aspects of the procedure over others. ICAS and CCAS exhibit a somewhat different layout of information as shown in Table 12.1 which provides a comparative picture of the sections and of their distribution in the two codes under analysis.

In the table, sections whose headings have an exact counterpart in the other code have been highlighted and variation in their position in the text indicated by the arrows connecting them. As can be seen from the table, the ICAS regulation is made up of two main parts, the 'Statutes of the Bodies Working for the Settlement of Sports-related Disputes' and the 'Procedural Rules' proper. CCAS has no statutory rules although Title I — 'The Chamber' provides a counterpart to point C in the ICAS Statute. The Procedural Rules, which is the part taken into consideration here, is made up in ICAS of six sections, A to G, and three appendices whereas the CCAS regulation is made up of four sections, Titles I to IV, and a separate schedule of costs thus leaving four sections for the rules for procedure proper.

The rule numbering in ICAS runs from 1 to 69; rules 1 to 26, belonging to the statutes, are preceded by the letter 'S' while the procedural rules, 27 to 69 are preceded by an 'R'. CCAS numbering runs from 1 to 29 each rule being indicated by the letters 'Art'. The number of rules dealing with the arbitration procedure proper in the two regulations are therefore 49 in ICAS versus 28 in CCAS.

Section headings and their sequencing in the text, in turn, seem to provide a different perspective on the way of conceiving the procedure. For example, the Italian CCAS, after Title 1, Art. 1–1.7, in which the nature, affiliation, composition and attributions of the Chamber are laid down, has three sections in sequence dealing with the different 'functions'

Table 12.1 Sections and their distribution in the two texts

ICAS (2000) (English and French)	CCAS (2002) (Italian)
Statutes of the Bodies Working for the Settlement of Sports-related Disputes A. Joint Dispositions B. The International Council of Arbitration for Sport (ICAS) **C. The Court of Arbitration for Sport (CAS)** D. Miscellaneous Provisions Statutory rules S1–26	**Title I. The Chamber of Conciliation and Arbitrations for Sport** Article 1
	Title II. Consultation Function Art. 2
(R42 under B below)	**Title III. Consultation Function** Art.s 3–6
Procedural Rules A. General Provisions Rules 27–37	**Title IV. Arbitration Function** Art.s 7–17
B. Special Provisions Applicable to the Ordinary Arbitration Proceedings R37–46	(cont.) Art.s 17–23
C. Special Provisions Applicable to the Appeal Arbitration Proceedings R47–59	(Not present)
D. Special Provisions Applicable to the Consultation Proceedings R60–63	
E. Interpretation R63	(Not present)
F. Costs of the Proceedings R64–66	(Art. 23 under IV. above)
G. Miscellaneous Provisions R67–69	**Title V. Miscellaneous Provisions** Art.s 24–29
	Schedule of dues, fees and costs of the Chamber
Appendix I. Standard Arbitration clauses	
Appendix II. Schedule of Arbitration costs	
Appendix III. Switzerland's Federal Code on Private International Law	

of the Chamber; these form the core of the regulation and follow a logical order of complexity of intervention, from simple consultation to arbitration via the intermediate step of conciliation. Miscellaneous provisions obviously conclude the regulation proper; the schedule of dues, fees and costs for the Chamber being presented as a separate part although, formally, not as an appendix. No further subheadings appear and, within sections, only the main articles have headings indicating the aspect of the procedure being dealt with.

ICAS is less linear in its conceptual layout. The rules concerning the nature, affiliation, composition and attributions of the Court are laid down in point C within the Statutes. But, C, further subdivided into 1. *Mission*, 2. *Arbitrators*, 3. *Organization of the CAS*, also introduces in point 2 (general) rules about the arbitrators, not given in the same position in CCAS. Further, the sub-headings relative to the five sections under the main 'Procedural Rules', excluding the final 'Miscellaneous Provision', i.e. *General Provisions, Special Provisions Applicable to the Ordinary Arbitration ACTICE Proceedings, Special Provisions Applicable to the Appeal Arbitration Proceedings, Special Provisions Applicable to the Consultation Proceedings, Interpretation, Costs of the Proceedings,* not only exhibit variation in order, but also provide a different picture of the proceedings as contemplated by the ICAS. For instance, *Consultation*, which in the Italian code opens the rule sequence, is provided for only in section D, after the general provisions and the provisions for ordinary and appeal arbitration have been established.

Besides location, variation is also found in the amount of space given to common aspects and in the procedures mentioned. *Conciliation*, which in CCAS forms step two, and to which a whole separate section is assigned, is dealt with in ICAS in one single rule (R42) within the ordinary arbitration proceedings. ICAS, on the other hand, assigns a whole separate section to *Costs* which in CCAS is reduced to one article (Art. 23) within the *Arbitration* section. ICAS further provides, in the appendices, the standard arbitration clauses to be inserted in contracts and the Swiss Federal Code on Private International Law. CCAS does not mention these two aspects, the standard arbitration clause being provided in the CONI Statute which forms a separate document, while it is, probably, given for granted that the applicable law is the Italian Code on Civil Procedure. Two further aspects, *Appeal Arbitration Proceedings* and *Interpretation* have no counterpart, anywhere, in the Italian regulation.

From the analysis of the general layout of the two codes, it thus appears that ICAS provides for aspects not touched upon by the Italian regulation and that different prominence and different weight is sometimes assigned to aspects which are common to both. Whether, and the extent to which, such diversities actually affect the arbitration practice in the two spheres of action or whether they are unsubstantial in the daily practice of experienced arbitrators cannot to be judged here, although, intuitively, they seem to point to differences in the way the whole procedure is conceived of by the issuing institutions.

Prominence

As it appears from the number of sections, their disposition in the text and the headings given, different prominence is assigned in the two codes to some aspects of the procedure over others.

The main, and probably most substantial, difference to be noticed is the sequence in which the *Consultation–Conciliation–Arbitration* sections are placed in the Italian regulation (Titles II–IV). Conceptually, consultation proceedings are somewhat disanchored from either conciliation or arbitration in that the concept of consultation does not imply open litigation, but simply requesting an advisory opinion on some legal matter which may or may not later lead to conciliation or arbitration, but not necessarily so. The placing of reference to consultation either before or after the other two kinds of proceedings does, therefore, not seem to particularly alter the general picture. Conciliation, on the other hand, takes place when litigation has already started. Conciliation proceedings refer to the action taken as a first attempt at settling a litigation amicably; in case of an agreement being reached through conciliation, an award is issued which states the terms of the agreement, thus taking the litigation to a (legal) end. The CCAS code requires that conciliation be attempted before any request for arbitration is filed in, as stated in Art. 3, where the general provisions for conciliation are laid out; 3(5) states that "An attempt at conciliation is obligatory before any arbitration proceedings is initiated". This is further reiterated in Art. 7, concerning the general provisions for the arbitration proceedings, where it is stated, in 7(6), that: "The arbitration proceedings can only be initiated after any previous attempt at conciliation according to the present Regulation has failed". This explains both the prominence given to the provisions for conciliation in a separate section, and the place they hold in the sequence of sections.

On the other hand, the fact that ICAS places the provisions relating to consultation only in a section following the three dedicated to the two kinds of arbitration contemplated and, in addition, deals with conciliation in one single rule within the provisions for ordinary arbitration, would seem to be indicative of greater importance assigned to arbitration in the practice of the international Court as against the other two aspects. The prominence of the arbitration function contemplated by the international Court is further reinforced by the presence of one section on provisions for the Appeal Arbitration Proceedings, which has no counterpart, anywhere, in the Italian regulation. Appeal arbitration, defined in ICAS (R47) as "appeal from the decision of a disciplinary tribunal or similar body of a federation, association or sports body ...", is not contemplated in CCAS since, according to the code for Civil Procedure, it can only be brought to a State Court of Appeal in the Italian system, it is therefore out of the CCAS jurisdiction.

Weight

The weight assigned within sections to a specific aspect was assessed in terms of the number of rules dealing with that aspect. This was applied particularly where substantial divergence was found, as in the case of *Consultation* and *Conciliation*, which although contemplated in both codes are dealt with somewhat differently. Table 12.2, provides a complete picture of the number of rules and paragraphs given to specific aspects within each relevant section in the two codes.

Consultation is dealt with in one single rule in CCAS Art. 2 (1–7) and in three in ICAS; ICAS headings to each rule also seem to indicate full-bodied proceedings rather than just general provisions as it would seem to be the case in CCAS.

Conciliation, on the other hand, is dealt with by ICAS in one single rule, R42, appearing as one of the points under *Arbitration Proceedings* whereas CCAS provides for it in four articles (3–6), subdivided into twenty-five paragraphs. The weight given to conciliation in CCAS thus reinforces the already mentioned importance attributed to it by the Italian Chamber. Much in the same way, the award is dealt with in one single rule (R46) in ICAS while CCAS provides for it in three articles (20–22) for a total of fifteen paragraphs. Given the disparity in the number of rules assigned, weight was further assessed in terms of the propositional content present in each rule or article in order to ascertain the amount and kind of information about the procedure provided. The Gricean maxim of quantity — "Make your contribution as informative as possible.

Table 12.2 Weight in terms of number of rules assigned to consultation and conciliation in the two codes

ICAS (200) (English and French	CCAS (2002) (Italian)
	Titolo II. Consultation Function Art. 2 Opinions given by the Chamber (2.1–2.7)
	Titolo III. Consultation Function Art. 3 Consultation proceedings (3.1–3.5) Art. 4 Consultation proceedings (4.1–4.9) Art. 5 Consultation meeting (5.1–5.8) Art. 6 Communications and time-limits in the conciliation proceedings (6.1–6.3)
Procedural Rules A. *General Provisions* R27 Application of the Rules R28 Seat R29 Language R30 Representation and assistance R31 Notifications and communications R32 Time-limit R33 Independence and qualifications of arbitrators R34 Challenge R35 Removal R36 Replacement R37 Provisional and conservatory measures	**Titolo IV. Arbitration Function** Art. 7 Conditions for arbitration (7.1–7.8) Art. 8 Request by appellant (8.1–8.4) Art. 9 Answer by respondent (9.1–9.5) Art. 10 Communications and time-limits in arbitration (10.1–10.3) Art. 11 Formation of the Panel Art. 12 Sole arbitrator (12.1–12.2) Art. 13 Arbitration board (13.1–13.4) Art. 14 Acceptance and declaration of independence by arbitrators (14.1–14.4) Art. 15 Challenge and substitution of arbitrators (15.1–15.9) Art. 16 Seat and Secretariat (16.1–16.2)
B. *Special Provisions Applicable to the Ordinary Arbitration Proceedings* R38 Request for arbitration R39 Initiation of the arbitration by the CAS and answer R40 Formation of the Panel (40.1–40.3) R41 Multiparty arbitration (41.1–41.4) R42 Conciliation R43 Confidentiality R44 Procedure before the Panel (44.1–44.5) R45 Law applicable to the merits R46 Award	Art. 17 Procedural rules (17.1–17.8) Art. 18 Hearings and minutes (18.1–18.8) Art. 19 Amiable composition before termination (19.1–19.4) Art. 20 Final decision and signing of award (20.1–20.5) Art. 21 Time-limit and filing of award (21.1–21.6) Art. 22 Content of award (22.1–22.4) Art. 23 Costs of proceedings (23.1–23.3)
D. *Special Provisions Applicable to the Consultation Proceedings* R60 Request for opinion R61 Initiation by the CAS R62 Opinion	

Do not be more informative than required" (Grice 1975: 45) — is likely to apply, particularly when, as in the drafting of legal documents, the objective of writing is clear, effective and efficient communication, as pointed out by Trosborg (1997: 136). This is more so when such documents constitute the basis for social action aimed at solving disputes through a speedy and more informal procedure than justice before a Court. Difference in the quantity and kind of information provided in specific rules common to both codes is therefore likely to be meaningful.

Weight in terms of kind and amount of subject matter dealt with

The quantity principle based on the number of rules proved not to be always indicative of unbalance in the aspects covered when these were analysed in terms of the amount and kind of information actually provided. In the case of consultation, for instance, the further analysis of the propositional content indicated that the difference in number of rules did not correspond to a substantial unbalance in the amount and kind of information provided, as shown in Table 12.3.

Table 12.3 Amount and kind of information provided about consultation

ICAS	CCAS
R60 <u>Request for Opinion</u> Bodies entitled to request opinion + kind of subject matter admitted for opinion + indications as to the filing in of request. R61 <u>Initiation by the CAS</u> Attributions of CAS President on: admissibility + formation of Panel and designation of president + formulation of questions for the Panel. Duty of president in forwarding to the Panel. R62 <u>Opinion</u> Admissibility of request for additional information + possibility of publicity of opinion on consent of the party + legal value of the opinion [non-binding award]	<u>Art. 2 Opinions rendered by the Chamber</u> 1. Legal value of the opinion [non-binding] + reference to the relevant art.s of CONI Statute. 2. Board charged with the formulation of questions + number and provenance of components. 3. Submission of preliminary opinion to the Chamber + question taken over by Chamber in case of request by three of its members. 4. Bodies entitled to request opinion. 5. Subject matter admitted for opinion. 6. Time sequence for payment of dues. 7. Subject matter not eligible for opinion.

A fair amount of variation was found, on the other hand, in the case of conciliation and award, where the Italian regulation is more detailed and punctual in providing for the procedural steps involved in these two phases of the proceedings. Tables 12.4 and 12.5 illustrate the imbalance found in the two regulations.

Table 12.4 Amount and kind of information provided about conciliation

ICAS	CCAS
R42 Conciliation Conciliation attempt by president of division, + conciliation attempt by Panel, + arbitral award.	**Title III. Conciliation function** Art. 3 Conciliation (3.1–3.5) 1. Definition of cases subject to conciliation 2. Initiation of request for conciliation 3. Further cases subject to conciliation 4. Exclusions 5. Obligatority of conciliation before arbitration Art. 4 Conciliation proceedings (4.1–4.9) 1. Time-limits for initiation 2. Nature and objective of conciliation 3. Appointment of conciliator 4. Duties of the parties 5. Initiation: duties of the appellant 6. Information to be included in request 7. Requirements about payment of administrative dues 8. Answer by respondent and time-limit for payment of administrative dues 9. Stage for appointment of conciliator Art. 5 Conciliation meeting (5.1–5.8) 1. Seat of meetings 2. Time-limit for first meeting 3. Nature of meetings (informal) 4. Presence of the parties 5. Admissibility of participation by more parties 6. Agreement: signing and enforcement 7. Closure of procedure in case of disagreement 8. Consequences of conciliation failure (none) Art. 6 Communications and time-limits in the conciliation proceedings (6.1–6.3) 1. Form of communications 2. Date of communication 3. Derogation from time-limits

Table 12.5 Kind and amount of information given about the Award

ICAS	CCAS
RCAS Award Made by majority decision, or by the President alone in absence of majority; + To be written, dated and signed; + Signature of sole President sufficient; + Final and binding; + Not challengeable except for people having habitual residence/domicile in Switzerland	**Art. 20 Decision making and signing of the Award** (20.1–20.5) Made by majority decision in presence of all components of the arbitral panel; + Written according to the norms of the Civil Procedural code; + Number of original copies required; + Possibility of signing at different times and places; + Indication of time and place of each member of the panel; + Final and binding from date of last signature; + Possibility of making public the final decision in case of urgency; + Need for the final decision and subsequent complete award to be signed by single arbitrator or by majority of panel; + When award signed only by majority, need for explicit declaration about presence of entire panel to the decision making and about unwillingness or inability to sign by minority members.
	Art. 21 Time limits and filing procedure (21.1–21.6) Time limit for filing the complete award; + Number of original copies required; + Communication to the parties; + Publication of Award; + Conditions of suspension of time limits; + Prorogation of time limits.
	Art. 22 Contents (22.1–22.4) Aspects to be dealt with in the award; + Possibility of partial award; + Time limits; + Attribution of fees and expenses to party/ parties.

ICAS provides scanty information, limited to a statement about the *possibility* of a first attempt to conciliation made by the president of the appropriate division and by the Panel afterwards. This is followed by a statement about the possibility for the eventual settlement to be embodied in an arbitral award. CCAS, on the other hand, provides detailed information about the whole procedure for conciliation from the definition of admissible cases and of exclusions (Art. 3) to the norms about the proceedings (Art. 4) and the conciliation meeting (Art. 5), up to the final formal aspects about form and time of the communications and eventual derogations from time-limits (Art. 6). CCAS, therefore, presents a full-bodied image of conciliation rather than just mentioning its possibility.

Much in the same way, a fair amount of detailed information is provided in CCAS about the award which, again, details a number of features pertaining to the process of decision making and issuing of the award not touched upon in ICAS. Even where dealing with the same aspects of the procedure, the two codes exhibit variation in approach, as is particularly evident in the specific norms for decision making and subsequent writing and signing of the award.

About decision making and signing, for instance, CCAS states in 20(1) that "the award is to be made by majority decision, in presence of the whole Panel", a concept reiterated in 20(5) which states that "when the award is signed only by the majority of the panel, it must contain a statement that the decision was taken in presence of all arbitrators and that the minority would not or could not sign". ICAS, on the other hand, states that the award "shall be made by a majority decision, or, in the absence of a majority, by the President alone ... The signature of the President of the Panel shall suffice." And, concerning the writing, CCAS (20.1) has "[the award] is to be written according to the norms of Art. 823 of the Code of Civil Procedure" and in (22.1) "The award must discuss all aspects of the dispute and state reasons for each of them" whereas ICAS simply states that "The award shall be written, dated and signed. Unless the parties agree otherwise, it shall briefly state reasons".

COMMENTS AND CONCLUSIONS

The international and Italian codes for sports-related arbitration were compared and contrasted in order to find out whether there might be loci of possible conflict between practice at international and regional level. The macro-textual analysis has looked at the general layout of the regulations in terms of number of sections, the headings given and their disposition in the text. The comparison has also focused in more detail on specific key aspects of the procedure where variation was most evident.

While it had initially been hypothesised that variation in provision making, particularly in the prominence and weight given to the information provided, might be indicative of corresponding variation in the procedure, the actual import of variation on the practice of international arbitration remains to be ascertained. The analysis has nonetheless made evident the existence of substantial variation in two codes relating to the same field of action and stemming out of similar legal civil law systems. It has also shown that variation exists not so much in the overall conceptual frame, as in the way that frame is interpreted in the drafting of specific regulations. Thus, it seems evident that the kind of variation examined is to be explained in terms of a number of socio-political factors among which the background legal context of action and the legal position of the issuing authorities within it play an important role. The way the rules for conciliation and arbitration are laid down in the two codes provides an interesting example of the impact of such factors on regulation drafting.

The Italian document stems from a public body regulated by the state law, as such, it is drafted according to the norms of the Italian Code of Civil Procedure, which is also explicitly mentioned in the case of the writing of the award. Probably for the same reason, the arbitration contemplated in it has a 'ritual' nature, i.e. it is a form of arbitration where the arbitrator acts as a proper judge and the award issued has the force of a court judgment, as against the 'irritual' form of arbitration in which the arbitrator is simply a 'compositeur' of litigation and the final award equals a contract. This may explain a number of features in the Italian Chamber's regulation, such as the punctiliousness in detailing the various steps and actions to be taken and the way in which they should be taken, which seem to relate to a preoccupation to formally ensuring a transparent 'public' ruling of the proceedings, a factor which is also typical of any Italian public document drafting.

The international regulation, on the other hand, stems out of a body — the international Court — which is part of an independent supranational organisation, thus not tied to any specific state law. Further, although adopting the Swiss Federal Code for its workings, reference is made only to the part of the code relative to the private sector. The freedom from the public sector ties no doubt allows more flexibility in regulation drafting, albeit within the limits posed by the private code and the need to ensure transparency to the proceedings. In addition, or probably as a consequence of that freedom, the international Court applies the 'irritual' form of arbitration, which requires less punctiliousness in detailing the various steps and actions to be taken and allows for the attribution of a higher degree of power to a single person representing authority. The manifest tendency of the ICAS regulation to attribute some kind of power or other to the president alone may be due to a preoccupation to ensure a smooth and speedy running of the proceedings, but supposedly could not be accepted in a document issued by a public body and has no counterpart in CCAS.

REFERENCES

Bhatia, V. K. and Candlin, C. N. (2004) Analysing Arbitration Laws across Legal Systems. In *Hermes* 32: 13–43.

Bhatia, V. K., Candlin, C. N., Engberg, J. and Trosborg, A. (eds.) (2003) *Multilingual and Multicultural Aspects of Legislation: An International Perspective*. Bern: Peter Lang.

Bhatia, V. K., Candlin, C. N. and Gotti, M. (eds.) (2003) *Legal Discourse in Multilingual and Multicultural Contexts: Arbitration Texts in Europe*. Bern: Peter Lang.

Evangelisti Allori, P. (2004) International Arbitration in Different Settings: Same or Different Practice? In Gotti, M. and Candlin, C. N. (eds.), *Intercultural Aspects of Specialized Communication*. Bern: Peter Lang.

Gotti, M. and Candlin, C. N. (eds.) (2004) *Intercultural Aspects of Specialized Communication*. Bern: Peter Lang.

Grice, P. 1975. Logic and Conversation, In Cole, P. and Morgan J. (eds.) *Syntax and Semantics III: Speech Acts* 41, 58. New York: Academic Press.

Shank, R. and Abelson, R. (1977) *Scripts, Plans, Goals and Understanding: An Enquiry into Human Knowledge Structures*. Hillsdale, NJ: Lawrence Erlbaum.

Swales, J. (1990) *Genre Analysis: English in Academic and Research Settings*. Cambridge: Cambridge University Press.

Trosborg, A. (1997) *Rhetorical Strategies in Legal Language*. Tübingen: Gunter Narr.

Van Dijk, T. A. (1977) *Text and Context*. London: Longman.

Van Dijk, T. A. and Kintsch, W. (1983) *Strategies of Discourse Comprehension*. London: Academic Press.

13

Implications of Legal Globalisation for Brazilian Legal Practice

Celina Frade

INTRODUCTION

Most commonly related to economics and the agenda of the so-called neo-liberalism,[1] the phenomenon of globalisation is in fact a part of more complex structural and strategic processes. It subsumes other subsystems — such as politics, education and law — and their actors acting globally on different spacio-time scales (Jessop 1999 and 2000).

Globalisation relies on two particular symbolic media of communication to mediate relations among institutions, organizations and actors on a global scale: law and language. In the first case, globalisation is legal-driven in its general intent to cover all legal relations within a global society. In the second case, globalisation is also discourse-driven insofar as language creates new words and terms for the representation of its ideas, the construction of its practices and the constitution of identities (Fairclough 2001).

As a natural complement to economic globalisation, legal globalisation constitutes the process of promoting the legal conditions for global trade and investment as the projection of their practices as universal and

1 Neo-liberalism can be described as "the hegemonic strategy economic globalization due to its support by leading international economic bodies (such as the OECD, IMF, and World Bank), its primacy in the United States (the still undisputed capitalist hegemony) and in other anglophone countries (notably Britain, Australia, New Zealand, and Canada), the significance of neo-liberal policy adjustments (even in the absence of a more radical neo-liberal regime change) in most other advanced capitalist economies, and its paradigmatic status for restructuring the post-socialist economies and integrating them into the global economy" (Jessop 1999)

'common sense'. Although clearly influenced by US legal approaches and legal English based on the common law tradition, the globalisation of law assumes its operational autonomy *vis-à-vis* other national laws. It does not exclude the possibility of reciprocal influences nor resistance to such (pre)dominance which "attempts to brake or guide it through various forms of strategic coordination" (Jessop 2000: 329). As a consequence, legal globalisation is changing the conditions under which national law firms and lawyers operate since nations can no longer view their laws in isolation.

In this chapter we analyse the implications of legal globalisation for Brazil's legal practice on various levels. As a Portuguese-speaking civil law developing country, Brazil is already fully integrated into global economy and now makes adjustments to comply with the latest requirements for getting legally global. We illustrate the claims with one of the most relevant contributions for inserting Brazil into legal globalization: the enactment of the Brazilian Arbitration Law 9.307/1996 (hereafter 'the Law')[2] and its implications on national legal practice, culture, discourse and education. On the one hand, national legal discourse tends to display a new texturing or "new making of meanings" to reflect the "generalized tensions between international practices and local traditions" (Fairclough 2001: 25–26). On the other hand, legal education and professional training calls for a new perspective with the purpose to train 'international lawyers' to achieve "core international legal competence" (Orban III 2001: 53).

The chapter is organized as follows. First, we make an attempt to define legal globalisation as a complement to economic globalisation. Next, we elaborate on the implications of legal globalization in Brazil on the organizational, procedural, and jurisdictional levels. On the discursive level, the trend is towards a new texturing so as to accommodate both national and global interests in legal texts. Then, we provide a more detailed analysis of the current context towards the internationalization of national legal education and professional training as a consequence of legal globalisation. We conclude by posing future challenges for our legal practice and for Brazilian linguistics and applied linguistics in a global legal environment.

2 The original text of the Brazilian Arbitration Law 9.307/1996 is available only in Portuguese in the issue of the *Official Gazette of the Federal Executive* [*Diário Oficial*], Section I, on 24 September 1996, page 18897. Due to its length, it has not been attached to this article.

LEGAL GLOBALISATION

Let us start making an attempt to throw some light on the "over-inflated, catchall quality" (Jessop 2000: 339) of the vogue term 'globalisation' most commonly associated with economic neo-liberalism. Far from being a simple and uniform phenomenon, globalisation involves both a complex combination of different structural and strategic processes and the restructuring in the network of social practices on spacio-temporal scales.

Structurally speaking, globalisation interrelates and interconnects several social systems of different degrees of importance, such as economy, law, education, science, politics and sport. Strategically speaking, globalisation refers to various actors' attempts to promote global coordination of activities in (but not necessarily across) different functional subsystems and/or the lifeworld[3] towards shareable global aims (Jessop 2000: 340). This combination of processes contributes to minimize socio-cultural variants and to eliminate the dominance of one system upon the other and include, among others, the internalization of national economic activities and multinationalization of national firms (see a complete account in Jessop 1999 and 2000). New forms of information, rapid advances in telecommunications and associated technologies (especially the Internet) have accelerated these processes and have "increasingly rendered insignificant the national boundaries that defined the period of economic nationalism" (Pinto 2002).

The neo-liberal agenda is also concerned with promoting the legal conditions for global trade and investment as the projection of its practices as universal and 'common sense'. Thus, as a complement to economic globalisation, legal globalisation refers to a combination of processes associated with a general intent to cover all legal relations and to make collectively binding decisions in the name of a global legal community.

Like all other phenomena resulting from globalisation, this combination of processes also involves a reordering in national legal discourses and also in the time-spatial scale of socio-legal relations among foreign corporations, law firms and legal practitioners — from national to global. Examples of fully global structural integration and strategic forms of coordination to achieve legal global aims will include: strategic

3 'Lifeworld' comprises "various social relations, identities, interests and values that stand outside and/or cut across specific systems rather than being anchored in them. It includes social relations such as gender, generation, etnicity, national identity, associational memberships, new social movements and so forth"(Jessop 2000: 332).

alliances of national law firms with global law firms, the acceptance of global legal norms in the solution of national issues, the new texturing of national laws towards harmonization for effective global communication and a new perspective for internationalizing national legal education. We will focus on these last two issues.

In an integrated globalised economy, institutionalized kinds of supranational laws (and procedures) have been developed to provide for their acceptance and uniformity in the regulation of issues which cannot be provided by national laws. This does not mean opposing national to global laws or rules but rather contributing to the coordination actions between them to compensate for "the progressive lack of structure of national laws" to meet global requirements (Garcez 1999: 193). Successful attempts to produce a set of global rules include, for example, the United Nations Convention on Contracts for the International Sales of Goods (CISG) and the United Nations Model Law on International Commercial Arbitration (UNCITRAL).

The ideal of achieving uniformity of laws implies the ideal of linguistic uniformity and the harmonization of legal education. The strategy for achieving linguistic uniformity is the widespread use of model laws, boilerplates, standard contracts and general conditions (van Houtte and Wautelet 2001: 93). The strategy for achieving the harmonization of legal education seems to be the dissemination of global communicative norms and genres "to reduce or even eliminate variation in people's ways of interacting", according to Cameron (2001: 81). In both cases, the US approaches based on common law tradition and legal English as the *lingua franca* prevail. For countries which use other legal systems and are not English speaking countries, like Brazil, the time has come to promote adjustments in their legal practice on various levels as we shall see next.

IMPLICATIONS OF LEGAL GLOBALIZATION IN BRAZIL

Over the past ten years, Brazil has been following strictly the adjustments dictated by the neo-liberal economic policy for restructuring the developing economies and integrating them into global economy.[4]

4 See a comprehensible account of Brazil's economic, legal and political structure in Frade (2003).

Likewise, national legal practice has been promoting adjustments on various levels to accommodate changes and innovations resulting from the reordering of legal practices from national to global in the material world and the relationship between them. Apart from innovations on the jurisdictional and procedural levels, which are beyond the scope of this article, relevant changes have also been occurring on the organizational, discursive and educational levels resulting in the emergence of a new legal culture in Brazil.

Global Alliances and the Emergence of a New Legal Culture

On the organization level, strategic alliances of national firms with international law firms confirm the trend of coordinating actions in and across globalised socio-cultural and legal sites. In Brazil, a specific law regulating the legal professional states that only members of the national bar association — OAB Ordem dos Advogados do Brasil — are allowed to engage in the practice of law in Brazilian territory and, consequently, that neither foreign legal consultants nor foreign law firms can render professional legal services or open offices here. Nonetheless, there is no impediment to a national law firm making strategic alliances with a foreign one provided that it keeps its local staff, clientele and policies while sharing the associate's international clientele and global policies. And that is what is happening with the major law firms in Brazil.

As Jessop (2000: 332) points out, the developments of these alliances tend to become "structurally coupled" through mutual adaptation to the changes in their environment generated by the operations of other systems — adaptations which are governed by each legal system's own operations code and organizational logic.

As far as arbitration is concerned, these strategic alliances have definitively contributed to its popularization in Brazil as the best chance for cost-effective resolution of commercial disputes and to the birth of an "arbitration culture" that has begun to flourish in many jurisdictions within and without the common law countries (see Zariski 2000 for more details on legal culture). As partners of global law firms, any Brazilian lawyer "may [now] be involved in a global transaction in which arbitration is the preferable means of dispute resolution" (Orban III 2001: 57) and thus have the opportunity to become more familiar with how a prototypical international arbitration is conducted independent from the national legal system. Also, the various arbitration rules that have been developed over time constitute a perfect guide to "what strategies can be employed to protect one's client's interests more effectively" (Woodbridge, Jr. and Mason 1999: 258) on both national and global level.

Although the classical lawsuit is still "deeply rooted in our legal culture, preventing an easy and quick access to justice" (Frade 2003: 19), the alternative for cost-effective resolution of commercial disputes through arbitration is giving birth to a "new disputing culture" towards mediation and arbitration in Brazil. This is happening not only within national legal practice and institutions but also within the "subjective perspective" (Zariski 2000) of Brazilian legal practitioners far as their new roles in legal globalisation are concerned. This fact is evidenced by the increasing number of lectures, courses and articles on arbitration delivered by expert lawyers not to mention the increase of arbitration chambers and national and foreign arbitral awards issued lately.

Thus what the Brazilian lawyer needs at the moment is to acquire appropriate communicative skills to cope with 'global' legal norms and genres which somehow involves "a one-way flow of expert knowledge from dominant to subaltern cultures" (Cameron 2001: 70). This means that at a minimum the Brazilian lawyer should know how the common law operates and what its key conceptual underpinnings are; become familiar with international standard legal genres (such as international contracts, laws and treaties) and with the art of negotiating in a global, cross-cultural setting (see Rodgers 1997) and be aware of the new texturing displayed in both national and international legal discourse to accommodate national and global space-times.

The New Texturing of National Legal Discourse

Fairclough (2003b) defines 'texturing' as "the 'work' that is done textually — the textual 'working up'" of the relationship between the 'global' and the national. Only recent has this feature of discourse become evident in Brazilian legal discourse such as international commercial contracts and the Law, which particularly brings together a relationship between international and national legal practice, rules and procedures enforced nationally. In this section we will consider how the national and global space-times are constructed and how they are textured together in Chapter 6 of the Law ('Recognition and Enforcement of Foreign Arbitration Awards'). Although the overall normative framework of the Law is national, this chapter provides for circumstances which may force its application into an international context with effects on the texturing of national legal discourse.

National and global spaces are represented as product, place, entity, recontextualization and process, depicted in Table 13.1:

Table 13.1 Representations of the national and global spaces in the Law

Representations of space	National	Global
Product	Foreign arbitration award(s)	Foreign arbitration award(s)
Place	Brazil Brazilian territory Brazilian consulate	Outside the national territory
Entity	Brazilian legal system Federal Supreme Court Brazilian party The parties	The courts sitting in the country where the arbitration award was handed down The parties
Recontextualization	Provisions of the Law Code of Civil Procedure Rules of public policy The laws to which the parties submitted themselves	International treaties The laws to which the parties submitted themselves The laws effective in the country where the arbitration award was handed down
Process	Recognition and enforcement of foreign arbitration awards Ratification of a foreign award	The procedural laws effective in the country where the arbitration procedure was conducted

Let us elaborate more on how these representations are constructed before analyzing how they are textured together. The product 'foreign arbitration award' must be effective to both spaces as it results from the process of an international arbitration agreed by the parties. National space is explicitly represented as a single place, 'Brazil' (or 'Brazilian') though it is implicitly evoked by some of its attributes such as 'Brazilian legal system' and 'Federal Supreme Court'. On the other hand, global space is undetermined ('outside the national territory') which accounts for the global character of the Law and implies the acceptance and validity of any award rendered abroad as long as it is conditioned by the provisions stated in the Law and/or others agreed by the parties and effective under the Brazilian legal system. Both spaces are also represented by the same entities 'the parties' engaged into an arbitration agreement, and the institutional bodies, here and abroad, involved in such agreement. It is worth noticing the ever-present national guardian of the state — the Federal Supreme Court — in a process that was supposed to "overcome state powers in dealing with private matters" (Frade 2003: 19).

National space, as a theoretical construct, is represented as recontextualizations by means of explicit and implicit reference to the provisions of the Law itself (intratextuality), as in 'the provisions contained in this Law' (Article 34); and explicit cross-referencing to other national legislation or legal texts or implicit shared knowledge of the meanings of legal principles, concepts and proceedings (intertextuality), as in 'the provisions contained in articles 483 and 484 of the Code of Civil Procedure) and 'goes against the Brazilian rules of public policy' (Article 39–II). In turn, global spaces are represented by the intertextual recontextualization of indeterminate laws and treaties so as to fit changing places and circumstances, as in 'international treaties' (Article 34) and 'the procedural laws effective in the country where the arbitration procedure was conducted" (Article 39, sole paragraph).

Spaces as represented as processes are "processes without human agency" (Fairclough 2003b), that is the actors in the processes are inanimate as 'Federal Supreme Court' (Article 35), 'by the interested party' (Article 37) and 'an offense to the Brazilian rules of public policy' (Article 39, sole paragraph). The processes are both material in that they "express the notion that some entity 'does' something — which may be 'done' to some other entity" (Halliday (1985: 103), as in 'shall be conditioned to' (Article 34), 'shall be solely subject to' (Article 35) and 'shall only be denied' (Article 38), and relational in that "one entity is used to identify another" (Halliday (1985: 103), as in 'shall be subject to its ratification' (Article 35) and 'shall not be deemed' (Article 39, sole paragraph).

The temporality of national and global relations in the chapter is predominantly future, as usual in legislation and contracts, and arbitrary in relation to ordering in sequence. The starting point of the sequence of events is the rendering of a foreign award stated in the Article 34 and afterwards there is no signalling of temporal sequence which may have legal effect on the process of recognition, enforcement and the ratification of the award. According to Hoey (2001: 75), this is a property of 'discourse colonies', types of text composed of sections "not affected by the sequence in which they are placed".

Turning to how global and national space-times are textured into a relationship, we notice that they are brought together by means of the

'Matching Relation', a type of clause relation whereby "we match things, actions, people, etc. for same and different" (Winter 1977: 6). As this type of relation does not involve ordering things, events or processes, the spaces are textured together with a view to "seeing what light they shed on each other" (Hoey 2001: 31).

In the chapter, the Matching Relation is signalled by what Winter (1979) calls 'replacement', a kind of parallelism of repeated items (constants) with additions or changes of information (variables) in the articles, as shown in Table 13.2:

Table 13.2 Replacement in Chapter 6

Constant	The recognition or enforcement of foreign arbitration awards in Brazil (Articles 34, 35, 38 and 40).	
Variables	Shall be conditional may only be denied	shall be solely subject to is denied

The Matching Relation of the chapter includes a relation of contrast to Chapter 5 which deals with domestic arbitration awards. The relation occurs when it answers the question 'In what aspects are the recognition and enforcement of foreign arbitration awards in Brazil different from the recognition and enforcement of domestic arbitration awards?' This relation of contrast is signalled by lexical items such as 'conditioned' and 'absence' (Article 34); 'indicate' and 'be substantiated by' (Article 37); 'no recognition or enforcement' (Article 39) 'may only be denied', 'if the recognition and enforcement is denied' etc).

The relationship of subordination of global space to national space is textured through its conditional on the Brazilian legal system (Article 34), the Code of Civil Procedure (Article 36 and 37) and on the whole process of recognition and enforcement of foreign awards in Brazil. This subordination can be somehow regarded as a form of resistance in order to maintain national sovereignty and legal culture within the dominant state-of-affairs of legal globalization. Having discussed new trends on organizational and discursive levels, we will now discuss the effects of legal globalization on national legal education and professional training.

THE INTERNATIONALIZATION OF NATIONAL LEGAL EDUCATION AND PROFESSIONAL TRAINING

On the legal educational and professional training levels, a new perspective is emerging to provide law students and legal professionals with specific legal practice to address matters and audience that transcend national boundaries as "domestic legal practice can no longer be clearly demarcated from international practice" (Orban III 2001: 50). Following the strict policy imposed by the Brazilian educational body concerning curricula, only recently has formal legal education made a move towards internationalization. Although still predominantly concerned with the civil law tradition and national legal subjects, law schools have been gradually updating their curricula so as to prepare students and professionals to meet the needs of the new global legal order.

Similarly, national legal education now increasingly incorporates more flexible and accessible post-graduation, specific subject-matter and online courses which include the basics of international legal knowledge, legal English, and also specialized international legal knowledge such as international contract law and international arbitration.

In addition to the traditional notions of grammatical and communicative competence, Bhatia (1997: 317) refers to 'generic competence' as a "more selective and specialized kind of competence" whereby a person is able to select the most suitable genre to achieve the communicative purposes in institutionalized and professional social contexts. Genre acquisition comprises at least three aspects: knowledge of the code or language, knowledge of the genre and its procedural, rhetorical and conceptual context and "genre ownership" through which not only do experts know how to use and read genre but also how to manipulate and exploit it (Bhatia 1997: 314).

A quite successful initiative in Brazil is the genre-based approach reading course for legal Brazilian professionals who negotiate international contracts in English by Frade (1998). The aim of the course is three-fold:

a. developing an understanding of how and why contracts are produced the way they are and how the genre relates to legal English as a whole;
b. developing the professionals' awareness of the regularity of patterning in English contracts, and
c. minimizing asymmetries in the reading and negotiating of international contracts on the part of Brazilian professionals towards foreign partners.

In the course, reading is not treated as an exercise in language practice only and provides legal practitioners with interactive strategies with the text so as to develop what Hoey (2001: 31) calls "the appropriate hypothesis-forming skills". The author claims that:

> as readers interact with a text they formulate hypotheses about how the text will develop, and that these hypotheses help them understand and interpret the text as they continue reading. Clearly, the [professional] needs to transfer the hypothesising skills s/he has in the first language to the second language.

Assuming that Brazilian professionals have already acquired a good ability with the language which thus does not constitute a potential obstacle to successful international communication in general, the course design was based on the learning-centered approach in Hutchinson and Waters (1996). After a detailed preliminary target analysis and a needs analysis, the course was organized into four integrated theoretical parts covering the following issues: (a) the scope of legal English, the socio-historical, linguistic and legal context of the language of contracts, the textual organization and the general characteristics of contracts; (b) the vocabulary and the syntax of contracts, with emphasis on the syntactic discontinuity; (c) cohesion and coherence in contracts, principles of legal interpretation; and (d) the organization of information (given-new) in contracts.

The theoretical framework is supplemented by practical and individual tasks and, for the intensive reading practice of various authentic clauses drawn from different types of commercial contracts. The clauses, as self-contained units, are classified into a syntactic typology and are displayed in an appendix:

a clauses initiating with subject,
b conditional clauses,
c clauses with long introductions,
d clauses with binomials and multinomials and
e parallel and itemized clauses.

The interaction between the reader and the clauses is processed by parsing the sentence with a marker: the reader identifies the subject (S), consider the verb (V) related to it and follow it up until they find the object or complement (O) and thus build the sentence "group by group or phrase by phrase as [they] go along" (Winter 1982: 28). The process of parsing turns the text as a site for interactions insofar as it sets up expectations in the reader's mind "and those expectations shape [his/her] interpretation of what comes next" (Hoey 2001: 22). Once identified and putting the SVO together, the reader is then asked to select and discriminate information contained in the clauses according to its legal relevance. Other reading strategies and interactive tasks include transforming clauses into a two-part interactive cognitive structure adapted from the easification device in Bhatia (1983, 1993, 1994), recognizing binomials and multinomials, finding references and adding headings to clauses and recognizing boilerplates.

An empirical research study was conducted in Frade (1999) in order to test the effectiveness of the approach used in the course design. In short, three informants, legal practitioners from a Brazilian law firm, were asked to talk about how they felt about reading international English contracts and what difficulties they faced in understanding and negotiating them. After the reading course, they were asked to read an original complex clause using the parsing and, once again, comment on how they interacted with it. Evidence showed that not only could the informants identify the main components of the clause but also had his/her expectations confirmed "on the basis of previous texts of the same kind" (Hoey 2001: 43). In addition to the research, written evaluations and subsequent feedback participants have shown that most of them succeed in acquiring the competence intended after taking the course.

Two complementary courses are being currently designed as the practice of instructing legal professionals in negotiating and legal drafting is also gaining ground in Brazil. The main purposes of these courses are to develop oral communication skills for the negotiation of international contracts in English in cross-cultural settings and audiences ('English for international negotiation'), and to teach the basics of contract drafting in English (Child 1992) and some rhetorical strategies (Trosborg 1997) so that native professionals can understand and handle adequate 'signals' of changes and additions in legal texts, such as international contracts, and thus maintain their generic integrity ('Basics of contract drafting in English').

Once the 'international legal culture' is acquired and retained, the next step for Brazilian professional is the "recontextualiation within organizations of discourses from the outside" (Fairclough 2003a), that is, the capacity of the professional to recontextualize the adequate communicative skills he/she has already acquired into the local context he/she is likely to operate within. Then, it can be introduced within the national law firms as new procedures, which might include new genres and new ways of legal services.

CONCLUSION

In this article we addressed some implications of legal globalization for Brazilian legal practice. Once 'accredited' to move from national to global economy scale, Brazil could no longer confine its economy and its legal practice "within a framework of national security" (Jessop 2000: 331).

National legal practice has adapted itself quite appropriately to accommodate changes and innovations resulting from the reordering of legal practices from national to global in the material world and the relationship between them. Brazilian legal professionals, national law firms and public and private institutions have been taking strategic coordinating actions towards seeking "closer integration with the dominant economic power" in order to increase their economic capacities and leverage to conquer (and somehow expand) global reach while seeking protection from global competition from various fronts (p. 345).

Although restricted to elite professional groups at present, in future the challenge is to incorporate the 'good' effects of legal globalization definitely into our legal practice: the implementation of a new government policy towards the internationalization of legal education, the increase of interaction between foreign and national law schools and the ease of access to specialized professional practice for those who work or aspire to work under legal globalization.

The challenge for Brazilian linguists and applied linguists is to "revisit our assumptions about the nature and scope of 'language teaching'" without the prevailing ideas about 'linguistic imperialism' (Cameron 2001: 71) and devote more attention and research on 'communication skills' for teaching and using foreign languages, mainly English, in the context of globalization in specific areas.

REFERENCES

Bhatia, V. K. (1983) Simplification v. Easification: The Case of Legal Texts. *Applies Linguistics*, 4(1): 42–54.

Bhatia, V. K. (1993) *Analysing Genre: Language Use in Professional Settings*. London: Longman.

Bhatia, V. K. (1994) Generic Integrity in Professional Discourse. In Gunnarsson, B. Linell, P. and Nordberg, B. (eds.), *Text and Talk in Professional Contexts*. ASLA:s skriftsrie 6, Uppsala, Sweden.

Bhatia, V. K. (1997) Introduction: Genre Analysis and World Englishes. *World Englishes* 16(3): 313–319.

Cameron, D. (2001) Globalisation and the Teaching of 'Communication Skills'. In Block, D. and Cameron, D. (orgs.), *Globalisation and Language Teaching*. New York: Routledge, 67–82.

Child, B. (1992) *Drafting Legal Documents: Materials and Problems*. 2nd ed. St. Paul, Minn.: West Pub.

Fairclough, N. (2001) *Discurso e mudança social*. [Discourse and social change]. Brasília: Editora UnB.

Fairclough, N. (2003a) Semiotic Aspects of Social Transformation and Learning, available at: http://www.ling.lancs.ac.uk/staff/norman/download.htm/.

Fairclough, N. (2003b) Critical Discourse Analysis in Researching Language in the New Capitalism: Overdetermination, Transdisciplinatiry and Textual Analysis, available at: http://www.ling.lancs.ac.uk/staff/norman/download.htm/.

Frade, C. (1998) *CLCI — curso de leitura de contratos internacionais*. [Reading international contracts]. Unpublished manuscript. Rio de Janeiro.

Frade, C. (1999) *O Contrato Velho-Novo e a Interpretação da Sentença Jurídica em Inglês* [The given-new contract and the interpretation of the legal clause in English]. Master Dissertation in Applied Linguistics, Faculty of Letters and Arts, Federal University of Rio de Janeiro, Brazil.

Frade, C. (2003) Introduction to the Legal System in Brazil. In Bhatia, V. K., Candlin, C. N., Engberg, J. and Trosborg, A. (eds.), *Multilingual and Multicultural Contexts of Legislation: An International Perspective*. Hamburg: Peter Lang GMBH, 1–24.

Garcez, J. M. R. (1999) *Arbitragem Internacional* [International arbitration]. In. Pucci, A. N. *et al* (orgs.), *A Arbitragem na Era da Globalização* [Arbitration in the era of globalisation]. Rio de Janeiro: Editora Forense, 163–201.

Halliday, M. A. K. (1985) *An Introduction to Functional Grammar*. London: Edward Arnold.

Hoey, M. (2001) *Textual Interaction: An Introduction to Written Discourse Analysis*. London and New York: Routledge.

Hutchinson, T. and Waters, A. (1996) *English for Specific Purposes*. Cambridge: Cambridge University Press.

Jessop, R. (1999) "Reflections on Globalisation and Its Il (logics)". Department of Sociology, Lancaster University, available at: www.comp.lancs.ac/uk/sociology/soc013rj.html/.

Jessop, R. (2000) The Crisis of National Spatio-Temporal Fix and the Tendential Ecological Dominance of Globalizing Capitalism, *International Journal of Urban and Regional Research*, 24 (2): 323–360.

Orban III, F. A. (2001) Legal Globalisation: The Challenges for In-House Counsel, *ACCA Docket* 19 (2): 48–62.

Pinto, D. (2002) Through the World's Eye: Governance in a Globalised World. *E Law — Murdoch University Electronic Journal of Law*, 9 (3): available at: http//www.murdoch.edu.au/elaw/issues/v9n3/pinto93nf.html/.

Rodgers, D. (1997) *English for International Negotiations: A Cross-Cultural Case Study Approach*. New York: St. Martin's Press.
Trosborg, A. (1997) *Rhetorical Strategies in Legal Language: Discourse Analysis of Statutes and Contracts*. Tübingen: Gunter Narr Verlag.
van Houtte, H. and Wautelet, P. (2001) International Lawyers and Uniform Law. In Drolshammer, J. and Pfeifer, M. (eds.), *The Internationalization of the Practice of Law*. The Netherlands: Kluwer International Law, 89–107.
Winter, E. (1977) A Clause-Relational Approach to English Texts: A Study of Some Predictive Lexical Items in Written Discourse. *Instructional Science* 6: 1–92.
Winter, E. (1979) Replacement as a Fundamental Function of the Sentence in Context. *Forum Linquisticum*, 4(2): 95–133.
Winter, E. (1982) *Towards a Contextual Grammar of English*. London: George Allen and Unwin.
Zariski, A. (2000) Disputing Culture: Lawyers and ADR. *E Law — Murdoch University Electronic Journal of Law*, 7(2) available at: http//www.murdoch.edu.au/elaw/issues/v7n2/zariski72_text.html

14

Translation in International Arbitration

Susan Šarčević

INTRODUCTION

Globalization and harmonization are dominant trends in international arbitration today. As a result of the globalization of international trade, the number of international disputes submitted to arbitration has increased tremendously in recent decades with actors from all continents speaking a multitude of languages. Thanks to the worldwide acceptance of international instruments, such as the New York Convention on the Recognition and Enforcement of Foreign Arbitral Awards and especially the UNCITRAL Model Law on International Commercial Arbitration, a high degree of harmonization has already been achieved in national arbitration laws. The Model Law has been accepted in whole or in part by a large number of states and jurisdictions, many of which have incorporated it into their national law, largely by an indirect process of translation. Though mostly behind the scenes, translation plays a vital role in numerous aspects of international arbitration, including the translation of legal documents for the proceedings, the translation of national arbitration laws into world languages, the translation of institutional procedural rules and standard arbitral clauses, the production of multilingual instruments of international arbitration law and others. This article intends to show that, despite the growing use of English, translation continues to make a significant contribution not only to the globalization but also to the harmonization of international arbitration. This is important because, as arbitration experts say, the future of international arbitration lies in its harmonization (Sanders 1999: 5; cf. Blessing 2000: 140–143).

CHOICE OF LANGUAGE AND TRANSLATION

Translation contributes to the globalization of arbitration by removing linguistic and cultural barriers, enabling parties from all nations to resolve international disputes by arbitration. In keeping with the principle of party autonomy, the parties agree to submit future disputes to arbitration; they choose the applicable law, the procedural rules, the arbitration site, the arbitrators, and the language of the arbitration, which comprises both its written and oral parts. Although arbitration institutions usually have one, two or three official languages, as a rule, the proceedings may be conducted in any language or languages chosen by the parties. For example, the official languages of the ICC International Court of Arbitration are English and French; however, Arabic, German, Italian, Japanese and Spanish are commonly used in practice as well (Bühler and Jarvin 2002: 214). The choice of language often influences the choice of arbitrators and both choices determine whether the translation of documents is necessary in order to guarantee due process. As a rule, a translation must be provided of any document not in the language of the arbitration; however, multilingual arbitrators sometimes accept documents in another language (Karrer 2004: 12). Any party challenging the accuracy of a translation submitted by the opposite party is obliged to provide another translation, usually at his own expense. The final decision on accuracy is made by the arbitrators (see Bühler and Jarvin 2002: 213–218).

Frequently the parties choose a neutral language, especially English, which is often the language of their contract, regardless of the law governing the contract. As in international contract law, English has also become the *lingua franca* of international arbitration. This obviously has advantages but also disadvantages for non-native speakers.[1] The fact that the parties, counsel and arbitrators often communicate (orally and in writing) in a language that is not their mother tongue increases the possibility of error and ambiguity, sometimes leading to new disputes. For example, the arbitral clause of a contract concluded in English

---

1 Abascal Zamora, professor and attorney from Mexico City, expressed regret that the commentaries, international case law and other books and journals on international commercial arbitration are "essentially produced in English and [are] thus accessible only to those who understand, read, translate and use that language". In his opinion, this excludes "practicing lawyers engaged in arranging contracts and advising clients, lawyers handling disputes at law between parties and judges needing to apply the [New York] Convention" (1999: 39–40).

between a Finnish and a Turkish corporation[2] contained, *inter alia*, the following:

> Place of Arbitration is Zurich, Switzerland, and the language shall be English unless otherwise decided by board of arbitrators.
>
> The Board of Arbitration shall take as base the provisions of this Contract and Turkish Laws in force.

The first sentence is clear; however, a dispute arose concerning the choice of law made by the parties in the second sentence. While claimant took the position that the key term *Turkish Laws* referred only to Turkish substantive law, defendant maintained that it referred to Turkish procedural law as well. After an exchange of pleadings on the issue, the majority of arbitrators concluded that the parties had not determined the arbitration procedure. The dissenting arbitrator maintained that the plural form implied that the parties had not intended to make a distinction between substantive and procedural law (Ehrat 1996: 228–231).

Everything begins with the agreement, including arbitration. Anxious to close the deal, the parties often disregard the importance of drafting a clear and proper arbitral clause. An expert from the Vienna International Arbitration Court reported that almost 50 per cent of the arbitral clauses submitted to that Centre are defective to the point that a court might consider them invalid (Melis 1999: 45). This indeed is alarming and has serious consequences for translation as well. Since translations of legal documents must accurately reproduce the originals, it is generally agreed that the quality of a translation can be no better than the original. Translators must refrain from making any corrections and clarifying any ambiguities, even if they think they know the intended meaning (see Harvey 2002: 181; in instruments of international law, see Šarčević 2000: 204).

STANDARD ARBITRAL CLAUSES AND INSTITUTIONAL PROCEDURAL RULES

As a safeguard against defective arbitral clauses, arbitration institutions have prepared multilingual standard clauses, which state the essential

2 *Osuuskunta METEX Andelslag ("METEX")* v. *Türkiye Elektrik Kurumu Genel Müdürlügu ("TEK")*, interlocutory decision of 28 August 1990; see Ehrat 1996: 228.

elements in clear and simple language, thus making them easily translatable. For example, parties wishing to make reference to ICC arbitration in their contracts are encouraged to use the following standard clause:

> All disputes arising out of or in connection with the present contract shall be finally settled under the Rules of Arbitration of the International Chamber of Commerce by one or more arbitrators appointed in accordance with the said Rules.
>
> Tous différends découlant du présent contrat ou en relation avec celui-ci seront tranchés définitivement suivant le Règlement d'arbitrage de la Chambre de commerce internationale par un ou plusieurs arbitres nommés conformément à ce Règlement.

The ICC standard clause has been translated and published by the ICC in 18 languages, also including Arabic, Chinese and Japanese, as well as Bulgarian, Dutch, German, Greek, Hungarian, Italian, Polish, Portuguese, Russian, Spanish, Turkish and even Thai and Vietnamese (*Rules of Arbitration*, ICC 2001: 8–11). The parties are reminded that, in addition to the above standard clause, it may be desirable to include a choice of law clause in the arbitration clause and to stipulate the number of arbitrators and the place and language of the arbitration, as in the first example cited above.

Anxious to become global centres of international dispute resolution, arbitration institutions have also translated their procedural rules into various languages and made them available on their web sites. For example, the web site of the German Institution of Arbitration (*Deutsche Institution für Schiedsgerichtsbarkeit* — DIS at www.dis-arb.de) contains translations of the German *Schiedsgerichtsordnung* 1998 in English, French, Russian and Spanish. Each text is identified as a "translation from German" and users are cautioned that "only the German text is authoritative". The bilingual (Chinese and English) web site of the China International Economic and Trade Arbitration Commission (CIETAC at www.cietac-sz.org.cn) is user friendly even for those with no command of Chinese. The CIETAC Arbitration Rules of 2000 are available in English; however, there is no indication that they are not authoritative. The web site of the ICC International Court of Arbitration (www.iccwbo.org) is also bilingual (French and English). Originally drafted in English, the new ICC Arbitration Rules of 1998 are currently online in Dutch, English, French, German, Japanese, Italian, Spanish,

Polish, Portuguese (Brazil) and Turkish. A note explains that the ICC Arbitration Rules have been translated into numerous languages but only the English and French texts are authoritative.

NATIONAL ARBITRATION LAWS

It is extremely important to distinguish between authoritative and non-authoritative language versions of legal instruments and use them accordingly. The fact that the term "translation" is used makes it clear that the particular text is non-authoritative and thus non-binding, i.e., not vested with the force of law. In states and jurisdictions with only one official language, all other language versions of national legislation have not been enacted by parliament; hence they are non-authoritative translations intended for information purposes only. Although such texts carry no weight for the purpose of interpretation by ordinary courts and arbitrators, they are frequently used by the parties, counsel and even by arbitrators. This is especially true in the case of the English translation of the national arbitration law of countries where English is not an official language. The fact that a translation is non-authoritative does not imply that the translator is subject to less stringent restrictions. Such translations must be accurate and reliable despite their non-authoritative status.[3] As a rule, translators are encouraged to preserve the textual symmetry to the extent possible; however, translations formulated in "natural" English, French or whatever the target language, secure user confidence, not literal translations (cf. Joseph 1995: 34). As for terminological considerations, terms should be chosen which make it clear that their meaning is derived from the source legal system. Accordingly, translators should use neutral terms instead of technical terms denoting concepts peculiar to the target language. On the other hand, if reference is made to a foreign concept, it is often better to borrow the foreign term rather than translate it. Mistakes occur when the translator is unaware of the legislative intent.

For example, the provision of the Swiss Private International Law Act on the right to a fair hearing (Art. 182(3) PIL Act) contains the terms

3 Sometimes the publications of non-authoritative translations contain a disclaimer. For example, the following statement appears in the foreword to *China Laws for Foreign Business* published in 1988 by C.C.H. Australia Ltd. and China Prospect Publishing House: "This publication (bilingual) is sold on the understanding that (1) the authors, editors and consultants are not responsible for the results of any actions taken on the basis of information in this work, nor for any errors or omissions ..." (in Šarčević 2000: 279).

procédure du contradictoire (FR) and *kontradiktorisches Verfahren* (DE). This is obviously a reference to foreign law since the concept is unknown in Swiss law. As experts point out, the use of the English term *adversarial proceedings* in the English translation of the Swiss Arbitration Association is misleading because the Swiss legislator did not have English adversarial proceedings in mind but rather the *principe du contradictoire* of French law (Schneider 2000: 414). The neutral term *contradictory proceedings* has been suggested instead; however, it would be ambiguous as it could be interpreted as a reference not only to French law but also to English law. Therefore, in my opinion, retaining the French term in the English translation would be the best solution in this case as it would be a clear reference to French law. Otherwise, a footnote could be used to clarify the reference of the ambiguous term.

The above example illustrates how difficult the decision-making process of legal translators can be, and, in particular, how risky it is when translators of legislation — even native speakers — have not participated in the drafting process and have no contact with the drafters of the authentic text or texts. Since the ultimate purpose of arbitration legislation is to resolve disputes, not to create new ones, translators must be able to foresee how the target text will be interpreted and applied by users of different legal, linguistic and cultural backgrounds (cf. Šarčević 2000: 72). This applies to both non-authoritative and authoritative translations.

Translations of legislation that have been enacted or authenticated by parliament are authoritative and thus legally binding. The term *authoritative translation* is a paradox because, from the legal point of view, the authenticated language versions of a legislative instrument are not referred to as translations but originals, even though they have been produced by translation. Today all the authentic texts of plurilingual legal instruments are usually equally authentic. Accordingly, each authentic text is deemed independent for the purpose of interpretation by the courts and no single text (not even the "real" original) should prevail in the event of an ambiguity or textual diversity between the various language versions.

Multilingualism in the law can be effective only if those affected by the instrument are guaranteed equality before the law, regardless of the language of the text. For this purpose, the authentic texts of a legal instrument are presumed to be equal in meaning, effect and intent; however, there is always a risk of linguistic diversity and error when translation is involved. Luckily some divergences and errors are harmless; however, others introduce ambiguity or are misleading, thus posing a threat to uniform interpretation and application. As a rule, using singular or plural is a matter of language and will not affect the results. On the other hand, translating *règles de droit* as *Recht* instead of *Rechtsregeln* changes the meaning of the choice of law clause. A broader term, *règles de droit* includes transnational rules of law, generally accepted principles, public international law, and trade usages or *lex mercatoria* (Blessing 2000: 122). Surprisingly, this mistake was made in the authentic German text of Art. 187(1) of the Swiss Private International Law Act, despite the parliamentary debate in French on that very issue (Blessing 2000: 167). The PIL Act, which contains the Swiss arbitration law, is one of the few instruments drafted partly in French and partly in German. (Šarčević: forthcoming) Since the Italian translation usually follows the German text, the same mistake occurs in the authentic Italian text, where the term *diritto* is used. While the error will not affect interpretation of the provision by Swiss courts and arbitrators familiar with the legislative intent, it could perhaps make a difference in cases where foreign courts and arbitrators rely on the German or Italian text when applying Swiss law.

MULTILATERAL INSTRUMENTS OF INTERNATIONAL LAW

The cause for concern is greater when a similar divergence exists in the authentic texts of multilateral instruments of international law, which are interpreted and applied by national courts and arbitrators from diverse legal systems and cultures. For example, the authentic English, French and Spanish texts of the choice of law provision in the Convention on the Settlement of Investment Disputes Between States and Nationals of Other States (known as the ICSID Convention of 1965) (Article 42(1)) contains minor textual divergences with regard to the role of international law. Whereas the English and Spanish texts use the same term for the parties' choice of law and international law (*rules* in the English text and *normas* in Spanish), the French text uses *règles* for the choice of law and *principes* for international law. According to experts, this subtle difference could lead to different results in arbitration practice (details in Reisman 2001: 586–589).

One of the advantages of international arbitration is that the disputes are not decided by national courts but by impartial arbitrators whom the parties trust. In most cases, the losing party recognizes the final award as binding and voluntarily complies with the ruling. Failing compliance on the part of the losing party, the winning party will be forced to request the national court in the country of enforcement to intervene and enforce the award. This is where the New York Convention comes into play, among other things, by providing uniform conditions for the enforcement of foreign awards. Adopted under the auspices of the United Nations, the New York Convention of 1958 is "drawn up" in five equally authentic language versions: Chinese, English, French, Russian and Spanish (Art. XVI).[4]

While the New York Convention has had overwhelming success in promoting legal certainty, there is a blemish on its record due to a divergence in the authentic texts on a small point that makes a big difference. Paragraph 1 of Article 5 provides five grounds for refusing the recognition and enforcement of a foreign award: invalidity of the arbitral agreement, violation of due process, excess of authority by the arbitral tribunal, irregularity as to the composition of the arbitral tribunal, or if the award has not yet become binding or has been set aside or suspended in the country where it was made. Since these grounds are not disputed, we need not examine that part of the text. Instead we focus our attention on the introductory part containing the operative part of the rule prescribing the action to be taken by the courts when one of the grounds for refusal is proven. The usual practice is that recognition and enforcement is *not refused unless* the defendant proves the existence of one of the grounds for refusal (Paulson 1996: 107). This is expressed in the French text with the expression *ne seront refusées* … *que si*, which is mandatory in the sense of *shall not be refused* … *unless*, thus obliging the court to deny enforcement in such cases:

> La reconnaissance et l'exécution de la sentence *ne seront refusées*, sur requête de la partie contre laquelle elle est invoquée, *que si cette partie fournit* à l'autorité compétente du pays où la reconnaissance et l'exécution sont demandées *la preuve* …

On the other hand, the English text uses the permissive *may be refused* … *only if* … , which could be interpreted to mean that the court is not required to reject an application for enforcement but may use its discretion to determine whether to enforce an award when one of the grounds for refusal is proven:

4 Arabic did not become an official language of the United Nations until 1973; see Tabory 1980: 7–9.

> Recognition and enforcement of the award *may be refused*, at the request of the party against whom it is invoked, *only if that party furnishes* to the competent authority where the recognition and enforcement is sought, *proof that* …

The Spanish text also contains a permissive: *solo se podra … si*:

> *Sólo se podrá denegar* el reconocimiento y la ejecución de la sentencia, a instancia de la parte contra la cual es invocada, *si esta parte prueba* ante la autoridad competente del país en que se pide el reconocimiento y la ejecución …

Similarly, the Russian text *может быть* expresses a permissive, as does the key expression in the Chinese text [*ke yi*] (Mandarin). In the event of any textual divergence or ambiguity, the courts are to consult each authentic text and reconcile the divergences, having regard for the object and purpose of the treaty. Sometimes, however, they rely on a single text, which in this case can lead to conflicting decisions in practice. The fact that four of the five authentic texts contain a permissive is not a conclusive argument for interpreting the rule as discretionary as the other texts may simply be aligned on the English text. More convincing is the fact that a proposal to formulate the English text as an obligation — *shall be refused … only if* — was rejected during the preparation of the Convention (see Paulson 1998: 227–230).

Some 25 years later the debate was reopened by the delegates who gathered in Vienna to prepare the UNCITRAL Model Law on International Commercial Arbitration, which is equally authentic in the six official languages of the United Nations. Article 36(1)(a) of the Model Law is modeled on Article V of the New York Convention with slight modifications.

> FR: La reconnaissance et l'exécution d'une sentence arbitrale, quel que soit le pays où elle a été rendue, *ne peut être refusée* par un tribunal *que*:
>
> EN: Recognition or enforcement of an arbitral award, irrespective of the country in which it was made, *may be refused only*:
>
> ES: *Sólo se podrà denegar* el reconocimiento o la ejecución de un laudo arbitral, cualquiera que sea el país en que se haya dictado:
>
> RU: В признанич или приведснии в исполнение арбитражного решеия, независимо от того, в какой стране оно было вынесено, <u>может быть отказано лишь</u>:

CH: [Zhi you zai xialie qingkuang sia cai ke jujue chengren huo zhixing bulun zai he guo zuochu de zhongcai caijue:]

Again the English wording *may be refused* was criticized as ambiguous. For the sake of certainty and predictability, the view prevailed that the court should not be given such discretion and that the interpretation could be made clear by changing the wording to *shall be refused*. At the next meeting, however, the Working Group rejected the change. Although the Report provides no explanation, it is assumed that the desire to align Article 36 on the New York Convention finally prevailed, as well as the desire to provide some flexibility, as regards individual reasons for refusal (Roth 2002: 1291). In the end, however, the French text was changed to correspond with the other authentic texts. Although a negation, the new wording *ne peut être refusée* makes the French provision discretionary.[5]

Notwithstanding the legislative history of rejecting applications for enforcement when one of the grounds for refusal exists, the High Court of Hong Kong interpreted the term *may* as discretionary in *Nanjing Cereals, Oils and Foodstuffs, Import & Export Corporation* v. *Luckmate Commodities Trading Ltd.*[6] Actually the Court found that defendant had had ample opportunity to present its evidence but had failed to do so; thus there was no ground for refusal. However, it added that, even if there were such a ground, it was at the court's discretion to grant enforcement because the Model Law provides that enforcement "may be refused" (Roth 2002: 1291). This opened Pandora's box, leading to a number of controversial decisions culminating in *Chromalloy Aeroservices* v. *Egypt*, where a US court used the discretionary *may* to grant enforcement to the US corporation, although the award had been made in Egypt and set aside by an Egyptian court (see Park 1999: 807).

FORMULATING MANDATORY AND DISCRETIONARY PROVISIONS

This illustrates how far-reaching the consequences can be when a provision is ambiguous as to whether it is mandatory or discretionary.

5 As Sullivan points out, "*pouvoir*" expresses discretion in French (1997: 84).

6 Decision of 16 December 1994, CLOUT Case 88, abstract and full text accessible at www.UNCITRAL.org under case law (CLOUT), UNCITRAL Index of the UNCITRAL Model Law on International Commercial Arbitration (A/CN.9/SER.C/INDEX/5).

Thus it follows that translators must be able to recognize whether a provision is mandatory or discretionary in the source text and possess the know-how to formulate the provision as such in the target language. However, this task is not always easy as drafting practices differ from jurisdiction to jurisdiction, sometimes even when the same language is used. In legislation written in English, one of the main sources of confusion is the overuse of "shall". For native speakers with legal training, "shall" is not ambiguous: It is used to impose obligations or to indicate the binding character of conditions or rules. Hence, "shall is always imperative in the sense that it imposes binding obligations or requirements" (Sullivan 1997: 86).[7] On the other hand, the use of the "legal shall" seems to be a constant source of ambiguity for non-native speakers, who often interpret it as future. According to common law drafting rules, a law speaks in the present tense even though the events described take place in the future. Thus the future tense is avoided in legislation. This, however, is clearly not the case in other jurisdictions, which follow their own drafting conventions. Today a growing number of jurisdictions prefer to express obligations less directly by using the present indicative. This is the case in French and Russian, whereas obligations in Spanish are expressed in the *futuro legislativo* (see Šarčević 2001: 102, note 16). The use of the present indicative makes it more difficult to determine whether a provision is mandatory and can be ambiguous if the legislative intent is not clear from the context. To remove all doubt as to the intent, drafters sometimes resort to the modal verb *devoir* in French.

A brief comparison of "shall" and its equivalents in French and Spanish in several provisions of the Model Law reveals the use of different drafting conventions. While the English and Spanish texts are consistent in their use of "shall" and *futuro legislativo*, the French text varies, using present indicative, present perfect, the modal verb *devoir* and even future tense. Nonetheless, the results are the same in the provisions cited below.

7 According to Sullivan, the interpretation question that arises in connection with "shall" regards the consequences of breaching the binding duty or ignoring the binding requirement. In other words, is a provision mandatory or directory? (1997: 86). Mandatory provisions are compulsory and non-compliance is punishable by sanction or may render the instrument or procedure invalid. Directory provisions should be complied with; however, the court may rule that non-compliance is a mere error without invalidating the instrument or procedure (Šarčević 2000: 138).

Art. 28(1)	The tribunal *shall decide* the dispute ...	Le tribunal arbitral *tranche* le différend ...	El tribunal arbitral *decidirá* el litigio ...
Art. 35(1)	An arbitral award ... *shall be recognised* as binding ...	La sentence arbitrale ... *est reconnue* comme ayant force obligatoire ...	Un laudo arbitral ... *será reconocido* como vinculante ...
Art. 35(2)	The party ... *shall supply* the ... original award ...	La partie ... *doit* en *fournir* l'original dûment ...	La parte ... *deberá presentar* el original debidamente...
Art. 35(2)	... the party *shall supply* a... translation ...	... la partie en *produira* une traduction ...	... la parte *deberá presentar* una traducción ...

Thus it follows that translators should strive to meet user expectations by using the drafting conventions common to the particular language. This also applies to non-authoritative translations of national legislation. In particular, problems of interpretation can arise in English translations if the indicative present is used instead of "shall" in mandatory provisions. It frequently occurs that non-native speakers translate obligations with "must" instead of "shall". Though unconventional (except in requirements), the use of "must" leaves no doubt as to the legislative intent and thus is not a threat to uniform interpretation. In fact, supporters of plain language drafting recommend that "must" *always* be used to express obligations. In their opinion, the use of "must" conveys the mandatory intent more clearly to the average citizen (Butt and Castle 2001: 98).[8]

TERMINOLOGICAL CONSIDERATIONS IN THE UNCITRAL MODEL LAW

To date, the UNCITRAL Model Law has been adopted either verbatim or with some modifications by almost 50 states and jurisdictions worldwide, including Hong Kong and Macau (see list at www.UNCITRAL.org under

8 On the other hand, the use of "should" is misleading and should be avoided in English translations of legislative texts. This could perhaps be interpreted as an attempt to express a directory rather than a mandatory provision; however, such usage is highly ambiguous (see previous note) and is not in keeping with drafting practices. "Should" is not used to formulate legal rules but to express non-binding recommendations.

Status of Texts). Most of the so-called Model Law States have incorporated the Model Law by enacting a separate new law for arbitration in general or one specifically for international commercial arbitration. The key to the impressive success of the Model Law lies in its flexibility and neutrality. In particular, care was taken to provide international arbitration standards with "neutral" solutions acceptable to parties from different legal systems, languages and cultures. To meet the expectations of users worldwide, the drafters used general language and neutral terminology that can be easily translated and has the same or nearly the same meaning in all official languages (Roth 2002: 1161). Needless to say, this has greatly facilitated the task of translating the Model Law into the various languages of the Model Law States. Each time the Model Law is transformed into national law, it is important to preserve language neutrality by avoiding the use of national terms having a special meaning in that national legal system.

Not surprisingly, the Model Law contains no system-bound terms that would limit aspects of its application to a particular legal system or systems. Since legal systems differ considerably as regards the taking of evidence, common law devices such as "discovery", "affidavit" and "deposition" have no place in the Model Law (3, English 1996 Act). Even the written submissions are designated by neutral terms: "statement of claim and defence" / "conclusion en demande et en defense" (Art. 23). Although the use of a technical term is avoided, sometimes the concept is included in a provision but described in neutral language. For example, Article 4 deals with the concept of "estoppel" but uses the descriptive paraphrase "waiver of right to object", hence the French: "renonciation au droit de faire objection". The provision then spells out in which instances a party is estopped, i.e., "shall be deemed to have waived his right to object". Even general principles known to most legal systems are described but not identified by name, thus facilitating translation into all languages and preserving neutrality. For example, Article 18 deals with the principle of due process under the heading "equal treatment of parties". The provision provides that "the parties shall be treated with equality and each party shall be given a full opportunity of presenting his case". Instead of stating that the violation of due process is a ground for refusal of recognition and enforcement, Article 36 specifies the situations amounting to a violation of due process: The enforcement of an arbitral award may be refused if "the party against whom the award is invoked was not given proper notice of the appointment of an arbitrator or of the arbitral proceedings or was otherwise unable to present his case".

An unusual technique, which I call doubling, is used in paragraph 3 of Article 28; here we find not one but two technical terms, one in Latin (*ex aequo et bono*), the other in French (*amiable compositeur*). The Spanish text uses the term *amigable componedor*, which is equivalent with *amiable compositeur*. Note that the connector is "or" not "and":

> EN: The arbitral tribunal shall decide *ex aequo et bono* or as *amiable compositeur* only if the parties have expressly authorized it to do so.
>
> FR: Le tribunal arbitral statue ex aequo et bono ou en qualité d'amiable compositeur uniquement si les parties l'y ont expressément autorisé.
>
> ES: El tribunal arbitral decidirá ex aequo et bono o como amigable componedor sólo si las partes le han sutorizako expresamente a hacerlo así.

As Roth puts it: "The authority to decide *ex aequo et bono* or as *amiable compositeur* indicates that the tribunal is not bound to apply specific rules of law, but may adjudicate the case according to what it deems *fair and equitable* under the given circumstances." Since there is no uniform designation for this type of arbitration in the various legal systems, both the Latin and the French terms are used, which are very similar in meaning (Roth 2002: 1256). In my opinion, this type of doubling is a unique means of promoting the uniform interpretation and application of a multilingual instrument in different legal systems and cultures throughout the world. It is interesting to note that the Egyptian Law on Arbitration attempts to define these terms, which are apparently lesser known in the Arab culture. No similar comments are found in the authentic Arabic text.

As a means of promoting harmonization, Model Law States are encouraged to follow the scheme and language of the authentic texts of the Model Law as closely as possible. While the use of general and neutral language has definitely enhanced the harmonization of international arbitration, it does not always result in uniform interpretation. In their attempt to use general, neutral and translatable language, the drafters of the Model Law left a number of matters open and did not address others. The number of definitions is notably small. For instance, there is no definition of the term *award*, nor are the terms *final award* and *binding award* defined. Widely accepted in arbitration, the principle of *res judicata* means that a final award by an arbitral tribunal is binding on the parties and can no longer be challenged or set aside or disputed in a second arbitration instance. Nonetheless, the Working Group did not accept a proposal to include a provision to the effect that an arbitral award made in accordance with Article 31 would be regarded as having the force of *res judicata*. The Latin term was rejected because it is not known in all legal systems. Moreover, proposals to define the notion of "final award" in neutral language as the award "intended to settle the dispute in full", the "final disposition of the substance of the dispute" or the award "which constitutes or completes the disposition of all claims submitted to arbitration" were rejected "for the sake of simplicity" (Roth 2002: 1269). Similarly, the Model Law does not define the point in time when the award becomes binding, thus leaving it to national courts to decide when "an arbitral award shall be recognized as binding" (Art. 36).

THE QUEST FOR HARMONIZATION

Despite its different origins, international arbitration has undergone an impressive degree of globalization and harmonization since the intensive discussions on the UNCITRAL Model Law. Nonetheless, most states agree that, in the interest of greater predictability and legal certainty, it is desirable to reach international consensus — albeit with certain slight variations — on the meaning of basic notions of international arbitration. A step in this direction was taken at the IFCAI's Conference in Hong Kong in November 1995 on the topic "Globalization and Harmonization of the Basic Notions in International Arbitration". The ICCA Conference in Seoul in October 1996 also dealt with this topic (Blessing 2000: 143). Recognizing language as a key factor in arbitration, lawyers and linguists have recently joined efforts to promote the harmonization of national arbitration laws in interdisciplinary conferences on law and language and in studies undertaken to identify legal, linguistic and cultural similarities and differences in national arbitration traditions.[9] As for translation, it plays a significant role in the harmonization process by enabling communication across diverse legal systems and cultures, promoting understanding and encouraging an increasing number of actors to reach consensus on international principles and standards for dispute resolution

9 For example, the International Conference on Law and Language in International Arbitration held 2–4 October 2003 at the City University of Hong Kong; also Bhatia, Candlin and Gotti (eds.) *Legal Discourse in Multilingual and Multicultural Contexts, Arbitration Texts in Europe*, 2003.

by arbitration. The ultimate goal in the quest for harmonization is for actors from all continents to speak their own language but share a common core of concepts, thus contributing to the development of a transnational arbitration law and an international arbitration culture.[10]

REFERENCES

Abascal, Z. and José M. (1999) Enhancing Dissemination of Information, Technical Assistance and Training. In *Enforcing Arbitration Awards under the New York Convention, Experience and Prospects*, New York: United Nations, 39–40.

Bhatia, V. K., Candlin, C. N. and Gotti, M. (eds.) (2003) *Legal Discourse in Multilingual and Multicultural Contexts: Arbitration Texts in Europe*, Bern: Peter Lang.

Blessing, M. (2000) Brief Review of International Developments; Globalisation and Harmonisation; Legislative Developments in Switzerland. In Berti, Stephen V. (ed.), *International Arbitration in Switzerland*, Basel-Geneva-Munich: Helbing and Lichtenhahn; and The Hague-London-Boston: Kluwer Law International, 63–139; 140–149; 156–170.

Bühler, M. and Jarvin, S. (2002) The Arbitration Rules of the International Chamber of Commerce. In Weigand, Frank-Bernd (ed.), *Practitioner's Handbook on International Arbitration*, München: Beck; Bruxelles: Bruylant; Wien: Manz; Bern: Stämpfli, 103–314.

Butt, P. and Castle, R. (2001) *Modern Legal Drafting, A Guide to Using Clearer Language*, Cambridge: University Press.

Ehrat, F. (1996) A Case Study: Turkey. In Blessing, Marc (ed.), *The New York Convention of 1958*, ASA Special Series No. 9, Zurich: Association Suisse de l'arbitrage, 225–237.

Harvey, M. (2002) What's So Special about Legal Translation? In *Meta* 47, 2: 177–185.

Joseph, J. E. (1995) Indeterminacy, Translation and the Law. In Morris, Marshall (ed.), *Translation and the Law*, Amsterdam: John Benjamins, 13–36.

Karrer, P. A. (2004) Arbitration and Language, Look for the Purpose. In *Croatian Arbitration Yearbook* 2: 7–14.

Melis, W. (1999) Considering the Advisability of Preparing an Additional Convention, Complementary to the New York Convention. In *Enforcing Arbitration Awards under the New York Convention, Experience and Prospects*, New York: United Nations, 44–46.

10 The latter is a reference to the ICCA Conference in Seoul and the proceedings: *Towards an International Arbitration Culture*, edited by Van den Berg 1998.

Park, W. W. (1999) Duty and Discretion in International Arbitration. In *The American Journal of International Law* 93, 4: 805–823.

Paulson, J. (1996) The New York Convention in International Practice — Problems of Assimilation. In Blessing, Marc (ed.), *The New York Convention of 1958*, ASA Special Series No. 9, Zurich: Association Suisse de l'arbitrage, 100–116.

Paulson, J. (1998) *May* or *Must* Under the New York Convention: An Exercise in Syntax and Linguistics. In 14 *Arbitration International*, 2, 227–230.

Reisman, W. M. (2001) The Regime for *Lacunae* in the ICSID Choice of Law Provision and the Question of its Threshold. In *Liber Amicorum Ibrahim F.I. Shihata*, 585–605.

Roth, M. (2002) The UNCITRAL Model Law on International Commercial Arbitration. In Weigand, Frank-Bernd (ed.), *Practitioner's Handbook on International Arbitration*, München: Beck; Bruxelles: Bruylant; Wien: Manz; Bern: Stämpfli, 1153–1294.

Rules of Arbitration, ICC International Court of Arbitration (2001) ICC: Paris.

Sanders, P. (1999) The Making of the Convention. In *Enforcing Arbitration Awards under the New York Convention, Experience and Prospects*, New York: United Nations, 3–5.

Schneider, M. E. (2000) Article 182. In Berti, S. V. (ed.), *International Arbitration in Switzerland*, Basel-Geneva-Munich: Helbing and Lichtenhahn; and The Hague-London-Boston: Kluwer Law International, 395–426.

Sullivan, R. (1997) *Statutory Interpretation*, Ontario: Irwin Law.

Šarčević, S. (2nd ed. 2000) *New Approach to Legal Translation*, The Hague-London-Boston: Kluwer Law International.

Šarčević, S. (2001) Translation Procedures of Legal Translators. In Šarčević, Susan (ed.), *Legal Translation, Preparation for Accession to the European Union*, Faculty of Law, Rijeka, 75–138.

Šarčević, S. (2005) The Quest for Legislative Bilingualism and Multilingualism: Co-drafting in Canada and Switzerland. In Gémar, Jean-Claude and Kasirer, Nicholas (eds.), *La jurilinguistique: Bilan et perspectives / Jurilinguistics. An Emerging Discipline between Language and Law*, Montréal: Thémis.

15

Translating Terminology in Arbitration Discourse

Marta Chroma

INTRODUCTION

Legal language has for decades been subject to the attention of both lawyers and linguists. While the lawyers have concentrated on how to express, and subsequently identify, legal information so that law may be applied, the linguists have focused on purely linguistic aspects, such as means of expressing a tone of normativity, or of serving frequently intended vagueness of legislative texts.

The purpose of the lawyers' research into the language has mostly been to achieve more efficient legal communication (*pro futuro* research): "If legal language is to become a clearer and more efficient means of communication, we need to identify the features that are most likely to impede comprehension" (Tiersma 2000: 203). In practice, law students and many law practitioners rely on just one outcome of such research, namely "legal writing" — books and manuals written by experienced lawyers (or in rare cases by lawyers with a linguistic background). Linguists have generally pursued a rather static (descriptive) approach (*pro praeterito*) in analyzing the linguistic tools employed in legal texts; however this approach has had little or no impact upon the drafting of subsequent legal texts. Within the understanding of linguists, language for law purposes (LLP) is used to facilitate communication within legal discourse. Legal language is a variety of language strongly determined by context and the particular discourse events with which it is linked. Research into this subsystem of language consists of describing and analyzing the selection, combination and use of existing morphological, lexical and syntactic units, structures and patterns that would best serve the specific stylistic, genre and discourse functions of a text in a concrete subject area and specific social context. The specificity of the discourse seems to be primarily a consequence of pragmatic considerations, reflecting the communicative purpose and needs of the users — both professionals in the respective subject field and, possibly, lay (or paralegal) persons working on legal assignments.

A third group of specialist professionals who engage in researching legal language are translators. Their methods should ideally combine the approaches of both lawyers and linguists, and be based on a comparison of the source and target languages, and source and target legal systems (*pro comparatione* research), so that the respective legal information may be effectively communicated to the ultimate recipient of the translated text: "Obviously the first stage in successful translation is to understand the source text fully. This is then followed by the production of a target text" (Alcaraz and Hughes 2002: 3).

The aim of this article is to provide a brief outline of terminological issues relevant for the translation of legislative texts dealing with the legal theme of arbitration.

TERMINOLOGY

General understanding

Terminology, in its most common meaning as a collection of terms which represent a system of concepts in an individual subject-field (Sager 1990: 3), is a part of vocabulary for specific purposes which has been extensively described, analyzed and standardized (ISO R 1087 1990). It should be noted, however, that almost all work on terminology pursued by ISO and their national affiliates has been aimed at what Bečka (1992: 73) calls "technological terms", designating phenomena of technological research and sciences. Not a lot has been accomplished in the area of researching into culturally deeply rooted legal terminologies although there are countries which pay respect to their language — or languages — of law, such as Canada, as evidenced by the bijural terminological research pursued by the Canadian Department of Justice.[1]

1 For more information see: http://www.canada.justice.gc.ca/en/ps/bj/harm/.

It has generally been agreed that terms designating concepts of any branch of knowledge should be accurate, concise, easy to spell and pronounce; and should allow the formation of derivatives and be linguistically correct (Felber 1984: 181–2). Thomas (1993: 46) suggests that, preferably, a term should also be monosemous (one meaning) and at the same time mononymous (one word), and be a member of a term system.

Terminology is traditionally considered to be the basis of any LSP (language for specific purposes) variety. Moreover, our own experience has suggested that lawyers without sufficient linguistic background training may use the concepts *terminology* and *LSP variety* indiscriminately, thus reducing the language of law to a mere set of legal terms. Considering the proportion of terminology and "non-terminology" in a subject-area text, Newmark (1988: 160) assumes that terminology makes up perhaps 5–10% of a text; our own data show that arbitration legislation is much richer with terms than those texts considered by Newmark. For example, the Arbitration Act 1996 (United Kingdom) contains about 22% of specialized terms; and terminology in the Federal Arbitration Act 1925, as amended (USA), makes up about 20% of the whole text. The lexis of the UNCITRAL Model Law on International Arbitration encompasses 21% of terminology; and terms in the European Convention on International Commercial Arbitration form 26% of the text. The difference in proportion of terms and non-terms in the Czech Act N. 216/1994 Sb. (Act providing for Arbitration Proceedings and Enforcement of Arbitral Awards) is even larger: 29% of the text is made up of specialised terminology.[2] Relatively high percentages of terminology contained within legislation may be the result of two major factors: (a) the existence of a high degree of repetitiveness of terms in legislative provisions; and (b) the fact that most terms are binominal and/or multiverbal phrases (not individual words).

Legal terminology

Law is the branch of humanities where mastery of its language most determines people's destinies. If an individual in a common law country

2 For the purposes of simple counting, only nominal terms were considered (including gerund); no terminological verbal constructions typical of the legal language of legislation were taken into account

hires an attorney who is able to persuade the jury of the innocence of his client, although the evidence suggests otherwise, s/he may escape serving many years in prison or paying sky-high damages. Such an extreme situation is not so frequent, one of the most famous cases being O. J. Simpson's criminal trial.[3] Due to significant differences between accusatorial and inquisitorial procedural principles in common law and continental law respectively, the art of persuasive legal reasoning and argumentation performed by lawyers is less valued within continental legal systems. However, the language of law plays a key role in these systems as well and Tiersma's conclusion (2000: 1) that "the law and its language affect the daily lives of virtually everyone in our society" is fully applicable to a continental law country such as the Czech Republic.

Linguists designate the specialist lexicon proper to, or typical of, some fields of knowledge as *terminology*, while lawyers tackling linguistic issues would ordinarily call this *technical vocabulary* (cf. Solan 1993: 130) or even *legalese* (cf. Goldstein and Lieberman 1991: 23) although legalese is also considered to be a style, not just a vocabulary. Tiersma (2000: 203) explains why it is difficult for lay people to comprehend the language of law. He emphasizes the role of technical vocabulary and as well as addressing the issue of there being often more than one meaning of one terminological unit:

> No doubt one of the things that makes legal languages hardest to understand is its unusual vocabulary. Although some technical terms are relatively well known (*defendant, judge, jury*), others are at best vaguely familiar to many people (*beyond reasonable doubt, negligence* or *wrongful imprisonment*). Further terms — legal homonyms — seem familiar but have unexpected meaning for the average person (as in *aggravation* or *file a complaint*). Still other vocabulary is a complete mystery to non-lawyers [...].

We would argue that what Tiersma (2000) calls "legal homonyms" are in fact examples of an extensive polysemy in legal language, rather than homonymy in its linguistic sense. Considering the issue of polysemy along with the above-mentioned proportion of terminological to non-terminological vocabulary in a legal text and the basic processes of translation, one may reasonably assume that a lack of familiarity with terminology in both the source and target languages as well as their exact

3 For more information on the trial transcripts see: http://simpson.walraven.org/.

meaning in the source and target legal systems can lead to a failure, or significant disruption, of interaction between the producer of the source text and the recipient of the target (i.e. translated) text.

The expression *term* in legal contexts has two different primary meanings, as (a) duration of time, and (b) a clause or provision in a legal instrument. Thus, law dictionaries, if mentioning a third, i.e. linguistic, meaning at all, attach it to the entry *term* as a marginal sub-entry *term of art* (cf. Mellinkoff 1993: 641, *Black's Law Dictionary* 1999: 1481) and explain it as a technical word with a specific meaning. Garner (1991: 184, 1995: 872) goes even further and distinguishes between a technical word ("jargonistic" term), and a term of art:

> Most 'lawyerly-words' are mere legaldegook, not irreducible terms of art that carry a meaning not otherwise to be precisely conveyed. Though we have hundreds of jargonistic terms, the common terms of art number fewer than fifty. [...] Many supposed terms of art are too imprecise to be properly so classed: *ratio decidendi* and *res judicata* have more than one layer of meaning; so do *common law* and *equity* (many more layers). Because such terms span an array of senses, the user should specify the sense in which the terms are used. We err to suppose that they are finely honed terms of art.

There are two more categories that should be considered in relation to legal terminology and its relevance for translation, namely *jargon* and *argot*. Czech linguists seem to be more rigorous than their English colleagues in distinguishing among *terminology* (a set of words having clearly defined meaning), *jargon* (a set of expressions and ways of its use by a certain group of persons), *slang* (the language of professional groups) and *argot* (usually the language of marginal social groups which is usually designated as *cant* in English understanding) (cf. for example, Čermák 1997: 57, 404). Such an approach is mostly based on a traditional distinction between (a) the standard (ie codified) Czech language taught and insisted on by most teachers in schools, and expected to be used in any public speeches or texts (terminology is a component part of its vocabulary), and (b) the common Czech language used in everyday life covering jargon, slang and possibly argot (cf. Danes 1999: 295). Thus written Czech law should, and essentially does, use only standardized (i.e. codified) language including terminology and should, but however partly fails to, avoid common language, i.e. jargon and slang. This approach seems to be quite essential in translation of legal texts from English to Czech: one should realize that whatever is written in legislation is official and codified both in the legal and linguistic senses of the word. The term 'arbitration' can be translated as a binominal term 'rozhodčí řízení' or simply 'arbitráž', the former being a term of legislation, the latter belonging to legal jargon. Where a translator's task is to translate, for example, the UNCITRAL Model Law into Czech he or she should refrain from using jargonistic expressions and should use only 'rozhodčí řízení' as an equivalent of 'arbitration', or 'rozhodce' for 'arbitrator', although another Czech equivalent 'arbitr' is often used by Czech lawyers in their casual communication.

Unlike Czech legal terminology denoting institutions and concepts of Czech law as a continental law derivative, English terminology within the Anglo-American system of law has to allow for designations of legal concepts and institutions of both common law and civil (continental) law, that is it has to accommodate two systems based on different legal principles. For example, the legislatures of Canada and Louisiana (USA) have to solve practical problems in their statutes as to how to make the concepts and institutions of common law and civil law (in both cases based on French law) compatible. Legislation in Louisiana has been published fully in English for many years; however, its basis was established by French law as early as in 1825, and in consequence introduced what were essentially European continental legal principles, concepts, institutions and terminology. These were transferred into the English language of common law as can be seen in the Louisiana Civil Code of 1996. Thus the work of contemporary legislators concentrates primarily on polishing English terminology whose origin lay in a more or less appropriate translation from French. The Canadian legislature faces a much more complicated task: legislation is published in two languages and both legal systems have been co-existing (Quebec law is constructed upon the basis of French law while the rest of Canada draws on common law). Extensive Canadian work in harmonizing common law and civil law English terminology is based primarily on a conceptual analysis of a limited number of basic terms as they exist and apply in both common law and civil (continental) systems of law; English and French are the means of communication in common law and civil law respectively. The approach has been purely legal, comparing intension of common law and civil law terms denoting the respective concept to be expressed in Canadian legislation which should be harmonized, i.e. to be comprehensible and applicable in both legal systems within Canada.

This internal conceptual conflict within English legal terminology may be quite insidious where there is a question of it being translated into other languages. One brief example of such a brief conceptual analysis can be given here, namely, the well-known phrase 'null and void':

- *UNCITRAL, Art. 16 (1):* "the contract is **null and void**"
- *Arbitration Act 1996 (UK), s. 9 (4)*: "that the arbitration agreement is **null and void**"
- *European Convention, Art. 5:* "the arbitration agreement was either non-existent or **null and void**"
- *Act N. 216/1994 Sb. (The Czech Arbitration Act), s 31 (b)*: "rozhodčí smlouva je z jiných du°vodu° **neplatná**".

Definitions of the phrase in law dictionaries:

- *Black's Law Dictionary*:

  null: having no legal effect; without binding force; the phrase *null and void* is a common redundancy; **void**: of no legal effect; null. [...] *void* can be properly applied only to those provisions that are of no effect whatsoever — those that are an absolute nullity.

- *Mellinkoff's Dictionary of American Legal Usage*:

  null and void: void and void, which is to say *void*. [...] *Null and void* is one of those once fashionable coupled synonyms that refuses to admit that it is dead. It has developed a flair of redundancy.

- *L.B. Curzon's Dictionary of Law*:

  null and void: having no force; invalid; **void**: without force; of no legal effect. [...] It is a nullity from its beginning.

- *B. Garner's Dictionary of Modern Legal Usage*:

  null (= void) is perfectly capable of standing alone; **null and void**: this doublet is old in law [...] and it is at worst a minor prolixity and a cliché; **void**: absolutely null.

Czech law uses two different expressions to denote that an act (such as a contract) is of no legal force, namely 'neplatný' and 'nicotný'; when translating a Czech legal text the English equivalents 'invalid' and 'null' (as if no act has been made) should be used respectively. The Czech legal theory distinguishes between an invalid act (made but materially defective thus invalid from the beginning) which can, however, have a certain legal effect (e.g. an action for damages in consequence of a defective act) and a nullity (no act has actually been made) which has no legal effect whatsoever (cf. Boguszak and Čapek 1997: 211). Moreover, there are two more distinguishing features attachable to 'neplatný', namely 'absolutně neplatný' (literally translated as 'absolutely invalid') and 'relativně neplatný' ('relatively invalid') the former meaning 'void' and the latter 'voidable'. 'Neplatný' alone in a legal text can stand for either phrase; however, if the term 'neplatný' occurs in legislation it will always mean 'invalid from the very beginning', i.e. 'void'.

In order to translate the above listed phrases from various examples of arbitration legislation a translator translating into the Czech language should know that

1. 'null and void' is a doublet (thus it should be treated as one attribute and not as two separate features);
2. its meaning is 'invalid from the beginning'; and
3. the Czech law uses 'neplatný' in the same and similar contexts.

The need for a conceptual approach to terminology in legal translation as well as in lexicography has been strongly supported and defended, for example, by Susan Šarčević (1989: 290). A conceptual analysis of seemingly equivalent terms in two or more different legal systems using two or more different languages as the vehicles of legal information is based on comparing the scope (intension), applicability (in various contexts and genres), and the purpose and effect of legal concepts. The first step, however, before any conceptual analysis may be pursued is that of finding such terms — in other words, to identify those expressions or phrases that may serve as possible equivalents in a specific situation and thus qualify for conceptual analysis. The easiest (but not always feasible) way of picking terminological pairs, triplets or even synonymical chains which are potentially equivalent, is to find an original text in the target language dealing with the same or similar topic as the source legal text, preferably of the same legal genre. For example, if the source text is a statute then the legal texts which we would need to search through for potential equivalents should also be statutes or texts of a similar nature (such as secondary legislation). This parallelism is necessary due to possible shifts in tenor of prescriptive and descriptive legal terms (for the distinction see below) between texts on the same topics but of different legal genres and different functions, such as a statute (primarily prescriptive terms) versus an explanatory memorandum (primarily descriptive terminology). We have already mentioned the distinction between the Czech 'rozhodčí řízení' as a term used in the Czech Arbitration Act (i.e. a term of art), and the expression 'arbitráž' (Czech legal jargon) found in the explanatory report accompanying that act throughout the legislative procedure in parliament.

Terminology in arbitration

Although we speak about the language of law, this does not necessarily mean that all terms used in legal texts are of legal origin. Arbitration, by its nature, belongs to the wider category of so-called alternative dispute resolution, which designation suggests that it constitutes an alternative to legal proceedings (i.e. proceedings before a court), and the parties may, if need be, have recourse to a court of law should they be dissatisfied with the award of an arbitrator. To compare some terms in arbitration that may be helpful to a translator of Czech arbitration law we chose two national and two international legislative texts: the British Arbitration Act 1996, the Federal Arbitration Act 1925 as amended (last amendment in 1990), the UNCITRAL Model Law on International Commercial Arbitration 1985, and the European Convention on International Commercial Arbitration 1965, which constituted the basic legal source for the Czech Arbitration Act 1994.

Terms used in arbitration may indeed be subdivided according to different criteria. They can be classified, for example, according to their:

a normativity (cf. Galinski 1982: 189);
b grammatical characteristics (cf. Hoffmann 1982: 399);
c lexical features;

or

d legal origin and distribution (i.e. which branch of law they originally belong to), and the identification of their illocutionary and tenor characteristics in their original legal branch and as borrowings in other branches.

Normativity of terminology

The normativity of terminology is extremely relevant for translation. Galinski (1982: 189) recognizes *descriptive terminology* as representing a descriptive norm of terms, i.e. their present usage, and *prescriptive terminology* as representing a prescriptive norm, i.e. one that is standardized and recommended for application by an authority. Applying this dichotomy to the language of arbitration, the prescriptive category of terminology would encompass those terms defined by and contained in arbitration statutes in individual countries or international conventions or model laws. Terms developed through case law and conventions would also fall into this category in common law countries (Tiersma 1999: 109). Descriptive terminology would, in addition to statutorily defined terms used in everyday legal practice, also contain legal jargon. Distinguishing between prescriptive and descriptive terminology is of vital importance where translation is considered. A translator unaware of this dichotomy may mistakenly choose a descriptive term in the target text to represent a prescriptive term used in the source text. An example may be given here: the English term 'arbitration clause' in a contract was translated by a professional translator as 'arbitrážní doložka', which can sometimes be heard in Czech legal jargon or used by the media; the prescriptive equivalent would be 'rozhodčí doložka', which is the term used in statutes.

Grammatical features

The grammatical characteristics of terms and terminological phrases may serve either as a distinctive feature with respect to the meaning (cf. different meanings of 'damage' and 'damages'), or may help to identify the meaning. Hoffmann (1982: 399) distinguishes four levels in relation to terms, namely *morphemic*, *categorial*, *lexemic* and *syntagmatic*.

One example relating to the morphemic level can be provided: the British Arbitration Act 1996 in Schedule 3, s.29 (2), referring to amendments to the Friendly Societies Act 1974, reads: "Any arbitrator, arbiter or umpire [...] may at the request of either party ...". One may question, with respect to the distinction between 'arbitrator' (coming through old French from Latin origins) and 'arbiter' (a purely Latin word), why the two nouns, distinguished by suffixes of the same kind, are used here. Do they denote different concepts? Or is 'arbitrator, arbiter or umpire' a typical example of legal triplets similar to, for example, 'form, manner and method' or 'right, title and interest', in private law? Technically speaking, both the terms 'arbitrator' and 'arbiter' denote the same general concept: a person with the power to decide disputes. What differs is the distribution of the term within law. Garner (1995: 73) points out:

> The terms overlap considerably and they cause confusion on both sides of the Atlantic. Yet when referring to legal arbitration, one should term the resolver of disputes the 'arbitrator' [...] Scottish law presents an exception: one appoints an 'arbiter' to hold an arbitration.

One can assume that this is the reason why both terms are used in the Friendly Societies Act 1974: the Act applies also to Scotland and most British statutes applicable to Scotland and Northern Ireland try to preserve the respective legal terminologies of the region if they differ from those used in England and Wales.

Countability may be the issue at the categorial level: a simple and one example of semantic difference can be given here:

'Authority' as an uncountable noun is found in Art. 6 of UNCITRAL Model Law: "A plea that the arbitral tribunal is exceeding the scope of its *authority* shall be raised. "Its countable counterpart is in Art. 9 of the European Convention: "... the composition of the arbitral *authority* or the arbitral procedure was not in accordance with the agreement of the parties ..." Although the problem would seem to be easy for a translator to solve, our own experience suggests that this has not always been the case: the former should be translated into Czech as 'pravomoc' and the latter as 'orgán'.

Lexical features

The level of lexis covers a wide range of features. Traditional understandings of terminology have been based on the assumption that terms should be both *mononymous*, i.e. that they should consist of one word, and at the same time they should be *monosemous*, i.e. bearing one meaning. Such a rule may generally apply to taxonomies, for example in criminal law, although not all crimes are naturally denoted by a one-word term (eg 'sexual assault' or 'forcible entry'). There are not many monosemous and mononymous terms in our field of research; 'arbitration' and 'arbitrator' are in fact the only representatives. Most Czech and English legal terms are multi-word expressions or phrases. A rough estimate of entries contained in *Black's Law Dictionary* (7th ed.) suggests that the proportions of one-word terms and multi-word terms in Anglo-American law are 33% and 67% respectively; the proportions in the most extensive *Czech Law Dictionary* are 26% of one-word terms and 74% of multi-word terms.

Polysemy, although undesirable, can be traced in different branches of law. Polysemy is more widely spread within English legal terminology than within Czech legal terminology, which fact relates to a higher occurrence of one-word terms in English than in Czech, and may correspond with the more frequent occurrence of polysemy in English for everyday purposes than in common Czech. For example, 'determination' in Art. 19 or Art. 10(2) (UNCITRAL) and 'determination' in Art. 2(d) are polysemes; the former means 'ascertainment' while the latter denotes the 'decision' of a body. Needless to say, distinguishing between the two meanings of one word in a concrete context is crucial for translation, as an inappropriate choice may mislead the recipient of the target legal text and lead to potentially negative consequences.

Synonymy is another lexical aspect of terminology. In their regular meaning, synonyms are two or more words (in the same language) which have the same general sense, but each of which possess meanings that are not shared by the other or others, or have different shades of meaning or implications pertinent to different contexts (OED, 2002). In a stricter sense, a synonym is a word which has the same meaning as another, something which Burton (1998: viii) calls 'exact' synonyms, and which practically does not exist in the language of both Czech and English law. Filipec and Čermák (1985: 133) emphasize two aspects which should be considered: (a) the intension (as the internal content of a notion or the sum of the attributes contained in it) which can be identical or variant, and (b) the distribution of synonyms. Where the synonyms are identical with respect to both intension and distribution, full (or 'exact' — see above) synonymy occurs; in all other cases there will be partial synonyms. Even if we find legal terms that enjoy identical meanings (i.e. the intension), their distribution will differ, for example they may be used in different contexts (e.g. 'service' and 'delivery' or 'self-government' and 'self-governance').

Three terms that may be considered synonyms in general language are used in the legal texts we analysed: 'proceedings', 'procedure' and 'process'. All three are contextualized by the attribute 'arbitral'.

The term 'arbitral proceedings' is used in the Arbitration Act 1996 and UNCITRAL Model Law to denote all acts and events between the time of the submission of a concrete dispute to arbitration and the time of the issuance of an arbitral award. This term is absent in the US Federal Arbitration Act, and occurs only once in the European Convention; other occurrences (five times) in the Convention relate to a modified version of the term but with the same meaning — 'arbitration proceedings'.

'Arbitral procedure' means a specific method or course of action in arbitration:

- *The Arbitration Act 1996 s.103 (2)*: "(e) that the composition of the arbitral tribunal or the **arbitral procedure** was not in accordance with the agreement of the parties ..."
- *UNCITRAL Model Law, Art. 34 (2)*: "(iv) the composition of the arbitral tribunal or the **arbitral procedure** was not in accordance with the agreement of the parties ..."
- *European Convention Art 9:* "(d) the composition of the arbitral authority or the **arbitral procedure** was not in accordance with the agreement of the parties ..." although in other articles (Art IV (b), Art V) the term is used in the meaning of a concrete case, i.e. in lieu of **arbitral proceedings**.

The only occurrence of 'arbitral process' can be found in the Arbitration Act 1996 s.12: (2), where it suggests a writ or other similar document issued during the arbitral proceedings:

> Any party to the arbitration agreement may apply for such an order (upon notice to the other parties), but only after a claim has arisen and after exhausting any available **arbitral process** for obtaining an extension of time.

We can easily conclude that these three terms, although they are understood as synonyms in general English and sometimes treated as such by non-native lawyers, cannot be considered as full, i.e. interchangeable, synonyms in English law, and therefore cannot be employed as synonyms in legal translation.

One more conclusion can be drawn from the foregoing which maintains Šarčević's conclusion (2001: 87): the use of different terms to express the same legal concept may be misleading, primarily for lawyers, as such use can imply that reference is being made to a different concept. The drafters of any piece of legislation whether national or international should strive to be consistent and precise in using only one term for each concept. We can see a certain degree of neglect in this respect even in the Arbitration Act 1996 and the European Convention ('arbitral' vs 'arbitration' proceedings), or the Federal Arbitration Act ('arbitral' vs. 'arbitration' agreement). The same rule applies to translators: they should be consistent in using one translational equivalent in the target text for one legal term in the source text; legal translators should not be creative, showing how many synonyms in the target legal language for one source language term they know, otherwise their translational product may result in significant confusion on the part of the target legal text recipients (mostly and primarily lawyers).

Classification of terms according to their legal origin

The fourth approach to classification of terms is based on their legal origin, distribution and the identification of their illocutionary force and their characteristic tenor. We can distinguish the following three groups:

a. terms applicable only to arbitration, such as 'arbitration', 'arbitrator';
b. terms belonging to other branches of law and employed in arbitration such as the procedural terms 'jurisdiction', 'objection', 'plea' or 'stay', as deployed in arbitration;
c. words of general import which have acquired a precisely defined meaning in law, such as 'writing' — used in all the four laws we examined.

The first category has already been dealt with above. The second group may be rather complex if considering translation into other languages.

Since arbitration is one type of alternative dispute resolution in general, it belongs, by its nature, to procedural rather than substantive law — i.e. its main purpose is to gain redress outside of court. Thus procedural concepts and vocabulary create a significant portion of arbitration lexis.

The term 'jurisdiction' is one of the core terms in procedural law; it is used in all the four arbitration legislative texts we examined. A translator should again be aware of the polysemic (or polysemous) nature of this term, misunderstandings of which may lead to different equivalents in different contexts. In law generally, 'jurisdiction' means the power to exercise judicial authority and can be translated as 'soudní pravomoc' or simply 'pravomoc' into Czech. Other equivalents will be used in translating compound terms, such as 'territorial jurisdiction' or 'subject-matter jurisdiction', where 'jurisdiction' means 'příslušnost' in Czech. In the examined arbitration legislation there are several occurrences of 'jurisdiction':

- *UNCITRAL Model Law, Chapter IV*: "to rule on **jurisdiction**"; "to have **jurisdiction**"; "a plea that the arbitral tribunal does not have **jurisdiction** shall be raised not later than ..."
- *Federal Arbitration Act, Sec. 4, 8* "the court having **jurisdiction**"; *Sec. 8* "to retain **jurisdiction**"; *Sec. 203* "to have original **jurisdiction**"
- *European Convention, Art. V:* "plea as to arbitral **jurisdiction**"; "arbitrator's **jurisdiction**"; "the arbitrator is alleged to have no **jurisdiction**"; "to rule on his own **jurisdiction**"
- *Arbitration Act 1996, Sec. 30* "to rule on its **jurisdiction**"; "**substantive jurisdiction**"; *Sec. 31* "tribunal's **jurisdiction**"; *Sec. 66* "to lack **substantive jurisdiction**"; *Sec. 87* "to exclude the **jurisdiction** of the court"

In the first three texts 'jurisdiction' is used as a monosemous term having the same meaning in all above listed occurrences and should be translated as '(soudní) pravomoc' in all the above contexts. There is one formal deviation, namely in the Arbitration Act 1996 (UK), where a binominal phrase 'substantive jurisdiction' is used. No available law dictionary provides definition or explanation of that terminological phrase; an extensive search into legislation available through the Internet has shown that such a binominal term is found only in the British Act. The analysis (both semantic and legal) suggests that 'substantive' refers to substantive law (stating rights, duties and powers in particular contexts); a conceptual analysis of Czech terminology in similar contexts helps to find an adequate translational equivalent — 'meritorní pravomoc', suggesting that a court or tribunal has the power to try the case. Therefore, we may conclude that 'jurisdiction' and 'substantive jurisdiction' in all the above listed examples designate the same concept, namely the power of a court or an arbitral tribunal, as the case may be, to deal with disputes submitted for arbitration. However it should be pointed out that such a conclusion for the purposes of translation can only be made upon a conceptual analysis of the particular terms in the source text and their potential equivalents in the target legal language.

Two more terms of procedural law should be mentioned — 'plea' and 'objection'. They are used in the following contexts:

- *UNCITRAL Model Law, Art. 16*: "a **plea** that the arbitral tribunal does not have jurisdiction"; *Art. 4*: "stating his **objection** to such non-compliance"; *Art. 16*: "**objections** with respect to the existence or validity of the arbitration agreement"

- *European Convention, Art. VI:* "a **plea** as to the jurisdiction of the court"
- *Arbitration Act 1996, Sec. 30:* "an **objection** that the arbitral tribunal lacks substantive jurisdiction"

As can be seen, the distribution of the two terms within the four examined pieces of legislation is unequal: the Federal Arbitration Act contains neither term, the European Convention provides only for 'a plea', contrasting with the Arbitration Act using solely an 'objection', and, eventually, the UNCITRAL Model Law employs both terms. A 'plea', by its nature, is a common-law term denoting a factual allegation offered in a case; as a multiverbal term it usually acquires its precise meaning in terminological phrases with premodifying or postmodifying attributes. 'Plea' in the above contexts always means the so-called 'jurisdictional plea' or 'plea to the jurisdiction', which is an objection to (the lack of) jurisdiction of the respective arbitrator, tribunal or court. The identical meaning of the two terms — 'plea' and 'objection' — in the respective contexts and the unmarked legal nature of the latter (as a general legal term not reduced to common law) might be reasons why the drafters of British Arbitration Act decided to use the term 'objection' in all relevant provisions. Thus, the Czech equivalent for both English terms is 'námitka' as an unmarked term of Czech law.

The last category are words of general import acquiring a precisely defined meaning in law; the expression 'writing', contrasted with 'written', deserves mentioning. The following occurrences can be traced in the laws examined:

- *UNCITRAL Model Law:*

  Art. 7 "The arbitration agreement shall be in **writing**"; *Art. 31* "The award shall be made in **writing**"; *Art. 35* "application in **writing**"

  Art. 3 "**written** communications"; *Art. 13* "a **written** statement"; *Art. 24* "**written** proceedings"; *Art. 26* "**written** or oral report"

- *The Federal Arbitration Act:*

  Sec. 2 "an agreement in **writing**"; *Sec. 4* "notice in **writing**"; *Sec. 7* "to summon in **writing** any person"

  Sec. 2 "a **written** provision in a contract"; *Sec. 4* "a **written** agreement for an arbitration"; *Sec. 13* "**written** extension of time"

- *European Convention*

  Art. I: "agreement is made in **writing**"

- *Arbitration Act 1996*

  Sec. 5 "the agreement is in **writing**"; "an agreement is evidenced in **writing**"; "References in this Part to anything being **written** or in **writing** include its being recorded by any means." *Sec. 14* "notice in **writing**"; *Sec. 16* "a request in **writing**"

  Sec. 5 "**written** submission"; *Sec. 6* "a **written** form of arbitration clause";

  Sec. 34 "**written** statements of claim", "**written** evidence".

As emphasized above, lawyers tend to find different meanings where words are different, and in consequence they tend to eschew creativity in using various synonyms to denote the same concept in different parts of their text. An experienced legal translator is perfectly aware of that rule and in consequence tries to identify the differences among synonyms in order to find a proper equivalent in the target language. However, the distinction 'in writing' — 'written' belongs to grammatical rather than semantic features of legal English, namely its tendency to nominalization. It should be noted that the postmodifying prepositional compound attribute 'in writing' is traditional, and therefore much more frequent in English legal texts, inducing a more formal tenor of legal discourse than its attributive past participle counterpart 'written'. Czech equivalents can follow their English patterns being 'v písemné podobě' and 'písemný' respectively.

CONCLUSIONS

It is clear from the foregoing that translators of legal texts regularly face a difficult task: that of identifying the exact meaning of information contained in the text which has been formed in one language within one legal context, and having to transfer that information into a different language and into a different legal context. The process of translation is a complex one, within which terminology plays a significant role as the main carrier of legal concepts and institutions. Although arbitration is by now an internationalized legal topic, there are still many lexical and terminological issues which are treated differently in different national legal systems. Extensive conceptual analysis of key, as well as collateral, terms needs to be undertaken so as to avoid the potential risk of choosing translational equivalents which would not be adequate in the target legal system and, in consequence, misleading or incomprehensible for the ultimate recipients.

REFERENCES

Alcaraz, E. and Hughes, B. (2003) *Legal Translation Explained*. Manchester: St. Jerome Publishing.

Bečka, J. (1992) *Česká stylistika*. Praha: Academia.

Boguszak, J. and Čapek, J. (1997) *Teorie práva*. Praha: Codex Bohemia.

Burton, W. C. (1998) *Burton's Legal Thesaurus*. New York: McGraw-Hill.

Curzon, L. B. (2002) *Dictionary of Law*. 6th ed., London: Longman.

Čermák, F. (1997) *Jazyk a jazykověda*. Praha: Pražská imaginace.

Daneš, F. (1999) Pojem spisovného jazyka v dnešních společenských podmínkách. In *Jazyk a text I*, část 2 Praha: Univerzita Karlova.

Felber, H. (1984) *Terminology Manual*. Paris: UNESCO and INFOTERM.

Filipec, J. and Čermák, F. (1985) *Česká lexikologie*. Studie a práce lingvistické. Praha: Academia.

Galinski, C. (1982) Standardization in Terminology: An Overview. In Nedobity, Wolfgang (ed.), *Terminologies for the Eighties, Infoterm Series* 7. Munich: K. G. Saur, 186–226.

Garner, B. A. (1991) *The Elements of Legal Style*. New York; Oxford: Oxford University Press.

Garner, B. A. (1995) *A Dictionary of Modern Legal Usage*. Oxford; New York: Oxford University Press.

Garner, B. A. (1999) *Black's Law Dictionary*. St. Paul: West Group Publishing.

Goldstein, T. and Lieberman, J. K. (1991) *The Lawyer's Guide to Writing Well*. Berkeley: University of California Press.

Hoffmann, L. (1982) Terminology and LSP. In Nedobity, Wolfgang (ed.), *Terminologies for the Eighties*, Infoterm Series 7 Munich: K. G. Saur.

International Organization for Standardization (ISO) (1990) R 1087. In *Terminology and Vocabulary*. Paris: ISO.

Mellinkoff, D. (1993) *Mellinkoff's Dictionary of American Legal Usage*. St. Paul: West Group Publishing.

Newmark, P. (1988) *A Textbook of Translation*. London: Prentice Hall.

Oxford English Dictionary. (2002) CDROM ed., Oxford: OUP.

Sager, J. C. (1990) *A Practical Course in Terminology Processing*. Amsterdam: John Benjamins.

Solan, L. M. (1993) *The Language of Judges*. Chicago: The University of Chicago Press.

Šarčević, S. (1989) Conceptual Dictionaries for Translation in the Field of Law. *International Journal of Lexicography* 2(4), Robert Ilson (ed.). Oxford: Oxford University Press.
Šarčević, S. (ed.) (2001) *Legal Translation: Preparation for Accession to the European Union*. Rijeka: University of Rijeka.
Thomas, P. (1993) Choosing Headwords from Language-for-Special-Purposes LSP: Collocations for Entry into a Terminology Data Bank (Term Bank). In Sonneveld, H. S. and Loening, K. L. (eds.), *Terminology: Applications in Interdisciplinary Communication*. Amsterdam: John Benjamins Publishing.
Tiersma, P. M. (1999) *Legal Language*. Chicago: University of Chicago Press.
Tiersma, P. M. (2000) *Legal Language*. Chicago and London: University of Chicago Press.

Examined laws:

Arbitration Act 1996 (United Kingdom).
Federal Arbitration Act 1925–1990 (USA).
UNCITRAL Model Law on International Commercial Arbitration 1985.
European Convention on International Commercial Arbitration 1965.
Act N. 216/1994 Sb. to regulate arbitration procedure and enforcement of arbitral awards (in Czech).

Index

AUTHOR INDEX

SUBJECT INDEX